The Law and Legitimacy of Imposed Constitutions

Constitutions are often seen as the product of the free will of a people exercising their constituent power. This, however, is not always the case, particularly when it comes to 'imposed constitutions'. In recent years there has been renewed interest in the idea of imposition in constitutional design, but the literature does not yet provide a comprehensive resource to understand the meanings, causes and consequences of an imposed constitution.

This volume examines the theoretical and practical questions emerging from what scholars have described as an imposed constitution. A diverse group of contributors interrogates the theory, forms and applications of imposed constitutions with the aim of refining our understanding of this variation on constitution-making. Divided into three parts, this book first considers the conceptualization of imposed constitutions, suggesting definitions, or corrections to the definition, of what exactly an imposed constitution is. The contributors then go on to explore the various ways in which constitutions are, and can be, imposed. The collection concludes by considering imposed constitutions that are currently in place in a number of polities worldwide, problematizing the consequences their imposition has caused. Cases are drawn from a broad range of countries with examples at both the national and supranational level.

This book addresses some of the most important issues discussed in contemporary constitutional law: the relationship between constituent and constituted power, the source of constitutional legitimacy, the challenge of foreign and expert intervention and the role of comparative constitutional studies in constitution-making. The volume will be a valuable resource for those interested in the phenomenon of imposed constitutionalism as well as anyone interested in the current trends in the study of comparative constitutional law.

Richard Albert, William Stamps Farish Professor of Law, The University of Texas at Austin; Co-Editor, Routledge Series on Comparative Constitutional Change; Book Reviews Editor, *American Journal of Comparative Law*.

Xenophon Contiades, Professor of Public Law, Panteion University; Managing Director of the Centre for European Constitutional Law, Athens, Greece; Co-Editor, Routledge Series on Comparative Constitutional Change.

Alkmene Fotiadou, Research Fellow, Centre for European Constitutional Law; Co-Editor, Routledge Series on Comparative Constitutional Change.

Comparative Constitutional Change

Comparative Constitutional Change has developed into a distinct field of constitutional law. It encompasses the study of constitutions through the way they change and covers a wide scope of topics and methodologies. Books in this series include work on developments in the functions of the constitution, the organization of powers and the protection of rights, as well as research that focuses on formal amendment rules and the relation between constituent and constituted power. The series includes comparative approaches along with books that focus on single jurisdictions, and brings together research monographs and edited collections which allow the expression of different schools of thought. While the focus is primarily on law, where relevant the series may also include political science, historical, philosophical and empirical approaches that explore constitutional change.

Series editors:

Xenophon Contiades is Professor of Public Law, Panteion University, Athens, Greece and Managing Director, Centre for European Constitutional Law, Athens, Greece.
Thomas Fleiner is Emeritus Professor of Law at the University of Fribourg, Switzerland.
Alkmene Fotiadou is Research Associate at the Centre for European Constitutional Law, Athens.
Richard Albert is William Stamps Farish Professor of Law at the University of Texas at Austin.

Also in the series:

New Challenges to Constitutional Adjudication in Europe
A Comparative Perspective
Edited by Zoltán Szente and Fruzsina Gárdos-Orosz

Participatory Constitutional Change
The People as Amenders of the Constitution
Edited by Xenophon Contiades and Alkmene Fotiadou

For more information about this series, please visit: www.routledge.com/Comparative-Constitutional-Change/book-series/COMPCONST

The Law and Legitimacy of Imposed Constitutions

Edited by Richard Albert, Xenophon Contiades and Alkmene Fotiadou

Routledge
Taylor & Francis Group
LONDON AND NEW YORK

First published 2019 by Routledge

2 Park Square, Milton Park, Abingdon, Oxfordshire OX14 4RN
52 Vanderbilt Avenue, New York, NY 10017

Routledge is an imprint of the Taylor & Francis Group, an informa business

First issued in paperback 2020

British Library Cataloguing-in-Publication Data
A catalogue record for this book is available from the British Library

Library of Congress Cataloging-in-Publication Data
A catalog record has been requested for this book

ISBN: 978-1-138-48898-4 (hbk)
ISBN: 978-0-367-51992-6 (pbk)

Typeset in Galliard
by Deanta Global Publishing Services, Chennai, India

Contents

Contributors

Richard Albert, William Stamps Farish Professor of Law, The University of Texas at Austin

Manon Bonnet, PhD candidate in Public Law, Aix-Marseille Univ, Université de Toulon, Univ. Pau & Pays Adour, CNRS, DICE, ILF, Aix-en-Provence, France

Graham Butler, Associate Professor of Law, Aarhus University

Xenophon Contiades, Professor of Public Law, Panteion University and Managing Director of the Centre for European Constitutional Law, Athens, Greece

Alkmene Fotiadou, Research Fellow, Centre for European Constitutional Law

James Fowkes, Professor of Foreign and International Law, Westfälisches Wilhelms-Universität Münster

Jörg Gerkrath, Professor of Public and European Law, University of Luxembourg

David S. Law, Charles Nagel Chair of Constitutional Law and Political Science, Washington University in Saint Louis; Sir Y.K. Pao Chair in Public Law, University of Hong Kong

Sanford Levinson, W. St. John Garwood and W. St. John Garwood, Jr. Centennial Chair in Law, The University of Texas Law School; Professor of Government, The University of Texas at Austin

Yota Negishi, Assistant Professor, Seinan Gakuin University

Antoni Abat i Ninet, Professor of Law, University of Copenhagen

Zoran Oklopcic, Associate Professor of Law and Legal Studies, Carleton University

Yaniv Roznai, Senior Lecturer in Law, The Radzyner Law School, Interdisciplinary Center Herzliya (IDC)

Introduction

Imposition in making and changing constitutions

Richard Albert, Xenophon Contiades† and Alkmene Fotiadou‡*

In our popular imagination, constitutions are celebrated as the product of the free will of a people exercising their sovereign power. It is taken for granted that modern constitutions are rooted in the consent of the governed, that they reflect a stable settlement among the people and that, as John Locke once wrote, they are the ultimate expression of the voluntary judgment of the people to 'enter into society to make one people, one body politic, under one supreme government'.[1] The most famous phrase in any constitution in the history of the world—'We the People', the preambular words that open the door to the United States Constitution—only reinforces this view.

And yet it is the rare constitution that springs directly in design and ratification from the considered judgment of the people themselves. Iceland came close in its failed but fascinating effort to crowdsource its new constitution in 2013.[2] Constitutions are more often the product of elite negotiations with no authentic representativeness. They may alternatively be held up as the result of mediated choices made on behalf of or in the name of the people, whether or not the people have in fact been consulted in a meaningful way. It is true, however, that constitutions are increasingly requiring some form of public approval before coming into force.[3]

Some constitutions can be described as 'imposed'. Precisely what is meant by imposition, however, can vary. Interrogating what imposition means is one principal purpose of this volume bringing together scholars to probe the law and

* William Stamps Farish Professor of Law, The University of Texas at Austin.
† Professor of Public Law, Panteion University of Social and Political Sciences.
‡ Research Fellow, Centre for European Constitutional Law.

1 John Locke, *Second Treatise of Government* (Indianapolis: Hackett Publishing Co, CB MacPherson ed 1980), at 47–48 (§89).

2 Hélène Landemore, 'The Icelandic Experience Challenges the View that Constitutional Process Must be Exclusionary and Secretive', *Democratic Audit UK*, July 23, 2014, online: http://www.democraticaudit.com/2014/07/23/the-icelandic-experience-challenges-the-view-that-constitutional-process-must-be-exclusionary-and-secretive.

3 *See* Tom Ginsburg, Zachary Elkins & Justin Blount, 'Does the Process of Constitution-Making Matter?' (2009) 55 *Annual Review of Law and Social Science* 23 at 57.

legitimacy of imposed constitutions. Another is to challenge the central presuppositions of imposition in constitution-making and -changing. And a third is to provide the field an informative and challenging resource for learning about imposed constitutions.

The idea of an imposed constitution evokes the thought of a charter of fundamental rules put into place after the conquest of one people by another. Hence Mark Tushnet's view that a constitution is imposed where 'a conquering power creates a constitution for its now-defeated enemy'.[4] An imposed constitution is associated with the violence of war, the high costs of surrender and the loss of sovereignty. Of all the spoils of war, there are fewer greater reminders of defeat than living under rules set by the victors, those rules sometimes requiring using a new language, paying homage to symbols, surrendering natural resources or even living under forms of enslavement.

Imposed constitutions raise something of a paradox: how can a set of basic social and political rules meant to govern a people ever legitimately be forced upon that people by another? The paradox itself raises questions, including what we understand to be the functions of a constitution, how we should regard a constitution that is created outside the jurisdiction it governs and why we value legitimacy as a feature of a constitution. There are answers to each of these questions, contestable though the answers may be, and we believe public law scholars would benefit from a sustained inquiry into them and their reasoning.

Constitutional imposition and fundamental concepts in public law

This book is about those who do not 'constitute themselves in writing', those who do not 'know themselves as the author'[5] of a constitution, but still are citizens in a constituted state. What happens when a nation has a constitution but lacks the memory of a self-constituting act? Memory is itself subject to perpetual revision and reformation. As Henry Rousso has remarked, 'memory is a mental representation of the past but it has only a partial rapport with the past'.[6] This memory has the power to legitimize or delegitimize the constitution. But in the context of imposed constitutions, memory is complicated by the disjunction between the authors of the constitution and those governed by it. Here the victors shape the narrative of the memories, of the myth-making that is an incident of constitution-making.

Neither viewed as the product of the free will of a people exercising constituent power nor indeed initially accepted as legitimate, imposed constitutions disturb the conventional narrative of the almost transcendent power of constitution-making

4 Mark Tushnet, 'Constitution-Making: An Introduction' (2013) 91 *Texas Law Review* 1983 at 1990.

5 *See* Anne Norton, 'Transubstantiation: The Dialectic of Constitutional Authority' (1998) 55 *University of Chicago Law Review* 458 at 459.

6 Henry Rousso, *The Haunting Past: History, Memory, and Justice in Contemporary France* (Philadelphia: University of Pennsylvania Press, 2002) at 4.

moments. These narratives pre-suppose twinned definitions of the 'people' and 'constituent power' that conceptualize national constitutions as resulting from the free exercise of constituent power by the people. Yet in recent years the divide between constituent and constituted power has come under reconsideration. And so have other fundamental concepts in public law, including the very idea of 'a people' making its own constitution, the modalities of formal and informal constitutional change and the liberal foundations of constitutionalism.

There are many reasons to study constitutional imposition. Constitution-making continues amid complex contexts of nation-building, sometimes in connection with war and sometimes not yet still with some form of what might be considered imposition. It no longer seems possible today for constitution-making to occur without external involvement. The lessons of conventionally imposed constitutions, then, are worth studying for their applications and caution in our present day. Any degree of imposition may be traumatic, and any measure of heteronomy in the exercise of the constituent power may prove difficult to justify in light of the modern appeal of popular constitution-making.

Constitutional imposition may impact implementation in various ways. A heteronomous set of rules may not fit well in the environment in which it is embedded. Provisions or principles that are unlikely to have been adopted by autochthonous drafters are forced upon a people, like a square peg into a round hole, but in conquest the formative rule of course is not law but power. Setting aside circumstances related to conquest and war, to what extent are global constitutional rules similar to a set of imposed constitutional rules? The rise of an industry of international constitutional advisors may have a similar effect insofar as the global menu of 'standardized constitutional items' has its origins not in local norms but in global expectations. Is there a legitimacy deficit in these standardized items or do they exude it? Equally noteworthy is that the moment of imposition is not limited to the founding moment of constitutional enactment. Sitting along a continuum between constitutional autonomy and constitutional heteronomy, constitutions can be imposed in periods of constitutional change. Varying degrees of heteronomy may therefore become apparent during constitutional amendment.

This volume embraces the contradictions, paradoxes and dilemmas in the study of imposed constitutions. The contributors revisit the concept from multiple perspectives and explore the legal, constitutional, political and historical aspects of traditional and novel forms of imposition. Fundamental concepts and constructs recur in different lights through the volume, including constituent and constituted power, local and international actors in constitution-making and constitutional change, the universality of constitutional principles and new forms of multi-level governance.

Interrogating imposition

One constitution in particular is usually identified as imposed: the Japanese Constitution. Adopted in 1946, it is the formalization of the Allied victory in

World War II. Immediately after the war, the Japanese government resisted calls to change its governing constitution, the Meiji Constitution, which had been in force since the late nineteenth century.[7] But General Douglas MacArthur, the Supreme Commander of the Allied Powers and the official overseer of the Japanese government, insisted that constitutional change was a necessary condition of Japan's surrender and of making good on the terms of the Potsdam Declaration.[8] The Japanese government ultimately relented and produced a draft.[9] Unsatisfied with the draft, MacArthur and his team produced their own draft, which was delivered to the Japanese government with instructions that it should be used as a basis for amending the Meiji Constitution according to the amendment process detailed in the Meiji Constitution itself, including action by the House of Representatives, the House of Peers, the Privy Council and the Emperor himself.[10] Still today, 70 years since its adoption, many refer to the Japanese Constitution as 'MacArthur's Constitution'.[11]

There are many other constitutions one might call 'imposed', including more recently the Iraqi Constitution.[12] Constitutions emerging from war-time conquests may be more specifically called 'occupation constitutions' to refer to 'constitutions drafted or adopted in the extreme condition of one state having explicit sovereign power over another'.[13] The imbalance of power that prevails between conquering and conquered states appears to be a core feature of imposed constitutions. But must war-time conquest be a necessary precursor to an imposed constitution?

Perhaps imposed constitutions can exist without a prior war. Consider Canada's *Constitution Act, 1982*, which includes the now-famous *Canadian Charter of Rights and Freedoms*.[14] It was negotiated and agreed to by first ministers—the prime minister and the provincial premiers—over the objection of Quebec's premier, who refused to consent to what has turned out to be a revolutionary set of new rules that have transformed Canadian law and society.[15] Surely from his view

7 Yasua Hasebe, 'Constitutional Borrowing and Political Theory' (2003) 1 *International Journal of Constitutional Law* 224 at 224 (2003).

8 *Ibid* at 225.

9 *Ibid*.

10 *Ibid*.

11 *See* Sandra Madsen, 'The Japanese Constitution and Self-Defense Forces: Prospects for a New Japanese Military Role' (1993) 3 *Transnational Law & Contemporary Problems* 549 at 555.

12 *See* Saad N. Jawad, 'The Iraqi Constitution: Structural Flaws and Political Implications', London School of Economics Middle East Center Paper Series 01, November 2013, online: http://eprints.lse.ac.uk/54927/1/SaadJawad_Iraqi_Constitution_LSE_Middle_East_Centre_WP01_Nov2013.pdf.

13 Tom Ginsburg, Zachary Elkins & James Melton, 'Baghdad, Tokyo, Kabul: Constitution Making in Occupied States' (2007) 49 *William & Mary Law Review* 1139 at 1140.

14 *Canadian* Charter *of Rights and Freedoms*, Part I of the Constitution Act, 1982, being Schedule B to the Canada Act 1982 (UK), 1982, c 11 (the 'Charter').

15 For a recent inquiry into Patriation, see Frédéric Bastien, *La Bataille de Londres* (Montreal: Les Éditions du Boréal, 2013).

and the view of his adherents, the *Constitution Act, 1982* seems imposed, even though there was no war to be won. What, then, distinguishes the imposition in Japan from the modern imposition in Canada?

In Germany, the end of World War II led to the formation of the Basic Law, a frequently referenced example of an imposed constitution. While the process of constitution-making was overseen by the Allied Powers, the drafting itself was primarily German in both the main and mundane. Not fully dictated nor directed by the occupiers, the new Basic Law was based on German models and traditions, and shaped by Germans themselves.[16] What makes this an imposed law? Is it the influence of outsiders in what we believe ought to be a process closed to them?

Return to the Iraqi Constitution. We think of it as an imposed constitution, and indeed it involved a dominant external actor. But it also involved a serious and authentic process of negotiation and cooperation. Unlike the conventional narrative of imposition, the process that yielded the Iraqi Constitution reflects a contemporary form of imposition, characterized by local input and cooperation, certainly with concessions and fewer choices, but also involving non-governmental organizations working alongside foreign actors and local elites in a process that can be fairly described as collaborative, albeit constrained by the reality of the recent war.[17] The best evidence of the influence of the local actors in the design of the Iraqi Constitution is the entrenchment of Islam as the official religion despite the dominant external actors being liberal democracies that would not adopt such an arrangement for themselves.

The origins of this volume

In May 2017, the Research Group on Constitution-Making and Constitutional Change of the International Association of Constitutional Law joined forces with the Centre for European Constitutional Law—Themistocles and Dimitris Tstatos Foundation and the Department of Law at the University of Nicosia to host an international symposium on 'Imposed Constitutions—Aspects of Imposed Constitutionalism' at the School of Law of the University of Nicosia in Cyprus. The purpose of the symposium was to bring together a group of constitutional scholars for a high-level discussion on theoretical and practical issues emerging from the enactment and operation of imposed constitutions. The group also considered particular examples of this phenomenon.

The symposium opened with an address from Demetris Syllouris, the President of the House of Representatives in Cyprus, and welcoming remarks from Achilles Emilianides, Dean of the University of Nicosia. The event proceeded over two days, with participants assigned to a variety of panels, including the making and

16 Frederick Schauer, 'On Migration of Constitutional Ideals' (2004) 37 *Connecticut Law Review* 907 at 908.

17 Noah Feldman, 'Imposed Constitutionalism' (2004) 37 *Connecticut Law Review* 857 at 859.

implementation of imposed constitutions, the imposition of constitutional principles and the theory of imposed constitutions. The symposium revealed for all to see the fascinating complexities of imposed constitutions and constitutionalism.

From the very beginning, the purpose of the symposium was to publish the best papers in a collection. The papers were therefore prepared with that objective in mind, and they now appear in this volume as chapters much improved and revised since their initial presentation in Nicosia.

Contents in context

The chapters in this volume raise new questions that have yet to receive the attention they deserve. They push us to reconsider what we have thus far thought to be true about imposed constitutions. Is there a difference between an imposed constitution and imposed constitutionalism? Can an imposed constitution ever be legitimate? Are imposed constitutions always created after conquest? Are all constitutions in some way imposed? Can there be such a thing as an internally imposed constitution? And how might we make sense of constitutions that are imposed with the consent of the governed?

The chapters highlight other questions. Is there a difference between octroyed and imposed constitutions? Must imposed constitutions always be ethically problematic? How might founding era American constitution-makers evaluate the Japanese Constitution they imposed following World War II? And is the imposed Constitution of Japan rooted in a persuasive understanding of constituent power? Is it possible to legitimate internationally imposed constitutions in the context of state building? Can there be supranational imposed constitutionalism, for instance in the context of the European Union? And what lessons can we draw from regions of the world where imposed constitutions are more common than not? These are only some of the questions addressed in this volume in an effort to break new ground in the study of an old but still fascinating subject, and yet one that remains understudied and undertheorized.

We have divided this volume into three parts. In the first part, on 'Theory', we gather chapters on the theoretical questions raised by the phenomenon of imposed constitutions. The authors consider how we should conceptualize imposed constitutions, they suggest definitions of imposed constitutions and they identify limitations to the existing literature in the field.

In the opening chapter, Xenophon Contiades and Alkmene Fotiadou explore *Imposed Constitutions: Heteronomy and (Un)amendabililty*. They offer a synthetic approach of different and often competing approaches to the notion of imposition. They have two objectives in their chapter. First, they delineate the notion of imposition—making the distinction between imposing a constitution and imposing constitutionalism. For them, it is important to distinguish between the two because it is a necessary distinction in the constitutional history of several countries. Second, they explore the relation among imposed constitutions, constitutional functions and constitutional change. What, they ask, is more important: the narrative of constituent power, or the functionality of a constitution—and how do these two interact? The conceptual lens of constitutional change shifts the focus to the way in which a constitution changes. They suggest that the way an imposed constitution can change, and how it has changed, defines both how a constitution operates and how it draws legitimacy.

Next, in *Imposed Constitutions and Romantic Constitutions*, David Law argues that the concept of an 'imposed constitution' implies a false dichotomy between 'imposed' and the political narrative about why a particular constitution is undeserving of acceptance. Such narratives, he contends, draw their power from a widespread and inaccurate romanticization of what constitutions are, and how they are created. Conversely, he suggests that a constitution that benefits from such a narrative might be called a 'romantic constitution'. As Law states, no constitution can in reality live up to such a narrative, but the application of the 'romantic' label—precisely like the 'imposed' label—depends as a practical matter on the narrative rather than the reality.

This provocative chapter breaks new ground by challenging the false dichotomy between 'imposed' and 'unimposed' constitutions, illustrating how possible definitions of 'imposed constitution' are all either ambiguous or untenable, highlighting the widespread yet frequently unchallenged romanticization of constitutions and constitution-making, and introducing an innovative distinction between 'romantic' and 'unromantic' constitutions, in lieu of what Law suggests is a problematic distinction between 'imposed' and 'unimposed' constitutions.

The following chapter, authored by Yaniv Roznai, offers a complementary view. In *Internally Imposed Constitutions*, Roznai argues that all constitutions are imposed. Even those constitutions that are not imposed by an external actor are imposed, he writes. He identifies four types of internal imposition: majoritarian imposition, generational imposition, elite imposition and judicial imposition. Roznai suggests that when it comes to 'old' constitutions, past generations impose the constitution on the current and future generations. Even with 'young' constitutions, during the constitution-making process there are always losing parties (usually minorities) upon which the majority imposes its values. Roznai moreover contends that in many cases constitution-making is elite-driven so that the elite impose the constitution on others. He also makes the case that even the judiciary can 'impose' the constitution on the polity. Like Law, Roznai stresses that the romantic vision of constitution-making is that the constitution is written, or at least ought to be written, by 'we the people'. He goes on to argue that no constitution in reality is or has been the result of an actual social contract because such unanimity is impossible in constitution-making. Roznai also distinguishes externally imposed from internally imposed constitutions, the former being a source of greater concern perhaps because the governed tend to regard outsiders as threats to their constitutional identity.

Next, in *Legal Theology in Imposed Constitutionalism*, Antoni Abat i Ninet focuses on the question of legitimacy, and asks how we can consider legitimate an imposed constitution and the subsequent constitutional principles, practices and values that go hand-in-hand with legal and political acculturation. As he explains, constitutional texts around the world are good examples of transposition and complicity of theological and juridical thoughts. Imposed constitutions are rules imposed for salvation for those 'Platonic Philosophers' who have 'seen the light' and know that *episteme* are paramount examples of legal and political theology. The chapter has two main sections. The first part is devoted to a fictitious example, the failure of Rawls' pretended state (Kazanistan) and how international military intervention, transition to democracy and foreign imposed constitution fits with theological experiences of 'apocalypses, the coming, redemption, and expiration'. The second discusses both the imposition of a constitution and constitutionalism. On the theme of imposed constitutionalism, Abat i Ninet reflects on the inconsistency of the idealistic discourse that permeates a constitutional text, the inability of an imposed text to be enveloped by principles that reflect the nation's fundamental concepts and finally the denaturalization of the understanding of a constitution as the juridification of the People or Nation.

The chapter is innovative because it engages the subject from the perspectives of legal theory and legal theology. Abat i Ninet identifies and explains the 'systemic inconsistencies' that imposed constitutionalism generates. Among these constitutional failures he highlights the unworkability of the idea of an implicit constitutional text (what he explains is the invisible ink of the norm), the impossibility of 'original' or 'purposive' interpretations of the constitution, the difficulty of accommodating aspirational principles, the denial of the right of self-determination and other dysfunctionalities related to the interpretation of an imposed constitutional text.

The second part on the 'Forms' of imposed constitutions contains chapters that explore the various ways in which constitutions are in fact imposed and can in theory be imposed.

In the first chapter in this part—*Constitutions Imposed with Consent?*—Richard Albert asks whether a constitution can be imposed with the consent of the peoples on which it is imposed. As he suggests, the conventional understanding of an imposed constitution—a constitution forced upon a people after war or conquest—rejects this possibility because the very nature of an imposed constitution denies that a community of peoples could ever divest itself of the power of self-determination associated with democratic constitution-making and -changing. Yet beyond contexts of war and conquest, Albert argues that we may consider constitutions to have been imposed also if they reflect some measure of heteronomy. Heteronomous constitutions are created, governed or adapted directly or indirectly by an external actor. He contends that this understanding of an imposed constitution accommodates both the conventional view of a constitution written or administered coercively by a victorious power for a vanquished state as well as those domestic constitutions born not of defeat but controlled in some way by an external actor invited by the governed to exercise constitution-level decision-making authority.

In this chapter, Albert identifies three categories of heteronomous constitutions imposed with consent—constitutions that are amended, adjudicated and interpreted by others beyond the jurisdictional sphere of those governed by the constitution. He argues that recognizing that a constitution can indeed be imposed with consent complicates our understanding of imposed constitutions, and forces us to confront the reality that extraterritorial actors can sometimes be invited to occupy a central place in domestic constitutional law.

In *Are 'Octroyed Constitutions' of the 19*th *Century to be Considered as Imposed Constitutions?*, Jörg Gerkrath considers the 'octroyed', 'conceded' or 'granted' constitutions of 19th century Europe whose common roots are to be found in the French 'Charte constitutionnelle' of 1814. These Charters, he notes, stem from a paternalistic process of domestic constitution-making engaged unilaterally by a monarch possessing the *de facto* constituent power and exercising it without the direct involvement of the people. Gerkrath argues that such octroyed constitutions, which should be contrasted with democratically established ones, nevertheless show a number of specific characteristics that distinguish them also from 'imposed constitutions' in the usual sense. Gerkrath explains that the expression "constitutional octroy' should not be used as a synonym for any process that leads to an 'imposed constitution". This chapter seeks to develop and validate or invalidate the value of a series of distinctive criteria and possible elements of a definition of 'octroyed' or 'granted' constitutions in order to underline their specificity—and to distinguish them from the class of constitutions that are better called 'imposed"

The chapter fills a void in the literature. Most existing works are based on the study of a single charter or an analysis of successive constitutions from a single country. The chapter applies the comparative method in order to develop legal criteria allowing to distinguish between 'octroyed' and 'imposed' constitutions. It is based on a thorough study of roughly one dozen granted constitutions from the 19th century, together highlighting the selected criteria that can distinguish these two forms of constitutions. Gerkrath makes frequent references to the constitutions of France 1814, Luxembourg 1841, Italy 1848, Austria 1849 and Prussia.

In the third and final chapter in Part II, we find Zoran Oklopcic's *Inter-Venire, Sed Ubi Ire?: 'Imposed' Constitutions, the 'Will of the People', and the Eye of the Beholder*. Oklopcic uses debates about 'imposed' constitutions as a foil, aiming to re-imagine the meaning of *Demos*, *Ethnos*, and *Nomos*, by looking at the acts of constitution-making through the eyes of a figure, which has, thus far, been ostracized from most constitutional theories. That figure, for Oklopcic, is *Xenos*, a particular kind of 'foreigner': an ambivalent and ambiguous powerful actor, who affects the formation of a constitutional order from without, without being in turn affected by the constitutional aspirations of those within. Oklopcic argues that a different approach to imposed constitution(alism) has to start looking at the scenes of constitution-making through *Xenos*' eyes, which he suggests is fruitful: it will allow scholars to come closer to a radically different way of looking at democratic self-government, national self-determination and the functions of international legal order; indicating at the same time an approach to sovereign peoplehood, orthogonal to most contemporary theories. Oklopcic argues that theorists have too narrowly understood the concept of 'imposed constitution' in one of two ways: either as a *normative oxymoron*, or as an *ontological pleonasm*—either as the ethically illegitimate, or as the logically inevitable outcome of constitution-making. He offers an alternative perspective.

The third part of this volume gathers together chapters on 'Applications'. The authors consider imposed constitutions currently in place in a number of polities worldwide, and they explore critically a number of consequences their imposition has caused.

Sanford Levinson reflects on Japan's restriction against maintaining a standing military in his chapter *On the Priority that Publius Gives to National Security in Constitutional Design: Reflections on the Longevity of Article 9 of the Japanese Constitution*. Levinson notes that many countries that have renounced aggressive warfare under the United Nations Charter have continued to maintain robust militaries, many with nuclear arsenals. Levinson uses the lens of American constitutional history, and more specifically of *The Federalist*, to consider Japan's Article 9 and its possible repeal. Highlighting a number of essays in *The Federalist*, Levinson contends that many of the framers of the United States Constitution argued for a strong centralized government with the capacity for self-preservation. Levinson argues that Article 9 limits Japan's ability as a sovereign state to protect itself, something which Publius would have found deeply problematic.

Next, in *The Constituent Power of the 'Imposed' Constitution of Japan: An Amalgam of Internationalised Revolutionary Power and Nationalist Devolutionary Power*, Yota Negishi argues that the Japanese Constitution is a hybrid model of an 'internationalised revolutionary power' and 'nationalistic devolutionary power'. As Negishi states, under the pre-war Meiji Constitution, constituent power was sanctified as 'imperial sovereignty' that embodied the culturally and historically constructed 'National Entity (Kokutai)'. Under the post-war Showa Constitution, however, the traditional principle was revolutionarily changed into popular sovereignty through the acceptance of the Potsdam Declaration, an international agreement. The 'internationalised revolutionary power' of the people has since become frozen and limited by basic human rights norms and the Kokutai concept has emerged to advocate a 'nationalist devolutionary power' for reversing the 'imposed' Constitution. Negishi's analysis provides a legal account for the contemporary ambivalent Japanese attitude between the post-war diplomatic subservience to the United States and the atavistic attempts to resurrect the pre-war values.

In her chapter on *The Legitimacy of Internationally Imposed Constitution-Making in the Context of State Building*, Manon Bonnet explores the legitimacy of the internationally imposed constitution-making processes in the context of state building. Starting from the assumption that the *pouvoir constituant* is held by the people, she questions the possibility of legitimating externally imposed constitutions. Bonnet's research is based on a comparative analysis of seven case studies: Afghanistan, Bosnia and Herzegovina, Cambodia, Iraq, Namibia, Sudan and Timor-Leste. She analyses the democratic and formal legitimacy of these processes by highlighting the different means of participation of the people in every step of the constitution-making process, from the context of peacebuilding operations to the adoption of the constitution and its implementation. Her chapter highlights the difficulty of addressing the questions of legitimacy and the perverse effects of international intervention in constitution-making processes. An important takeaway from her chapter is that although legitimacy is often considered one of the key markers of a successful constitutional transition, a look at a few case studies in international practice shows just how little attention is given to the need for legitimacy by the institutions designing and executing these processes. Her chapter aims to provide an overview of relevant tools to improve the level of legitimacy of imposed processes while questioning their very capacity to be legitimate.

In the second-to-last chapter in this part, entitled *A Post-National Legal Order: Does the European Union Have an Imposed Constitution?*, Graham Butler considers whether the foundational steps in forming the European Union have made it a form of imposed constitutionalism. He argues that while Union membership is a voluntary exercise, it is an expression of integration into a larger community of like-minded states. Regionally, this exercise of internal integration occurred through various means. Legally, the signing of treaties between European states that founded the Union was a fine balance between constitutionalism that was imposed, as opposed to self-imposed. Whether this constitutionalizing process stemmed from the Union's judicial political actors is largely irrelevant, given that the nature of European constitutionalism appears evident. Graham raises a number of important questions for consideration: Can constitutionalism in the EU be considered imposed? Who is imposing these actions? And who will sustain the constitutionalism? This chapter explores the constitutionalizing process of European integration through a supranational organization model, putting into perspective the intersection of imposed constitutionalism and supranationalism.

In the final chapter of this part and also of the volume, James Fowkes begins his exposition on *Texts in a Time of Imposition: Lessons from Two Imposed Constitutions in Africa* from the proposition that so much has been imposed on Africa that studying imposed constitutions on the continent can seem like an exercise in the obvious. He recognizes that, indeed, sometimes it is. But he invites us to see that African cases are of a richness that has been neglected by comparative constitutional law. His chapter reports on research into two Anglophone case studies, Liberia and Botswana. Each is dominated by one imposed text, the 1847 Constitution in the case of Liberia, in force until 1980, and the 1966 Botswana Constitution, which remains in operation today. Both are unusually long-lived for an imposed text in Africa. Both are independence constitutions drafted in a colonial context, but in each case this external relation is accompanied by significant local agency and by complex internal political patterns, including oppressive ones. He complicates our understanding of an 'imposed constitution' by suggesting that coming to terms with the nuances of these neglected cases offers several useful lessons about what an adequate concept of an 'imposed constitution' should look like.

New ground and new learning

Despite the prevalence of imposition throughout history, there has been little written on imposed constitutions in the conceptual, historical, theoretical and practical ways offered in this volume. More than simply offering conclusions about imposed constitutions, this volume seeks to further complicate the conventional understanding of an imposed constitution as the product of conquest. We also aspire in this volume to shed light on the existing ambiguities in the study of imposed constitutionalism, and in the end to create a resource that will serve as a useful guide in the field for understanding the idea of an imposed constitution, as well as its unresolved internal tensions.

Part I

Theory

1 Imposed constitutions

Heteronomy and (un)amendability

*Xenophon Contiades and Alkmene Fotiadou**

Introduction

Do imposed constitutions exist 'merely in the mind which contemplates them'?[1] In other words, is constitutional imposition an intangible notion able to provide a specific definition of what an imposed constitution is?

The paradox of 'imposed constitutionalism' is that although the argument that 'the very concept of an 'imposed' constitution lacks explanatory or analytical value because it rests upon a false dichotomy between 'imposed' and 'unimposed' constitutions'[2] is appealing from a theoretical aspect, the concept of imposed constitutions is deeply imbedded in the history of countries that experienced the making of their constitution as a story of external imposition.[3] To begin with, making the distinction between imposing a constitution and imposing constitutionalism is crucial for explaining the recent trend of theoretically deconstructing the concept of imposed constitutions, while at the same time the idea of imposed constitutions is central in the constitutional narratives of several countries. Imposed constitutions and imposed constitutionalism are not the same thing: The notion of the imposed constitution refers to the document whereas imposed constitutionalism refers to principles and values enshrined in the document.

This chapter aims to explore the notion of 'imposed constitutions' offering a synthetic approach of different and often competing approaches. It begins by analyzing the imposition continuum. Along the two ends of the imposition continuum (constitutional autonomy and constitutional heteronomy) lie principles and values that are considered to be sine qua non of constitutions, external expert advice, consultation and external involvement that may amount to constitution

* Xenophon Contiades, Professor of Public Law, Panteion University of Social and Political Sciences (Athens, Greece) and Managing Director of the Centre for European Constitutional Law. Alkmene Fotiadou, Dr.iur. and Research Associate at the Centre for European Constitutional Law (Athens, Greece).

1 D Hume, *Of the Standard of Taste: Post-Modern Times Aesthetic Classics* (The Birmingham Free Press, 2013).

2 D Law, 'The Myth of the Imposed Constitution' in D Galligan and M Versteeg (Eds), *The Social and Political Foundations of Constitutions* (CUP, 2013) 241–50.

3 On the Notion of the 'External' see Z Oklopcic, 'Inter-venire, sed ubi ire?' (Chapter 7) in this volume.

drafting. The second part probes whether there is such a thing as an uncorrectable birth defect which will inevitably tint future constitutional life. The third part traces different sources of constitutional legitimacy attempting to find the correlations between constitutional imposition, amendability and functionality. The fourth part explores the process of promoting and 'selling' a constitution to an audience, which it names constitutional marketing. To do so, it examines the construction of memory during the moment of constitutional enactment and the ways in which this memory impacts how a constitution is perceived in the case the memory of the constituent moment is a memory of imposition. The fifth part addresses the connection between constitutional imposition and constitutional change, arguing that imposition is better understood not by exploring constitution-making but by focusing on constitutional change and amendability. The conceptual lens of constitutional change shifts the focus to the way in which a constitution changes. In that sense, how an imposed constitution can change and how it has changed defines both the way a constitution operates and how it draws legitimacy.

As this chapter delineates the relation between imposed constitutions, constitutional functions and constitutional change, the question emerges of what is more important: the narrative of constituent power or the functionality of a constitution, and how the two interact. The distinction between imposing a constitution and imposing constitutionalism reaches beyond distinguishing the written document and the principles it enshrines. The 'who, when, how and why' questions have to be addressed to explain the distinction.

The constitutional imposition continuum

Constitutional imposition is a continuum, not a dichotomy. Constitutions exist along the continuum of imposition, whose poles are constitutional autonomy and constitutional heteronomy. Autonomy as the end of the imposition continuum refers to the collective awareness that 'society has created its own laws', an explicit knowledge of self-institution through rules also enabling future alteration.[4] Heteronomy, regulation by another, is the other end of the continuum. Both, however, entail not only the act of enacting, but also a sense of awareness. Along this continuum lie, thus, not only actions but the perception of these actions as well.

Rules and standards exist along a continuum of discretion where standards may become more rule-like and rules can become more standard-like through application and exceptions.[5] In a like manner, a heteronomous constitution may move along the continuum through formal and informal change, while autonomous constitutions may also be applied and interpreted in such ways as to lose, or be perceived as having lost, their autonomy.

4 C Castoriadis, 'The imaginary institution of society', available at: http://base.mayfirst.org/wp-content/uploads/2013/03/cornelius-castoriadis-the-imaginary-institution.pdf accessed 4 December 2017.

5 K M Sullivan, 'Foreword – The Supreme Court, 1991 Term: The Justices of Rules and Standards' (1992) 106 *Harv L Rev* 22, 27–56.

The notion of 'another', which is crucial in the perception of the imposition continuum, also varies in degrees. The crucial distinction appears to be the one between the 'who' and the 'what'. According to Blound, Elkins and Ginsburg, 'international constraints on constitution-making can range in their intensity and degree of "coordination" ranging from borrowing to imposition'.[6] Constitutional borrowing and even the involvement of external experts may be the decision of internal constitution makers. Even in case it results from the need to abide by international standards of constitution-making, self-discipline in the exercise of constituent power differs from full-fledged imposition. From that aspect, it might fall into the category of imposition with consent,[7] in which case the question is whether such consent differentiates the way in which the constitution is perceived.

In case, however, imposition suggests a heterochthonous constitution,[8] it is crucial to distinguish between an external actor who plays a major part in writing and enacting a constitution, as opposed to external influencers who play a less succinct role. The balance between fact and emotion may determine the placement of a constitution along the imposition continuum.

The question which emerges by placing constitutions along the imposition continuum is whether imposition is so fluid as to render all constitutions imposed to a certain degree and in that sense imposition becomes self-nullified and empty of meaning. If everything is imposed, nothing is truly imposed.

Yaniv Roznai's analysis pins down four types of internal imposition: generational imposition, majoritarian imposition, elite imposition and judicial imposition.[9] The constitution-making act always entails a certain degree of imposition as it is meant to bind not only the bearers of constituent power but also others, not only in time present but also in time future. This may indicate two things. Firstly, that internal imposition does not impact constitutional legitimacy to the extent that external imposition does. In that sense, the degree of imposition correlates with the degree of legitimacy loss.

Secondly, imposition (both internal and external) depends on the degree of constitutional rigidity: not only who makes, but also who can change, a constitution matters. Institutional rigidities put in place primarily by formal amendment rules interacting with factual rigidities determine how difficult it is to change constitutions.[10] The degree which something is imposed on someone depends on their ability to alter it. The capacity to change the constitution may negate imposition, or rather remedy its legitimacy flaw. As Rosalind Dixon and Adrienne Stone explain, amendment procedures by providing an 'ongoing popular participation',

6 J Blound, Z Elkins and T Ginsburg, 'Does the Process of Constitution-Making Matter?' in T Ginsburg, *Comparative Constitutional Design* (CUP, 2012) 40.

7 R Albert, 'Constitutions imposed with consent?' (Chapter 5), in this volume.

8 PC Oliver, 'Autochthonous Constitutions' (July 11, 2017) in R Grote, F Lachenmann and R Wolfrum (Eds), *Max Planck Encyclopedia of Comparative Constitutional Law* (Oxford University Press, 2016).

9 Y Roznai, 'Internally imposed constitutions' (Chapter 3), in this volume.

10 See X Contiades and A Fotiadou, 'Models of Constitutional Change' in X Contiades (Eds), *Engineering Constitutional Change. A Comparative Perspective on Europe, Canada and the USA* (Routledge, 2012) 417.

'confer legitimacy not only on changes to the Constitution' but 'also to the status quo'.[11]

Uncorrectable constitutional birth defects

The dark side of the strong symbolic meaning flowing from the constituent power imagery is that it allows infinitely attributing present-time problems to flaws in the past exercise of constituent powers.

Imposition is a memory which is often subject to restructuring, and can be brought back and influence the present at any moment, especially stressful ones. Recent examples are illuminating. During the turmoil in Spain with regard to the possibility of Catalonian secession, the blame game targeted the Constitution. It has been argued that "Historically, the Spanish constitution of 1978 is a product of a transition to democracy and, far from being the result of a deliberation of free and equal citizens, it was negotiated in the shadow of a possible return of Francoist forces, and in particular the possibility of a military coup (a very real threat, as the actual *coup d'état* in 1981 demonstrated)….A document which, at the time, was accepted by many merely for fear of the alternatives, does not have a particularly strong claim to authority four decades later."[12] The constitutional emphasis on the unity of Spain and the weak status of the autonomous regions are thus attributed to the faulty constituent moment background. Although the Spanish Constitution is characterized by a high level of rigidity, this analysis is somewhat disquieting. During the financial crisis, a fast-track procedure which took only thirty-two days from the submission of the proposal was used to enshrine the balanced budget rule in the Constitution.[13] The amendment took place through a fast-track procedure set out in art 166 of the Constitution and was allowed to happen because both dominant parliamentary groups co-operated in the proposal for this amendment. Both parties had requested that the amendment be processed by the emergency procedure and approved in a single reading.

So, the notoriously stringent amending formula allowed even a fast-track process of constitutional change as far as strong consensus existed. A constitutional response to the challenge of the financial crisis, using the symbolic force of the constitution, was possible. How and why then can the Constitution of Spain still be revisited as a product of transition accepted through some sort of psychological coercion and thus be ill-suited to control the secessionist crisis? Why does there appear to be a

11 R Dixon and A Stone, 'Constitutional Amendment and Political Constitutionalism: A Philosophical and Comparative Reflection' in D Dyzenhaus and M Thorburn (Eds), *Philosophical Foundations of Constitutional Law* (Oxford University Press, 2016) 95.

12 N Krisch, 'Law, legitimacy and popular sovereignty in question', available at: http://verfassungsblog.de/the-spanish-constitutional-crisis-law-legitimacy-and-popular-sovereignty-in-question/ accessed 30 October 2017.

13 See M Estrada-Cañamares and L Díez Sánchez, 'Constitutional change through the Euro crisis law: Spain', available at: http://eurocrisislaw.eui.eu/country/spain/topic/euro-plus-pact and X Contiades and A Fotiadou, 'The Resilient Constitution: Lessons from the Financial Crisis' in A Herwig and M Simoncini (Eds), *Law and the Management of Disasters. The Challenge of Resilience* (Routledge, 2017) 189.

presumption of irrelevance due to a tainted constituent moment despite the prescribed, and applied when deemed necessary, possibility of constitutional change?

The example of Iceland is even more puzzling. Iceland attracted remarkable attention due to an innovative, experimental participatory process of crowdsourcing constitution-writing. The experiment did not succeed in producing a constitution and yet it triggered a novel debate about alternative ways of constitutional design. The requirement of constitutional reform appeared strong because the Constitution still had the 'flavour' of an imposed constitution despite important amendments with regard to the organization of the Althingi and human rights protection. There was thus a necessity for a 'written and adopted unanimously new comprehensive document that matches the nature of an independent republic'.[14] Large parts of the Constitution of Iceland had remained unchanged from the time when Iceland had received its first Constitution from the King of Denmark in 1874. In 1944, when Iceland broke off the union with Denmark at the peak of World War II, only minimal amendments were made to the constitution to accomplish the passage from a constitutional monarchy to a republic.[15] The memory of a long-gone imposed constitution still haunted the collective perception of constitutional legitimacy and when a crisis broke out this perception turned to a pressing need to revisit the constitution.

A juxtaposition with constitutions traditionally viewed as imposed is helpful to probe into backward- and forward-looking framing of the moment of imposition as juridically/politically consequential. Perhaps the most oft-used example of an imposed constitution is that of Japan. The Constitution of Japan of 1946 was imposed by the occupying forces on the Japanese Government after World War II. Under orders of General MacArthur, the General Headquarters of the Supreme Commander produced a draft constitution and pressured the Japanese government to revise the then-existing constitution accordingly.[16] Although the striking feature appears at first glance to be imposition, the truly impressive element is speed in constitution-making. As Blound, Ginsburg and Elkins vividly described, 'a small group of American bureaucrats for the occupying authorities drafted the basic form of Japan's Constitution a little more than a week, and the entire process including elections, legislative deliberation and approval by the emperor took a mere eight months'. Not even the pretence of constitution-making rituals were

14 B Thor Bergsson and P Blokker, 'The Constitutional Experiment in Iceland' (September 4, 2013) in K Pocza (ed), *Verfassunggebung in konsolidierten Demokratien: Neubeginn oder Verfall eines Systems?*, (Nomos Verlag, forthcoming), available at: https://ssrn.com/abstract=2320748, accessed 4 December 2017; B Thorarensen, 'The People's Contribution to Constitutional Changes. Writing, Advising or Approving? – Lessons from Iceland' in X Contiades and A Fotiadou (Eds), *Participatory Constitutional Change: The People as Amenders of the Constitution* (Routledge, 2017) 106.

15 See B Thorarensen, 'The Impact of the Financial Crisis on Icelandic Constitutional Law: Legislative Reforms, Judicial Review and Revision of the Constitution' in X Contiades (ed), *Constitutions in the Global Financial Crisis. A Comparative Analysis* (Ashgate, 2013) 274.

16 See Y Hasebe, 'Imposed Constitutions (constitutions octroyées)' in R Grote, F Lachenmann and R Wolfrum (Eds), *Max Planck Encyclopedia of Comparative Constitutional Law* (n 8), available at: http://oxcon.ouplaw.com/view/10.1093/law-mpeccol/law-mpeccol-e21 accessed 10 September 2017.

abided by and yet this paradoxical constitution is at the same time the archetype of an imposed constitution and the negation of constitutional imposition.

A possible explanation for the longevity of Japan's Constitution explored by D. Law is that it was never truly imposed. According to this approach, Contemporaneous public opinion data strongly supports the view that General MacArthur's constitutional maneuvering is best understood not as an act of imposition upon "Japan" as a whole, but rather as an act of agenda control that bypassed elite resistance in favour of a document that enjoyed widespread popular support.

It is tempting to think that if a constitution works, it cannot be actually imposed, even though it may correspond to the basic features of the definition of an imposed constitution. Lack of legitimacy of the highest norm should impede its functionality. If there is no such thing as a truly imposed constitution then at the descriptive, rather than the existential level, the category of imposed constitutions may be viewed as useless. Adversely, constituent power exercised by the people is equally susceptible to deconstruction. Descriptive typologies of imposition that occurs during constitution-making may be created, as Roznai's analysis most vividly proves. Everything is in a sense imposed, which renders imposition trivial or even irrelevant. The question here is whether the demystification of the constituent moment can offer redeeming consolation to those who perceive their constitution as imposed to the degree that they stop focusing on how it was made and turn toward the way it actually works.[17]

The Constitution of Cyprus can also be described as an archetypal paradigm of an imposed constitution. It fulfils all the requirements of imposition to the extent that it constitutes a challenge to the trend of questioning whether the category of imposed constitutions actually exists. Both the historical facts and the way the Constitution of Cyprus is perceived by the people point to the direction of the heteronomy end of the imposition continuum.

The constitutional structure of the Republic of Cyprus was created by the Zurich agreements signed on 11 February 1959 by the prime ministers of Greece and Turkey. The agreements were subsequently approved by the UK Prime Minister and representatives of the Greek Cypriot and Turkish Cypriot communities, eight days later, on 19 February 1959 in London. The agreements were approved on the same day by the Parliament of England, which unanimously expressed satisfaction, and by the Turkish National Assembly despite the intense criticism. The Greek Parliament, on the other hand, did not expressly ratify the agreements. However, they were implicitly approved through the rejection of a motion of censure with regard to the Zurich–Honduras terms and the overall management of the Cyprus problem.

17 On how constituent power is exercised in practice see J Widner and X Contiades, 'Constitution-Writing Process' in M Tushnet, T Fleiner and C Saunders (Eds), *Routledge Handbook of Constitutional Law* (Routledge, 2013).

The United Nations Mediator on Cyprus characterized the arrangements as a 'constitutional oddity' very difficult to maintain in the future. Indeed, the Cypriot Constitution was designed to serve as a compromise between two communities. It created an independent State, where the rights of the minority were entrenched to ensure their effective participation in governance at all levels and in every instance. To attain this objective, the three interested States (Greece, Turkey and Great Britain) were given extraordinary powers of intervention in case of a constitutional anomaly.[18] Nonetheless, the constitutional design underestimated the prerequisites for stability and functionality. The Constitution was lengthy, detailed and difficult to change. In retrospect, the danger of constitutional paralysis seems to have been inherent in the features of the constitution.

And indeed paralysis soon followed: following a period of tension and armed conflict between the two communities, the Turkish-Cypriots withdrew from the government, thus rendering the executive, legislative and judicial branch incapable of any decision-making.

An extra feature complementing constitutional imposition in the example of Cyprus is difficulty of constitutional change. The amendment formula is stringent and does not allow recourse to the people excluding the majority rule, aiming thus to solidify the system safeguarded by the three foreign guarantor States. Constitutional amendment was possible through a separate community two-thirds majority in the House of Representatives, and there is a long list of eternity clauses. This deadlock had led President Makarios to propose several amendments to the Constitution that were rejected by Turkey. Constitutional detail can also serve as a form of rigidity,[19] which if used in combination and not as an alternative to stringent amendment rules may result in extreme difficulty of change.

The legal way out of the impasse was provided in the seminal Ibrahim[20] case which allowed the constitutional system to continue functioning through a construction of the doctrine of necessity to match the situation. Following the intercommunal conflict in 1963–64, Law No. 33/64 was enacted in order to address the enormous constitutional and legal difficulties that arose in the functioning of the State, by the withdrawal of the Turkish Ministers, MPs and Judges from its institutions.[21] The Court ruled that the above-mentioned Law 33/64 was constitutional under the doctrine of necessity.

18 C Kombos, 'Developments in Cypriot Constitutional Law' in R Albert, D Landau, P Faraguna and S Drugda (Eds), *Global Review of Constitutional Law* (2016) 52, available at: http://www.bc.edu/centers/cloughcenter/about/annual-report/i-connect.html accessed 4 December 2017. See also 'Report of the United Nations Mediator on Cyprus to the Secretary-General', available at: http://www.securitycouncilreport.org/atf/cf/{65BFCF9B-6D27-4E9C-8CD3-CF6E4FF96FF9}/Cyprus%20S6253.pdf accessed 4 December 2017.

19 M Vesteeg and E Zackin, 'Constitutions Un-Entrenched: Toward an Alternative Theory of Constitutional Design' *Am Pol Sci Rev* (forthcoming).

20 Mustafa Ibrahim and others, '[1964] Cyprus Law Reports 195', available at: http://www.uniset.ca/other/cs2/1964CLR195.html accessed 4 December 2017.

21 *Attorney General of the Republic v Ibrahim and Others* [1964] CLR, 195.

The basic rationale of the Ibrahim case is based on the idea that a constitutional crisis that could endanger the existence of the State could not have been predicted or constitutionally anticipated; thus provisions to effectively deal with the situation were not in place and a declaration of a state of emergency provided for in art 183 of the Constitution was not sufficient to address the situation. Nonetheless, the law of necessity stemmed from the imposed and rigid Constitution, and was thereby integral to the Constitution, implied in art 179, according to which the Constitution is the supreme source of law. The law of necessity was thus conceptualized as an integral part of the constitution.[22]

There appears to be an obvious paradox in the idea that during the enactment of the constitution the possibility of an impasse was inconceivable. Rather adversely, in reality the situation and the mode of constitution-making had all the ingredients for dysfunctionality. Nonetheless, the fiction of unpredictability allowed the invocation of necessity, which enabled the constitutional order to demonstrate resilience in the face of crisis. Through the passage of years, the law of necessity became a substitute for normal channels of constitutional change. 'The invocation of the law of necessity, for over fifty years, can be regarded as a constitutional "anomaly" but this, in fact, saved the Republic of Cyprus and allowed the continuation of the smooth functioning of the three powers of the state, despite the enormous difficulties'.[23]

After the events of 1963 and the withdrawal of the fifteen Turkish Cypriot Representatives, the Parliament amended the Constitution, evoking the law of necessity several times.

- In 1989 to modernize family law.
- In 1996, extending the right of citizens to vote in general elections to the minimum age of 18 instead of 21 and to replace the by-election provided for filling a vacancy in the Parliament, introducing a provision for the vacant seat to be filled by the first runner-up of the same party.
- In 2002 the Constitution was amended to comply with the provisions of the acquis communautaire, ensuring the independence of the Central Bank.
- In 2006, as a result of the accession of the Republic of Cyprus to the European Union, the supremacy of European Communities and European Union law was recognized to enable Cyprus to respond successfully to its commitments stemming from the accession, as well as to its international commitments.
- In 2010 an amendment regulating the possibility of intervention during the exercise of the right to communication was introduced.
- In 2013 the Constitution was amended to enable the Republic of Cyprus to fully comply with its commitments as a member state of the European

22 Kombos (n 18) 54.

23 See M M Nicolatos, 'Austerity measures and economic crisis. The case of Cyprus. A judges's approach', available at: http://www.venice.coe.int/webforms/documents/default.aspx?pdffile=CDL-LA(2014)011-e accessed 4 December 2017.

Union, with regard to the provisions for the European arrest warrant and the procedures of handing over citizens between EU member states.

- In 2015 an amendment of the Constitution was adopted to set up an Administrative Court, aimed to reduce the burden of work of the Supreme Court to speed up the administration of justice.[24]

The following thoughts expressed in the case of Ibrahim are characteristic of the over-rigidity problem.

> The Cyprus Constitution contains very rigid provisions for its future amendment – and even this in certain non-basic respects only. It affords no possibility for amendment as far as basic Articles are concerned. Regarding its basic provisions, in respect of matters which were incorporated from the Agreement in Zurich, no amendment is possible not even by unanimous consensus of all members of the House of Representatives. Thus, it has been deprived of the opportunity of representing the sovereign will of the people of the country at any given time and this is a vital and decisive difference between this Constitution and other written constitutions, which are subject to amendment, through processes ensuring the exercise of the sovereign will of the people of each country, so as to ensure that they give continuous expression to such will, on which after all their supremacy depends.

It is to be reasonably concluded from the foregoing that the Constitution of Cyprus, though invested with the sanctity of a supreme law, under art 179, is found not to be in reality compatible with the principles which led Marshall C.J. to propound the doctrine of the supreme law in *Marbury v Madison*. It cannot, in reality, be regarded as the ultimate outcome of the exercise of the "original right" of the Cyprus people "to establish, for their future government, such principles, as, in their opinion, shall most conduce to their own happiness" – in the same manner as Marshall, C.J., was, in *Marbury v Madison*, entitled to regard the constitution of his own country as being the product of the will of its people. Extreme difficulty of change augments the heteronomy defect.

David Law disentangles the myth of the imposed Constitution of Japan by reference to the Sherlock Holmes mystery of the curious incident of the dog in the night-time: 'Postwar constitutionalism in Japan can be likened to the story of the dog that did not bark: the absence of the most routine forms of constitutional change is a source of mystery'.[25] In the case of Cyprus, which is as characteristic of imposition, yet underexplored compared with the case of Japan, the dog did bark: the constitution evolved through the odd use of the necessity doctrine, which made possible the protection of the rule of law in the constitutional order and allowed the endurance of the constitution despite its functional and symbolic shortcomings, while it did not provide the pretext for

24 Kombos (n 18).
25 Law (n 2) 239.

the limitation of human rights. Emilianides describes the way the constitutional order operates as 'transcending' the Constitution, which captures the odd way the Constitution of Cyprus is on one hand indeed perceived by the people as imposed and yet it is valued for what it safeguards and is allowed to evolve through the doctrine of necessity.[26]

Imposition, amendability and functionality: The matrix of constitutional legitimacy

Is constituent power the ultimate source of legitimacy, or is constitutional change able to supply an alternative equally potent source?

Constitutional legitimacy may stem from functionality ensured or enhanced through constitutional amendments.[27] A working constitution capable of performing efficient constitutional functions is not only the key element for a functioning legal order, but it is also a tangible notion.[28] Formal constitutional change enables people to revisit their constitution through the exercise of constituted amending power. Constitutions draw legitimacy through this process, which in turn allows them to perform their functions better.[29]

Constitutional quality is inescapably context-sensitive. It depends on the ability of a constitution to perform its functions in a given environment. Thus, it depends on deciding the functions required from a constitution and the analysis of the environment in which they are performed. Functions may vary and so do environments. In longstanding democracies, the constitutional functions which take priority are different than the ones that matter in post-conflict or more turbulent environments. The authority of a constitution depends in large measure on how it can be made to matter through the successful regulation of politics.[30] In post-conflict environments where the possibility of full-fledged imposition is high and varying degrees of external influence or intervention more than likely, the stakes of constitution-making are very high. In that context, focus on the mechanisms of future change may not be a top priority although they may prove crucial for future functionality and evolving legitimacy.

In post-conflict environments, distinct constitutional functions are expected of constitutions impacting the way they are perceived by the people. During transitions besides the traditional constitutional functions, certain additional

26 A Emilianides, *Η υπέρβαση του Κυπριακού Συντάγματος [Trancending the Constitution of Cyprus* (Sakkoulas Publications S.A., 2006) (in Greek).

27 X Contiades and A Fotiadou, 'The Emergence of Comparative Constitutional Amendment as a New Discipline: Towards a Paradigm Shift (Conclusion)' in R Albert, X Contiades and A Fotiadou (Eds), *The Foundations and Traditions of Constitutional Amendment* (Hart Publishing, 2017).

28 X Contiades and A Fotiadou, 'Amendment-Metrics: The Good, the Bad and the Frequently Amended Constitution' in R Albert, X Contiades and A Fotiadou (Eds), *The Foundations and Traditions of Constitutional Amendment* (n 27) 239.

29 Contiades and Fotiadou (n 27).

30 M Tushnet, *Why the Constitution Matters* (Yale University Press, 2010).

functions are expected, which correspond to the aspirations of the people. The first function is the reduction of violence and conflict calming. Creating institutions through which conflicts are conducted in accordance to rules and away from the streets is crucial in such constitution-making processes.[31] However, it is possible that focusing on the importance of this function may result in paying little attention to the quality of constitution-writing.[32] Bad writing, however, causes difficulties in applying the constitution at a later point where more traditional constitutional functions gain importance. Furthermore, the urgency of the situation may suggest that constitutional imposition is the only way to achieve this function, which allows little thinking about future legitimacy and constitutional birth defects that may hinder a healthy constitutional life.

A second function expected of constitutions is building cohesion in deeply divided societies. Harmonizing religious, social and ethnic differences is a difficult challenge, especially in conditions that stimulate and intensify conflicts. The question here is whether cohesion-building is best achieved through constitutional moments with all their glamour (and clamour) or through incrementalism.[33] Forcing majoritarian decisions on values and goals at constitution-making moments may further differences instead of bridging them, and allow them to linger on unexpressed, yet ready to ignite, for an infinite period of time. Hence, allowing the possibility of evolutionary constitutional change has a better chance of success. Incremental change may result from a variety of reasons, e.g. abstract language often leaves room for such change. Nonetheless, by relaxing the foremost institutional rigidity which stems from the amending formula, incrementalism is encouraged to happen through formal constitutional paths, which is a condition fostering constitutionalism especially when it is in the making. The pragmatic demystifying approach to constituent power during transitions is inclusiveness.[34] Active inclusion encompasses the creation of effective channels of communication between decision makers and constituents in constitution-making moments. Targeted inclusion entails taking into consideration all voices, especially those expressing unconventional views, including those challenging traditional conceptions of liberal democracy.[35] Inclusiveness may counterbalance external involvement, which is standard practice in transitions. External participation in constitution-making can result in clumsy constitutional borrowing. Provisions may not match the requirements of a given

31 See J Widner, 'Constitution-Writing in Post-Conflict Settings', (2008) *Wm & Mary L Rev* 49, 1513–1541.

32 E Afsah, 'Constitution-Making in Islamic Countries: A Theoretical Framework' in R Grote and T Röder (Eds), *Constitution-Making in Islamic Countries: Between Upheaval and Continuity* (Oxford University Press, 2010) 475.

33 See H Lerner, *Making Constitutions in Deeply Divided Societies* (CUP, 2011).

34 J. Elster, 'The Optimal Design of a Constituent Assembly' in H Landemore and J Elster (Eds), *Collective Wisdom: Principles and Mechanisms* (CUP, 2014).

35 International IDEA Institute for Democracy and Electoral Assistance, *The Global State of Democracy. Exploring Democracy's Resilience* 252 (IDEA, 2017), available at: https://www.idea.int/gsod/files/IDEA-GSOD-2017-REPORT-EN.pdf accessed 4 December 2017.

environment, being either out of context or 'superior to those that the drafters have the resources or knowledge to engineer for themselves'.[36] It is possible that problems generated by lack of inclusiveness or bad design choices can be remedied through change.

In the midst of political and social turmoil it is difficult for drafters to envisage a future where the amendment rate is expressive of the overall function of a constitution and of the way in which it is perceived, that is, as a truly higher law or as a code.[37] Still, keeping in mind that the degree of difficulty of the amending process influences the whole constitution and most importantly its future chance of acquiring legitimacy is helpful. Transition examples such as Eastern Europe, Iraq or Afghanistan, where constitution-making does not coincide with entrenchment of a final document produced by a sovereign people, can be useful.[38] The possibility of interim constitutions is an option, where the functions expected of the constitution can be narrowly tailored to the transition.[39] Temporary constitutions change the way in which constitutions relate to the passage of time and they help slow down time at moments of constitution-making when time accelerates. Thus, they may provide extra time for building political institutions. Being ephemeral by definition does not aim to establish long-lasting constitutional values. It is exactly this divergence from the ordinary conceptualization of the constitution that renders them useful in very particular situations. Nonetheless, the option of temporary constitutions did not become a default option negating the phenomenon of imposing constitutions aimed to last. The degree of constitutional flexibility thus may also serve as an alternative to temporality.

According to traditional constitutional scholarship, drafters face a trilemma. They may put in place a stringent formula aimed to a high rigidity level, they may adopt a relaxed formula that shall facilitate future amendments or they may opt for temporary constitution with an expiry date. The first two options lead to a further dilemma regarding the enshrinement of eternity clauses as part of the amending formula. In case material limits are enshrined some issues are placed beyond the grasp of the majority, whereas if only procedural limits are set up, regardless of the degree of rigidity they create, everything is renegotiable.

Before engaging into writing the amending formula it is crucial to be conscious of how relative the abstract concepts of rigidity and flexibility are, especially when approached solely on the basis of the formula wording. The same mechanisms may work quite differently and produce diverse results in combination with institutional and factual rigidities. Whether the constitution shall include deferral

36 Blound, Elkins and Ginsburg (n 6) 49.

37 See D S Lutz, 'Toward a Theory of Constitutional Amendment' (1994) *Am Pol Sci Rev* 88, 355–370.

38 See V Jackson, 'What's in a Name? Reflections on Timing, Naming, and Constitution-Making' (2008) *Wm. and Mary L Rev* 49, 1249–1305.

39 A Arato, *Constitution Making Under Occupation: The Politics of Imposed Revolution in Iraq* (CUP, 2009); A Arato, 'Interim Imposition' (2004) *Ethics and International Affairs* 18(3), 25–50.

clauses expressively postponing decisions on certain subject-matters,[40] how the electoral law shall impact representation in the Parliament, that is, the body having a crucial if not deciding role in constitutional revision, and how constitutional review is set up interact with the formula. Factual rigidities are also important. Whether a constitutional culture already exists or is it in the making after years of autocracy, how the party system works, how divided a society is and what are the sources of such divisions, and how reconcilable the overall values of the population are with the traditional concepts of human rights protection such as, e.g., religious freedom, non-discrimination, equality of sexes etc. are decisive. In case external constitutional imposition plays a central role in constitution-making, the amending formula may serve an additional purpose: providing a channel for incremental legitimacy building. Imposition consciousness, in light of past experience, may lead to an intentional correlation between the degree of imposition and the degree of intended constitutional flexibility. Allowing constitutional change may counterbalance imposition, modifying the perception of heteronomy and thus also altering the perception of the constitution.

Creating formal channels of constitutional change has a different weight in situations where it is predictable that major constitutional changes may be sought in the near future. In case formal channels allow such changes to be made in conformity with amendment rules, constitutional replacement can be avoided.[41] Abiding by rules is a constitutional ethos-building factor, as it impacts the symbolic function of the constitution as well as the normativity of the document that sets out the basic rules of the polity. The impossibility of achieving formal change when required due to stringency of the amendment prerequisites may lead to informal change, such as informal amendment through jurisprudence or consensual political bypass by way of interpretation. This, however, is only possible when the infrastructure for so doing already exists. When it does not, which is the case in regime transitions, the impossibility of formal change results in violations or replacements that may harm the transition process and hinder the formation of constitutional legitimacy. If these options are also unavailable, the absence of channels of change may totally estrange people from the Constitution.

Formal amendment rules interact with multiple external factors, established patterns of negotiation, as well as with the existence of veto players. Choices between pursuing stability or flexibility do not have to be one-sided; combinations are also possible, and reform procedures can be blended with adaptation procedures.[42] How legitimacy shall be ensured for future constitutional changes is an important consideration that must always govern the choice of amending

40 R Dixon and T Ginsburg, 'Deciding Not to Decide: Deferral in Constitutional Design' (2012) *Int'l J Const'l L* 9, 636–672.

41 See R Dixon, 'Constitutional Amendment Rules: A Comparative Perspective' in T Ginsburg and R Dixon (Eds), *Comparative Constitutional Law* (Edward Edgar Publishing Ltd, 2011) 104.

42 N Behnke and A Benz, 'The Politics of Constitutional Change between Reform and Evolution' (2009) *Publius* 39, 213–240.

mechanisms. Legitimacy of future constitutional change as an ownership-building mechanism in the case of imposed constitutions is a context-specific mechanism aimed to transform heteronomy to autonomy.

Constitutional marketing and construction of memory

The enactment of a constitution constructs a memory.[43] The democratic pedigree of a constitution is established at that moment. In the collective imagination of a people the constituent moment is 'the juristic expression of the democratic impetus'.[44] The memory of this moment is intertwined with the symbolic power of the constitution and lingers on although the constitution may change in multifarious manners and directions depending on the amendment model a constitutional order can be classified in. The constitutional document inescapably reflects the memory of the constituent moment, which is however subject to perpetual revision and reformation. 'Memory is a mental representation of the past but it has only a partial rapport with the past'.[45] This memory has the power to legitimize or delegitimize the constitution but can also be reformed and revisited in such ways as to influence constitutional legitimacy positively or negatively.

Unlike the more mundane constituted power, constituent power appears to retain its mythical dimension. Amplified in aged constitutions by time and distance, the primordial constitution-making moment holds strong symbolic power.

Noah Feldman observes that the theoretical and practical distinction about imposing constitutions today as opposed to past imposition is that 'it takes place against a backdrop of widespread commitment to democratic self-determination'.[46] In that sense this is a conceptual lens through which to look at the past. The flip side of focusing on the founding moment of a constitution as a source of legitimacy is scrutiny of the distant constituent power for the detection of flaws whenever some sort of crisis puts constitutional legitimacy to test. The constituent moment creates in its own temporality a break from the past and yet a bridge from the past to the present and the future, while it also creates a memory. This memory defines how the constitution is perceived by the people and how they feel about it.

Constitutional marketing is the process of promoting and 'selling' a constitution to an audience. Pitching the product matters but maintaining a long-term relationship with the audience matters too. The saga of constituent power renders constitutions attractive to their target audience. Constitutional faith is created

43 C Dupre and J Yeh, 'Constitutions and Legitimacy Over Time' in C Saunders, T Fleiner and M Tushnet (Eds), *Routledge Handbook of Constitutional Law* (n 17) 45.

44 M Loughlin, *The Idea of Public Law* (OUP, 2004) 100.

45 Henry Rousso, *The Haunting Past: History, Memory, and Justice in Contemporary France*, (University of Pennsylvania Press, 2002), 4, Renáta Uitz, *Constitutions, Courts, and History: Historical Narratives in Constitutional Adjudication*, (Central European University Press, 2005), p. 241.

46 N Feldman, 'Imposed Constitutionalism' (2005) *Conn L Rev* 37, 857–890.

through belief in the idealized exercise of constituent power and the legitimacy of the constitution increases. The symbolic function of constitutions is interrelated to constitutional faith and the way in which people envisage the(ir) constitution. What does the modifier 'their' entail? Is longevity of the product good for marketing? The motto 'established in 1789', for example, may sound impressive and give the customer security. Still, does longevity of a product matter more than its relevance or functionality? Is it possible to market a constitution that has weaknesses with regard to the mode of its enactment if it possesses virtues that enable it to serve valuable functions? Does the democratic pedigree matter more than the actual functioning of democratic procedures put in place by a constitution?

Constitutions exist in people's imagination and emotions quite apart from their actual use in ordering people's affairs.[47] It is this imagination and these emotions that are the target of constitutional marketing. The sense of awareness that accompanies autonomy and the knowledge of self-institution also has to do with feeling and imagination. The idea that the constituent power belongs to the people is the default conceptualization about constitution-making so any departure from that scheme becomes very difficult to market.[48]

Constitutional marketing has a unique role in the context of rising populism. Narratives about the constitution are central in populist discourse and any degree of heteronomy may be used as the basis for deconstructing constitutional faith.

According to Tom Ginsburg, we have entered 'an era of populist backlash against international commitments in many countries. Populism is a complex phenomenon, with myriad causes, but one theme that unites its various exponents is a distrust of elites, including foreign policy elites'.[49] An issue set persistently by modern aspects of populism is the process of constitutional backslide. In a sense, backslide can be viewed as the opposite route of the ownership process of an imposed constitution. An imposed constitution may develop gradually into a document that ensures the limitation of government and slowly integrates into the constitutional order it aimed to form, thus acquiring legitimacy.[50]

47 'Constitutions, like all creations of the human mind and the human will, have an existence in men's imagination and men's emotions quite apart from their actual use in ordering men's affairs.' M Lerner, 'Constitution and Court as Symbols' (1937) *Yale LJ* 46, 1290–1319.

48 See Hasebe (n 16).

49 T Ginsburg, 'Constitutions and Foreign Relations Law: The Dynamics of Substitutes and Complements' (2017) 111 *AJIL* 326, 330, available at: https://www.cambridge.org/core/journals/american-journal-of-international-law/article/constitutions-and-foreign-relations-law-the-dynamics-of-substitutes-and-complements/ABCB9603E7AB21DA5E-1C3AF2494FFCBD/core-reader, available at: https://www.cambridge.org/core/services/aop-cambridge-core/content/view/ABCB9603E7AB21DA5E1C3AF2494FFCBD/S2398772317000897a.pdf/constitutions_and_foreign_relations_law_the_dynamics_of_substitutes_and_complements.pdf accessed 4 December 2017.

50 On the sources of constitutional legitimacy see M Hartwig, 'What Legitimises a National Constitution? On the Importance of International Embedding' in A von Bogdandy and P Sonnevend (Eds), *Constitutional Crisis in the European Constitutional Area* (Nomos, 2015) 322.

Constitutional resilience may result from the ability of an imposed constitution to perform its functions overcoming the obstacle of its original handicap and thus allow the operation of the legal order.[51] Adversely, a constitutional order may move away from constitutionalism through gradual and often legal or constitutional steps. Kim Lane Scheppele describes a political shift in which the global/local political spectrum is replacing the left/right spectrum: 'The local side of the spectrum emphasizes the exclusiveness of community, importance of loyalty and distinctive values; the global side emphasizes global interconnectedness, cosmopolitanism and universal values'.[52] Distrust of experts, global values and interconnectedness create an environment where any degree of imposition through the work of experts and international consultation or the mere adoption of global constitutional values may trigger a narrative able to negatively tint even a working constitution.

Quite interestingly, the term ownership was used with regard to the Memoranda of Understanding signed between crisis-struck countries and international lenders during the global financial crisis. Although such Memoranda imposed measures with the consent of the weaker signing party, talk about the importance of ownership of the measures is a reminder that the new aspects of heteronomy revive older notions regarding sources of legitimacy. Heteronomy is hard to market.

The EU itself can be viewed as a 'gradualising process of imposed constitutionalism where multiple influences shape the constitutionalism and legalism of the European Union'.[53] Adherence by certain principles is a kind of imposition – the exact kind that Eurosceptics use in narratives. The gradual osmosis of values, which to some is a desideratum, is in the eyes of others heteronomy. The example of Cyprus is here relevant: the law of necessity was used to make possible amending the heteronomous constitution in order to allow responding to the requirements of the accession to the EU. EU principles and values can hardly be perceived as imposed juxtaposed to the mummified, extra rigid imposed constitution.

Populism thrives on narratives and in the realm of constitutional narratives prominence is given to the importance of constituent power.[54] Emphasis on the

51 X Contiades and A Fotiadou, 'On Resilience of Constitutions: What Makes Constitutions Resistant to External Shocks?' (2015) *ICL Journal* 9(1), 3–26.

52 K L Scheppele, 'Autocratic Legalism', available at: https://blogs.eui.eu/constitutionalism-politics-working-group/populist-constitutionalism-6-kim-lane-scheppele-autocratic-legalism accessed 28 November 2017.

53 G Butler, 'A post-national legal order', Chapter 11 in this volume.

54 Paul Blokker suggests that 'Populists seem to prefer an instrumentalist approach to constitution-making and constitutional revision, in which constitutional norms are not higher "framework" norms, but rather evaluated on the basis of the extent to which they promote the majority interest.' See P Blokker, 'The Populist Threat to Democratic Constitutionalism' (*blogs.eui.eu*, 14 November 2017) available at: https://blogs.eui.eu/constitutionalism-politics-working-group/populist-constitutionalism-4-populist-threat-democratic-constitutionalism/ accessed 5 December 2017.

majority interest, often expressed through favouring referendums as a means of constitutional change, may exploit any perceived constitutional weakness in that direction. Negative marketing targeting constitutions may tap into the people's negative emotions and target the symbolic value of a constitution.

Imposition as unchangeability

Continuity of imposition stems from the lack of formal and informal channels of change. Changeability is not the same as temporality. Once the option of a temporal, imposed constitution is rejected, the relation of the constitution to the passage of time depends on the availability of channels of change. Constitutions are defined by the way in which they change.[55] Constitutions are works in process and as such, what defines them most is their change, or the exact opposite – lack of change. Constitutional imposition is not an imaginary condition. It pre-supposes a distinct and real moment of heteronomy that creates an indelible memory. Nonetheless, it is continuity of heteronomy that should matter most in defining a constitution as imposed upon the people, which equals absence of autonomous constitutional change.

Amendability has become a basic feature of constitutions, signifying but also building constitutional identity. How (un)amendable a constitution is, is a focal point for understanding not only how it was conceptualized by its framers, but also the way it is applied in practice, and the role of political and constitutional actors involved in constitutional change.[56] Octroyed constitutions granted to the people by the monarch derived their legitimacy from divine sources,[57] and as such were defiant to change by the people. Formal amendment rules most often echo the memory of the amendment moment. 'A semantic memory of the constituent episode, but also an implicit memory without awareness, is embedded in the wording of each amendment formula'.[58] Amendment rules create a link between the past, the present and the future, determine whether the constitution shall convey the image of a quasi-religious or that of a mundane document and may monitor the way people feel about the constitution, rendering it user friendly and transformable or a distant object of worship.

Imposed constitutions differ from the default conceptualization of the constituent moment. Consensus, even if present as in the case of imposed constitutions with consent, is not equivalent to 'by the people'.[59] A perplexed amendment

55 A constitution can be defined 'as its process of amendment', H Finer, *Theory and Practice of Modern Government* (Henry Holt & Company, 1949) 127. See also R Albert, 'The State of the Art in Constitutional Amendment' in R Albert, X Contiades and A Fotiadou (Eds), *The Foundations and Traditions of Constitutional Amendment* (n 27).

56 Contiades and Fotiadou (n 27).

57 J Gerkrath, 'Are "octroyed constitutions" of the 19th Century to be considered as imposed constitutions?', Chapter 6 in this volume.

58 Contiades and Fotiadou (n 27).

59 R Albert, 'Constitutions imposed with consent?', Chapter 5 in this volume.

formula, thus, in the context of imposed constitutions, cannot aim to replicate a democratic ritual, but instead solidifies heteronomy. Stringency blocks the possibility of formal amendment rules performing a function tailored for imposed documents: the gradual passage towards autonomy through formal constitutional change. Stringency may deprive also the possibility of legitimation through chosen inertia and preservation, diminishing the choice not to amend the constitution to inability to change it. It is possible that during constitutional enactment, participatory processes may even undermine constitutional legitimacy through procedural malfunctions.[60] Nonetheless, nothing surpasses the handicap, which has a document perceived as imposed with regard to legal, sociological and moral legitimacy.[61]

Constitutional rigidities, which are the different shapes in which hindrances to constitutional change appear, encompass multiple parameters that influence constitutional change. Institutional rigidities are institutionally embedded ways of increasing the level of difficulty in enacting constitutional change. Formal amendment rules, the system of government and the judicial review system fall into this category. Factual rigidities are sources of impediments to constitutional change situated in the practices, attitudes and behaviour patterns of different actors which emerge through the application of institutional requirements or stem directly from the political, legal or social culture and constitutional ethos.[62] With regard to imposed constitutions, extra rigidities appear. Designated actors of formal change may differ and it is possible that the continuance of external involvement adds veto players. Rigidities stemming from culture are particularly important in post-conflict situations, while the aim of imposed constitutionalism may be to shape a new constitutional culture.

In the examples of Japan and Cyprus, the conundrum lies in the way their constitutions evolved through time and not in the way and the reasons of their enactment. 'By any standard, the longevity of the Kenpo has been remarkable. That longevity becomes even harder to fathom, however, if one accepts the conventional narrative that the Kenpo was imposed on an unwilling nation by force', writes David Law.[63] The answer to the question of whether a constitution is imposed appears to lie in how and why it has or has not changed after its enactment.

Shifting the centre of attention from constituent to amending power and from constitutional enactment to constitutional change, both formal and informal, allows revisiting the concept of constitutional imposition.

60 For example, malfunctions of the comment process 'popular participation may undermine the very legitimacy it is supposed to generate', M Tushnet, 'Constitution-Making: An Introduction' (2013) *Tex L Rev* 1983, 1999.

61 RH Fallon Jr, 'Legitimacy and the Constitution' (2005) *Harv L Rev* 118(6), 1787–1853.

62 Contiades and Fotiadou (n 10) 459.

63 Law (n 25).

Conclusion: Imposition as identity

> Begin with an individual, and before you know it you find that you have created a type; begin with a type, and you find that you have created – nothing.
>
> F. Scott Fitzgerald, 'The Rich Boy'

When the analysis of imposed constitutionalism begins with the effort to explain the category of imposed constitutions, it seems doomed to create nothing. Once focus is placed on a particular constitution conceptualized as imposed by the citizens of the legal order whose ground rules it sets out, the elements of imposition begin to acquire form.

Michel Rosenfeld writes that constitutional identity like national identity 'can be conceived as belonging to a collective-self'. Connected with the fact of having a constitution, the content of the constitution and the context in which the constitution operates, constitutional identity relates to change through an enduring image through or despite inevitable change.[64]

Constitutions characterized as imposed exist along a 'continuum of imposition', its poles being constitutional autonomy and constitutional heteronomy. The sense of awareness of autonomy and the knowledge of self-institution is a memory and an image of selfhood. Constitutions are part of people's collective and individual imagination and emotions quite apart from their actual functions. The placement of a constitution along the imposition continuum depends on a combination of fact and emotion. Most importantly, it also depends on the possibility of change, who and how can change the constitution impact imposition. Amendment procedures that allow popular participation are a source of legitimacy to change but also to lack of constitutional change. Channels of informal change may enhance constitutional workability, which is also a source of legitimacy. Constitutional imposition is a distinct constitutional identity belonging to a collective self and is interrelated with context, culture and imagination.

Shifting the focus of attention to constitutional change, and viewing it as a source of legitimacy equal and competitive to the original exercise of constituent power, provides a novel conceptual lens for understanding constitutional imposition as a combination of fact and emotion.

64 M Rosenfeld, 'Constitutional Identity' in M Rosenfeld and A Sajo, *The Oxford Handbook of Comparative Constitutional Law* (OUP, 2013) 757.

2 Imposed constitutions and romantic constitutions

*David S. Law**

I Introduction: Romanticizing and delegitimating narratives

At first blush, the concept of an "imposed constitution" seems straightforward: surely it is simply, as its name implies, a constitution that is imposed. Its adoption was involuntary, and its legitimacy is therefore suspect. From a liberal perspective, there is no greater sin than lack of consent, and therefore, an imposed constitution—born in sin—lacks legitimacy from the outset.

If only it were so simple. Each part of this formulation begs a host of questions, starting with the word "imposed". What counts as imposition? Does it matter who is doing the imposing, or upon whom the constitution is imposed? If a nineteenth-century European monarch, or a modern-day military junta in Myanmar or Thailand, promulgates a constitution without genuine public support or approval, is that an "imposed constitution"? What about a constitution devised and adopted by a Shi'ite minority against the wishes of a Sunni majority? If these situations involve "imposition", does the "imposition" disappear if a majority favors the constitution? What about a constitution that is ratified by Canada's English-speaking provinces but bitterly resisted by the French-speaking province? Or a constitution adopted by a white majority that permits black slavery? Or any constitution that is imposed by one portion of society upon another or, indeed, any constitution that commands less than unanimous support? Why is a constitution imposed upon a minority not an "imposed" constitution? Is it not the case that every single constitution in the world is "imposed" from the perspective of at least some people? And if there are always people who experience a constitution as "nonconsensual" or "imposed", then how can any constitution escape the "imposed constitution" label?

* © David S Law, 2018. Thanks to Xenophon Contiades and Alkmene Fotiadou for organizing a conference on the fascinating, recurring, and problematic concept of imposed constitutions, and for their very helpful suggestions and conversations about this chapter in particular; to Malcolm Langford, Chien-Chih Lin, Peter and Einar Lorentzen, Yaniv Roznai, Alex Schwartz, and Po Jen Yap for invaluable suggestions and feedback; and to Karen Tsang and Lorraine Wu for indefatigable research assistance. All infelicities are mine and mine alone.

One might try to salvage the concept by saying that "imposition" refers to a constitution foisted *by outsiders* upon a particular community.[1] But this simple definition, too, is riddled with difficulties and raises more questions than it answers. Who counts as an "outsider", and what kind of involvement by "outsiders" causes a constitution to count as "imposed"? What if the government opposes the constitution as a foreign imposition, but the people embrace it? Is it still imposed in that case? Why should it matter if those doing the imposing are "outsiders" (whatever that means)? What if anything is qualitatively worse about a constitution imposed by outsiders as opposed to oppression at the hands of one's neighbors?

The fundamental problem with the concept of an "imposed constitution" is not simply that the concept is difficult to define. It is, rather, that the concept implies a false dichotomy between "imposed" and "unimposed" constitutions:

> Constitution-making routinely implicates multiple authors, constituencies, and narratives in a process that is part negotiation, part dialectic, and part coercion. This multiplicity of participants and processes renders the distinction between "imposed" and "unimposed" constitutions highly arbitrary. On the one hand, even an ostensibly imposed constitution can reflect a considerable measure of local input and influence. ... On the other hand, elements of imposition and alienation are arguably endemic to all constitutions, regardless of how or where they are authored.[2]

The result is a concept that is incoherent and unstable. The problem is not simply that scholars cannot agree on a definition, or that there are competing definitions (as in the case of essentially contested concepts such as "democracy" or "rule of law"), but rather that the concept cannot be defined and applied in a logical and consistent manner. Depending upon how the concept is defined, either there are no genuinely imposed constitutions, or all constitutions are imposed. There is no stable middle ground.

Simply because the "imposed constitution" concept is incoherent does not mean, however, that it serves no purpose. The concept serves rhetorical functions in political and constitutional discourse and plays a central role in the construction of constitutional narratives. Its lack of descriptive or analytical value does not detract from its rhetorical or narrative value. The true test of a constitutional narrative—the story that is told about a constitution—is its ability to shape how the constitution is perceived,

1 *See, e.g.*, Noah Feldman, 'Imposed Constitutionalism' (2005) 37 *Connecticut Law Review* 858, 859 ("Today a new constitution must be understood as locally produced to acquire legitimacy.").

2 David S Law, 'The Myth of the Imposed Constitution' in Denis Galligan and Mila Versteeg (eds), *Social and Political Foundations of Constitutions* (CUP 2013) 239, 264. Yaniv Roznai's contribution to this volume (Chapter 3) explores at greater length the ubiquity of constitutional imposition and the various forms that constitutional imposition can take.

not its descriptive accuracy. Whether it is flattering or unflattering, the narrative surrounding a particular constitution will often be highly selective and inaccurate.

Most obviously, the "imposed constitution" label serves as a potent pejorative that can be used to delegitimate an existing constitution. Its value is not as an analytical concept that helps us to understand or explain things more clearly, but rather as a pejorative label used as part of a narrative about why a particular constitution is undeserving of acceptance, affinity, or allegiance. To say that a constitution is "imposed" is to undermine its legitimacy, in a very literal sense, by casting aspersions upon its parentage. An imposed constitution is an illegitimate constitution in more than one sense of the word: it is unworthy of acceptance and of questionable parentage.

Japan illustrates this usage of the term. For decades, the right-wing Liberal Democratic Party (LDP)—which has held power almost continuously since the mid-1950s—has sought to amend Japan's post-war constitution, the 1947 *Nihonkoku Kenpō*.[3] Japanese conservatives seek in particular to deemphasize individual rights, give a more prominent role to the emperor and, last but not least, dilute the pacifist provisions that bar remilitarization. To this end, one of their main rhetorical moves has been to depict the *Kenpō* as having been "imposed" by the occupying powers and therefore illegitimate and in need of revision. Thus, in Japan, one's position on whether the *Kenpō* was imposed is a proxy for one's views on whether the *Kenpō* should be amended, which in turn is a fairly good indicator of one's position on the political spectrum.[4]

Not only have Japanese conservatives failed to secure their desired amendments, but the *Kenpō* has at this point lasted longer without amendment than any other constitution in the world. It is more than fair to ask how a supposedly involuntary or "imposed" constitution could last so long in the hands of a democratic society with the power to amend its constitution at any time. The principal reason why the Japanese right has failed for decades to amend the *Kenpō* is the same reason why it is wrong to describe the *Kenpō* as "imposed": the *Kenpō* has, from the outset, enjoyed strong popular support and, in that sense, was never truly "imposed" upon the Japanese people.[5] Alas, American pride has

3 Shigenori Matsui, *The Constitution of Japan: A Contextual Analysis* (Hart 2011) 55–56; Roger W Bowen and Joel J Kassiola, *Japan's Dysfunctional Democracy: The Liberal Democratic Party and Structural Corruption* (Routledge 2016) 9.

4 The extent to which characterization of the *Kenpō* as "imposed" serves as a proxy for the desirability of constitutional amendment is evident from the clashing views and rationales on display in the Final Report of the Diet's Research Commission on the Constitution. See Research Commission on the Constitution, The House of Representatives: *Final Report* (April 2005) xi–xxi, 285–90.

5 Law, 'The Myth of the Imposed Constitution' (n 2), at 253–54 (citing, inter alia, Japanese public opinion polls taken in the aftermath of World War II). Moreover, support for amendment appears to be falling rather than rising. A poll conducted by Japan's national broadcaster NHK reveals that as of 2016, only 26% of the Japanese population supports constitutional revision, as compared to 41% in 2006. Yasuo Hasebe, 'Book Review: Making We the People: Democratic Constitutional Founding in Postwar Japan and South Korea' (2016) 11 *Asian Journal of Comparative Law* 329, 331 n.10.

played directly (and perhaps unwittingly) into the hands of the Japanese right: Americans are flattered by, and therefore happy to perpetuate, a narrative that depicts them as the authors of a successful and long-lived constitution, but this same narrative is cultivated by the Japanese right to undermine and repudiate the very same constitution.[6]

An analogy might be made to the role of the term "judicial activism" in American popular and political discourse. To the extent that it can be defined at all—say, as unseemly willingness to depart from settled law—it is a form of behavior in which judges on both the left and right engage. However, it is mainly liberal judges who are lambasted for "judicial activism" in practice. Likewise, all constitutions are in fact imposed in some way or to some degree, but in practice, only certain constitutions are depicted as imposed. Much like the term "judicial activism"—which is applied on a selective and ideological basis to attack liberal judges, even though it is far from unique to liberal judges—the term "imposed constitution" is used to problematize and villainize particular instances of behavior that is in fact endemic.

The "imposed constitution" label has pejorative power only by dint of an inarticulate, widely shared, and descriptively inaccurate romanticization of what constitutions are and how they are created. Some constitutions are demonized; others are romanticized. Whereas some constitutions are the object of delegitimating narratives that depict them as "imposed", others are the object of romanticizing narratives that idealize them as "unimposed", or indigenous, or the product of an act of self-determination, or an expression of the nation's fundamental identity and defining ideals. Application of the "imposed constitution" label may have little to do with whether the constitution was "imposed" in any literal sense, for all constitutions are "imposed" upon at least some people. Instead, the perception of a constitution as "unimposed" or "imposed" is mainly the product of either a romanticizing or delegitimating narrative.

II Romantic versus unromantic constitutions

Wrestling with an unstable and perhaps even imaginary distinction between "imposed" and "unimposed" constitutions serves the interests of neither descriptive accuracy nor conceptual clarity. More useful from a scholarly perspective would be terminology that highlights—and thus exposes to critique—the underlying romanticization of some constitutions and delegitimation of others. In lieu of stigmatizing certain constitutions as "imposed" on shaky factual and conceptual grounds, it might be more accurate to identify and problematize certain

6 The right-wing Liberal Democratic Party is so keen to advance this narrative that it has published a comic book that depicts the *Kenpō* as a foreign imposition and thus a source of embarrassment and outrage. Colin PA Jones, 'The LDP's comic appeal for constitutional change falls flat' *Japan Times* (Tokyo, 25 July 2015) https://www.japantimes.co.jp/community/2015/07/15/issues/ldps-comic-appeal-constitutional-change-falls-flat accessed 16 May 2018.

constitutions as "romantic" because their origin stories paint a fantastical picture of consent and autochthony. The operative distinction is not between "imposed" and "unimposed" constitutions, but rather between constitutions that benefit from a romanticizing narrative and those that do not. In other words, we ought to be distinguishing between *romantic* and *unromantic* constitutions.

When the narrative surrounding the origins or character of a constitution does not fit our idealized notions of how constitutions are supposed to be made or what they are supposed to do, the result might be called an "unromantic constitution". Conversely, when the prevailing narrative depicts the constitution as local and consensual in origin and character, the result is a "romantic constitution". In reality, no narrative of this kind can be trusted because no constitution can live up to such a narrative. But the point of constitutional narrative—whether of the romanticizing or delegitimating variety—is not descriptive accuracy, but rather something more like myth-making or political persuasion.

A romantic constitution is the product of a kind of immaculate conception. It is born free of imposition or coercion, in a magical land beyond the realm of power politics and foreign influence, in which free and equal members of an inclusive yet distinctive community engage in constitution-making that somehow manages to address the nation's unique needs and express the nation's unique identity while also respecting a generic checklist of global norms—electoral democracy, fundamental human rights, the rule of law, and so forth.

An imposed constitution cannot be a romantic constitution. One of the primary ways in which we romanticize constitutions is by insisting that they should, and do, express the distinctive identity, character, and values of the nations that adopt them.[7] The nation speaks through its constitution, and the nation must speak for itself. An imposed constitution puts words in a nation's mouth; it

7 *See, e.g.*, Vicki C Jackson, *Constitutional Engagement in a Transnational Era* (OUP 2010) 155 (characterizing constitutions as "forms of national self-expression"); Nico Krisch, 'The Case for Pluralism in Postnational Law' in Gráinne de Búrca and JHH Weiler (eds), *The Worlds of European Constitutionalism* (CUP 2012) 203, 207 (observing that, although constitutions "may entrench universal values", "they typically also give expression to particularist ones, thus restating the distinct foundations of the polity and sometimes allowing for a deepening of the national community through attachment to common values and institutions"); Mark Tushnet, 'The Possibilities of Comparative Constitutional Law' (1999) 108 *Yale Law Journal* 1225, 1269–70 (employing the term "expressivism" to describe the long-held view that "constitutions emerge out of each nation's distinctive history and express its distinctive character"). The view that constitutions should and do embody distinctive national characteristics has a long and distinguished pedigree dating back at least as far as Montesquieu. *See* Otto Kahn-Freund, 'On Uses and Misuses of Comparative Law' (1974) 37 *Modern Law Review* 1, 6 (quoting Montesquieu's *Spirit of the Laws*) ("Les lois politiques et civiles de chaque nation … doivent être tellement propres au peuple pour lequel elles sont faites, que c'est un grand hazard si celles d'une nation peuvent convenir à une autre."); Vlad Perju, 'Constitutional Transplants, Borrowing, and Migrations' in Michel Rosenfeld and András Sajó (eds), *The Oxford Handbook of Comparative Constitutional Law* (OUP 2012) 1304, 1309 (identifying Montesquieu, Hegel, and Savigny with the "mirror theory of law" that views a legal system as reflecting "the spirit of the community").

cannot speak for a nation and therefore cannot perform the crucial function of defining and grounding a nation's identity.

The ideal traits associated with romantic constitutions are, in reality, unattainable. Imposition is unavoidable because constitution-making produces winners and losers. Meanwhile, a fully indigenous constitution that expresses what makes the nation unique, yet also checks all the right boxes—in other words, a constitution that is familiar and generic, yet distinctive and unique—is a contradiction in terms. A constitution that checks all the right boxes will, by definition, differ only at the margins. The notion that constitutions are instruments of self-expression is difficult to swallow in light of how formulaic they happen to be and how much they regurgitate boilerplate language. There are standard ways of writing a constitution.[8] Significant variation exists, to be sure, but even the variations tend to be relatively systematic and predictable. Countries do not randomly combine rights in their constitutions, for example, but instead bundle them together in predictable ways.[9] Even the parts of a constitution that are supposedly decorative and expressive—the parts that lend themselves to flights of fancy and pure narrative—recycle familiar elements into familiar patterns.[10] Ultimately, however, it does not matter whether a constitution actually warrants a particular romanticizing (or delegitimating) narrative. What marks a constitution as "romantic" (or "imposed") is the perception and not the reality.

The arguments used to demonize a constitution are the mirror image of the arguments used to romanticize a constitution. Imposed constitutions and romantic constitutions are flip sides of the same coin. In storytelling, every hero needs a villain—the antagonist who must be overcome in order for the hero to demonstrate heroism. Likewise, good constitutions can only be defined in opposition to bad constitutions. Every idealizing constitutional narrative needs its bogeyman. There can be no hero without a villain; there can be no romantic constitutions without imposed constitutions. In constitutional storytelling, outsiders make for exceptionally convenient villains, and thus a constitution imposed by outsiders is readily demonized as an "imposed constitution". The imposition that occurs when one faction of society imposes a constitution upon another faction, by contrast, does not fit the storyline and is thus cut from the narrative.

8 *See, e.g.*, Chibli Mallat, *Philosophy of Nonviolence: Revolution, Constitutionalism, and Justice Beyond the Middle East* (OUP 2015) 157–62 (suggesting that constitutions are "dull" documents to write because they follow a "universal template" that can be boiled down to a single acronym, "LEJ(F)ARC": Legislative power, Executive power, Judicial power, Federalism (in parentheses because it is the only truly optional element in the template), Amendment, Ratification, and the rights of the Citizen).

9 David S Law and Mila Versteeg, 'The Evolution and Ideology of Global Constitutionalism' (2011) 99 *California Law Review* 1163, 1170, 1212 (finding as an empirical matter that variation along two dimensions—"libertarian" versus "statist", and "generic" versus "esoteric"—explains 90% of the variation in the content of bills of rights).

10 David S Law, 'Constitutional Archetypes' (2017) 95 *Texas Law Review* 153 (finding as an empirical matter that even preambles fall into a handful of basic ideological molds or archetypes at the linguistic level).

In Jungian psychology, the shadow is the unconscious but omnipresent side of oneself that the conscious self, the ego, seeks to suppress and deny. It is the embodiment of all that the conscious self finds unacceptable yet is nevertheless omnipresent; the shadow "personifies everything that the subject refuses to acknowledge about himself".[11] Every constitution is Janus-faced; every constitution has its shadow. The idea of an imposed constitution is an affront in part because it reminds us of something in our own constitutions that we prefer not to confront, and that we paper over with romanticizing narrative. Viewed from one angle, a constitution can satisfy our desires for self-expression, nationhood, community, identity, recognition, legitimacy, and approval. Viewed from another angle, a constitution is an instrument of coercion, imposition, oppression, and alienation from the community and the state. Which aspect we see is a function of the narrative that we choose to tell about the constitution and the aspects that we choose to emphasize. But the materials needed to construct either narrative are always close at hand.

Most constitutional narratives are flattering rather than unflattering, legitimating rather than delegitimating. The typical constitutional narrative is flattering because the constitution is a symbol of the state, and a regime that wishes to legitimate itself will therefore seek to romanticize rather than demonize the constitution. Japan is an exception. There are definitely national symbols that the Japanese right wishes to celebrate and elevate; it is simply that the *Nihonkoku Kenpō* is not one of them. The right is enamored with other symbols, such as the "rising sun" flag of Imperial Japan[12] and the national anthem. The association of these symbols with Japanese militarism simultaneously endears them to the Japanese right and repels the Japanese left. For the left, by contrast, the *Kenpō* symbolizes Japan's post-war pacifism, commitment to internationalism, and repudiation of militarism and ultra-nationalism. Thus, "Protect the Constitution" has for years been the rallying cry of the left rather than the right.[13] Decades of rule by the conservative LDP, however, have ensured the continued prominence of the demonizing narrative in Japanese popular and political discourse.[14]

Taiwan is another exception. The Republic of China (ROC) Constitution of 1947, which remains in force in Taiwan, is a holdover from the Kuomintang (Nationalist) government of pre-Communist China, which lost control of everything except a handful of islands including Taiwan. The result is that Taiwan's

11 CG Jung, 'The Archetypes and the Collective Unconscious', in *Collected Works of CG Jung* (Princeton University Press 1969) 284.

12 Adam Taylor, 'Japan has a flag problem too' *Washington Post* (Washington, 27 June 2015) https://www.washingtonpost.com/news/worldviews/wp/2015/06/27/japan-has-a-flag-problem-too accessed 16 May 2018 (likening the "Rising Sun" flag to the Confederate flag in certain respects).

13 Arthur Stockwin and Kweku Ampiah, *Rethinking Japan: The Politics of Contested Nationalism* (Lexington 2017) 117 (quoting a poster distributed by the Japan Socialist Party, which was for decades Japan's main opposition party).

14 See n 6 and accompanying text (discussing the LDP's propaganda efforts).

constitution symbolizes a country—China—from which many Taiwanese wish to dissociate themselves.[15] The ROC Constitution was written for a vast and diverse territory controlled largely by rival warlords, not an affluent and democratic island-state with roughly the population of Australia. The definition of the nation found in the formal constitution does not match the reality of the nation's constitutional practice or political existence, and the result is a high level of what might be called constitutional dissonance.[16]

Taiwanese alienation from a constitution that was designed with a very different country and a very different time in mind is thus entirely understandable. It is no surprise that the ROC Constitution is the subject of a delegitimating narrative that portrays it as an "imposed constitution".[17] Whether the label actually fits is open to debate, however, as the facts are even more complicated than in the case of Japan. Legally speaking, Taiwan was a part of China at the time—indeed, it sent delegates to the constituent assembly that adopted the ROC Constitution—and the Kuomintang government did not invade or occupy Taiwan but rather retreated to Taiwan.[18] On these facts, "refugee constitution" might be a more apt label than "imposed constitution": the ROC Constitution sought sanctuary in Taiwan, only to find that its presence breeds discomfort, if not resentment, in its new home.

But there is yet another twist to the story. Even if the ROC Constitution was not *initially* imposed on Taiwan by the Kuomintang government, one might argue that it is *currently* imposed on Taiwan by an overbearing neighbor. China might view Taiwan's adoption of a new, tailor-made constitution as a step toward a formal declaration of independence, which could in turn trigger an attack on Taiwan.[19] In other words, regardless of whether Taiwan was under external

15 See Yen-Tu Su and Chien-Chih Lin, 'Taiwan' in David S Law and Holning Lau and Alex Schwartz (eds), *The Oxford Handbook of Constitutional Law in Asia* (forthcoming OUP 2019).

16 Wen-Chen Chang and David S Law, 'Constitutional Dissonance in China' in Gary Jacobsohn and Miguel Schor (eds), *Comparative Constitutional Theory* (Elgar 2018) 476, 507–08 (defining "constitutional dissonance" as divergence between the formal constitution and the actual practice of constitutionalism that generates creative tension and necessitates adaptation of an informal or "small-c" variety).

17 *See, e.g.*, Jiunn-rong Yeh, *The Constitution of Taiwan* (Hart 2016) 24–30; Su and Lin (n 15); Yasuo Hasebe, 'Imposed Constitutions (constitutions octroyées)' in Rainer Grote and others (eds), *Max Planck Encyclopedia of Comparative Constitutional Law* (OUP 2017) (last updated July 2016).

18 Jiunn-Rong Yeh and Wen-Chen Chang, 'The Emergence of East Asian Constitutionalism: Features in Comparison' (2011) 59 *American Journal of Comparative Law* 805, 819–20 (arguing that the participation of the Taiwanese delegates in the constituent assembly was "largely symbolic", and describing the ROC Constitution as an "instrument of annexation").

19 Zachary Elkins, Tom Ginsburg and James Melton, *The Endurance of National Constitutions* (CUP 2009) 174; Chien-Chih Lin, 'Survival of the Fittest(?): The Endurance of the ROC Constitution and the Constitution of Japan' (2014) 62 *American Journal of Comparative Law* 775, 803–04.

pressure to ***adopt*** the ROC Constitution, it is currently under external pressure to ***retain*** the ROC Constitution.

Even from this condensed account, it should be clear that the "imposed constitution" label cannot begin to do justice to the convoluted history and politics behind the ROC Constitution. Complex constitutional politics do not lend themselves to simple dichotomies between, for example, "imposed" and "unimposed" constitutions. This is true of Taiwan, and—as will be seen below[20]—it holds true for Japan as well. But it is nevertheless entirely predictable that many in both Taiwan and Japan reach for the "imposed constitution" label. People are bound to do so because the label is a standard trope of delegitimating narratives. In constitutional discourse, the "imposed constitution" label is a slur, and the use of slurs does not always yield to descriptive or analytical rigor.

III A typology of possible definitions

An "imposed constitution" might be defined in terms of either, or both, of the following criteria. First, the concept explicitly incorporates the idea of imposition, which implies that the people who are bound by the constitution had it forced upon them without their consent. Second, the manner in which the "imposed constitution" label has been applied by scholars suggests that the concept might also imply the influence or involvement of outsiders. The supposedly classic examples of imposed constitutions—Japan, Iraq, Afghanistan, and the American South after the Civil War[21]—mostly involve outside influence of some kind (although the correct application of the "inside"/"outside" distinction is hardly self-evident in the American example). In other words, a constitution that has been imposed in a literal sense nevertheless does not count as an "imposed constitution" unless the imposition is in some sense at the hands of outsiders. Thus, for example, the Constitution of the Democratic People's Republic of Korea is "imposed" in a literal sense on the North Korean population, but it nevertheless might not count as an "imposed constitution" because it is indigenous or autochthonous in origin (meaning that it was authored and imposed by North Koreans). Indeed, one might even argue that outside influence is, by itself, sufficient to render a constitution "imposed", regardless of consent. [22]

Conceivably, there might also be a relevant distinction to be drawn between the drafting and adoption stages of a constitution. It might be suggested, for example, that outside influence is acceptable at one stage but amounts to an "imposition" at the other stage. Combining these criteria yields a two-by-two table of possible definitional approaches (Table 2.1). A plausible definition of the

20 See Part V.B.

21 Feldman (n 1) 858–59; Frederick Schauer, 'On the Migration of Constitutional Ideas' (2005) 37 *Connecticut Law Review* 907, 907–09.

22 See Richard Albert's contribution (Chapter 5) to this volume (characterizing Canada's post-1931, pre-1982 constitution as an example of a constitution that is "imposed with consent").

Table 2.1 Possible approaches to defining "imposed constitution"

	A. Drafting stage	*B. Adoption stage*
1. Lack of consent	1A (not a conceptually viable definition)	1B (indeterminate definition: could be either overbroad or underbroad)
2. Outside influence	2A (massively overbroad definition)	2B (potentially overbroad definition)

"imposed constitution" concept might span more than one cell but is unlikely to transcend these criteria altogether.

The definitions in each row share certain problems in common. Those in row 1 presuppose a viable distinction between consensual and nonconsensual constitutions, whereas those in row 2 presuppose a viable distinction between constitutions made under "outside influence" and those made free of "outside influence". Both distinctions are deeply problematic in light of two basic facts. First, imposition is ubiquitous. Constitutions are never supported by everyone. Every constitution can be expected to arouse feelings of resentment or imposition at some point among some people. Second, outside influence is also ubiquitous. Constitutions are never completely original. There is no such thing as a constitution that is fully indigenous or free of outside influence.

There are also difficulties specific to the definitions in each cell. Definition 1A makes little sense because the concept of consent does not seem applicable to the mere drafting of a constitution. The whole point of having an adoption stage as well as a drafting stage is to provide an opportunity for the expression or withholding of approval. If the people are free to veto a constitution at the adoption stage, there is no obvious reason why they must also possess a veto at the drafting stage lest the constitution be viewed as "imposed". The main problem with definition 1B, by contrast, is that it is indeterminate: it may encompass either too many constitutions or too few constitutions, depending upon what qualifies as "consent" as opposed to "imposition". This problem is explored in Part IV.

Definition 2A—outside influence at the drafting stage—is massively overbroad for the simple reason already noted: there is no such thing as a constitution that is wholly indigenous in content. To say that any constitution drafted with foreign influence is an "imposed constitution" is to say that all constitutions are imposed. That leaves Definition 2B—outside influence at the adoption stage—as the most plausible candidate. Even in this scenario, however, questions must be raised about the applicability of the "imposed constitution" label. *Upon whom* was the constitution imposed? *Why* was the constitution imposed? Is the constitution *still* imposed? On the one hand, if these factors are relevant, then even a constitution imposed pursuant to military occupation might not qualify as "imposed". On the other hand, if these factors are all irrelevant, then even seemingly innocent constitutions generated by nation-building or peacemaking efforts pursuant to international law might qualify as "imposed". The difficulties surrounding Definitions 2A and 2B are discussed in Parts V.A and V.B, respectively.

IV The ubiquity of imposition

No constitution enjoys the unanimous support or consent of all those who must live under it. The politics of constitution-making are like any other kind of politics: there are invariably both winners and losers, and the losers may resent the outcome. Constitutions are routinely the product of bargaining among political actors of unequal strength. Some of the most intensely affected parties may be underrepresented in the constitution-making process or even excluded entirely. Moreover, even if genuine participation in the process is available on generous terms, there is still no guarantee that all sides will view the results of the process as entitled to their acceptance and obedience. And even if—counterfactually, implausibly—a society were to reach consensus on the adoption of a constitution, would the entrenchment of that constitution not count as imposition upon future generations? The result is that even constitutions that are not generally considered to be imposed are, in a very real sense, imposed upon at least some people, some of the time.

One perfectly reasonable response to this conundrum is simply to give up and acknowledge that all constitutions are "imposed", in which case the concept of "imposed constitutions" does not seem especially meaningful.[23] Another response is to try to salvage the concept by distinguishing "adequate" consent from "inadequate" consent. To do so requires that we answer two questions. First, whose consent is required? Who is entitled to have a say in the adoption of a constitution? Second, how much consent is required? If a minority resents or rejects the constitution, does that mean the constitution is imposed?

A Whose consent is needed?

The question of whose support or consent is necessary and sufficient for a constitution to escape categorization as "imposed" is not trivial. Is it the people who must consent, or is it the state? Suppose, for instance, that a monarch decrees a constitution without any pretense of public input or approval—a common historical occurrence. Or suppose that the French or Dutch government ratifies a constitution for the European Union in the face of strong domestic opposition—not a farfetched hypothetical. In both scenarios, the regime is acting in accordance with the law, and there is no imposition upon the regime, but the regime is imposing upon the people. Are the wishes of the people irrelevant to the question of whether the constitution was "imposed"?

To say that only the state needs to consent cuts against orthodox constitutional and political theory. From a liberal perspective—which respects the autonomy of the individual from the state—it is awkward to argue that imposition only

23 Yaniv Roznai's chapter flirts with this conclusion: his "basic argument is that there are many ways and degrees of imposition and *all constitutions can be considered as imposed* to some extent" (emphasis in original). See also Hasebe, 'Imposed Constitutions (constitutions octroyées)' (n 17) ("Whether a constitution is imposed or not is a question of degree, not of kind".).

counts as "imposition" when it happens to the abstract entity known as the state, and not when it happens to actual people. It is even more difficult to deem the wishes of the people irrelevant in matters of constitution-making if one subscribes to the fairly standard view that the power to create a constitution—*le pouvoir constituant*—belongs to the people, not the state (which is itself merely a creation of the people).[24] These normative considerations may help to explain why scholars have categorized constitutions handed down by monarchs—or *constitutions octroyées*—as imposed.[25] If there is to be consent that confers legitimacy on a constitution, it is difficult to avoid the conclusion that the consent in question must ultimately be—whether directly or indirectly—the consent of actual people.

To say that a constitution requires the consent of "the people", however, is to beg the question of who counts as "the people". Is it everyone who must abide by the constitution in question, or just a subset of the population? Political elites? Certain vocal or influential constituencies? Or a larger but still politically privileged subset of the population—call it the political community, or the citizenry, or the "polity"? If the distinction is between citizens and non-citizens, then why do some people get to be "citizens" and thus have a say in matters of government, while others do not? To those who are disenfranchised, do we have anything more convincing or satisfying to say than the mere tautology that "your views do not count because those of us whose views count have decided that your views do not count"?

Consider, for example, a scenario in which the white male inhabitants of a heavily agrarian society from centuries ago foist upon the members of a highly diverse, post-industrial society a constitution that contains irrelevant, unrealistic, and even immoral provisions.[26] Not only is this constitution initially adopted without the participation of over half the adult population (namely, blacks and women), but it endorses the enslavement of roughly one-fifth of the population. In other words, the adoption of this constitution combined "generational imposition" (imposition by a past generation upon the present generation) with "elite imposition" (imposition by privileged white males upon the rest of society).[27] Over time, the constitution also comes to be imposed upon the indigenous peoples of the country, even though it was never supposed to apply to them.[28]

24 Tamara El Khoury, 'Pouvoir Constituant' in *Max Planck Encyclopedia of Comparative Constitutional Law* (n 17) (last updated December 2017).

25 *See, e.g.*, Hasebe, 'Imposed Constitutions (constitutions octroyées)' (n 17) ¶ 2; Claude Klein and András Sajó, 'Constitution-Making: Process and Substance' in *The Oxford Handbook of Comparative Constitutional Law* (n 7) 432. Jörg Gerkrath's chapter in this volume on the subject of "Octroyed Constitutions" takes issue with this view (Chapter 6).

26 This paragraph is adapted from Law, 'The Myth of the Imposed Constitution' (n 2) 265.

27 See Yaniv Roznai's chapter in this volume (Chapter 3).

28 James A Poore III, 'The Constitution of the United States Applies to Indian Tribes' (1998) 59 *Montana Law Review* 51, at 53, 55, 57–69 (describing the "complete defeasance of retained tribal power and retained sovereignty"); Philip P Frickey, 'Domesticating Federal Indian Law' (1996) 81 *Minnesota Law Review* 31, 31–32, 39, 55 (observing that Native American tribes, once described as "domestic dependent nations" that retained sovereignty, have become subject to the "plenary" and "essentially unlimited power of Congress").

Finally, as if to ensure that it will not be adjusted to reflect the needs and wishes of the polity, this constitution entrenches itself by raising a variety of obstacles to amendment.[29]

If this is what passes for the consent of "the people", then it is hard to defend the implicit definition of "the people". Such a definition of "the people" leaves out an awful lot of actual people, all of whom could justifiably complain as a result that the constitution was imposed upon them. It is no coincidence that those who were disenfranchised also fared the worst under this constitution. Yet the U.S. Constitution—the obvious inspiration for this not very hypothetical scenario—is virtually the archetypal example of a revered and highly legitimate constitution. Few, if any, would call it the textbook example of an "imposed constitution".

There is one respect in which scholars have no difficulty accepting that the U.S. Constitution was "imposed", and that is with respect to the breakaway states of the Confederacy.[30] But why should the U.S. Constitution be considered "imposed" *only* with respect to the former Confederate states? One possible move would be to say that the "imposed constitution" concept implies the involvement of outsiders, and that outsiders were not responsible in any meaningful sense for drafting or adopting the Constitution in 1787. But the American example illustrates the difficulty of relying on a distinction between insiders and outsiders. Such a distinction is difficult to apply in the context of civil war or revolution, which by definition pit fellow countrymen against one another. It is not just the Civil War that divided Americans against each other in armed conflict, but also the American Revolution. At the time that the Constitution was framed, many still pined for British rule. For the hundreds of thousands of people—roughly one-fifth of the white population[31]—who opposed independence, the American Revolution and the ensuing adoption of a national constitution surely constituted an "imposition" in every sense of the word. How can it be that those who favored secession from the United States were victims of an "imposed constitution", but those who opposed secession from Britain were not?

Another possible move would be to argue that the "imposed constitution" concept implies imposition following some kind of military conflict. But this argument, likewise, fails to impress. It is hard to argue that the War of Independence was any less of a military conflict than the Civil War, or that the losing side felt less imposed upon. But more importantly, at a conceptual level, it is unclear why military defeat should be the sine qua non of constitutional imposition. Why should it matter whether imposition occurs as a consequence of military defeat, or instead as a consequence of systemic disenfranchisement and oppression? Why are only those who fought for slavery viewed as having to endure an imposed constitution, but not the slaves themselves? Would it not be more accurate to

29 Law, 'The Myth of the Imposed Constitution' (n 2) 265.

30 Feldman (n 1) 589, 883–84; Schauer (n 21) 908; Hasebe, 'Imposed Constitutions (constitutions octroyées)' (n 17) ¶ 4.

31 Gordon S Wood, *The Radicalism of the American Revolution* (Vintage Books 1991) 176.

say that the U.S. Constitution was from the outset an "imposed constitution", and that the Civil War merely shifted the burden of imposition from one group (slaves) to another (white southerners)?

Perhaps the most viable explanation would be that the labeling of the U.S. Constitution is the product of a romanticizing narrative, not the application of principled distinctions to fact. The labeling of the U.S. Constitution as "unimposed" is difficult to explain or justify on purely factual or conceptual grounds because the U.S. Constitution has been heavily romanticized: it is perceived through a gauzy filter of patriotism, nation-building narrative, and wishful thinking. In other words, the U.S. Constitution is not viewed as an "imposed constitution" because it is, instead, a romantic constitution. If the "imposed constitution" label seems inapplicable to the U.S. Constitution, that may have less to do with whether it was actually imposed and more to do with the story that we tell about the U.S. Constitution. The same could be said of other constitutions. If the *Nihonkoku Kenpō* is described as "imposed", that may have less to do with whether the *Kenpō* was actually imposed and more to do with whether the story of its "imposition" advances the interests of the storyteller or pleases the ear of the listener.

B How much consent is needed?

What quantum of support is necessary before we can say that a constitution is accepted rather than imposed? Majority support is often equated with popular approval. The practical reasons for doing so are obvious. In any society of even moderate size or diversity, unanimity is a practical impossibility; some lower threshold is a practical necessity if political decisionmaking is to occur. Supermajority rule is common for decisions that are fundamental in nature or difficult to reverse, such as constitutional revision. Supermajority requirements seem especially appropriate in the area of constitutional law. Insofar as the whole point of a constitution is to restrain majoritarian excess and protect minorities, some higher threshold, or something approaching consensus, might be indispensable.

But why should anything less than consensus count as anything other than imposition, from the perspective of those on the losing side? Even a supermajority requirement merely ensures that those on the imposing end outnumber those on the receiving end. Majority rule—or indeed anything short of a unanimity requirement—is a form of imposition on minorities. The only question is the size of the losing minority. In other contexts, nonunanimous decisions can perhaps be defended as legitimate and thus not "imposed" if the decisionmaking procedures have been agreed and accepted in advance. This defense is unavailable, however, when the decisionmaking rules themselves are at issue—which is precisely the case when it comes to constitution-making.

Whatever the requisite level of support, it is far from clear as an empirical matter whether most constitutions would be capable of meeting it. To be sure, mechanisms for registering public sentiment are common, but only one-third of the world's constitutions require direct public input in the form of a popular ratification requirement.[32] Instead, the public is usually expected to register its views indirectly, via the election of representatives, to a constituent assembly or legislature. But the use of such procedures may not be reliable evidence of strong and genuine support for a constitution. Those who impose constitutions can be expected to muster at least a veneer of procedural regularity and popular support. A military junta that does not tolerate opposition, for example, may nevertheless make a point of holding a popular referendum when it comes time to adopt a constitution that legitimates its rule, as happened in Myanmar in 2008[33] and Thailand in 2016.[34] Even the paradigmatic "imposed constitution"—the *Nihonkoku Kenpō*—was adopted by a popularly elected legislature acting free of overt coercion.

V The ubiquity of outside influence

A Outside influence on constitutional drafting

It is not clear as a logical or normative matter why the authorship of a constitution should be relevant to the question of whether it was "imposed". Regardless of who is nominally responsible for drafting a constitution, the content of the document will reflect heavy outside influence. Constitutional borrowing—or constitutional migration, or constitutional isomorphism, whichever term one prefers—is ubiquitous.[35]

Perhaps the solution is to say that a constitution should be deemed "imposed" only when outsiders inject themselves into the drafting process, and not when they are invited to assist in the drafting—which is an utterly routine occurrence.[36] At the extreme, insiders might even prefer to have the constitution drafted by outsiders. In the case of Malaysia's 1957 independence constitution, for example, the leaders of Malaysia's dominant political coalition argued for the exclusion of local participants from the drafting process on the ground that foreigners would be more neutral.[37] Their wish was granted: ultimately, no one from Malaysia served on the British-led drafting commission.[38] Given the strong local support

32 Tom Ginsburg, Zachary Elkins and Justin Blount, 'Does the Process of Constitution-Making Matter?' (2009) 5 *Annual Review of Law and Social Science* 201, 205.

33 Melissa Crouch, 'Myanmar' in *The Oxford Handbook of Constitutional Law in Asia* (n 15).

34 Khemthong Tonsakulrungruang, 'Thailand' in *The Oxford Handbook of Constitutional Law in Asia* (n 15).

35 See nn 8–9 and accompanying text.

36 *See, e.g.*, Paul Craig, 'Transnational Constitution-Making: The Contribution of the Venice Commission on Law and Democracy' (2017) 2 *UC Irvine Journal of International, Transnational, and Comparative Law* 57; Tom Ginsburg, 'Constitutional Advice and Transnational Legal Order' (2017) 2 *UC Irvine Journal of International, Transnational, and Comparative Law* 5 (discussing the existence of a "transnational legal order" of constitution-making organizations (such as IDEA, the UN, and the Venice Commission) and consultants).

37 Kristen Stilt, 'Contextualizing Constitutional Islam: The Malayan Experience', (2015) 13 *International Journal of Constitutional Law* 403, 414.

38 Ibid.

for foreign authorship—not to mention extensive local consultation and the nearly unanimous approval of the resulting document by Malaysia's own legislature[39]—it seems difficult to argue that the Malaysian constitution was "imposed" simply because foreigners were responsible for its drafting.

A distinction between invited and uninvited outside involvement might also make sense of the classification of the paradigmatic "imposed constitution", the 1947 *Nihonkoku Kenpō*, which presents a clear-cut case of foreign intervention in the drafting of a constitution. Unbeknownst not only to the Japanese people, but also to the other Allied powers and even to General MacArthur's superiors in Washington—and following two embarrassing failures on the Japanese side[40]—MacArthur's team secretly produced its own draft then pressured the Japanese Cabinet to claim authorship.

Nevertheless, this move is problematic on multiple levels. First, it requires us to distinguish between "insiders" and "outsiders". Second, it then requires us to further distinguish between "invited" outside involvement and "uninvited" outside involvement. Both of these distinctions, in turn, are open to a combination of conceptual, practical, and normative objections.

1. The insider/outsider distinction.—It is standard for constitutions to be made in the name of "We the People". But this standard formulation begs the question of who counts as "We the People" and who does not. Those who fall within the scope of "We the People" not only assert the power and the right to make a constitution; they also assert the power and the right to exclude those who do not belong to "We the People". For every "us", there must also be a "them". Who, then, is entitled to participate in constitution-making, and who is not? What set of persons is entitled to engage in political self-determination, to the exclusion of others? In other words, who is an "insider" and who is an "outsider"?

The answer is potentially arbitrary, if not circular. Political communities are made, not found. The difference between "us" and "them" is not a naturally occurring phenomenon, like a river or a snowflake or a rock. A constitution constitutes the very people in whose name it is made.[41] "We the People" make the constitution, but it is the constitution that defines who "We the People" are and distinguishes "us" from "them". In other words, the insider/outsider distinction is constructed through the same exercise of constitution-making power that the insider/outsider distinction is supposed to justify.

The insider/outsider distinction is likely to be especially difficult to apply in cases of internal conflict, such as revolution, civil war, or efforts at secession—all

39 Andrew Harding, *The Constitution of Malaysia: A Contextual Analysis* (Hart 2012) 33.

40 The first attempt failed when Prince Konoe, a former prime minister who had been tapped by the Americans to produce a draft, killed himself after learning he would face prosecution for war crimes. The second attempt by the Shidehara Cabinet was cut short by the Americans when a leaked draft was savaged in the press for the sheer inadequacy of its reforms. See Law, 'Myth of the Imposed Constitution' (n 2), at 255.

41 Chaihark Hahm and Sung Ho Kim, *Making We the People: Democratic Constitutional Founding in Postwar Japan and South Korea* (CUP 2015) 9, 53–57.

of which are frequent catalysts of constitutional change.[42] In cases of traditional interstate conflict, it is possible to fall back on preexisting political boundaries as the basis for determining whose involvement is legitimate and whose is not. In cases of internal strife, however, there is no agreement on who counts as "us" and who counts as "them"; the meaning of "We the People" is itself at issue. Indeed, the very characterization of revolution or civil war as *internal* strife highlights the difficulty of drawing a line between "us" and "them".

2. The invited/uninvited distinction.—Even assuming that the insider/outsider distinction can be sorted out, there remains the problem of distinguishing "bad" or "uninvited" outside imposition from "good" or "invited" outside assistance. As a practical matter, the distinction between invited and uninvited involvement may not be a good indication of whether outside imposition is occurring. There is nothing contradictory about a country simultaneously inviting the international community to help create its new constitution, for example, and resenting the involvement of the international community. States that are fragile, impoverished, post-conflict, or otherwise starved for international recognition and assistance are especially likely to need new constitutions. But they may also have little practical choice but to "voluntarily invite" outside help in order to satisfy key external audiences. To do otherwise is to bite the hand that feeds.

Looming over both the insider/outsider and invited/uninvited distinctions, however, is a fundamental philosophical objection. Simply put, why should foreign involvement in the drafting of a constitution—whether by invitation or otherwise—be relevant at all to the question of whether the constitution was "imposed"? If members of the community (however defined) acquiesce or consent to a constitution, how can the identity or nationality of the author somehow render it "imposed"? Why should it matter if a constitution was handed down by General MacArthur, or Napoleon—or fell off the back of a truck, or was found at the bottom of a box of Cracker Jack—as long as the people who must abide by it, approve of it? What reason is there for treating foreign authorship as a form of original sin that cannot be expunged by the liberal cure-all of consent?

One may as well ask why it is deemed so important for people to experience a sense of ownership when it comes to their constitution,[43] or for constitutions to express national identity or character. The answer to all of these questions probably lies to a large extent in the fetishization of autochthony, which is in turn central to the romanticization of constitutions. The making of a romantic constitution—the transmutation of a dry, formulaic legal document into a romantic symbol of the nation—involves first and foremost celebration of an idealized notion of the constitution, as opposed to the actual constitution.

42 See text accompanying nn 30–31 (discussing the examples of the American Revolution and Civil War).

43 *See, e.g.*, Feldman (n 1) 859 ("Today a new constitution must be understood as locally produced to acquire legitimacy".).

The constitution must be placed on a pedestal and swaddled in a suitably flattering narrative. Once the constitution becomes an object of national storytelling or myth-making, it becomes irresistible to romanticize the constitution by projecting onto it a variety of qualities that are not there, or to gloss over the very real shortcomings of the constitution. Reality is sacrificed to romance.

Part of the romanticization of a constitution is its treatment as a symbol of the nation, if not the sacred object at the heart of a civic religion.[44] In the United States, the President does not pledge to defend or uphold the nation, or the flag, or God; indeed, the President is not even required to believe in God.[45] Rather, from the President's oath of office to the immigrant's oath of citizenship, it is the Constitution that is the object and locus of loyalty. In Norway, the sole holiday of a patriotic variety is the celebration of the country's 1814 constitution, which enjoys the status of a "national myth".[46] For purposes of sacralizing, it is particularly helpful if the constitution is old—the older, the better. The U.S. Constitution is the oldest constitution in the world; the Norwegian Constitution, the second-oldest. An old constitution can be a source of pride because it is evidence of stability and continuity. But that is not the only reason why old constitutions are cherished. When it comes to constitutions, age is a good thing in and of itself. Like the medieval castles of Europe, old constitutions gain a certain romantic appeal, not because they are especially well suited to today's needs or conditions, but simply because they are old. Constitutions that are old lend themselves naturally to veneration.

The need to idealize is heightened with old constitutions, however, because old constitutions are prone to contain material that, in hindsight, looks anachronistic or downright embarrassing. In such cases, the most serious obstacle to the romanticization of the constitution may be the constitution itself. Republicans demonstrated this fact in spectacular fashion when they sought to wrap themselves in the nation's holy scripture by orchestrating a public reading of the U.S. Constitution on the floor of the U.S. Congress—only to discover that it behooved them to skip over the three-fifths clause.[47] Their mistake was to draw attention to what the Constitution actually says, instead of merely basking in the

44 Sanford Levinson, *Constitutional Faith* (2011 edn, Princeton University Press) 10–12; Sanford Levinson, '"The Constitution" in Civil Religion' (1979) *Supreme Court Review* 123, 123–24.

45 U.S. Const. Art. II, § 1, cl.8 ("I do solemnly swear (or affirm) that I will faithfully execute the Office of President of the United States, and will to the best of my Ability, preserve, protect and defend the Constitution of the United States".).

46 Karen Gammelgaard and Eirik Holmøyvik, 'The Norwegian Constitution as Text' in Karen Gammelgard and Eirik Holmøyvik (eds), *Writing Democracy: The Norwegian Constitution 1814–2014* (Berghahn 2015) 2.

47 "Representatives and direct Taxes shall be apportioned among the several States which may be included within this Union, according to their respective Numbers, which shall be determined by adding to the whole Number of free Persons, including those bound to Service for a Term of Years, and excluding Indians not taxed, three fifths of all other Persons." U.S. Const. art. I, § 2, cl. 3; see Evan McMorris-Santoro, 'House Reading Amended Slavery-Free Constitution This Morning', https://talkingpointsmemo.com/dc/house-reading-amended-slavery-free-constitution-this-morning.

warm, gauzy feelings that surround the Constitution. The safest way to celebrate a romantic constitution, they learned, is to censor it.

It is perhaps even harder to explain the pride that Norwegians take in their constitution without resort to constitutional romanticization. For over thirty years, their constitution—their national pride and joy—formally prohibited Jews; through the mid-1950s, it condemned Jesuits by name.[48] Indeed, the text was not even written in Norwegian, but in the language of the ruling Danes who had dominated Norway for centuries.[49] Only when Denmark attempted to hand over Norway to Sweden like a used plaything did the Norwegians declare independence and write a constitution—at which point they were promptly defeated by the Swedes and forced to revise their brand new constitution to acknowledge the king of Sweden as their head of state.[50] On these facts, how did this constitution become the incarnation of national pride and identity rather than, say, a potential source of mild embarrassment that forces its admirers to plead the finer points of Scandinavian history and linguistics?

The obvious answer is that constitutional romanticization involves a form of selective blindness. Much can and must be deemphasized or overlooked for the sake of romance—including the constitution itself. When it comes to a romantic constitution, ignorance is bliss: dwelling on the actual content would only get in the way of the narrative. The less we actually know about a constitution—warts and all—the easier it becomes to celebrate the version of the constitution that we have constructed for ourselves. In courtship, romance thrives on a sense of mystery. In the case of constitutions, romance thrives on ignorance.

Perhaps the most important part, however, of constitutional romanticization—the one thing that every romantic constitution needs—is an origin story. And any good origin story demands a homegrown hero. In this type of story, the constitution could be the crystallization of generations of wisdom and tradition, or the hard-won fruit of revolutionary struggle and liberation. But what it cannot be, in this type of story, is the spawn of foreigners. The role of the foreigner is that of the villain.

48 Article 2 of the 1814 Constitution read: "Jews are excluded from the kingdom. Jesuits and Monks are not to be tolerated." After several years of struggle, the prohibition against Jews was repealed in 1851. Samuel Abrahamsen, 'The Exclusion Clause of Jews in the Norwegian Constitution of May 17, 1814' (1968) 30 *Jewish Social Studies* 67, 69. Only in 1956 was the anti-Jesuit provision finally eliminated, just in time to permit ratification of the European Convention on Human Rights. Bernt T Oftestad, 'Norway and the Jesuit Order: A History of Anti-Catholicism' (2013) 31 *European Studies* 209, at 210, 218–19.

49 There were good reasons for the use of the Danish written language, but these reasons all seem to reflect, directly or indirectly, Denmark's heavy influence over Norway or Norway's lack of distinctiveness from Denmark. See Gammelgaard and Holmøyvik (n 46) 4 (noting that all those with power in Norwegian society used Danish, and that Norwegians "did not regard Danish as foreign" until around 1850, when "the campaign for a distinct Norwegian language began").

50 Øyvind Eitrheim and Jan Tore Klovland and Lars Fredrik Øksendal, *A Monetary History of Norway, 1816–2016* (CUP 2017) 47.

B Outside influence on constitutional adoption

If there is anything that can be described with confidence as an "imposed constitution", it is surely the situation in which adoption of a constitution is compelled by a foreign government. The extreme case is an "occupation constitution"—namely, a constitution fashioned by, then adopted under pressure from, occupying forces.[51] Over the last two centuries, around forty constitutions—or roughly seven percent of all new constitutions—have been adopted under occupation or shortly thereafter.[52] It is not difficult to see why Japan's post-war constitution is the paradigmatic example: General MacArthur was willing and able to impose his will, and there is no question that he did so when it came time for Japan to adopt a new constitution.

Upon closer examination, however, it is not clear whether even the *Nihonkoku Kenpō* ought to be described as "imposed". There are three questions to be asked of any supposedly "imposed" constitution—even an occupation constitution. First, *upon whom* was it imposed? Second, *why* was it imposed? Third, is it *still* imposed? The answers to all three of these questions weigh against describing the *Kenpō* as imposed. The *Kenpō* was imposed upon Japan's political leadership, but not on the Japanese people.[53] By and large, the goals of the drafters matched the wishes of the public. And precisely because the *Kenpō* gave the people what they wanted, the people have embraced the *Kenpō*. That embrace has outlasted any foreign influence by decades. Whatever happened in the 1940s, it no longer makes sense to describe the *Kenpō* as "imposed" because, for seventy years and counting, its continuing existence has been a matter of choice.

Having been led into devastation and defeat, the Japanese people were understandably keen to revise the arrangements that had so badly disappointed them. The draft produced at General MacArthur's direction aimed to put an end to the imperialism and militarism that had led Japan into a disastrous war; to democratize the country; and to protect individual rights, among other things. These reforms were intended to enjoy—and by every indication did enjoy—public support. The constitutional reforms with the greatest popular

51 Ginsburg, Elkins and Blount (n 32) 208; Zachary Elkins, Tom Ginsburg and James Melton, 'Baghdad, Tokyo, Kabul: Constitution Making in Occupied States' (2008) *William and Mary Law Review* 1139.

52 Elkins, Ginsburg and Melton (n 51) 1141, 1152, 1154 (counting 42 occupation constitutions from 1816 through 2008, out of a total of 801 new, 90 interim, and 57 reinstated constitutions); Elkins and others (n 19) 119 (same).

53 *See, e.g.*, Shojiro Sakaguchi, *The 'Militant Democracy' Principle in Modern Democracies* (Routledge 2009) 235, 239 (contrasting the imposition of the 1946 constitution "on an extremely reluctant conservative Japanese government" with the "overwhelmingly favourable [...] reaction of the Japanese people to the new constitution"); Yasuo Hasebe, 'Constitutional Borrowing and Political Theory' (2003) 1 *International Journal of Constitutional Law* 224, 225–26 (arguing that, "although the new Constitution was indeed imposed upon the government, it is not true that it was imposed against the will of the Japanese people").

support, according to public opinion polls, all made their way in some form into the American draft.[54]

Indeed, the Japanese people were more faithfully served by the American drafters than by their own government. A draft produced by the Shidehara Cabinet leaked to the press and was roundly criticized for introducing only minor changes. The realization that the locally produced draft lacked public support was an explicit factor in both MacArthur's decision to produce his own draft, and the Shidehara Cabinet's grudging decision to present the American draft as their own.[55] Fresh elections were held; at this point, the Americans deliberately receded into the background, and the newly elected representatives debated it, made a few more changes, and ultimately voted by a large margin to adopt it.[56]

General MacArthur left Japan in 1951. Since that time, the Japanese people have had decades in which to change their "imposed" constitution and have chosen to do precisely nothing about it. They are not imprisoned within an "imposed" constitutional framework because they themselves hold the key to changing it. If the Japanese have not changed their constitution since then, the most likely explanation is that they accept it and support it in its current form—which, by and large, they do.[57] It is not external imposition, but rather the lack of domestic support for amendment—combined with the requirement that amendments must be approved in a referendum[58]—that has long prevented Japan's ruling conservatives from making their move. And popular contentment with the *Kenpō* in its current form should come as no surprise in light of the decades of peace and enormous prosperity that have followed its adoption.

The classification of the *Nihonkoku Kenpō* as "imposed" raises the full panoply of questions that have been rehearsed thus far. Why is a constitution imposed upon a nation's government, but embraced by the nation's people, a clear case of an "imposed" constitution? Are we to infer that the views of the people matter less than the views of the politicians? Is the fact that a constitution was made with the wishes of the people squarely in mind irrelevant to the question of whether it was "imposed"? What is special about the moment of adoption if a constitution can subsequently be changed and replaced? Even assuming that a constitution was initially "imposed" in some sense, why attach any greater normative significance or meaning to the moment of creation than to the countless opportunities to amend or replace that follow? Why is consent after the fact not sufficient to

54 Law, 'The Myth of the Imposed Constitution' (n 2) 253–55 (citing, inter alia, public opinion polls conducted in 1945 and 1946). Indeed, the Americans were so confident of public support for their own draft that MacArthur responded to the Japanese government's initial objections by threatening to "take the constitution to the people directly and make it a live issue in the forthcoming [election] campaign in order that the people will have the opportunity to enact the constitution". Ibid 257.

55 Ibid 243, 257.

56 Ibid 257–58.

57 *See* n 5.

58 Nihonkoku Kenpō art. 96 (1947).

validate a constitution? If the people have the power to replace a constitution but choose not to do so, how then can the constitution be described as "imposed"? If the *Nihonkoku Kenpō* cannot be said to enjoy popular consent or approval—after seventy unbroken years without a single amendment, longer than any other constitution in the world—then what constitution does?

The answer lies, again, in the demands of constitutional narrative. Foreign imposition is treated as a form of original sin because the moment of framing occupies a special place in constitutional storytelling. The origin story is the most important story of all. But if imposition is an ineradicable stain upon the soul of the constitution, then every constitution is born in a state of sin because every constitution entails a degree of imposition. The distinction between imposed and unimposed constitutions deserves to be viewed with suspicion because its value is more rhetorical than descriptive. Japan's constitution suffers from a delegitimating narrative that depicts it as "imposed", and therefore illegitimate, because that is what serves the interests of Japanese politicians who engage in constitutional storytelling.

Conversely, ideological and political considerations can lead us to overlook actual imposition. These days, external imposition of a constitution is unlikely to take the form of a conquering state unilaterally imposing its will on a weak or vulnerable state in the aftermath of war. The modern-day version of constitutional imposition is laundered through the post-war international legal order, with its emphasis on international organizations and multilateralism. Its targets are still weak and vulnerable states—states like South Sudan, or East Timor, or Yemen, or the various shards of the former Yugoslavia—although they may be weak or vulnerable for reasons other than traditional interstate conflict. And in lieu of an aggressor state unilaterally exercising hard power, we are likely instead to observe the international community exercising soft power and acting through international bodies to pressure fragile, impoverished, and/or post-conflict states to draft and adopt constitutions that reflect global norms (especially of the human rights variety). It is hard to believe that, when it comes time to writing their constitutions, countries that depend critically on the assistance of foreign powers and international organizations are free to repudiate the goals and values of their foreign benefactors.[59] Perhaps the main difference between Imposition 1.0 and Imposition 2.0 is that Imposition 2.0 occurs under the banner of international law, not military conquest.

The problem is that this new, genteel variety of constitutional imposition conflicts with the fetishization of constitutional autochthony. If constitutional autochthony is to mean anything at all, it must mean that countries are free to reject global norms in favor of local traditions and values. It cannot possibly mean that countries can only adopt constitutions that express and reflect local traditions and values if, and only if, those traditions and values are endorsed or shared by

59 Feldman (n 1) 868; Mark W Janis, 'Human Rights and Imposed Constitutions' (2004) 37 *Connecticut Law Review* 955, 956.

the global community. In that case, the only local values that a constitution could express—the only permissible form of constitutional autochthony—would be the parroting of global norms that are not distinctive or unique at all. For example, if constitution-makers in Yemen argue that equal rights for women are incompatible with longstanding practices and deeply held beliefs regarding the place and function of women in society, respect for constitutional autochthony dictates that they be entitled to reject equal rights for women. We cannot have it both ways and say that we support constitutional autochthony only insofar as it leads to the adoption of global norms, for that is simply not autochthony. It is the equivalent of Henry Ford's edict that car buyers can choose any color of Model T that they want, as long as it is black.

If we are serious about valorizing autochthony, we must expect that some countries will entrench genuine, long-held traditions and values that grate against the liberal norms ordinarily identified with constitutionalism and human rights. Democracy suffers from the well-known flaw that, if voters are allowed to choose freely for themselves, they may opt for an illiberal or authoritarian regime. Likewise, constitutional autochthony suffers from the flaw that, if countries are allowed to freely write their own constitutions, they may opt for illiberal or authoritarian arrangements. In Nepal, for example, constitutional autochthony could license a combination of a hereditary caste system, entrenched dominance of a conservative brand of Hinduism, a ban on the conversion of Hindus, a hereditary monarchy, and the subordination of women, to name just a few possibilities.[60]

What are we to do, then, if constitutional autochthony means rejection of democracy or the rule of law or international human rights norms, in favor of hereditary monarchy (which by definition tends to be deeply rooted in history and tradition), or a hereditary caste system (ditto), or a mandatory state-imposed religion (ditto again), or traditional gender roles (which are called "traditional" for a reason)? Should we sing the praises of such a constitution because it is genuinely indigenous? Or are we prepared instead to ram global human rights norms down the throats of the hidebound natives who do not share the same values? If so, will we be open in perpetuity to the accusation of having "imposed" the constitution in question? Will the constitution forever suffer an insurmountable, irremediable lack of legitimacy because it was "imposed" ab initio, no matter how local sensibilities evolve in the future?

What matters more to us: respect for distinctiveness of the national community and for local ownership of the constitution? Or compliance with what hegemonic states—the wealthy, powerful, and mostly Western states in a position to impose their norms on others—characterize as fundamental universal norms? If the latter, are we prepared to confess to constitutional imposition?

60 See Mara Malagodi, 'Constitutional History and Constitutional Migration: Nepal', in David S Law (ed), *Constitutionalism in Context* (forthcoming CUP 2019).

Conclusion

The concept of an "imposed constitution" implies some combination of involuntariness and outside influence. But what constitution is not characterized by a degree of involuntariness or outside influence? There is no such thing as a constitution created free of imposition or coercion, or in a wholly indigenous manner. To call a constitution "imposed" is to say that not everyone supported the constitution—which is to describe every constitution in existence. Only some constitutions, however, are the subject of delegitimating narratives that depict them as "imposed". More often, constitutions are cherished as symbols of nationhood and idealized by romanticizing narratives that impart an impossible combination of virtues. The type of narrative surrounding a constitution has more to do with national myth-making or political argumentation than the application of a coherent and clearly defined dichotomy between imposed and unimposed constitutions. Some of the stories that we tell about constitutions are flattering; others are not. What such stories tend to share in common, however, is that they are both selective and reductive. Constitutions come to us deeply enmeshed in politics, and it is unlikely that those politics can ever be reduced to a single word—be it "autochthonous", or "indigenous", or "imposed".

3 Internally imposed constitutions

*Yaniv Roznai**

'in constitutional terms, all constitutions... [are] imposed'

(Philipp Zorn)[1]

I Introduction

One of the basic ideas behind a national constitution is that it is *autochthonous*, either as it results from the national 'spirit' or presupposes a group of people who possesses constituent power and create the constitution.[2] A constitution thus reflects a certain place at a certain time.[3] 'Every nation', in the words of Hegel,

* An earlier version of this article was presented at the international conference: 'Imposed Constitutions: Aspects of Imposed Constitutionalism', held at the School of Law of the University of Nicosia in collaboration with the Research Group on Constitution-Making and Constitutional Change of the International Association of Constitutional Law and the Centre for European Constitutional Law (5–6 May 2017). I would like to thank Xenophon Contiades and Alkmene Fotiadou for their organization and the conference's participants for their comments. Special gratitude goes to the participants of the panel on 'Imposed Constitutions: Theory Revisited', Jörg Gerkrath, Richard Albert, Zoran Oklopcic, and David Law, for a discussion that has surely improved this chapter. It was also presented at the 2018 ICON-S Annual Conference, which took place at Hong Kong University (25–27 June 2018). I would like to thank the participants of the panel on 'constitutionalism and constitutional actors in comparative perspective', Mila Versteeg, Yvonne Tew, and the discussant Samuel Issacharoff, for a rich and useful debate. I would also like to send my appreciation to Adam Shinar, Hillel Sommer, Oren Tamir and the reviewer for extremely useful comments. As no one *imposed* upon me any parts of this chapter, I bear full responsibility for errors.

1 Philipp Zorn, *Das Staatsrecht des Deutschen Reiches*, Vol. 1 (Guttentag, 2nd ed. 1895) 109; cited in Dieter Grimm, *Constitutionalism: Past, Present and Future* (OUP 2016) 114.

2 Mark Tushnet, 'Constitution' in Michel Rosenfeld and András Sajó (eds), *The Oxford Handbook of Comparative Constitutional Law* (OUP 212) 217, 218–219. See also Peter C Oliver, 'Autochthonous Constitutions', in *Max Planck Encyclopedia of Comparative Constitutional Law* (July 2016): '"Autochthony" refers to the fact that a constitution is, legally speaking, 'home grown' or rooted in native soil. By this it is meant that the constitution owes its validity and authority to local legal factors, rather than to the fact of enactment by a foreign legal process'.

3 Beau Breslin, *From Words to Worlds – Exploring Constitutional Functionality* (John Hopkins University Press 2009) 17.

'has the constitution which suits it and belongs to it',[4] and accordingly a constitution cannot be imposed upon a nation from the outside:

> Napoleon insisted upon giving to the Spanish a constitution a priori, but the project failed. A constitution is not a mere manufacture, but the work of centuries; it is the idea and the consciousness of what is reasonable, in so far as it is developed in a people. Hence no constitution is merely created. That which Napoleon gave to the Spanish was more rational than what they had before, yet they viewed it as something foreign to them, and rejected it because they were not sufficiently developed. In a constitution a people must embody their sense of right and reproduce their conditions. Otherwise the constitution may exist externally, but it has no significance or truth.[5]

Hegel refers to the Bayonne Constitution Napoleon imposed on Spain in 1808 that remained a dead letter and was replaced in 1812 by a new one after the fall of Napoleon's rule.[6] Indeed, from traditional constitutional theory perspective, due to a strong sense of locality or a people's attachment to the constitution, there is an objection to an 'imposed constitution' which can be generally defined as 'a written constitution [that] is imposed on a people without their full agreement. Strictly speaking, the 'full agreement' will require that a majority of the people expressly consent to a constitution through a formal procedure. However, at least some part of the people may acquiesce'.[7]

This chapter seeks to challenge the 'imposed constitutionalism' debate by providing a critical view of the objections toward 'externally imposed constitutions'.[8] In order to do so, we have to first understand the term 'imposed'. According to the *Oxford Dictionary of English*, the word *impose* comes from French *imposer* (influenced by old French *poser* – 'to place'), from Latin *imponere* which means to put upon, to inflict. It means to 'force (an unwelcome decision or ruling) on someone'

4 G. W. F. Hegel, *Philosophy of Right* (S. W. Dyde trs., originally published by George Bell & sons, 1896, Dover Publications, INC 2005) 160 para 274.

5 Ibid.

6 See Brian R. Hamnett, 'Constitutional Theory and Political Reality: Liberalism, Traditionalism and the Spanish Cortes, 1810–1814' (1977) 49(1) *The Journal of Modern History* D1071, D1079; Emilio La Parra López, 'The Monarchy at Bayonne and the Constitution of Cadiz' in Michael Broers, Peter Hicks and Agustin Guimerá (eds), *The Napoleonic Empire and the New European Political Culture. War, Culture and Society, 1750–1850* (Palgrave Macmillan 2012). See, interestingly, Henry Bertram Hill, 'The Constitutions of Continental Europe: 1789–1813' (1936) 8(1) *The Journal of Modern History* 82, 91 (writing that 'Spanish collections of constitutions begin with 1812 and omit the Napoleonic constitution of 1808').

7 Yasuo Hasebe, 'Imposed Constitutions (constitutions octroyées)', *Max Planck Encyclopedia of Comparative Constitutional Law* (July 2016).

8 I am less interested in the question whether indeed external intervention in constitution-making process or to what extent such intervention can be considered as 'constitutional imposition', but rather accept as a given the claim that such constitutions are to some extent imposed.

or 'to put (a restriction) in place'.[9] Imposed constitutions, for our purpose, thus mean *constitutions that are forced upon or put in place for a people.* Whereas constitutional literature has so far focused on constitutions that were imposed from outsiders, such as occupying powers, strictly speaking, there is nothing necessarily foreign or external that characterizes the notion of imposed constitutions. While some constitutions were externally imposed, for instance after armed conflicts by the victorious parties or under occupation,[10] all constitutions are internally imposed or at the very least have some elements of imposition. This thus raises the question: why do we regard external imposition as problematic but internal imposition as unproblematic or less problematic? Is it simply due to the notion of the 'nation-state'? But if what that is troubling with imposed constitutions is the lack of people's consent to the constitution then why do we give a short-shrift to other instances of imposition? Thus, the basic argument of this chapter is that there are many ways and degrees of impositions and *all constitutions can be considered as imposed* to some extent, i.e. have some characteristics of imposition. If this is the case, then the objections to externally imposed constitutions are overrated. When considering imposed constitutionalism, one has to consider the *degree* of imposition in addition to the *source* of imposition (external/internal).

The chapter advances the argument as follows: Section II reviews the common external element in the imposed constitutionalism debate. Section III provides a typology of internally imposed constitutions. It analyzes four types of internally imposed constitutions: 'Old' constitutions by which past generations impose the constitution on current and future generations ('Generational Imposition'); constitution-making processes in which the majority imposes upon a minority its values ('Majoritarian Imposition'); constitution-making processes that are elite-driven in which an elite group imposes the constitution upon the rest ('Elite Imposition'); and a constitution-making process that is judicially driven, in which the court brings about a constitutional revolution ('Judicially Imposed'). Section IV evaluates the idea of 'we the people' as the generative principle undergirding the discussion which causes anxiety about external constitutional intervention. Yet elements of imposition appear also in internally made constitutions. Therefore, this section calls to shift the focus from the *sources* of imposition to an examination of the *degree* to which a constitution is imposed. Section V concludes.

II The common external element in imposed constitutions

Inherent to the concept of imposed constitution is the supposition that the constitution is created by constituent power that belongs to 'the people'.[11]

9 Angus Stevenson (ed), *Oxford Dictionary of English* (OUP 2010) 879.

10 See infra section II.

11 On perceptions of constituent power see Martin Loughlin, 'The Concept of Constituent Power' (2014) 13(2) *Eur J Pol Theory* 218; Joel Colón-Ríos, 'Five Conceptions of Constituent Power' (2014) 130(2) *LQR* 306; Mikael Spång, *Constituent Power and Constitutional*

For that reason, historically, monarchical constitutions that a monarch or a prince 'graciously' granted to his subjects ('constitution octroyée') are also often considered a type of imposed constitution.[12] An oft-cited example is the 1814 French Charter granted to the people by Louis XVIII.[13] After 1814, this 'top-down' model of constitutionalization became a monarchical-constitutional model in various Europan states.[14]

Contemporary debates on imposed constitutions focus on constitutions that are regarded as imposed from the outside. The classic example is the Japanese Constitution of 1946,[15] which was the product of Supreme Allied Commander General Douglas MacArthur under the auspices of U.S. occupation rather than the internal Japanese decision-making process.[16] Another often mentioned example is the 1949 post-WWII German Basic Law. Whereas the constitution-making process drew mainly from German models and traditions, it was initiated and closely observed by the occupying Allied powers. The military governors of Germany prescribed basic constitutional principles, namely democracy, federalism, and individual rights, with which the new constitution had to comply and which provided

Order – Above, Within and Beside the Constitution (Palgrave Macmillan 2014); Yaniv Roznai, '"We the People", "Oui, the People", and the Collective Body: Perceptions of Constituent Power', in Gary Jacobsohn and Miguel Schor (eds), *Comparative Constitutional Theory* (Edward Elgar 2018) 295; Andrew Arato, *Adventures of Constituent Power* (CUP 2017).

12 Lieber termed this 'a chartered constitution', which he regarded as a compact between the ruler and the people. See Francis Lieber, *Legal and Political Hermeneutics, or Principles of Interpretation and Construction in Law and Politics* (Charles C. Little 1839) 174. For an examination see Jörg Gerkrath, 'Are Octroyed Constitutions of the 19th Century to be Considered as Imposed Constitutions?' in this vol.

13 The Preamble to the Constitutional Charter of 4 June 1814 explicitly stated that 'Thus willingly, and by the free exercise of our royal authority, we have granted this constitutional charter to our subjects'. See Pamela M. Pilbeam, *The Constitutional Monarchy in France, 1814–48* (Routledge 2014) 93.

14 See Markus J. Prutsch, '"Monarchical Constitutionalism" in Post-Napoleonic Europe' in Kelly L. Grotke and Markus J. Prutsch (eds), *Constitutionalism, Legitimacy, and Power: Nineteenth-Century Experiences* (OUP 2014) 69, 77.

15 See Jon Elster, 'Ways of Constitution-Making' in Axel Hadenius (eds), *Democracy's Victory and Crisis* (CUP 1997) 123, 127: "'MacArthur's Japanese constitution" from 1946 provides an example of a constitution imposed, in its smallest detail, by a foreign power'. However, see David S. Law, 'The Myth of the Imposed Constitution', in Denis Galligan and Mila Versteeg (eds), *The Social and Political Foundations of Constitutions* (CUP 2013) 239, 264 (claiming that the notion that constitutionalism in postwar Japan has been the story of the imposition and internalization of an alien document is both inadequate and misleading.)

16 On the constitution-making process, see Ray A. Moore and Donald L. Robinson, *Partners for Democracy Crafting – The New Japanese State under MacArthur* (OUP 2002). See also Dale M. Hellegers, *We the Japanese People: World War II and the Origins of the Japanese Constitution* (Stanford University Press 2001); Chaihark Hahm and Sung Ho Kim, *Making We The People – Democratic Constitutional Founding in Postwar Japan and South Korea* (CUP 2015).

the Parliamentary Council (Parlamentarischer Rat) parameters for the making of the Basic Law.[17] Moreover, the final product was subject to Allied approval.[18]

Sujit Choudhry describes the basic pattern:

> A foreign power would design the institutional and legal architecture of another political community without its consent. The constitution was presented as a fait accompli. Local participation – there was usually some – did not entail meaningful, substantive decision-making power. Rather, it was directed at ensuring the acquiescence of local elites, with fundamental questions of constitutional choice safely remaining in foreign hands.[19]

This was the prevailing debate surrounding imposed constitutions, regarded by some as 'intervention through constitution-making',[20] which was considered a rare phenomenon.[21]

Another type of imposed constitutions concerns constitution-making processes that even if not being conducted directly by foreign powers takes place under occupation with great external influence and pressure.[22] Noah Feldman describes this type of imposition as a 'sophisticated form of imposed constitutionalism':

> Old-fashioned imposed constitutionalism, it would seem, is dead. Or is it? Although the wholesale imposition of an entire constitutional order is increasingly rare, constitutions are being drafted and adopted in the shadow of the gun. In the last decade, in the former Yugoslavia, East Timor, Afghanistan,

17 François Venter, *Constitutional Comparison – Japan, Germany, Canada and South Africa as Constitutional States* (Kluwer Law International 2000) 26, 31; François Venter, 'Constitution Making and the Legitimacy of the Constitution', in Antero Jyranki (ed), *National Constitutions in the Era of Integration* (Kluwer Law 1999) 9, 16.

18 Axel Tschentscher, *The Basic Law (Grundgesetz) 2016: The Constitution of the Federal Republic of Germany (May 23rd, 1949) – Introduction and Translation* 16–17 (3rd ed., BoD – Books on Demand 2016) (mentioning that the allied powers frequently interfered with the drafting and claiming that 'the result set into force in 1949 cannot easily be understood as an expression of the German People's constitution making power (*pouvoir constituant*)'.)

19 Sujit Choudhry, 'Old Imperial Dilemmas and the New Nation-Building: Constitutive Constitutional Politics in Multinational Polities' (2004–2005) 37 *Conn L Rev* 933.

20 Viktor Mayer-Schönberger, 'Into the Heart of the State: Intervention through Constitution-Making' (1994) 8 *Temple Int'l & Com LJ* 315.

21 Frederick Schauer, 'On the Migration of Constitutional Ideas' (2004–2005) 37 *Conn L Rev* 907, 909.

22 See Andrew Arato, 'Post-Sovereign Constitution-Making and Its Pathology in Iraq' (2006) 51 NYLS Rev 535; Philipp Dann and Zaid Al-Ali, 'The Internationalized Pouvoir Constituant – Constitution-Making Under External Influence in Iraq, Sudan and East Timor' (2006) 10 Max Planck UNYB *423*; Alexandra Kemmerer, 'The Pouvoir Constituant in Times of Transition – A Comment on Andrew Arato and Philipp Dann' (2008) 18 Demokratie in der Weltgesellschaft, Soziale Welt; Zachary Elkins, Tom Ginsburg and James Melton, 'Baghdad, Tokyo, Kabul...: Constitution Making in Occupied States' (2008) 49 Will & Mary L Rev 1139; Andrew Arato, Constitution-Making under Occupation: The Politics of Imposed Revolution in Iraq (CUP 2009).

and, yes, Iraq, interim or permanent constitutions have been drafted under conditions of de facto or de jure occupation.[23]

These constitution-making processes were essentially local yet included substantial external intervention and pressure by international organizations and foreign powers.

Another sophisticated form, rather unique, of imposed constitutions might be the constitutions of independent entities created as part of multilateral agreements. For example, the Zurich Treaty of 1959, in which Greece, Turkey, and Great Britain guaranteed Cyprus' independence, territorial integrity, and security, was incorporated within the Constitution of 1960 (Art. 181).[24] Another possible example is the Sino-British Joint Declaration of 1984, which established basic policies of China regarding Hong Kong as formulated in Hong Kong's Basic Law of 1990.[25]

Modern constitution-making processes now include more delicate forms of external involvement. One such form is the contemporary practice of nondomestic actors, such as the United Nations Development Program or the International Institute for Democracy and Electoral Assistance (IDEA), giving advice to domestic actors engaged in constitution-making.[26] The European Commission for Democracy Through Law ('the Venice Commission') can be regarded as another example for an external body that provides advice and assistance in domestic constitutional reforms.[27] Another form might be the invitation of extra-territorial actors to participate in the making of domestic constitutional law, not necessarily during formal constitutional making, but also in constitutional amendments, constitutional adjudication, and interpretation.[28]

23 Noah Feldman, 'Imposed Constitutionalism' (2005) 37 *Conn L Rev* 857, 858.

24 Catherine D. Papastathopoulos, 'Constitutionalism and Communalism: The Case of Cyprus' (1965) 16(1) *Univ Toronto LJ* 118, 139. Art. 182.1 declares unamendable the treaty's basic articles.

25 Yash Ghai, 'The Legal Foundations of Hong Kong's Autonomy: Building on Sand', 29(1) *Asia Pacific Journal of Public Administration* (2007) 3, 7.

26 Carina B. Gouvêa, The United Nations' Interventions in the Constitution-Making Process in the States in Political Transition: Facing the Legitimacy Problem of the Constitutional Charters (21 June 2017), https://ssrn.com/abstract=2990485; Mark Tushnet, 'Observations on The Politics of "Best Practices" in Constitutional Advice Giving' (2015) 50 *Wake Forest L Rev* 843.

27 See e.g. Maartje De Visser, 'A Critical Assessment of the Role of the Venice Commission in Processes of Domestic Constitutional Reform' (2015) 63(4) *AJCL* 963.

28 Richard Albert, 'Constitutions Imposed with Consent?' in this vol. On 'extra-territorial' forms of constitutional interpretation see also Rosalind Dixon and Vicki C. Jackson, 'Constitutions Inside Out: Outsider Interventions in Domestic Constitutional Contests" (2013) 38 *Wake Forest L Rev* 149. Like formal constitution making, constitutional mechanisms such as adjudication and amendment can also bring about constitutional transformations. See Yaniv Roznai, 'Constitutional Transformations: The Case of Hungary' in David Law (ed), *Constitutionalism in Context* (CUP, forthcoming 2019).

In light of these external forces which are at work during constitution-making processes, Zoran Oklopcic claimed that constituent power – the generative force behind constitution-making – must be regarded in an 'enlarged perception of the geographical theatre' to include also political powers which work also externally to the political boundaries.[29] Regardless of the theoretical implications of imposed constitutionalism to the concept of constituent power, this chapter claims that the element of imposition is not unique to external interventions in constitution-making and exists, to various degrees, also in internal constitution-making.

III Internally imposed constitutions

This chapter focuses on, what I term, internally imposed constitutions. Thus, a good starting point is Mark Janis' definition of imposed constitutionalism, which is wider than merely externally imposed constitutions:

> By 'imposed' we might mean that 'constitutionalism' may be imposed either by a conqueror of a nation on a nation or by a conqueror of a nation on a nation with some degree of consent of the conquered nation (or at least by the elite of a conquered nation) or by an international or multilateral organization on a nation with or without the consent of the conquered nation (or its elite) or by a majority of a nation on the minority of a nation or by the elite of a nation on the non-elite of a nation.[30]

Janis adds to external forms of imposed constitutions two examples of internally imposed constitutions: majority imposition over minority and elite imposition over non-elite. I extend this definitial list even more to add two additional forms: generational and judicial forms of imposition. This provides a typology of internally imposed constitutions.

A Generational imposition

In his *Rights of Man*, Thomas Paine wrote that 'every age and generation must be as free to act for itself … [I]t is the living, and not the dead, that are to be accommodated'.[31] Thomas Jefferson expressed a similar notion in his famous correspondence with James Madison from 6 September 1789, in which Jefferson argued that because each generation is free to decide its form of government,

29 Zoran Oklopcic, 'Constitutional (Re)Vision: Sovereign Peoples, New Constituent Powers, and the Formation of Constitutional Orders in the Balkans' (2012) 19(1) *Constellations* 81. See also Hans Agné, 'Democratic Founding: We the People and the Others' (2012) 10(3) *Int'l J Const L* 836.

30 Mark W. Janis, 'Human Rights and Imposed Constitutions' (2004–2005) 37 *Conn L Rev* 955, 956.

31 Thomas Paine, *Rights of Man, Common Sense, and Other Political Writings* (M. Philip ed., OUP 1998) 91–92.

constitutions should be rewritten every generation. The dead should not govern the living since 'the earth belongs always to the living generation'.[32]

However, if one takes the U.S. Constitution as an example, there is the known problem that the people responsible for the constitution-making are long gone, yet their creation still binds the 'living people'. For that reason, David Strauss declared, 'we are talking about they the people, not we the people, and that does not sound very democratic'.[33] In other words, the American people live by a constitution *imposed* upon them over two hundred years ago. Walter Murphy once described it by using an interesting analogue: 'insofar as a constitution is a covenant by which a group of people agree to (re)transform themselves into a nation, it may function for the founding generation like a marriage … for later generations, a constitution may operate more as an arranged marriage in which consent is passive, for the degree of choice is then typically limited'.[34] The inadequate consent is the key feature.

This aspect of imposed constitutions focuses on the well-known difficulty in constitutional theory of the 'dead hand of the past'. According to this difficulty, constitutional entrenchment causes to the present and future generations to be ruled by the 'dead hand' of their ancestors. The 'dead hand' difficulty mostly refers to constitutional entrenchment in the form of special or super majority requirements for constitutional amendments but also to originalism as a theory of constitutional interpretation, according to which the constitution should be interpreted in keeping with the original intent or meaning of those who are often long gone.[35] This difficulty is of course aggravated the older a constitution gets.[36]

32 Lance Banning, *Jefferson and Madison: Three Conversations from the Founding* (Rowman & Littlefield 1995) 29. Sunstein describes this notion as Jefferson's main democratic concern toward constitutionalism. See Cass R. Sunstein, 'Constitutions and Democracies: An Epilogue' in Jon Elster and Rune Slagstad (eds), *Constitutionalism and Democracy* (CUP 1988) 327.

33 David A. Strauss, 'We the People, They the People, and the Puzzle of Democratic Constitutionalism' (2013) 91 *Texas L Rev* 1969. Indeed, Elster describes the paradox of democracy in the following terms: 'each generation wants to be free to bind its successors, while not being bound by its predecessors'. See Jon Elster, *Ulysses and the Sirens: Studies in Rationality and Irrationality* (CUP 1979) 93.

34 Walter F. Murphy, 'Constitutions, Constitutionalism and Democracy' in Douglas Greenberg et al. (eds), *Constitutionalism and Democracy – Transitions in the Contemporary World* (OUP 1993) 3, 9.

35 See Michael J. Klarman, 'Antifidelity' (1997) 70 *S Cal L Rev* 381, 382; Michael J. Klarman, 'Majoritarian Judicial Review: The Entrenchment Problem' (1997) 85 *Geo LJ* 491, 508–9; Michael W. McConnell, 'Textualism and the Dead Hand of the Past' (1998) 60 *Geo Wash L Rev* 1127–28; Adam M. Samaha, 'Dead Hand Arguments and Constitutional Interpretation' (2008) 108 *Colum L Rev* 606; John O. McGinnis and Michael B. Rappaport, 'Originalism and the Good Constitution' (2010) 98 *Geo LJ* 1693, 1752.

36 Indeed, old constitutions in particular raise unique and important questions for constitutionalism, judicial review and interpretation. See Elvind Smith (ed), *Constitutional Justice Under Old Constitutions* (Kluwer Law International 1995).

The problem of the theory of imposed constitutionalism is particularly acute when the constitution fixes and establishes non-neutral principles, and protects values and interests of the day, such as state religion or special status to the then prevailing interest groups. As András Sajó describes:

> [O]ne cannot deny that constitutions tend to impose more than just freedom of self-determination on future generations. Future generations are further constrained by preceding generations, as the latter may create constitutional laws which may preempt the possibilities and rights of future generations. … This indicates that the present generation inevitably imposes its scheme or vision upon future generations, and the constitution-making generation … has a particularly strong impact on future generations.[37]

However, one may claim, modern constitutions include mechanisms for their modifications, so there is no imposition at all. The people are always free to amend the constitution. This is only partially correct.

First, there is a cognitive 'status quo bias', which refers to the irrational tendency to prefer the existing state of affairs.[38] This bias applies also to constitutional design and constitutional change. Ozan Varol demonstrates how people tend to be biased against novel ideas that generate uncertainty about their consequences, and 'existing constitutional provisions enjoy a first-mover advantage' not only because their repeated application elevates them to a higher position. The longer the provision exists the longer the bias.[39] Elkins, Ginsburg and Melton demonstrate this 'constitutional stickiness' by revealing that the removal and addition of rights from constitutions are extremely rare.[40]

Second, indeed constitutional amendment formulas manage to relax the dead hand difficulty by allowing future generations to change the constitution. Yet at the same time they create or enhance the difficulty by requiring an often-formidable or extremely cumbersome procedure for amending the constitution.[41] As flexible constitutions relax the dead-hand difficulty,[42] the more difficult it is to amend the constitution, the stronger is the element of imposition because the

37 András Sajó, 'Preferred Generations: A Paradox of Restoration Constitutions' (1992–1993) 14 *Cardozo L Rev* 847, 848–851.

38 Viktor J. Vanberg, 'The Status Quo in Contractarian-Constitutionalist Perspective' (2004) 15 *Const Pol Econ* 153.

39 Ozan O. Varol, 'Constitutional Stickiness' (2016) 49 *UC Davis L Rev* 899, 938–939.

40 Zachary Elkins, Tom Ginsburg and James Melton, 'Time and Constitutional Efficacy' in Tom Ginsburg and Aziz Z. Huq (eds), *Assessing Constitutional Performance* (CUP 2016) 233, 247–250.

41 Lawrence G. Sager, 'The Dead Hand and Constitutional Amendment' (1995–1996) 19 *Harv J L & Pub Pol'y* 275. See generally Richard Albert, 'The Structure of Constitutional Amendment Rules' (2014) 49 *Wake Forest L Rev* 913; Richard Albert, 'The Difficulty of Constitutional Amendment in Canada' (2015) 53(1) *Alberta L Rev* 85.

42 Mila Versteeg and Emily Zackin, 'Constitutions Unentrenched: Toward an Alternative Theory of Constitutional Design' (2016) 110(4) *Am Pol Sci Rev* 657, 660.

ability of the people to choose the constitutional rules and values based upon which they live is more limited. Even if the constitution-making generation ratified the constitutional choice by a supermajority referendum that manifests the consent of the governed at the time of ratification, an extremely rigid constitution established in the past can barely be regarded as manifesting the current consent of the governed.[43]

Third, it is true, as Elster writes, that 'constitutions are usually designed to make it difficult to change their provisions, compared to ordinary legislation, but not impossible'.[44] Nonetheless, many constitutions include not only procedural entrenchment that requires special majorities for their revision but also absolute entrenchment in the form of 'eternity clauses' or 'unamendable provisions' that completely protect certain principles, rules or institutions from change.[45] Moreover, these provisions are often enforced through substantive judicial review of constitutional amendments.[46]

By preventing current and future generations from amending certain parts of the constitution, unamendable provisions exacerbate the 'dead hand' difficulty and obstructs what might be viewed as healthy social development. When the constitution cannot be changed with the changing values of society, then it does not protect the values that society believes in, but instead, simply imposes upon the current generation the values of past ones. Unamendability is the strongest 'precommitment' device.[47] Consequently, Richard Albert claims that as the most acute manifestation of the dead hand problem, unamendable constitutional provisions create a democratic deficit as to the current and future generations, and are 'deeply troubling for democratic theory, and doubly troubling for democratic practice'.[48]

Take the example of Turkey, in which secularism is an unamendable constitutional principle in the constitutional order since the early years of the Republic founded in 1923 by Atatürk. The founder's choice of secularism, even if politically desirable and correct, did not correspond with society's values, which caused

43 Walter Dellinger, 'The Legitimacy of Constitutional Change: Rethinking the Amendment Process' (1983) 97 *Harv L Rev* 386, 386–87.

44 Jon Elster, *Ulysses Unbound* (CUP 2000) 94.

45 See Christoph Bezemek, 'Constitutional Core(s): Amendments, Entrenchments, Eternities and Beyond Prolegomena to a Theory of Normative Volatility' (2011) *J Juris* 517.

46 See Gary J. Jacobsohn, 'An Unconstitutional Constitution? A Comparative Perspective' (2006) 4(3) *Int'l J Const L* 460; Aharon Barak, 'Unconstitutional Constitutional Amendments' (2011) 44(3) *Isr L Rev* 321; Gábor Halmai, 'Unconstitutional Constitutional Amendments: Constitutional Courts as Guardians of the Constitution?' (2012) 19(2) *Constellations* 182; Yaniv Roznai, 'Unconstitutional Constitutional Amendments – The Migration and Success of a Constitutional Idea' (2013) 61(3) *Am J Comp L* 657.

47 Richard Albert, 'The Expressive Function of Constitutional Amendment Rules' (2013) 59 *McGill LJ* 225, 233.

48 Richard Albert, 'Constitutional Handcuffs' (2010) 42 *Ariz St LJ* 663, 667.

a continuing struggle of the secular character of the states.[49] When a nation (in this case predominantly Muslim) is bound by unamendable constitutional principles (in this case secularism) enshrined in the past, this imposition creates grave democratic challenges.[50]

For Elisha Mulford, an unamendable constitution is 'the worst tyranny of time, or rather the very tyranny of time. It makes an earthly providence of a convention which has adjourned without day. It places the sceptre over a free people in the hands of dead men, and the only office left to the people is to build thrones out of the stones of their sepulchres'.[51] I have elsewhere described this as 'necrocracy' rather than democracy.[52] Conversely, entrenchment provides stability, allows to focus on every-day politics, and can build national support for its protected values.[53] It can also protect minority rights and basic principles against hasty majoritarian impulse and short-term political gains and protect future generations from, what Holmes describes as 'being sold into slavery'.[54] In the end, entrenchment allows to maintain and reform the fundamental principles and institutions in a self-conscious manner.[55] George Mader summarizes this positive aspect of unamendability:

> Unamendable provisions provide maximum stability and permanent settling of basic questions, enabling all of the benefits associated with reliance. They also provide maximum restraint on any impulsive, destructive passions of majorities and even supermajorities. And if carefully written, unamendable provisions may be the most effective means of preventing future generations from harming even later generations.[56]

49 Yaniv Roznai, 'Negotiating the Eternal: The Paradox of Entrenching Secularism in Constitutions' 2017(2) *Mich St L Rev* 253, 270–276, 306–307. On unamendability and religion-secularism in general see Richard Albert and Yaniv Roznai, 'Religion, Secularism and Limitations on Constitutional Amendment' in Rex Ahdar (ed), *Research Handbook on Law and Religion* (Edward Elgar, 2018) ch. 8.

50 See Svetlana Tyulkina, *Militant Democracy: Undemocratic Political Parties and Beyond* (Routledge 2015) 181: 'The idea of secularism, which is being shielded from any public debate, was introduced into Turkish society in the 1920s. ... it is time to reconsider the ideas introduces some 100 years ago to see if they are still compatible with major democratic principles accepted by society'.

51 Elisha Mulford, *The Nation: The Foundations of Civil Order and Political Life in the United States* (Hurd and Houghton 1870) 155.

52 Yaniv Roznai, 'Necrocracy or Democracy? Assessing Objections to Constitutional Unamendability' in Richard Albert and Bertil Emrah Oder (eds), *An Unamendable Constitution? Unamendability in Constitutional Democracies* (Springer, 2018) 29.

53 McGinnis & Rappaport, Originalism (n 35) 1753.

54 Stephen Holmes, *Passions and Constraint – On the Theory of Liberal Democracy* (University of Chicago Press 1995) 162; See also Stephen Holmes, 'Precommitment and the Paradox of Democracy' in Elster and Slagstad (n 32) 195.

55 Christopher L. Eisgruber, 'The Living Hand of the Past: History and Constitutional Justice' (1997) 65 *Fordham L Rev* 1611, 1616.

56 George Mader, 'Generation Gaps and Ties That Bind: Constitutional Commitments and the Framers' Bequest of Unamendable Provisions' (2017) 60(2) *Howard L Rev* 483, 510.

This section does not provide a normative claim on whether mechanisms of entrenchment, eternity, and alike are good or bad.[57] It merely aims to describe the intergenerational imposition inherent in some constitutions. Of course, one also has to consider the fact that the median lifespan of national constitutions is a mere nineteen years,[58] which relaxes to some extent (and bearing in mind constitutional stickiness) the idea of the 'dead hand of the past' as binding future generations.

B Majoritarian imposition

Constitutions are made through some kind of decision-making procedures in which choices are ultimately made among various alternatives and preferences. Whether these are constitutional conventions, constituent assemblies, normal legislatures, or the executive,[59] there are always winners and losers. It is hard to imagine a constitution that is constituted in a complete consensus. Those who lose the constitutional battle remain bound by the winner's decision.[60] And in democracy the winner is, naturally, the majority or a super-majority. Indeed, democracy presents the 'permanent loser' problem – those who are regularly the minority will regularly lose the constitutional-political battles.[61] Majority rule may thus produce a kind of what Alexis de Tocqueville called 'the tyranny of the majority' – the oppression of minority groups.[62] John Stuart Mill refers to this risk in terms of imposition referring to the need to protect 'against the tendency of society to impose…its own ideas and practices as rules of conduct on those who dissent from them'.[63] Of course, the majority principle acts as a principle of legitimation to impose conformity.[64] Yet, the important element, for our matter, is that of imposition:

57 For an analysis see (2018) 1 *Intergenerational Justice Review* 3–41 with the following contributions: Jörg Tremmel, 'Constitutions as Intergenerational Contracts: Flexible or Fixed?'; Richard Albert, 'Constitutions as Handcuffs'; and Konstantin Chatziathanasiou 'Constitutions as Chains? On the Intergenerational Challenges of Constitution-Making'. See also Elai Katz, 'On Amending Constitutions: The Legality and Legitimacy of Constitutional Entrenchment' (1995–96) 29 *Colum J L & Soc Probs* 251.

58 Zachary Elkins, Tom Ginsburg and James Melton, *The Endurance of National Constitutions* (CUP 2009) 129.

59 See e.g. Andrew Arato, 'Forms of Constitution Making and Theories of Democracy' (1995–1996) 17 *Cardozo L Rev* 191.

60 Feldman (n 23) 863.

61 See Feldman (n 23) 864. See also Noah Feldman, 'Imposed Constitutions and Established Religion' (2006) 4(3) *Rev Faith & Int'l Aff* 3, 6.

62 Alexis de Tocqueville, *Democracy in America* (The Lawbook Exchange, Ltd., 1838) 252. On different conceptions of tyranny of the majority see Donald L. Beahm, *Conceptions of and Corrections to Majoritarian Tyranny* (Lexington Books 2002).

63 John Stuart Mill, *'On Liberty' and Other Writings* (CUP 1989) 8.

64 Giovanni Sartori, 'The Theory of Democracy Revisited' in Ricardo Blaug and John Schwarzmantel (eds), *Democracy – A Reader* (2nd ed., Columbia University Press 2016) 183, 194.

> Voting is an imposition of a will over a will. When a decision is reached by voting, some people must submit to an opinion different from theirs or to a decision contrary to their interest. … Voting generates winners and losers, and it authorizes the winners to impose their will, even if within constraints, on the losers.[65]

There are many examples of majoritarian imposition of constitutional norms. For example, regardless of the moral question, one can consider the case of the American Civil War after which the majority (the victorious North) imposed constitutional compliance – in this case abolition – on the losing minority side (the South).[66] As Ackerman describes, the triumphant Republican Congress excluded representatives from the Southern states, and proposed that the Fourteenth Amendment should be ratified, which ten of the eleven Southern states rejected due to their exclusion from deliberations and voting on the proposal. In 1867, Congress enacted a series of Reconstruction Acts, which divided the ten Southern states into five military districts under Union Army control. The commanding Generals were authorized to call new constitutional conventions and supervised the elections to those conventions. Moreover, not only did Congress inspect whether newly enacted state constitutions were truly 'republican', but Southern representatives were allowed to be admitted into Congress only after the state legislature ratified the Fourteenth Amendment.[67]

The second type of internally imposed constitutions is therefore majoritarian (or super-majoritarian) impositions; the majority imposes upon a minority its constitutional preferences. There are various means of shielding majoritarian preferences in the constitution. I shall briefly mention here two such mechanisms.

The first is constitutional unamendability, described above. Often, political actors use constitutional unamendability in order to preserve power asymmetry.

65 Adam Przeworski, 'Minimalist Conception of Democracy: A Defense' in Ian Shapiro and Casiano Hacker-Cordón (eds), *Democracy's Values* (CUP 1999) 23, 47.

66 Lani Guinier, *The Tyranny of the Majority, Fundamental Fairness in Represented Democracy* (Free Press 1994) 103.

67 Bruce Ackerman, *We the People Vol. 2 Transformation* (Harvard University Press 1998) 110. Christopher Green notes, however that: 'Importantly, the Constitution was not imposed on the South, or on Territories, or on prospective officials today, utterly without their consent. The South was told to ratify the Fourteenth Amendment, as a pledge of loyalty, if they wanted to be represented in Congress. Those in territories are told to agree to the Constitution if they want to be in the Union. The current generation is told (by Article VI's oath requirement) to be bound to support the Constitution if they want to be officials. These acts of consent may not amount to the sort of self-government that can legitimate Reconstruction, the lessened federal rights of those living in territories, or the inter-generationally-imposed Constitution in the eyes of our preferred democratic theory. But it might be possible to understand the obligations of those who have agreed to such impositions, even while we bracket the issue of the political principles that should govern the propriety of state-to-territory, North-to-South, or intergenerational assertions of authority themselves' See Christopher R. Green, 'Loyal Denominatorism and the Fourteenth Amendment: Normative Defense and Implications' (2018) 13 *Duke J Const L & Pub Pol* 167, 200–201.

The majority entrenches in the constitution its existing political preferences in a way that if they subsequently become a minority, their preferences would be protected against future alterations.[68] Elsewhere, I gave two examples for such a use: the French unamendability of republicanism, which marked the triumph of the republicans over the monarchists, and the Mexican unamendability of confederalism, which marked the victory of the Mexican federal party over the centralists after a long struggle that existed between the two parties over the country's formation.[69]

The second mechanism is banning political parties. Often, constitutions block, in advance, political associations which strive for a revolutionary change in the nation's identity.[70] This is another mechanism to block political movements (usually extreme) which do not fit within the dominant narrative of the polity. Take, for example, Section 7(a) of the Israeli Basic Law: the Knesset, which determines the standards for banning candidates and parties.[71] Among other things, Section 7(a) stipulates that a candidates' list shall not participate in elections to the Knesset if the objects or actions of the list include 'negation of the existence of the State of Israel as a Jewish and democratic state'. Mazen Masri claims that Section 7(a)'s exclusions have implications for who is included in 'the people' in Israel and especially affect the perception Palestinian citizens have of their constitutional membership.[72] While this is surely a very complex issue, simply put, according to Section 7(a), the constitutional values of 'Jewish and Democratic' are imposed on the Arab minority allegedly without the legal means to change it.[73]

In that respect, constitutional unamendability and banning political parties are similar; both impose a certain constitutional identity or constitutional preference

68 Jack Knight, 'Institutionalizing Constitutional Interpretation' in John Ferejohn, Jack N. Rakive and Jonathan Riley (eds), *Constitutional Culture and Democratic* Rule (CUP 2001) 361, 367.

69 Yaniv Roznai, 'Unamendability and The Genetic Code of the Constitution' (2015) 27(2) *Eur Rev Pub L* 775, 803 and references therein.

70 See e.g. Tyulkina (n 50); Walter F. Murphy, 'Excluding Political Parties: Problems for Democratic and Constitutional Theory' in Paul Kirchhof and Donald P. Kommers (eds), *Germany and its Basic Law* (Nomos Verlagsgesellschaft 1993) 173.

71 See generally Mordechai Kremnitzer, 'Disqualification of Lists and Parties: The Israeli Case', in András Sajó (ed), *Militant Democracy* (Eleven International Publishing 2004) 157; Suzie Navot, 'Fighting Terrorism in the Political Arena" The Banning of Political Parties' (2008) 14(6) *Party Politics* 91.

72 Mazen Masri, *The Dynamics of Exclusionary Constitutionalism: Israel as a Jewish and Democratic State* (Hart Publishing 2017) 151–153.

73 See Hilly Moodrick-Even Khen, *National Identities and the Right to Self-Determination of Peoples: 'Civic -Nationalism -Plus' in Israel and Other Multinational States* (Brill 2016) 105–106: 'several laws – among them, a Basic Law... determine, with a perpetual intent, Israel's character as a 'Jewish-democratic state.' ... The characterization of Israel as a Jewish (and democratic) state is thus considered a legal fundamental principle of the Israeli state. ... while the Jewish nationality is assimilated within the overall nationalistic characterization of Israel as a Jewish state ... Israel does not intend to incorporate Arab nationality in the definition of the state's character...'

without the possibility to modify them. The latter places the bar ex-ante and the former ex-post.[74]

The notion of majoritarian-imposed constitution is indeed extremely important for deeply divided societies with clear majority and minority groups. Analyzing constitutional nationalism and legal exclusion in Nepal, Mara Malagodi demonstrates how the 1990 constitution of Nepal enshrined certain national narratives: Hinduism, the Shah Monarchy and Nepali language, thereby reflecting the hegemony of a particular social group over other groups which, in light of the monolithic constitutional definition of the nation, were legally excluded.[75]

While it is true that nowadays constitution-making 'takes place against a backdrop of widespread commitment to democratic self-determination',[76] as Sandy Levinson replies concerning the right of 'national self-determination', 'almost all countries…are in fact 'multinational' and thus involve, as a matter of brute fact, the subordination of one or another … 'nations' to the single nation or coalition of nations that possesses political power'.[77] Indeed, in reality, 'nation-state' in the sense of homogenous population in terms of language, religion, and ethnicity does not exist.[78] The subordination of some groups to other's constitutional values is a clear manifestation of majoritarian imposed constitutionalism.

C Elite impositions

The U.S. Constitution declares that it was established by 'We the People'. Many other constitutions have followed this declaration.[79] But was it an act of we the people? According to estimations, only 2.5% of the population of the United States at the time voted in favour of ratifying the Constitution (since only property-holding adult white males were empowered, and not all of them supported ratification).[80] It is therefore certainly doubtful whether the individuals responsible for the Constitution represented the people of their time.[81] If the elite puts in place a constitution for the rest of the polity, is this not a type of imposition?

74 On this relationship see Rivka Weill, 'On the Nexus of Eternity Clauses, Proportional Representation, and Banned Political Parties' (2017) 16 *Election L J* 237.
75 Mara Malagodi, 'Constitutional Change and the Quest for Legal Inclusion in Nepal' in Colin Harvey and Alex Schwartz (eds), *Rights in Divided Societies* (Hart Publishing 2012) 169, 180.
76 Feldman (n 23) 859.
77 Sanford Levinson, 'Imposed Constitutionalism: Some Reflections' (2004–2005) 37 *Conn L Rev* 921, 930.
78 H. Patrick Glenn, *The Cosmopolitan State* (OUP 2013).
79 Denis J. Galligan, 'The Sovereignty Deficit of Modern Constitutions' (2013) 33(4) *OJLS* 703. On the global influences on constitutional preambles see Tom Ginsburg, Daniel Rockmore and Nick Foti, 'We the Peoples: The Global Origins of Constitutional Preambles' (2014) 46 *Geo Wash Int'l L Rev* 305.
80 Larry G. Simon, 'The Authority of the Framers of the Constitution: Can Originalist Interpretation Be Justified?' (1985) 73 *Cal L Rev* 1482, 1498–1500.
81 Strauss (n 33) 1969.

Much of the constitutional literature on constitution-making and constitutional change these days focuses on public or popular participation.[82] But elites take an important role in constitution-making.[83] Indeed, one of the constitution-making features is elites since the people themselves cannot bargain over a constitution and must choose a representative elite to draft the new constitutional document.[84]

An example of elite imposition might be the constitution-making in France in 1958 as Elster describes. At first, de Gaulle wanted a carte blanche in drafting the new constitution and presenting it to ratification by a referendum. When this encountered opposition, he established a consultive constitutional committee that deliberated his draft and made non-binding recommendations to him, practically all of which he disregarded. True, the constitutional adoption was accompanied with a plebiscite, but with no real democratic participation in the constitution-making process.[85] Thus the French Constitution of 1958 was written by de Gaulle and was 'tailor-made' for him.[86]

Elite self-dealing is common in constitution-making. In Venezuela, Hugo Chavez captured the electoral majority in a constituent assembly and then forced through a partisan constitution.[87] In East Timor, the Fretilin Party dominated the elections to the constituent assembly and then proceeded to draft a constitution in their own interests.[88] William Partlett recently demonstrated how across the former Soviet Union, extraordinary constitution-making institutions were 'democratic' mechanisms for legalizing partisan and rights-limiting constitutions, and rather than providing the people meaningful input in the constitution drafting

82 See Angela M. Banks, 'Expanding Participation in Constitution Making: Challenges and Opportunities' (2008) 49 *Wm & Mary L Rev* 1043, 1050; Kostas Chryssogonos, 'Popular Involvement in Constitution-Making' (2008) 20(4) *Eur Rev Pub L* 1299; Tom Ginsburg, Zachary Elkins and Justin Blount, 'Does the Process of Constitution-Making Matter?' (2009) 5 *Ann Rev L Soc Sci* 201; Xenophon Contiades and Alkmene Fotiadou (eds), *Participatory Constitutional Change – The People as Amenders of the Constitution* (Routledge 2017).

83 See Rafael Lopez-Pintor, 'Mass and Elite Perspectives in the Process of Transition to Democracy' in Enrique Balayra (ed), *Comparing New Democracies: Transition and Consolidation in Mediterranean Europe and the Southern Cone* (Westview Press 1987) 79; John Higley and Michael G. Burton, 'The Elite Variable in Democratic Transitions and Breakdowns' (1989) 54 *Am Soc Rev* 17.

84 William Partlett, 'The Elite Threat to Constitutional Transitions' (2016) 56 *Va J Int'l L* 407, 417.

85 Jon Elster, 'Deliberation and Constitution-Making', in *Deliberative Democracy* (Jon Elster ed., CUP 1998) 99. Elster notes that de Gaulle would not have decided upon the referendum if there had been a real chance of him losing it.

86 Jon Elster, 'Afterword the making of postcommunist presidencies' in Ray Taras (ed), *Postcommunist Presidents* (CUP 1997) 225, 233.

87 Allan R. Brewer-Carias, 'The 1999 Venezuelan Constitution-Making Process as an Instrument for Framing the Development of an Authoritarian Political Regime' in Laurel E. Miller (ed), *Framing the State in Times of Transition: Case Studies in Constitution Making* (USIP Press Books 2010) 505, 512; cited in Partlett (n 84) 455.

88 Louis Aucoin and Michele Brandt, 'East Timor's Constitutional Passage to Independence' in Miller ibid at 245, 270; cited in Partlett (n 84) 455.

they enabled elite self-dealing in the constitution-making and perpetuated public exclusion and alienation.[89]

Africa's constitution-making experiences that followed the 1960s political independence is noteworthy in that respect. The constitutions of many African states were the products of constituent assemblies, parliamentary committees, special task forces or tribunals, or a mere handful of lawyers and politicians, and the process included depoliticization of the people, the establishment of corrupt despotic regimes, the privatization of the state, and coercion by political elites.[90] For example, Julius Ihonvbere describes the Nigerian state as controlled by 'a weak, factionalised, corrupt and largely unproductive elite'.[91] According to Ihonvbere, in Nigeria, the draft constitution was never widely debated or voted upon and was in fact kept by the government as a secret from the Nigerian people.[92] The constitution, in other words, was not imposed from the outside but internally by an elite.

The reality is that many constitutions were not adopted with direct popular ratification. Popular participation is many times completely absent or merely formal. As Claude Klein and András Sajó note, 'The "people" is not sufficiently structured to develop a constitution, nor are empirical people very welcome by the actual constitution-making elite'.[93] Albert describes this crucial element in constitution-making: 'The people are more often than not represented by executives who negotiate constitutions as elite bargains, by legislators who vote on a package of proposals, by Constituent Assembly members who deliberate on and debate the content of constitutions, and sometimes by one or more of these groups of representatives in some special sequence or combination'.[94] It is mostly an elite, not 'we the people' that makes the constitution.[95]

Again, I am not arguing in favour or against elite constitution-making. Some theorists claim that since constitution-making involves the creation of long-term rules and principles, constitution-making should include elite decision-making that is often considered less self-interested than ordinary politics.[96] My claim is merely that often, when a small elite decides upon the constitutional

89 Partlett (n 84) 445.

90 Julius O Ihonvbere, 'How to Make an Undemocratic Constitution: The Nigerian Example' (2000) 21(2) *Third World Q* 343, 344–346.

91 Ibid.

92 Ibid.

93 Claude Klein and András Sajó, 'Constitution-Making: Process and Substance' in Rosenfeld and Sajó (n 2) 419, 424.

94 Richard Albert, 'Constitutional Amendment and Dismemberment' (2018) 43(1) *Yale J Int'l L* 1, 13.

95 Klein and Sajó (n 93) remark that 'for a theory of constitutionalism, it is not the democratic nature of the participation through constituent bodies and referenda that matters, but the lack of unilateral imposition'.

96 Elster (n 85) 105.

scheme that would bind the entire society, this can be regarded as another form of imposed constitutionalism.[97]

D Judicial imposition

The final example of internally imposed constitution is that which is imposed by the judiciary, as exemplified in Israel. Interestingly, the beginning of Israel's constitutional history resembles externally imposed constitutionalism. UN General Assembly's Resolution 181 (II) on 'Future government of Palestine' of 1947 declared the termination of the mandate over Palestine and the establishment of Arab and Jewish states. The resolution then stipulated the requirement that each state shall, 'not later than two months after the withdrawal of the armed forces of the mandatory Power, hold elections to the Constituent Assembly which shall be conducted on democratic lines'.[98] It also explicitly stipulated that the new democratic constitutions 'shall embody' sections of the resolution regarding Holy Places and Religious and Minority Rights, and include provisions regarding universal suffrage for a legislative body and guarantee various human rights and fundamental freedoms.[99] The future constitution and its basic principles were imposed by the United Nations. Accordingly, the Israeli Declaration of Independence explicitly called for elections to a constituent assembly for the purpose of making a formal constitution. Yet, from May 1949 until June 1950, the Israeli Parliament (the Knesset) was at the centre of debates surrounding the question whether or not to adopt a constitution.[100] As disagreements persisted, the inability to reach an agreement led to the adoption of a compromise formula proposed by Knesset Member Yizhar Harari, according to which the constitution-making process would evolve in stages, in the shape of basic laws that, at the end of the process, would be unified to a full formal constitution. The constitution-making process became an incremental enterprise.[101] Since the 1950 Harari compromise to the early 1990s, the Knesset enacted several institutional basic laws that regulated only governmental structure and institutions. The legal status of these basic laws was considered equivalent to ordinary legislation. In all these years, Israel lacked a formal Bill of Rights and the prevailing approach was that of 'parliamentary sovereignty' – the Knesset had no limitations on its

97 Ihonvbere (n 90) groups these African elite-driven constitutions together with imposed constitutions due to similar features, mainly: 'The hallmark of imposed, elite-driven or top-down constitutions is that they are never subjected to popular debates or referenda'.

98 UN General Assembly, A/RES/181(II), 29 November 1947, para. 9, https://unispal.un.org/DPA/DPR/unispal.nsf/0/7F0AF2BD897689B785256C330061D253

99 Ibid para 10.

100 See Philippa Strum, 'The Road Not Taken: Constitutional Non-Decision Making in 1948–1950 and Its Impact on Civil Liberties in the Israeli Political Culture' in S. Ilan Troen and Noah Lucas (eds), *Israel – The First Decade of Independence* (State University of New York Press 1995) 83.

101 Hanna Lerner, *Making Constitutions in Deeply Divided Societies* (CUP 2011) Ch 3.

legislative powers.[102] The Knesset, which holds both legislative and constituent powers,[103] has failed to compete the constitution-making process.

In the early 1990s, Basic-Law: Human and Citizen Rights was proposed but in light of opposition was not adopted. Thereafter, Knesset-Member Prof. Amnon Rubinstein selected out of the draft bill several rights which were considered non-controversial: dignity, occupation, speech, and movement. He intentionally left out equality and freedom of religion, which were considered problematic from religious perspectives.[104] In 1992, the Knesset adopted Basic Law: Human Dignity and Liberty, and Basic Law: Freedom of Occupation. The two basic laws now constitute a partially entrenched bill of rights.[105] The enactment of the basic laws on human rights did not initially mark a radical shift in the understanding of constitutionalism in Israel and the legal status of these basic laws was unclear. Also, there was no wide public or political debate as for any special significance in the enactment of these two basic laws. In other words, there was no 'constitutional moment'.[106]

It was only in 1995, with a judicial decision of monumental significance – the Mizrahi Bank Case,[107] that a 'constitutional revolution' has materialized. In this decision, comparable to the 'Marbury' model',[108] the Israeli Supreme Court ruled that the Knesset holds constituent authority and therefore the basic laws carry a supreme constitutional status; that the Knesset has only limited legislative powers; and that the court possesses the authority to conduct judicial review of legislation and invalidate laws that contradict the substantive provisions established in the basic laws. This produced a radical change in the overall structure of Israeli constitutional law as subsequent to this judicial decision, Israel was transformed

102 Suzie Navot, *The Constitution of Israel – A Contextual Analysis* (Hart Publishing 2014) 17; Adam Shinar, 'Accidental Constitutionalism: The Political Foundations and Implications of Israeli Constitution-Making' in Dennis Galligan and Mila Versteeg (eds), *The Social and Political Foundations of Constitutions* (CUP 2013). The lack of a Bill of Rights did not prevent the Supreme Court from protecting individual rights, through interpretive means. See Amos Shapira, 'Judicial Review without a Constitution: The Israeli Paradox' (1983) 56 *Temp LQ* 405.

103 Suzie Navot, 'Israel', in *How Constitutions Change – A Comparative Study* (Dawn Oliver and Carlo Fusaro eds., 2011) 191.

104 Navot (n 102) 26–27.

105 See Aharon Barak, 'The Constitutional Revolution: Israel's Basic Laws' (1992–1993) 4 *Const F* 83; David Kretzmer, 'The New Basic Laws on Human Rights: A Mini-Revolution in Israeli Constitutional Law' (1992) 26 *Isr L Rev* 238.

106 Gideon Sapir, 'Constitutional Revolutions: Israel as a Case-Study' (2009) 5(4) *Int'l J L in Context* 355, 364.

107 CA 6821/93 *United Mizrahi Bank Ltd. v. Migdal Cooperative Village*, 49(4) P.D. 221 (1995). See Suzie Navot, 'Mizrahi Bank Case (Isr)' *Max Planck Encyclopedia of Comparative Constitutional Law* (February 2016).

108 See Yoram Rabin and Arnon Gutfeld, 'Marbury v. Madison and its Impact on the Israeli Constitutional Law' (2007) 15 *U Miami Int'l & Comp L Rev* 303; Daphne Barak-Erez, 'From an Unwritten to a Written Constitution: The Israeli challenge in American Perspective' (1994) 26 *Colum Hum Rts L Rev* 309; Rivka Weill, 'Hybrid Constitutionalism: The Israeli Case for Judicial Review and Why We Should Care' (2012) 30 *Berkeley J Int'l L* 349.

from a 'parliamentary sovereignty' system to a 'constitutional democracy' backed with a strong judicial review. Since the basic laws did not grant court explicit authority to review and invalidate legislation, the existence and scope of constitutional judicial review in Israel have been harshly contested.[109]

The story does not end here. In a series of judicial decisions which have followed the United Mizrahi Bank case, the Supreme Court ruled that even though certain fundamental rights were not explicitly included in the two basic laws on human rights (intentionally, recall), they should be inferred from 'human dignity', which is explicitly protected in Basic Law: Human Dignity and Freedom. Based on such broad interpretation of human dignity, the Supreme Court has ruled that certain aspects of the right to equality and freedom of expression carry a constitutional status.[110] Accordingly, a new legislation that would violate equality would have to meet the terms set forth in Basic Law: Human Dignity and Freedom. Suzie Navot claims that 'this dramatic development is surely a revolution in itself'.[111] Israel's constitution, in many aspects, was judge-made.[112]

Of course, one may argue that this is not the case of imposed constitutionalism since if the Knesset wishes, it can now amend the basic laws and abolish or limit judicial review and the constitutional guarantees. From a purely formalistic perspective this is correct. However, politically and legitimacy-wise, and considering the notion of path dependence, the Supreme Court's actions managed to set a new constitutional status quo, which, as time passes, has become less and less susceptible to an opposing political action.[113]

Implicit constitutional unamendability is another form of judicial imposition. In the section on 'generational imposition', I mentioned constitutional unamendability – limits to formal constitutional change – as one form of constitutional imposition. Often, unamendability is derived not from explicit constitutional provisions but derived by courts implicitly from the constitution. Indeed, courts around the world have declared that the constitution contains a set of core constitutional values that are implicitly unamenable.[114] The most famous example is the Indian Basic Structure, developed by the Indian Supreme court, and according to which, the constitutional amendment power does not include the power

109 Amnon Reichman, 'Judicial Constitution Making in a Divided Society: The Israeli Case' in Diana Kapiszewski, Gordon Silverstein and Robert Kagan (eds), *Consequential Courts: Judicial Roles in Global Perspective* (CUP 2013) 233, 245–258.

110 See HCJ 6427/02 Movement for Government Quality in Israel v. The Knesset, ver 61(1), 619 (2006) (regarding equality); HCJ 10203/03 The National Census LtD v Attorney General (Nevo, 20 August 2008) (regarding political expression).

111 Navot (n 102) 235.

112 See Moshe Landau, 'Judicial Enactment of a Constitution to Israel' (1996) 3 *Mishpat Umimshal* 697 [Heb.].

113 Ori Aronson, 'Why Hasn't the Knesset Repealed Basic Law: Human Dignity and Liberty–On the Status Quo as Counter-Majoritarian Difficulty' (2014) 37 *Tel Aviv UL Rev* 509 [Heb.].

114 Yaniv Roznai, *Unconstitutional Constitutional Amendments – The Limits of Amendment Powers* (OUP 2017) 39–70.

to abrogate or change the identity of the constitution or its basic features.[115] The doctrine now includes, as basic features of a liberal democracy, the principles of supremacy of the Constitution, the rule of law, separation of powers, judicial review, judicial independence, human dignity, national unity and integrity, free and fair elections, federalism, and secularism.[116]

As unamendability blocks any constitutional manner of amending certain principles designated as unchangeable, implicit unamendability, judicially-made, allegedly imposes certain constitutional principles on current and future generations.[117]

IV Imposition: A matter of degree not only of source

The origins or source of a constitution cannot provide absolute guarantee to its success. A constitution drafted through a participatory process might not endure for long or be accepted while even externally imposed constitutions, due to their conflict-reducing effects, may gain acceptance and legitimacy.[118] Indeed, David Law claimed that the case of Japan demonstrates that the support of the public can be sufficient to overcome 'foreign authorship stigma'.[119] Moreover, Tushnet notes that the complex history of so-called imposed constitutions suggests the possibility that a constitution that is really 'good' can produce stability even without substantial public or elite buy-in at its inception.[120] Why is then the panic surrounding externally imposed constitutions?

One possible explanation derives from Schmitt's overarching understanding of the political realm: 'The specific political distinction to which political actions and motives can be reduced is that between friend and enemy'.[121] We regard outsiders as enemies, threats to our particular constitutional identity; whereas internal imposition is considered less severe because it comes, in a way, from 'us' and not 'them'. We believe (or want to believe) that the constitution is ought to be written by 'we the people' (and within 'we', I also include our political representatives). Indeed, the fear surrounding external imposed constitutions derives from the fact that 'today a new constitution must be understood as locally produced to acquire legitimacy. Thus, the question of who imposes the constitution might have a normative importance by affecting constitutional legitimacy.'[122]

115 Kesavananda Bharati v. State of Kerala, AIR 1973 SC 1461.
116 On the doctrine, see Sudhir Krishnaswamy, *Democracy and Constitutionalism in India: A Study of the Basic Structure Doctrine* (OUP 2010).
117 And is therefore in clear tension with the basic notion of democratic self-government. See Melissa Schwartzberg, *Democracy and Legal Change* (CUP 2009) 2. On the risks of judges-made implicit unamendability see also Rehan Abeyratne, 'Giving Structure to the Basic Structure Doctrine' (2017) 1(2) *Indian L Rev* 182–189.
118 Klein and Sajó (n 93) 424.
119 Law (n 15) 242.
120 Tushnet (n 26) 851.
121 Carl Schmitt, *The Concept of the Political* (trans. George Schwab, University of Chicago Press, 1996) 26–27.
122 Feldman (n 23) 859.

However, what about constitutions enacted dozens and hundreds of years ago? These documents still symbolize 'we the people' if one accepts Jed Rubenfeld's articulation that true sovereignty – we the people – is generational. Freedom and democracy is a complex project of living a set of commitments that people write themselves into overtime and that link past, present, and future generations.[123] Thus, the question of who imposes the constitution might matter symbolically and conceptually, especially if we think of constitutionalism as an exclusively national achievement.

Finally, the source question might matter epistemically or informationally. External or foreign imposers might know either more or less about the conditions of the relevant country compared with internal imposers such as majorities, elites, or courts. As Lanni and Vermeule note, 'an outsider will lack adequate information about the polity for which he is to design a constitution'.[124] Of course, as even they note, in the modern world, it is fairly easy for outsiders as founders to acquire information regarding the polity for which they constitute.[125] Moreover, current external constitution-makers possess and may acquire far more information regarding current country and its conditions than what past-generations could have imagined two hundred years ago.

There are two main problems with the externally imposed constitutionalism debate. First, it holds a romantic view of how constitutions are made arguing implicitly that externally imposed constitutionalism does not correspond with this vision. However, as David Law points out, instead of a romantic notion of constitution-making enacted by 'we the people', we must consciously acknowledge the fact that constitution-making processes regularly involve various authors, negotiations, and – very often – coercion.[126] As I have tried to demonstrate throughout this chapter, even locally made constitutions which were not imposed from the outside carry elements of imposition; be it past generations who impose on the current and future generations, a majority that imposes upon a minority, an elite that imposes upon the rest, or even the judiciary. And each element of imposition can be to various degrees. What is the majority by which the constitution was imposed upon the minority? Was the losing minority homogeneous or simply a collection of different individuals? Were the arrangements incorporated by the elites meant to serve self-interests or wide long-term interests? Was there any popular involvement? At what stage (before, during, or after the process)? These and other questions may be important for understanding the extent of the constitutional imposition.

Secondly, the scholarship on imposed constitutions has thus far focused exclusively on the constitution-making moment (point A); whether there was an actual involvement or consent of domestic actors and peoples. The focus, however,

123 Jed Rubenfeld, *Freedom and Time* (Yale University Press 2001).

124 For a discussion, see Adriaan Lanni and Adrian Vermeule, 'Constitutional Design in The Ancient World' (2012) *Stan. L. Rev.* 907, 934.

125 Ibid 934–5.

126 David Law, 'Is There Such a Thing as an Imposed Constitution?' in this vol.

should be both on point A and on the ability to change the constitution at any given moment (point B). Compare the following two constitutions: the first is a constitution imposed from the outside but is very flexible and allows a change in an ordinary majority through a regular legislative process. The second is a constitution which was adopted domestically through a general acceptance of the people in a national referendum 230 years ago, but includes a very rigid, almost impossible, amendment process.[127] The former, although imposed at the time of the promulgation from the outside, carries a less severe component of imposition than the latter, which even if it was not imposed at all at the time of its adoption for later generation should be considered as imposed.

As both external and internal constitutions carry elements of imposition, instead of focusing exclusively on the source of the imposition, it is more useful to ask ourselves which factors should weigh in when evaluating constitutional imposition. For example, we must consider the extent of the imposition, and not only at the time of the promulgation or adoption of the constitution but in light of the constitutional mechanisms that can hinder or facilitate constitutional change and adaptation. Impositions must be examined over time.

V Conclusion: 'If you accept the Torah, it is good, and if not, there will be your burial place'

The story of the Jewish people receiving the Torah – the first constitution[128] – raises fundamental questions about the theory of imposed constitutionalism. The book of Exodus tells us the following story of Mount Sinai, in which the people waited for three days to receive the constitution, and on the third day the ceremony began in awesome grandeur with 'thunder and lightning and a thick cloud upon the mount'.[129] When Moses brought the people to meet God, 'Mount Sinai was altogether on a smoke, because the LORD descended upon it in fire', and then Moses went up the Mount to receive the Torah.[130]

A deep question behind the story is whether the acceptance of the Torah was coerced upon the people. According to a famous statement in the Talmud Bavli, when God gave Israel the Torah he suspended Mount Sinai over their heads and coerced them into the covenant: 'This teaches that the Holy One, blessed be He, overturned the mountain upon them like an cask, and said to them, 'If you accept the Torah, it is good; if not, this will be your burial place'.[131] The Rabbis rejected

127 Yaniv Roznai, 'Constitutions, Rigid(entrenched)/Flexible' in Rainer Grote et al (eds), *The Max Planck Encyclopedia of Comparative Constitutional Law* (OUP 2018).
128 Cf. Bernard M. Levinson, 'The First Constitution: Rethinking the Origins of Rule of Law and Separation of Powers in Light of Deuteronomy' (2006) 27(4) *Cardozo L Rev* 1853.
129 Exodus 19:7–20.
130 Ibid.
131 Talmud Bavli Shabbat 88a. See Shmuel Yosef Agnon, *Present at Sinai: The Giving of the Law* (Jewish Publication Society, 2002) 114.

this interpretation, according to which the Jews did not have a real choice but to accept the Torah, since a covenant cannot exist without a voluntary acceptance.[132]

Nevertheless, is there ever a full acceptance of constitutions? All constitutions have certain elements of imposition. As Lars Udehn correctly writes:

> No state and no constitution is, or was, the result of an actual social contract and unanimity is impossible in constitutional, as in other, matters. All constitutions are imposed; in most cases by a minority, nowadays more often by a majority. In some countries, the passing of a constitution even requires something more than a simple majority, but unanimity – never.[133]

Imposed constitutionalism is thus a matter of degree not of a kind.[134] This chapter demonstrates various types of what I have termed internally imposed constitutions. With this in mind, it becomes less a matter of which actors initiate, observe, and approve the constitution – external or internal. We need to free ourselves from focusing solely on questions of origin of the imposition and extend our focus to the extent to which constitutional norms are binding upon us, to what extent these correspond with society's values, and to what extent can the people amend and reform the constitution in a self-conscious manner if they so wish.

132 Rabbi Jonathan Sacks, *A Letter in the Scroll: Understanding Our Jewish Identity and Exploring the Legacy of the World's Oldest Religion* (Simon and Schuster 2004) 24.

133 Lars Udehn, *The Limits of Public Choice: A Sociological Critique of the Economic Theory of Politics* (Routledge 2002) 180.

134 See, in a similar vein, Hasebe (n 7).

4 Legal theology in imposed constitutionalism

Antoni Abat i Ninet†

Introduction

> "A constitution is meant to express the will of the people, understood in a majoritarian or super-majoritarian fashion".[1]

The focus of this chapter is the question of legitimacy, and how we can consider legitimate an imposed constitution and the subsequent constitutional principles, practices and values that go hand-in-hand with the legal and political acculturation. Constitutional texts around the world are good examples of transposition and complicity of theological and juridical thoughts. Legal theology implies the application of religious phenomena, theories and concepts to achieve undisputed legal legitimacy. Imposed constitutions as rules imposed for salvation for those "Platonic Philosophes" who have seen the "light", that know the *episteme*, are paramount examples of legal and political theology.

For the purpose of this chapter, imposed constitutions are political and legal norms of a state enacted and enforced without the free and full agreement of the demos. The chapter analyses different scenarios of foreign imposition that are not interchangeable; intervention to promote democracy differs from an intervention to promote constitutionalism. Even then both elements (democracy and constitutionalism) tend to merge under the political system "Liberal Constitutional Democracies" that is used to justify military interventions.

The chapter has two main sections. The first one is devoted to a fictitious example, the failure of Rawls' pretended state (Kazanistan) and how the international military intervention, transition to democracy and foreign imposed constitution fits with theological experiences of "apocalypses, the coming, redemption and expiation". The second section discusses both the imposition of a constitution and constitutionalism. The examples that the drafters of Kazanistan's constitution analysed are "successful" imposed texts such as in Germany and Japan, where both constitutions were made by elites under the humiliating supervision of foreign occupiers, and more concretely, by military conquerors. "Unsuccessful"

† In memory of Tzvetan Todorov

1 Daniel Markovits, 'Democratic Disobedience' (2005) 114 *Yale Law Journal* 1897

examples are those of Iraq, Timor, Somalia and Afghanistan, states or failed states unable to enforce laws and to use legitimate force over their populations. The comparative analysis aims to obtain valid inputs for the imposed constitutional text.

On the theme of imposed constitutionalism, the chapter reflects on the inconsistency of the idealistic discourse that permeates a constitutional text; the inability of an imposed text to be enveloped by principles that reflect the nation's fundamental concepts; and finally, the denaturalisation of the understanding of a constitution as the juridification of the People or Nation. Related to the topic of imposed constitutionalism, the chapter focuses on the systemic inconsistencies that imposed constitutionalism generates, such as the unviability of the idea of an implicit constitutional text (invisible ink of the norm); the impossibility of "original" or "purposive" interpretations of the constitution, the impossibility to accommodate aspirational principles, the denial of the right of self-determination and other dysfunctionalities related to the interpretation of an imposed text.

The collapse of Kazanistan as a biblical episode

Apocalypse

> Then I kept looking because of the sound of the boastful words which the horn was speaking; I kept looking until the beast was slain, and its body was destroyed and given to the burning fire.[2]

In the year 2033, a fierce economic and political crisis is affecting Kazanistan, Rawls's pretended Islamic "Decent Hierarchical People".[3] According to Rawls, the invented state is a country with a political system that does not institute the separation between religion and state, where Islam is the favoured religion and only Muslims can hold upper positions of political authority and influence the government's main decisions and policies, including foreign affairs.[4] Rawls indicates that the rulers of Kazanistan have not sought empire and territory due to an interpretation of the *Jihad*, in a moral sense, and not military.[5] This is known as *al-Jihād al-Akbar* and is mainly based on the interpretation of Sufi authors.[6] The spiritual struggling summarised with the answer that the Prophet Muhammad gave to the question, what is the most meritorious *jihād*? The Prophet replied, "A just word in the presence of a tyrannical ruler".[7]

Rawls continues stating that in Kazanistan, the Muslim rulers have long held the view that all members of society naturally want to be loyal members of the

2 Book of Daniel, 7:11
3 John Rawls, *The Law of Peoples* (Cambridge (MA), Harvard University Press 1999)
4 Ibid 75
5 Ibid 76
6 John Renard, 'Al-Jihād al-Akbar: Notes on a theme in Islamic spirituality' [1988] *The Muslim World* 225
7 Ibid 229

state into which they are born.[8] The state seems to be a non-liberal but non-authoritarian constitutional entity because its basic institutional design does not accommodate liberal constitutional principles such as the rule of law, parliamentarianism, separation of powers or substantial degree of independence of the judiciary. The fictitious Rawlsian state does not have aggressive aims, and recognises that it must gain its legitimate ends through diplomacy and its system of law secured for all the people what have come to be human rights.[9] It also has a sense of tolerance and respect to the minorities found in our utopic scenario that is similar to Islam centuries ago in the Ottoman Empire, or al-Andalus, and the principles exposed by Roy Mottahedeh on his Islamic theory of toleration.[10]

In a non-democratic state such as Kazanistan, the immediate consequence of a fierce economic downturn crack is political instability and contestation to the unelected leaders, followed by the first signs of democracy. The response of the leaders of states like the one imagined by Rawls remains uncertain and impossible to predict in the very first instance. Unlike in other outlaw states were the reaction is extreme violence, or in liberal peoples where the response will be democratic elections and profound economic reforms, instability in decent hierarchical peoples, such as Kazanistan, may provoke a shift of the state's political nature. The dissimilar political outcomes of the events labelled as the Arab Spring seem to evidence this point.[11]

After new massive demonstrations and a consequent repressive governmental response, Rawls' "Liberal peoples" or constitutional democracies start to plot a position against the leaders of Kazanistan. Critical diplomatic negotiations to stop violence failed and summary trials and more repression are the responses of the authoritarian government. For the benefit of the main argument of the book and playing with this uncertainty, suppose that Kazanistan goes through more episodes of explicit violence and repression, and the immediate declaration of the state of emergency. The state is facing an apocalyptic scenario, such as what happened in Libya, Syria, Somalia, Bosnia Herzegovina, Armenia or Rwanda.

To this, the League of Nations in a Rawlsian sense, the United Nations, reacts *a posteriori*, with more economic sanctions and blockages, as if only the regime were going to suffer the goods scarcity. The civil war came suddenly and Kazanistan is divided in cities, towns and streets according to where loyalties lie. The ending of the regime seems to be possible. As Feldman correctly remarks

8 Rawls (n 3) 77

9 Ibid 65

10 Rawls (n 3) 76 and Roy Mottahedeh, 'Towards an Islamic Theory of Toleration' in Tore Lindholm and Kari Vogt (eds), *Islamic Law Reform and Human Rights* (Oslo, Nordic Human Rights Publications 1993). See also Abat i Ninet, A, "The Administration of Justice in al-Andalus and the Principles of Justice in Constitutional Democracies", *Journal of International Law and Islamic Law*, vol. 1/2018

11 Abat i Ninet A and Tushnet, M, *The Arab Spring – An Essay on Revolution and Constitutionalism* (Edward Elgar 2015); Sultany, N, *Law and Revolution: Legitimacy and Constitutionalism after the Arab Spring* (Oxford University Press 2017)

for the case of Iraq, an important predictor of the nation building after a military intervention is the way the old regime ended, either by internal collapse or by overwhelming military force.[12] The way a regime is also a potential risk factor to end up into a failed state; this risk is superior in countries under the great influence of the effects of colonisation on the sense of self.

Kazanistan is facing an apocalyptic scenario. The religious-secular analogy when talking about the apocalypse is related in the books of the exodus, Ezra, Daniel, Enoch and also in Christian mysticism, such as the Revelation of John in the New Testament. In the apocalyptic stance, there is always the hope that God will act in favour of its people in a moment of oppression, as during the period of slavery in Egypt, the exile of Babylon and in the persecution in the Seleucid era. The hope is that the good will prevail over bad, and that the Messiah will come to initiate the millennium and the nonbelievers will be thrown into the lake of fire and sulphur.

Grotius, one of the founders of the Bauhaus, said to a generation of artists at the end of the First World War: "A world has been destroyed; we must seek a radical solution".[13] The apocalyptic experience, misery and despair seem also to be common elements preceding some of the international operations and Grotius' words reflect the reality faced by the people of Sierra Leone, Somalia, Ruanda, Kosovo but also today's Syria.

"The Coming"

> Then I heard a loud voice from the temple saying to the seven angels, "Go, poured out the seven bowls of God's wrath on the earth."[14]

After several weeks of military campaign, in a very Abrahamic sense, the "forces of good" defeated the "forces of evil" and the transition to a constitutional democracy is about to start in Kazanistan. Now, the "saviours" will meet in London, Paris or New York with "the recognised elites" to establish the sets of principles that the post-apocalyptic state must contain in order to expiate the state and its political system. The meeting will establish the conditions of the redemption and the eschatological effects of the intervention. The military operation determines the final events; the *tabula rasa* is followed by a consequent constitutional guidance or imposition, normally behind the backs of the people and in the best case scenario with the complicity of the local elites. The idea is to purge any remnants of the former regime. This conception is installed in the collective psyche of the international and domestic sides of international interventions, and it requires a

12 Noah Feldman, *What we Owe Iraq: War and the Ethics of Nation Building* (Princeton University Press 2006) 4

13 Robert W Jenson, 'Apocalyptic and Messianism in Twentieth Century German Theology' in Wayne Cristaudo and Wendy Baker (eds), *Messianism, Apocalypse and Redemption in 20th Century German Thought* (Australia, ATF Press 2006) 4

14 Book of the Revelation 16:16

military defeat of the former order to materialise the final events, and to avoid any sort of *transactional* justice instead of a *transitional* justice.

U.N. interventions normatively have very ambitious objectives, meaning that transitional administration, peace operations, security, governance, peace enforcement, justice, exit strategies and so forth,[15] at least in the last decades, refer to a greater and vague goal, "nation building". Just a century ago Lawrence remarked: despite the concrete typology of intervention it always implies force, or a threat of force, in case the dictates of the intervening power are disregarded... There can be no intervention without on the one hand, the presence of force, naked or veiled, and on the other hand, the absence of consent on the part of the combatants.[16] This statement is valid today and the forced intervention strengthens the messianic connotations. The change caused by the arrival of a "Messiah" which is responsible for the establishment of a new order will give rise to a utopian world. Force helps not only to purge and defeat the former order; but it also provides gravity to the change.

In our fictitious scenario of Kazanistan, the League of Nations, following the Rawlsian essay, will respond with coercive measures that imply tacit or explicit military intervention and the use of force. Even that, agreed or not, the U.N. Charter limits the use of force to the inherent right of self-defence and humanitarian work, with the exception of the collective coercive action.[17] The vague interpretation of this norm seems to prove, once again, the non-legal character of international norms. Instead, its dependence on politics, social and economic casuistry which was formally delimited beyond the point at which legal argument was supposed to stop in order to remain "legal".[18]

The vagueness also brings out the paradoxical character of the obligation placed upon states to observe human rights. It also calls into question the permeability of the principle of the rule of law of international charters and treaties.

The international community have a broad rational set of criteria to appraise when "intervention" is warranted.[19] However, the answer may also vary depending on the type of "intervention". When military force is used, the arguments of legitimacy are normative, and also non-normative (economic, geopolitical, imperialistic, moral and others), so that the realistic school of thought correctly points out that the *real politik* is what really matters in the international arena, where

15 Simon Chesterman, *You, The People: The United Nations, Transitional Administration, and State-Building* (Oxford Scholarship Online 2004) 237–238

16 T.J. Lawrence, *The Principles of International Law* (London, 7th ed, Macmillan & Co. 1927) 120

17 See Charter of United Nations, Chapter VII and article 51. It is questionable within the international community whether humanitarian intervention is allowed; if at all, it is certainly not allowed by the Charter of United Nations but as a development of customary international law

18 Martti Koskenniemi, *From Apology to Utopia, The Structure of International Legal Argument* (Cambridge University Press 2005)

19 See e.g. U.N. Secretary-General, *A More Secure World: Our Shared Responsibility,* 207, U.N. Doc A/59/565, (Dec. 2, 2004)

neither morals nor law have a place. Every decision somehow is made based on national interests.[20]

In this sense, laws on war are related to imposed constitutionalism when the latter is a consequence of a military intervention. The legal corpus and principles on Ius ad, in and post bellum, may affect not only the way that a constitution is imposed, but also some future constitutional matters.

Authorisation and sovereignty of the state are relevant when talking about intervention in constitutional democracies; for instance, helping a democratic government to respond to a coup d'état ("upon request" of the state), but as Walzer states, military operations that consist of defending people against their own state, necessarily undermine political sovereignty and integrity, they meet a higher burden of justification.[21] A concern that Rawls also expresses when talking about occupation is "the enemy's people are not to be held as slaves or serfs surrender, or denied in due time full liberties".[22] Yet, when talking about non-democratic regimes, the burden of justification seems to be lower. In any case, when there is no domestic authorisation, the sacred concept of state sovereignty is violated in the name of other sacred notions.

International interventions are not easy tasks and the models used to justify interventions are not always compatible. Feldman evidences this fact when explaining how his colleagues consulted a sort of international intervention to guide the Iraqi constitutional draft in 2003. His colleagues were reading books on the American occupation and reconstruction of Germany and Japan, despite the fact that each occupational situation seems to have its owns challenges and own casuistry.[23] Another question that transcends is the reason that justifies the occupation;[24] as the response to a military attack and the aftermath of a world war (Japan and Germany), to stop an ethnical cleansing or genocide (Kosovo), preventive self-protection (cause alleged in the Iraqi invasion).

The justification of the military intervention is also relevant in the post-war conduct that must be consistent with the justificatory end of the operation. As Bass stated, the *jus post bellum* is related with *jus ad bellum*, in that declared ends that justify a war, whether to stop a genocide or prevent aggression– impose obligations on belligerent powers to try, even after the conclusion of the war, to bring the desired outcome.[25]

20 Henry Shue and David Rodin (eds), *Preemption: Military Action and Moral Justification* (Oxford University Press 2007)

21 Seth Lazar, 'War' [2016] The Stanford Encyclopedia of Philosophy https://plato.stanford.edu/entries/war/ accessed 19 June 2017. See also Walzer, M, *Just and Unjust Wars: A Moral Argument with Historical Illustrations*, (Basic Book 1997) and Walzer, M, "Responsibility and Proportionality in State and Non-state Wars", *Parameters*, 2009, pp. 40–52

22 Rawls (n 3) 98

23 Feldman, *What We Owe Iraq: War and the Ethics of Nation Building* (n 12) 1

24 Ibid 2

25 Gary J Bass, 'Jus Post Bellum' [2004] *Philosophy and Public Affairs* 385, 386

After the coming of the international forces, we move to a different component of just war theory, the *jus post bellum* or what happens after war. This might be true in theory, but after the interventions in Kosovo, Iraq[26] and the Russian invasion of Crimea in 2014, the "saviours" have normatively transgressed the basic requirements established internationally after World War II. The lack of objective elements and normative consensus to support the interventions was evident in these military interventions, where the political justification was stronger than the normative argumentation. Some of the leading forces in international military operations killed the international norm that ruled these interventions and conferred legitimacy to these ultimate actions.

Therefore, and due to the link between the different elements of the theory of just war, if *jus ad bellum* is transgressed, *jus post bellum* is distorted, then the political and economic outcomes are the superior motivation of the intervention. At the same time, these examples have shown the inefficacy and incapability of these potencies to put into place constitutional democracies, rule of law and human rights. In other words, the normative transgression has brought up a fake messiah, instead of a saviour, that comes with constitutional democracies, human rights, rule of law and other related principles.[27]

Despite the uncertain legitimacy of some international military interventions, Chesterman remarks that the primary barrier to establishing transitional administration-type operations in areas such as Somalia, Western Sahara, and the Democratic Republic of the Congo has less to do with the difficulty of such operations than with the absence of political will to commit resources to undertake them.[28]

In our fictitious case-scenario, the process of intervention will also aim at forming a constitutional democratisation process. The people of Kazanistan, whether they believe in the secular "Messiah" or not, are going to accept the "coming" and its consequences despite the authenticity and legitimacy of the interveners. As what occurred with the Libyan Political Agreement signed on 17 December 2015, the implementation of the agreement of Kazanistan will also seek to provide the tools needed to address potential challenges. Among these challenges are: fighting terrorism, reforming and building state institutions,

26 See the Iraq Inquiry or "Chicot report" http://www.iraqinquiry.org.uk/media/247921/the-report-of-the-iraq-inquiry_executive-summary.pdf accessed 20 June 2017

27 A question underlies the entire discussion is whether a forcible intervention of a foreign state can actually bring about democracy in general – and a stable democracy in particular – especially where a social and cultural basis for democracy was lacking in the first place. See e.g. Nanda, Ved P. Agora: U.S. Forces in Panama: Defenders, Aggressors or Human Rights Activists? (The Validity of United States Intervention in Panama Under International Law), 84 *Am. J. Intl Law* 494 (1990); Varayudej, S, *The Right to Democracy in International Law: Its Implications for Asia*, 12 Ann. Surv. Int'l & Comp. L. 1 (2006)

28 Chesterman (n 15) 15. On the move from the legality to legitimacy of humanitarian intervention see Roberts, A, Legality vs. Legitimacy: Can Uses of Force Be Illegal but Justified? In: Alston, Philip and MacDonald, Euan, (eds.) *Human Rights, Intervention, and the Use of Force* (Oxford University Press, 2008)

stimulating economic growth, confronting the phenomenon of illegal migration and consolidating the human rights throughout the country.[29] A similar agreement is expected in Kazanistan and another consequence of the "coming" will be imposed constitutionalism as happened previously in other occupied countries, such as the former Yugoslavia, East Timor, Afghanistan or Iraq.[30]

The degree of involvement of the domestic actors in this process is a key determinant for the success in the constitutional-democratic-human rights evangelical mission. Even though an imposed constitution can be a noble endeavour, an aspirational or programmatic constitution reflecting the aspirations of others is not the solution to a land destroyed economically, morally and in terms of identity.

Redemption through constitutional imposition

> Say therefore to the Israelites, "I am the Lord, and I will free you from the burdens of the Egyptians and deliver you from slave"/ry to them. I will redeem you with an outstretched arm and with mighty acts of judgment. I will take you as my people, and I will be your God. You shall know that I am the Lord your God, who has freed you from the burdens of the Egyptians. I will bring you into the land that I swore to give to Abraham, Isaac, and Jacob; I will give it to you for a possession. I am the Lord".[31]

The concept of redemption has different meanings, but the most common is related to free someone or a group of persons of suffering; as the Christian dogma states, Jesus died on the cross to save humanity. In theology, the question is if redemption is the entrance of the spirit (*Geist*) into human life. An analogical question that can arise before and after the military intervention in a state is if Kazanistan can be redeemed after the military intervention throughout a constitutional imposition.

As a part of the path to redemption and salvation, the new imposed constitution of Kazanistan (ideally) is going to be drafted in a way that gives a substantial role to local participation, but it will also experience large intervention and pressure imposed from outside to produce constitutional outcomes preferred by international actors to acquire a "reasonably just" constitutional regime.[32] Experience shows that according to the contemporary sense of imposed constitutions, constitutional drafting is understood by all participants as a negotiation among political elites and occupying power and international organisations capable of exerting pressure.[33] The participation of domestic elites in the drafting of the text depends on diverse external factors. Domestic intellectuals in exile who

29 See Libyan Political Agreement, 17 December 2015 https://www.un.org/press/en/2015/sc12185.doc.htm accessed 20 June 2017

30 Noah Feldman, 'imposed constitutionalism' [2004–2005] *Connecticut Law Review* 857

31 Exodus 6:1–8

32 Ibid

33 Ibid 881

contested the authoritarian government are welcomed back by the constitutional imposers despite the risk of denaturalisation that a long period of exile may cause.

Yet, the struggle of constitutionalism in the Islamic states such as Kazanistan is intimately related to the multifaceted nature of Islam and the manifold political and legal positions taken by the different Islamic movements. In addition, the requirements of democracy, human rights, and liberal constitutionalism can never obviate the colonialism that denied human rights to human beings.[34] As Sartre states, in the colonies the native was considered subhuman – the Declaration of Human Rights did not apply to him; he was forsaken, without protection.[35] What matters is the appearance or perception that the constituent power is domestic, despite the fact that the constituent moment is a consequence of a foreign intervention and international actors are supervising not only the constitution, but the constitutional process and the nation "building".

The process of foreign constitutional imposition is also accompanied with a strong degree of acculturation. The implementation of some of the constitutional principles can be disrespectful with some of the inner trends of constitutional identity. In discussions on nation-building, it is often expressed as the need to "build up" and "modernise" state institutions. Constitutions and constitutionalism have often been used to inoculate non-Western countries and ex-colonies with this "modernity". In Islamic countries, as the one outlined by Rawls, this process has proven far from unproblematic, in part due to the troubled relations between constitutionalism and religion. The dose of "modernism" comes inoculated through the new coloniser's rationality. As Adorno and Horkheimer pose, the self-destruction of Western reason is grounded in historical and fateful dialectic between the domination of external nature and society. They trace enlightenment, which split these spheres apart, turning back into its mythical roots. Enlightenment and myth, therefore, are not irreconcilable opposites, but dialectically mediated qualities of both real and intellectual life.[36]

Constitutions and constitutionalism are tools to implement legal and political rationality. Constitutions are the reason; and legal reasoning comes from the top of the legal-political pyramid. Weber analysed how formal and substantive rationality affects both theocratic and secular law, with the particular feature that distinguishes modern secular law being formal and logical rationality.[37] Weber's work, although almost a century old, still seems to be valid today when talking about the Islamic countries, where theocratic and secular law coexist. Constitutions have their own empire; and they do not concede superior rule, only coexistence.

34 On Islamic Constitutionalism, see Brown, N, *Constitutions in a Non-Constitutional World, Arab Basic Laws and the Prospects for Accountable Government,* (SUNY Press 2002)

35 Jean Paul Sartre, 'Introduction' in Albert Memmi, *the Colonizer and the Colonized* (Boston, Beacon Press 1965) 24

36 Max Horkheimer and Theodor Adorno, *Dialektik der Aufklärung: Philosophische Fragmente* (Frankfurt am Main, S. Fischer Verlag 1969)

37 Max Weber, *Economy and Society* (University of California Press 1978) 809

Some basic problems can arise when this highest legal norm is imposed by others and distinct cultures.

In Kazanistan, a state with a Muslim majority, many citizens will often want Islam to have some official role in state governance, beyond mere symbolism. Such a role for Islam may potentially, though not necessarily, trench upon full equality in the legal order that may emerge.[38] The drafters of the new constitution will face the debate on how to accommodate Islamic law in the constitution. It is not habitual that *Shari'a* will replace the constitution, but the constitution integrates some standards drawn from Islamic law and should indeed refer directly to Islamic law as a source of law with application to either legislation, judicial review or both.[39] However, where *Shari'a* plays both a substantive and an institutional role in its constitutionalism, it thus raises the possibility that some of its applications in public law will be illiberal. Are international actors willing to establish an illiberal constitutional system after a military intervention?

The constitutional theology and constitutional imposition is also an imposed narrative. Analysing the processes of "democratisation" and transformation into liberal regimes, we can observe how deep the liberal intervention of the foreign victor potencies was and the nature of this political involvement. As with the coming of the Messiah, the forces of good are going to redeem the country of all its sins. The "salvation" is associated with the fulfilment of the duties by the vanquished, which are basically related with the restoration and reparation of the damages. Restraint should be the rule of the restoration performed by the victors. As Bass states, only in cases of genocidal states, which cannot be said to have any legitimacy; foreigners have a duty to reconstruct the genocidal state.[40]

Imposing a constitution, a narrative, a reason and an identity

The imposition of a constitutional text also entails the imposition of a concrete narrative of winners and losers, faithful and unfaithful, or in a very Schmittean sense, friends and enemies in a political sense. A constitution shapes the character of society and its aspirations, lays the foundation for social values, and set goals, obligations and trends.[41] A constitution expresses national agreement and seeks to establish the nation's fundamental values, covenants and social viewpoints.[42] How can an imposed text fulfil these essences? The imposition of a constitutional text is not aseptic but it always implies and causes political, legal, cultural and sociological reasons and effects.

For the purpose of this work, two German terms, "*Grundnorm*", used as a synonym of constitution or basic norm, and "*Verrechtlichung*" (juridification),

38 Feldman 'imposed constitutionalism' (n 30) 860
39 Ibid 861
40 Bass (n 25) 412
41 Aharon Barak, *Purposive Interpretation in Law* (Princeton University Press 2015) 370
42 Ibid 372

reflect some of the implications of a constitutional imposition and the denaturalisation of the understanding of what is a constitution. The first term "*Grund*" can be translated into English as "ground", "cause", "foundation" or "reason". Each of them represents a valid claim of the meanings of a constitution and the power that entails. In our case study, the implications are an imposed "foundation" and imposed "reason" to another people or community. A constitution is simply a set of political norms organising the politics of a community; imposition is not that traumatic. The second German term, "*Verrechtlichung*", in the situation of constitutional imposition, implies that the new higher legal norm juridifies foreign political decisions, a new political unit by a new people.

The *Bünderszentrale fur Politiche Bildung*, a federal public authority providing citizenship education and information on political issues in Germany, defines the term in two ways: "1: expressing the fact that in modern countries, the area of action in all spheres of life is increasingly affected by laws, ordinances, decrees, norms and 2: But it also results from the fact that increasingly political decisions are shifting to the legal level".[43] As Ackerman states for the constitution (in the US) as the juridification of the identity of a people and the starting point of their consideration as a people. Can an external imposed juridification through the constitution be effective? Is the constitution really so transcendent? The answer depends on the very particular casuistry. In this sense, constitutions in Germany and Japan did not reflect the starting point of a new people, but a new political era, a new political identity for the pre-existent communities. In other case scenarios, when the constitution, as a founding norm that grounds the independence of a new community, the situation is different. In *post bellum* scenarios, the imposed text will aim to represent this new starting point erasing any authoritarian constitutional influence, a sort of tabula rasa in the Aristotelian sense where the tablet is now scribed by the imposers.[44]

The constitutional imposition also generates some *systemic inconsistencies or limitations*, such as the limits of an "originalist" and "purposive" interpretations of the constitution; the impossibility to accommodate founding aspirational principles and other dysfunctionalities related to the interpretation of an imposed text (such as the principle of proportionality and the need of balance). However, imposed constitutionalism corresponds with an objective purposive interpretation which refers to more general principles that the Constitution should fulfil in a democracy.

On the account of the purpose of a norm, Barak distinguishes between subjective and objective purpose.[45] The subjective purpose is the authorial content.

43 The *Bunderszentrale fur Politiche Bildung* : 1-soll zum Ausdruck bringen, dass in modernen Staaten der Handlungsraum in allen Lebensbereichen zunehmend durch Gesetze, Verordnungen, Erlasse, Normierungen; 2-Resultiert aber auch daher, dass zunehmend politische Entscheidungen auf die rechtliche Ebene verlager

44 Aristotle, *De Anima (on the Soul)* (Penguin Classics 1987)

45 Barak, *Purposive Interpretation in Law* (n 41) 88. See also, Aharon Barak, *Proportionality, Constitutional Rights and Their Limitations* (Cambridge University Press 2012) 49

The interpreter of a norm seeks the meaning that best realises the intent of the author. The objective constitutes the values, goals, interests, policies, aims and function that the text should actualise in democracy.[46] A constitution is the product of the history of a people and a nation. We can derive its subjective purpose from the history of the procedures by which the constitution was founded and the intent of the authors.[47]The foundations of purpose and the purposive interpretation of the text is conditioned by the imposition and its effects *in aeternum*. Who is capable of knowing the intention and purpose of the imposers? The temporary solution to safeguard a purposive and original interpretation is to place magistrates in the constitutional/supreme court who know the imposer's logic. As happens in Bosnia and Herzegovina where the Constitutional Court has nine judges, four members shall be selected by the House of Representatives of the Federation, and two members by the Assembly of the Republika Srpska. The remaining three members shall be selected by the President of the European Court of Human Rights after consultation with the Presidency.[48]

The limitations to an originalist interpretation are also evident. How can a Magistrate, after some generations, establish the meaning of the (imposed) constitution if the text is the result of a different legal and political culture? Which are the documents that the judge would need to scrutinise to apply correctly the constitution? What documents are going to check Kazanistan's chief justice homologue to Chief Justice William Howard Taft?[49] What evidence should be examined to develop a background understanding of the topic under dispute? If the constitutional imposers come from different nationalities and dissimilar legal genealogies and traditions, the task is simply impossible.

A third concept that might dysfunction in imposed scenarios is the traditional theory of the *pouvoir constituant originaire*. The constituent power is the faculty to draft a constitutional text. A power that classically was unlimited, despite that some constitutions were attached to meta-constitutional principles, a sort of constitutional identity that established legal boundaries to the drafting. Boundaries and principles that do not apply in imposed constitutions.

Since the American and French revolutions, to talk about constituent power was to talk about (representative) democracy.[50] The mysteries and mysticism that involve the constituent power are annulled with the act of imposition. Imposition implies necessarily theoretical and practical effects on the binding character of the constitution (*the constitution is binding because it is the incarnation of the people*)

46 Barak, *Purposive Interpretation in Law* (n 41) 90

47 Ibid 377

48 Article VI. I of the Constitution of Bosnia and Herzegovina of 1995. On the Judges in the Court of Bosnia see Schwartz, A, "*International Judges on Constitutional Courts: Cautionary Evidence from Post-Conflict Bosnia*", Law & Social Inquiry (22 November 2017)

49 Antonin Scalia, 'Originalism: The Lesser Evil' (1988–1989) 57 *University of Cincinnati Law Review* 849

50 Antonio Negri, *Insurgencies: Constituent Power and the Modern State* (Maurizia Boscagli tr, University of Minnesota Press 1999) 1

and its authority, (the authority is rooted in the authorship of the creator of the constitution).[51]

The idea of the people as constituent power, as the agents and creators of the constitutional Order, is familiar in American constitutionalism. "We the people" is a strong fiction that has persisted since the draft of the American revolutionary constitution in the unconscious of natural and naturalised US citizens. This amazing technique of legislative building has been the essence and core of the American condition and evidences some of the main features of US revolutionary constitution making. The statement "we the people" is the best consolidation of the democratic sovereignty fiction, one that imposed constitutionalism extinguishes. We the people *of where*? In order to form a more perfect Union, establish justice, insure domestic tranquillity, provide for common defence, promote the general welfare and secure the blessings of liberty to *you* and *your* "Prosperity", do ordain and establish the constitution for Kazanistan.[52]

The drafters of the first modern constitution decided to affirm "we the people" because they knew the strong meaning of this statement. It included not only the entire present population, but also future generations. Its immense inclusive strength has effective consequences in terms of national identity and popular involvement. The fiction includes the participation of domestic actors in the constitutional drafting. Using Ackerman's terminology, can the constitutional canon formation be imposed? Being the official canon, the body of texts that conventional legal theory emphasises as central.[53] Can the nation centred self-understanding of a concrete people be imposed? Can this self-understanding be built up in opposition to the constitution?

French revolutionaries are also familiar with the concept of constituent power and its national nature. The "constituent power" (*pouvoir constituant)* enthrones the "Nation" in its sovereign place. Sieyès synthesises in a sentence the contradiction of imposed constitutionalism, when he states: "If we lack a constitution, then a constitution must be made, and the Nation alone has the right to do so".[54] Constitutional laws are positive laws emanating from the will of the Nation, regulating the organisation and functions of the legislative body.[55] Following this unique and exclusive role of the Nation in the constituent process, Carré de Malberg affirms that the Nation alone, unified and personified in the state, is the

51 Ulrich K Preuss, 'The Exercise of Constituent Power in Central and Eastern Europe' in Martin Loughlin and Neil Walker (eds), *The Paradox of Constitutionalism, Constituent Power and Constitutional Form* (Oxford University Press, 2007) 211

52 Regarding the question "we the people of where" see the discussion on the need to provide a new conceptualisation of constituent power that can encompass external and international involvement in constitution-making. See e.g. Agne, H, 'Democratic Founding: We The People and the Others' 10(3) *ICON* 836 (2012)

53 Bruce Ackerman, *We the People Vol. 3: The Civil Rights Revolution* (Harvard University Press 2014) 32

54 Emmanuel Sieyès, *Qu'est-ce que le Tiers état?* (Paris, Ed. du Boucher 2002)

55 Ibid

subject of the public authority, and the constitution is the channel through which this authority is communicated in its exercise with the organs of the state.[56] Only the state, as the personification of the national community has an own will, a will that results from the constitutional organisation of the community.[57] Therefore, in national terms, the constitutional imposition also has (national/community) identity implications. The Nation in imposed scenarios is not the one drafting the text, is not the one self-determined. The two kinds of identity in relation to selfhood distinguished by Ricouer are not respected; *Ipséité, Idem* identity is the identity of something that is always the same and *Mêmeté, ipse* identity is sameness across and through change.[58]

On the other hand, imposed constitutionalism would fit perfectly with a different understanding of the constituent power, what Walker defines as a post-constituent constitutionalism or non-constituent constitutionalism.[59] This new constitutionalism tries to remain open to the myriad ways in which different constitutional forms – static and dynamic, pedigree identifying and system realising 0150 may interact over time to tap into the fuller potential of the shifting title of constituent power.[60]

Imposed rule of recognition: which group grounds the constitution? In addition, which group is going to recognise the imposed constitution as a valid norm? Hart told us that law is a kind of norm ultimately grounded in official practice.[61] The author considered a community that does not have a legal system and then invites the reader to ponder the various social problems that would arise in that group, and how the introduction of certain rules would resolve these difficulties.[62] Legal rights, duties, liberties, powers, liabilities, immunities and disabilities that exist in each legal system are just those putative rights, duties, etc. that are validated by what Hart called the rule of recognition: the rule for identifying law that is accepted as the ultimate rule by officials in the legal system, particularly judges.[63]

56 Raymond Carré de Malberg, *Contribution à la Théorie Générale de l'État, spécialement d'après les données fournies par le Droit Constitutionel Français* (Recueil Sirey 1923) 484
57 Ibid 500
58 Paul Ricoeur, *Oneself as Another* (Kathleen Blamey tr, University of Chicago Press 1992)
59 Neil Walker, 'Post-Constituent Constitutionalism? The Case of the European Union', in Loughlin Martin and Walker Neil (eds), *The Paradox of Constitutionalism, Constituent Power and Constitutional Form* (Oxford University Press 2007) 248
60 Ibid 264
61 H. L. A. Hart, *The Concept of Law* (Oxford, Clarendon press 1986) as quoted in M. D. Adler, 'Popular Constitutionalism and the Rule of Recognition: Whose Practices Ground US Law?' (2006) 100 *Northwestern University Law Review* 719
62 S.J. Shapiro, 'What Is the Rule of Recognition (and Does It Exist)?' (2008) 184 Yale Law School: Public Law & Legal Theory Research Paper Series https://www.researchgate.net/profile/Scott_Shapiro2/publication/228177339_9_What_Is_the_Rule_of_Recognition_And_Does_It_Exist/links/553f62970cf23e796bfb39d5.pdf accessed 19 June 2017
63 Adler, 'Popular Constitutionalism and the Rule of Recognition: Whose Practices Ground US Law?' (n 61), 722

In Hart's account, citizens' beliefs about the role of voting and other forms of popular political expression in constitutional decision making are necessarily legally irrelevant, in the absence of some validation of those beliefs by officials.[64] Citizens have no legal role in constitutional decision making unless officials come to believe that they do or at least come to accept other rules from which a citizen role is derivable.[65]

Is it possible to legitimatise an imposed constitution throughout the rule of recognition? The answer, following Hart's theory, depends on whether the elites believe in the text, something that MacArthur understood in Japan. In the case that we consider that the rule of recognition should include the demos as "recognizer" and not only the elites, the constitution, also in imposed scenarios, will need to recognise the right of self-determination in a broader sense, and include democratic means to at least legitimise the text.

The locution "the people" enhances a constitutional text and not the opposite. No constitution determines who "the people" are, but the opposite, a people defines and creates a constitution. This statement only appears once the act of national self-definition has been invoked in the constitutional text. This strengthens the concept of "the people" as something unitary, as a single entity without divisions, in which the institutions should not be assigned to groups or sectors of the whole, but individuals acting on behalf of the ideal "people".

The denial of the right of self-determination is also another major systemic limitation that imposed constitutionalism implies. Not surprisingly, the goal of constitutionalism is to facilitate self-determination fully and in the most inclusive sense.[66] Self-determination is essential to the development of constitutionalism including fundamental rights, principles, institutions and authority to govern.[67] And that constitutionalism, subject to certain initial conditions, has a long-term tendency to serve the interests of liberty and equality.[68]

Self-determination is a mother-right, or in Feldman's words a "right of rights", it enables the recognition, accommodation and later enforcement of constitutional rights. It is only respecting self-determination that imposed constitutionalism seems to be justified. Whether imposition and self-determination are compatible is contestable. Noah Feldman and Richard Albert's definition of heteronomous scale and heteronomous constitutions open this possibility.[69] I am more sceptical because it is hard to conceive self-determination, when a foreign power designs your constitution and institutional framework, or as Sujit Choudry expresses, when the constitution is presented as a *fait accompli* and fundamental

64 Ibid

65 Ibid 725

66 Feldman, 'imposed constitutionalism' (n 30) 881

67 Ibid. On the denial of self determination contributing to the denial of human rights, see, Wall, I.R., *Human Rights and Constituent Power without Model or Warranty* (Routledge 2012)

68 Ibid 889

69 Ibid and Richard Albert, 'Constitutions imposed with consent?', Chapter 6 in this volume

questions of constitutional choice safely remaining in foreign hands.[70] However, if the imposed constitutionalism came in response to a previous repressive/occupation/dictatorial regime, this could actually mean the fulfilment – not denial – of self-determination, in a deeper sense.

Despite the differences that Feldman remarks between ancient and contemporary constitutional imposition, there are some elements in common, a sort of "constituent pack". This legal and political set includes mandatory ratification of international treaties, international control and presence (military, economic and political), constitutional accommodation of eternal clauses (as in Japan and Germany), a new version of the rule of law fused with democracy, and human rights and federalism that deserves a special mention.

When the constitution is imposed onto a state composed by multiple territorial sub-state units with competing nation-building projects that pull in opposite directions, federalism has been always the proposed "solution". Federalism can be a long-term interest solution for some cases but for others it can turn into a "problem" that can vitiate completely a constitutional project. In this sense, and for different reasons, federalism has not worked for the Kurdish minority in Iraq, as it did not work for Kosovo, Ethiopia or Somalia even though neighbouring countries have been pushing their proxies to accept clan-federalism. For these cases, a more durable and stable solution for the state might be to accept the right of self-determination of the sub-state entities and the establishment of a constitutional pact as a clarity bill (following the Canadian example) that the parties will respect.

Conclusion

As Fitzpatrick remarks: "With occidental political formation, the paradigm of law is the law of the sovereign nation state. Thence, law is a dependent creation of this particular new idol, this theological phantasm".[71] The imposition of a constitution appears to be an instrument of this new idol that guides societies towards democracy, human rights, constitutionalism and the rule of law. The imposed rule of law is guiding us to the secular-political Arcadia. The imposition is justified by the imposer for the sake, benefit and "civilization" of the imposed. Answering the question that Feldman poses: "what, if anything, is wrong with imposed constitutionalism, postmodern style"?[72] Devastating Napoleonic occupation of the Iberian Peninsula also modernised the state, ended the Ancient Regime and introduced the values of the French enlightenment. A different question is whether the modern sense of imposed constitutionalism is a legitimate way to inflict democratic and liberal constitutionalism. At least this seems to be

70 Sujit Choudry, 'Old Imperial Dilemmas and the New Nation-Building: Constitutive Constitutional Politics in Multinational Polities' [2004–2005] *Connecticut Law Review* 934

71 Peter Fitzpatrick, 'Legal Theology: Law, Modernity and the Sacred' (2009) 32 *Seattle University Law Review* 341

72 Feldman 'imposed constitutionalism' (n 30) 879

a paradox but it is not so difficult to conceive. Transitions to democracy are normally undemocratic paths to democracy, therefore, the claim would be that imposed constitutions can be unconstitutional paths to constitutionalism. Thus, the potential of this path to constitutionalism depends on the degree of imposition, the ex-ante participation of domestic elites and the ex-post democratic validation of the constitution.

When a constitution is imposed abruptly, limiting the right of self-determination and excluding without participation of locals in the decision making power, the imposition could be more related to colonialisation and neo-colonialism than to liberalism, democracy and constitutionalism. In that case, the imposition of liberal constitutional values resembles Francisco de Vitoria's justification of the colonial subordination derived for the *ius gentium* and the evangelisation of unbelievers by Christian and civilised nations.[73] Using Sartre's words on colonisation, to impose a constitution denying the right of self-determination contributes to the denial of human rights to human beings who have been by violence, and keeps them by force in a state of misery and ignorance.[74]

This piece, that proposes a theological analysis of a political/constitutional phenomenon, ends with a moral. Each process of constitutional imposition needs to be contextualised and individualised to consider its adequacy and legitimacy. However, giving economic possibilities and prosperity to domestic elites and private enterprises (an Iraqi Volkswagen or a Bosnian Bayern) instead of exploding natural resources and giving economic privileges to foreign victors will be determinant to build up a liberal constitutional democracy; a scenario that prioritises Aristotle's zoon ekonomikon over zoon politikon.[75]

Bibliography

Abat i Ninet A, "The Administration of Justice in al-Andalus and the Principles of Justice in Constitutional Democracies", Journal of International Law and Islamic Law, vol. 1/2018

Abat i Ninet A and Tushnet M, *The Arab Spring – An Essay on Revolution and Constitutionalism* (Edward Elgar 2015)

Ackerman B, *We the People Vol. 3: The Civil Rights Revolution* (Harvard University Press 2014)

Adler M D, 'Popular Constitutionalism and the Rule of Recognition: Whose Practices Ground US Law?' (2006) 100 Northwestern University Law review

Agne H, "*Democratic Founding: We The People and the Others*" 10(3) ICON 836 (2012)

Albert R, 'Constitutions imposed with consent?', Chapter 5 in this volume

73 Francisco de Vitoria, 'On the Law of War' in Anthony Pagden and Jeremy Lawrance (eds) *Political Writings* (Cambridge University Press 1991)

74 Sartre (n 35) 24

75 Jan Klabbers, 'Hannah Arendt and the Languages of Global Governance' in Marco Goldoni and Christopher Mc Corkindale (eds), *Hannah Arendt and the Law* (Oxford, Hart Publishing 2012) 247

Aristotle, *De Anima (on the Soul)* (Penguin Classics 1987)
Article VI. I of the Constitution of Bosnia and Herzegovina of 1995
Baker W (eds), *Messianism, Apocalypse and Redemption in 20th Century German Thought* (Australia, ATF Press 2006)
Barak A, *Proportionality, Constitutional Rights and Their Limitations* (Cambridge University Press 2012)
Barak A, *Purposive Interpretation in Law* (Princeton University Press 2015)
Bass G J, 'Jus Post Bellum' [2004] Philosophy and Public Affairs 385
Brown N, *Constitutions in a Non-Constitutional World, Arab Basic Laws and the Prospects for Accountable Government*, (SUNY Press 2002)
Carré de Malberg R, *Contribution à la Théorie Générale de l'État, spécialement d'après les données fournies par le Droit Constitutionel Français* (Recueil Sirey 1923)
Chesterman S, *You, The People: The United Nations, Transitional Administration, and State-Building* (Oxford Scholarship Online 2004)
'Chicot report' http://www.iraqinquiry.org.uk/media/247921/the-report-of-the-iraq-inquiry_executive-summary.pdf accessed 23 June 2017
Choudry S, 'Old Imperial Dilemmas and the New Nation-Building: Constitutive Constitutional Politics in Multinational Polities' [2004–2005] Connecticut Law Review 934
De Vitoria F, 'On the Law of War' in Anthony Pagden and Jeremy Lawrance (eds) Political Writings (Cambridge University Press 1991)
'Description of Dialectic of Enlightenment' (Stanford University Press) http://www.sup.org/books/title/?id=1103 accessed 23 June 2017
Feldman N, 'imposed constitutionalism' [2004–2005] Connecticut Law Review 857
Feldman N, *What We Owe Iraq: War and the Ethics of Nation Building* (Princeton University Press 2006)
Fitzpatrick P, 'Legal Theology: Law, Modernity and the Sacred' (2009) 32 Seattle University Law Review
Hart H L A, *The Concept of Law* (Oxford, Clarendon Press 1986)
Horkheimer M and Adorno T, 'Dialektik der Aufklärung: Philosophische Fragmente' (Frankfurt am Main, S. Fischer Verlag 1969)
Jenson RW, 'Apocalyptic and Messianism in Twentieth-Century German Theology' in Wayne Cristaudo and Wendy Baker (eds), *Messianism, Apocalypse and Redemption in 20th Century German Thought* (Australia, ATF Press 2006)
Klabbers J, 'Hannah Arendt and the Languages of Global Governance' in Marco Goldoni and Christopher McCorkindale (eds), *Hannah Arendt and the Law* (Oxford, Hart Publishing 2012)
Koskenniemi M, *From Apology to Utopia, The Structure of International Legal Argument* (Cambridge University Press 2005)
Lawrence T J, *The Principles of International Law* (London, 7th ed, Macmillan & Co. 1927)
Lazar S, 'War' [2016] The Stanford Encyclopedia of Philosophy https://plato.stanford.edu/entries/war/ accessed 19 June 2017
'Libyan Political Agreement of 17 December 2015' (United Nations 2015) https://www.un.org/press/en/2015/sc12185.doc.htm accessed 20 June 2017
Markovits D, 'Democratic Disobedience' (2005) 114 Yale Law Journal 1897
Mottahedeh R, 'Towards an Islamic Theory of Toleration' in Tore Lindholm and Kari Vogt (eds), *Islamic Law Reform and Human Rights* (Oslo, Nordic Human Rights Publications 1993)

Nanda, Ved P, Agora: U.S. Forces in Panama: Defenders, Aggressors or Human Rights Activists? (The Validity of United States Intervention in Panama Under International Law), 84 AM. J. INT'L L. 494 (1990)

Negri A, *Insurgencies: Constituent Power and the Modern State* (Maurizia Boscagli tr, University of Minnesota Press 1999)

Preuss U K, 'The Exercise of Constituent Power in Central and Eastern Europe' in Martin Loughlin and Neil Walker (eds), *The Paradox of Constitutionalism, Constituent Power and Constitutional Form* (Oxford University Press, 2007

Rawls J, *The Law of Peoples* (Cambridge (MA), Harvard University Press 1999)

Renard J, 'Al-Jihād al-Akbar: Notes on a theme in Islamic spirituality' [1988] The Muslim World

Ricoeur P, *Oneself as Another* (Kathleen Blamey tr, University of Chicago Press 1992)

Roberts A, Legality vs. Legitimacy: Can Uses of Force Be Illegal but Justified? In: Alston, Philip and MacDonald, Euan, (eds.) Human Rights, Intervention, and the Use of Force (Oxford University Press, 2008)

Sartre J P, 'introduction' in Albert Memmi, *The Colonizer and the Colonized* (Boston, Beacon Press 1965)

Scalia A, 'Originalism: The Lesser Evil' (1988–1989) 57 University of Cincinnati Law Review

Schwartz A, "*International Judges on Constitutional Courts: Cautionary Evidence from Post-Conflict Bosnia*", Law & Social Inquiry (22 November 2017)

Shapiro S J, 'What Is the Rule of Recognition (and Does It Exist)?' (2008) 184 Yale Law School: Public Law & Legal Theory Research paper Series https://www.researchgate.net/profile/Scott_Shapiro2/publication/228177339_9_What_Is_the_Rule_of_Recognition_And_Does_It_Exist/links/553f62970cf23e796bfb39d5.pdf accessed 19 June 2017

Shue H and Rodin D (eds), *Preemption: Military Action and Moral Justification* (Oxford University Press 2007)

Sieyès E, *Qu'est-ce que le Tiers état?* (Paris, Ed. du Boucher 2002)

Sultany N, *Law and Revolution: Legitimacy and Constitutionalism after the Arab Spring* (Oxford University Press 2017)

Varayudej S, *The Right to Democracy in International Law: Its Implications for Asia*, 12 Ann. Surv. Int'l & Comp. L. 1 (2006)

Walker N, 'Post-Constituent Constitutionalism? The Case of the European Union', in Loughlin Martin and Walker N (eds), *The Paradox of Constitutionalism, Constituent Power and Constitutional Form* (Oxford University Press 2007)

Wall I R, Human Rights and Constituent Power without Model or Warranty (Routledge 2012)

Weber M, *Economy and Society* (University of California Press 1978)

Part II

Forms

5 Constitutions imposed with consent?

*Richard Albert**

The Japanese Constitution is widely viewed as the paradigmatic example of an "imposed" constitution.[1] We know, however, that the 1946 Japanese Constitution was adopted with some input and consent from Japanese political actors, a fact that weakens the all-too-common claim that the post-war Japanese Constitution was an entirely foreign imposition.[2] In fact, what we today identify as the Japanese Constitution was an omnibus package of constitutional amendments to the 1889 Meiji Constitution—a set of reforms that were approved by local actors according to the formal rules of constitutional amendment codified in the old constitution.[3] Other constitutions similarly described as imposed—but equally complicated in the extent to which they were forced by one nation upon another—include the German Basic Law, the reconstructed United States Constitution, and the Constitutions of Bulgaria, the Philippines and Western Samoa.[4] These constitutions, none imposed in the ordinary sense of the term as it

* For helpful feedback, I am grateful to the participants at the international symposium on 'Imposed Constitutions,' held in Nicosia, Cyprus, on May 5–6, 2017. I am also grateful to a reviewer who provided detailed comments on an earlier draft of this chapter.

1 *See* Axel Berkofsky, 'Japan's US-'Imposed' Post War Constitution: How, Why and What For?' in Silvio Beretta et al, eds, *Italy and Japan: How Similar Are They?* (Milan: Springer 2014) 67 at 87; Zachary Elkins et al, 'Baghdad, Tokyo, Kabul.... Constitution Making in Occupied States' (2008) 49 *William & Mary Law Review* 1139 at 1157; Sylvia Brown Hamano, 'Incomplete Revolutions and Not So Alien Transplants: The Japanese Constitution and Human Rights (1999) 1 *University of Pennsylvania Journal of Constitutional Law* 415 at 415; Frederick Schauer, 'On the Migration of Constitutional Ideas' (2005) 37 *Connecticut Law Review* 907 at 907–08.

2 *See* David S. Law, 'The Myth of the Imposed Constitution' in Denis Galligan & Mila Versteeg, eds, *The Social and Political Foundations of Constitutions* (Cambridge: Cambridge University Press 2013) 239 at 241–50; Mark Tushnet, 'Constitution' in Michel Rosenfeld & András Sajó, *The Oxford Handbook of Comparative Constitutional Law* (Oxford: Oxford University Press 2012) 217 at 221.

3 *See* Robert E. Ward, 'The Origins of the Present Japanese Constitution' (1956) 50 *American Political Science Review* 980 at 1004 n59.

4 Viktor Mayer-Schönberber, 'Into the Heart of the State: Intervention Through Constitution-Making' (1994) 8 *Temple International & Comparative Law Journal* 315 at 318–25; Schauer, *supra* n 1, at 907–08.

is used today, raise a difficult question: what makes a constitution imposed rather than indigenous?

Imposed constitutions sit along a scale of heteronomy. Heteronomy is the condition of being under the rule of another. One state or entity can rule another in several ways. For example, one may rule another directly by force or coercion through occupation or control. Or one may rule another indirectly through formal or informal means by exercising persuasive or peremptory constitution-level decision-making authority. Along this scale of heteronomy, many constitutions that we might not otherwise consider imposed reveal tinges if not full colors of imposition. Heteronomous constitutions are created, governed or adapted directly or indirectly by an external actor. This understanding of an imposed constitution accommodates the conventional understanding of a constitution written or administered coercively by a victorious power for a state vanquished after war or conquest. Yet this understanding of an imposed constitution as rooted in heteronomy also incorporates those constitutions not born of defeat.

In this chapter, I focus on a particular kind of heteronomous constitution: a constitution that has been imposed with the consent of the peoples on which it has been imposed, meaning that the state has voluntary shared or fully ceded the constitution-making or -changing power to an external actor. What matters here is that the decision-maker is foreign, answers to constituents based abroad, and is neither constituted, selected nor legitimated by domestic institutions. I identify three categories of constitutions imposed with consent—constitutions that are amended, adjudicated and interpreted by others—none quite the paradigmatic model of an indigenous constitution born of and governed by local actors but each one more a function of self-determined choice than a constitution imposed in war or conquest.

I use three case studies to illustrate how a constitution can be imposed with the consent of the peoples it governs. I draw from the Constitutions of Canada, Grenada and South Africa. These are by no means an exhaustive catalogue of constitutions we may describe as having been imposed "with consent" in some way or another. I have chosen these three constitutions in particular because they illustrate three quite different forms of heteronomy yet are all three part of the Commonwealth. I use these three constitutions as a springboard to make one general point: recognizing that a constitution can be imposed with consent complicates our understanding of imposed constitutions and forces us to confront the reality that extraterritorial actors can sometimes be invited to occupy a central place in domestic constitutional law.

The Parliament of the United Kingdom and the Canadian Constitution

A constitution can be imposed with consent where a state requests that an external actor amend its constitution on its behalf. Relying on another state to amend one's own constitution creates a heteronomous relationship. Here, the external amending actors exercise constitution-level decision-making authority over the domestic political actors who rely on the former to formalize changes to their constitution. This heteronomous relationship is of course qualitatively different from the subjugation that defines the relationship between states in the context of conquest. Yet the estrangement of the amendment power from the home state to an external actor creates an indirect form of imposition. I show how with reference to the estrangement of the amendment power from Canadian political actors to the Parliament of the United Kingdom.

Constitutional amendment in the founding Canadian Constitution

The founding Constitution of Canada—the *British North America Act, 1867*, since renamed the *Constitution Act, 1867*[5]—is unique among the constitutions of the world. As Jamie Cameron has observed, it is one of the few not to formally codify rules for its own amendment.[6] It took more than one century for Canada to finally acquire formal amendment rules that would allow domestic political actors to amend the Canadian Constitution on their own.[7] In the years prior to 1982, formal amendments to the Constitution were made by another country—an extraordinary arrangement that Canada had in fact requested of its own volition.[8]

With few exceptions, the power to amend the Constitution of Canada belonged to the Parliament of the United Kingdom.[9] Canadian political actors could not lawfully amend their constitutional text without first requesting the change from the United Kingdom and then waiting for it to be made. Here is how one Canadian prime minister described the unusual reality that Canada was unable to amend its own constitution without the intervention of another country:

> The Canadian Constitution of 1867 was the first to provide "dominion status" within the British Empire. But in blazing that path, our Fathers of Confederation incurred some of the penalties of pioneering: no amending procedure was provided in the British North America Act. ... [T]he omission was almost immediately a source of some uncertainty; after the great strides toward sovereignty during and after the first World War, it became a matter of growing embarrassment.[10]

5 Constitution Act, 1867, 30 & 31 Victoria, c 3 (U.K.) ['*Constitution Act, 1867*'].
6 Jamie Cameron, 'Legality, Legitimacy and Constitutional Amendment in Canada' in Richard Albert & David R. Cameron, eds, *Canada in the World: Comparative Perspectives on the Canadian Constitution* (Cambridge: Cambridge University Press 2017) 98 at 98.
7 Richard Albert, 'The Conventions of Constitutional Amendment in Canada' (2016) 53 *Osgoode Hall Law Journal* 399 at 416.
8 Richard Albert, 'Constitutional Amendment and Dismemberment' (2018) 43 *Yale Journal of International Law* 1 at 35–38.
9 *See* Constitution Act, 1867, s. 92(1) (authorizing provincial legislatures to amend their own provincial constitution); s. 101 (authorizing Parliament of Canada to amend the Constitution as to certain judicial matters).
10 Lester B. Pearson, 'Introduction' in Guy Favreau, *The Amendment of the Constitution of Canada* (Ottawa: Queen's Printer 1965) at vii ['Favreau Report'].

It is not an exaggeration to call this arrangement an "embarrassment," as the prime minister did at the time. The power to amend one's constitution is a marker of sovereignty, and we must question where sovereignty resides when this power is alienated from the people whom the constitution governs.[11] And yet one conceivably could claim that this arrangement was an appropriate means of ensuring that Commonwealth states were afforded protections under law.

From 1867 through 1965, the Parliament of the United Kingdom amended the *Constitution Act, 1867* a total of 22 times.[12] Some amendments were relatively minor, for example the repeal of obsolete provisions in the original document.[13] Some were relatively more important, including an amendment to extend the life of the war-time Parliament,[14] to grant legislative representation in Parliament to territories,[15] or to change the tenure of office for judges.[16] And some introduced fundamental changes to Canada, for instance the creation of new provinces.[17] But all of them were made in the same way: by formal law-making outside Canada.

There is a reason why the Constitution of Canada could be amended only by the Parliament of the United Kingdom: the Constitution was itself an Act of Parliament. The Parliament of the United Kingdom had passed the Canadian Constitution into existence as an ordinary law. And as an Act of Parliament, both the theory and doctrine of legal continuity required that only Parliament could make amendments to it. Canada's beginnings may today strike us as odd but Peter Russell reminds us that the Canadian and British political actors who negotiated Confederation saw this arrangement as completely reasonable: "the Fathers of Confederation assumed throughout that Canada's Constitution would take the form of an imperial statute and, as such, would be formally amended by the British Parliament."[18] As the years wore on, however, the estrangement of the amendment power became a problem. According to Nadia Verrelli, this arrangement was "at best, an inconvenience, and

11 Richard Albert, 'Constitutional Handcuffs' (2010) 42 *Arizona State Law Journal* 663 at 665. The European Union (EU) complicates this view insofar as its Member States must conform to the standards, rules and values enshrined in the EU treaties. Indeed it is accepted that Member States are not fully sovereign, that the powers of Member States are curtailed in important ways, and that supranational rules may take priority over national law. On one view, this arrangement is itself heteronomous: Member States have ceded a lot of ground to the EU. On another, the choice of Member States to accede to the European Union and everything accession entails is made by the Member States themselves in full understanding of the consequences, expectations and requirements that follow from it.

12 Favreau Report at 4–7.

13 *See* Statute Law Revision Act, 1893 (repealing obsolete provisions of the *Constitution Act, 1867*); Statute Law Revision Act, 1950 (same).

14 *See* British North America Act, 1916.

15 *See* British North America Act, 1886.

16 *See* British North America Act, 1960.

17 *See* British North America Act, (ratifying Manitoba Act); British North America Act, 1949 (confirming Terms of Union between Canada and Newfoundland).

18 Peter H. Russell, *Constitutional Odyssey: Can Canadians Become a Sovereign People?* (Toronto: University of Toronto Press 1992) at 27.

at worst, a national embarrassment as it continued to indicate that Canada's nation-building project was incomplete."[19]

As Canada matured into more of an independent state and less of a colonial possession, the arrangement began to evolve.[20] Eventually the Parliament of the United Kingdom would not choose independently to exercise its amending power over the Canadian Constitution. From 1895 onward, the Parliament of the United Kingdom would amend the Canadian Constitution only at the request of Canada, as expressed by a resolution adopted by a majority of the Parliament of Canada, styled a "joint Address of the Canadian House of Commons and Senate to the Crown."[21] What resulted was a division of amendment powers between approval and formalization: Canadian political actors would negotiate the amendment among themselves before reaching approval on what it should say and they would subsequently request its codification by the Parliament of the United Kingdom, which would in turn invariably formalize the amendment into the Constitution of Canada by passing a simple law.[22]

Decolonization and disagreement

The critical point has so far remained unstated: at an historic moment when the Parliament of the United Kingdom was ready to cede its amendment power, Canada refused to accept it and instead asked the United Kingdom to retain the power to amend the Canadian Constitution. The year was 1931, when the Parliament of the United Kingdom passed the Statute of Westminster, written to formalize the decolonization of Australia, the Irish Free State, Newfoundland, New Zealand, South Africa and Canada.[23] The Statute put an end to the power of the Parliament of the United Kingdom to legislate on behalf of Canada and the other jurisdictions, called "dominions":

> No law and no provision of any law made after the commencement of this Act by the Parliament of a Dominion shall be void or inoperative on the ground that it is repugnant to the law of England, or to the provisions of any existing or future Act of Parliament of the United Kingdom, or to any order, rule or regulation made under any such Act, and the powers of the Parliament of a

19 Nadia Verrelli, 'Searching for an Amending Formula: The 115-Year Journey' in Emmett Macfarlane, *Constitutional Amendment in Canada* (Toronto: University of Toronto Press 2016) 19 at 19.

20 *See* Richard Albert, 'The Difficulty of Constitutional Amendment in Canada' (2015) 53 *Alberta Law Review* 85 at 108–09.

21 Favreau Report at 15.

22 One of the most important questions in Canadian political history concerned the quantum of political agreement needed in Canada to authorize the domestic Parliament to request a formal amendment involving matters of federal-provincial interest. The Canadian Supreme Court answered this question in connection with the patriation of the Canadian Constitution in 1982. *See* Reference re: Resolution to amend the Constitution, [1981] 1 SCR 753.

23 Statute of Westminster, 1931, c 4, 22 Geo 5.

> Dominion shall include the power to repeal or amend any such Act, order, rule or regulation in so far as the same is part of the law of the Dominion.[24]

From this point forward, Canada and the other dominions could pass laws of their own without worry that they would be declared "void" or "inoperative" for conflicting with the laws of the United Kingdom. More importantly, the Statute of Westminster authorized the dominions to "amend" any Act of Parliament that had been passed as their law, namely law passed by the Parliament of the United Kingdom for the dominions as their founding constitutional texts.

But the Parliament of the United Kingdom made an exception to this rule when it passed the Statute of Westminster. It expressly denied Canada the power to amend the *British North America Act, 1867* and all subsequent constitutional acts that had been passed as amendments to the founding constitutional text. London instead retained the power of amendment for itself:

> Nothing in this Act shall be deemed to apply to the repeal, amendment or alteration of the British North America Acts, 1867 to 1930, or any order, rule or regulation made thereunder. … The powers conferred by this Act upon the Parliament of Canada or upon the legislatures of the Provinces shall be restricted to the enactment of laws in relation to matters within the competence of the Parliament of Canada or of any of the legislatures of the Provinces respectively.[25]

Although Australia, South Africa and the other dominions were given the power to amend their own constitutions, the Statute of Westminster withheld the same power from Canada. The plain language of the Statute did not authorize the "repeal, amendment or alteration of the British North America Acts, 1867 to 1930" by anyone other than the Parliament of the United Kingdom. Canadian actors could continue to pass laws within their sphere of jurisdiction under the *British North America Acts* but they generally could not make changes to those Acts. This Canadian exception to the devolution of the amendment power was peculiar but it was not without reason.

To understand the reason why, we must turn to the Balfour Declaration in 1926. The Declaration defined Great Britain and the dominions as equals, describing them as

> autonomous Communities within the British Empire, equal in status, in no way subordinate one to another in any aspect of their domestic or external affairs, though united by a common allegiance to the Crown, and freely associated as members of the British Commonwealth of Nations.[26]

Equality entailed by implication an end to the power of the Parliament of the United Kingdom over the affairs of the dominions. But before Parliament could

24 *Ibid* s 2(2).
25 *Ibid* ss 7(1), 7(3).
26 Balfour Declaration, pt II (1926).

divest itself of its extraterritorial legislative power in the case of the dominions, political actors within each of the dominions had to reach some agreement as to how they would govern themselves without the involvement of Parliament.

In Canada's case, the questions of self-governance centered on the amendment formula: by what quantum of agreement would political actors agree to amend the Constitution, would the majorities vary according to the subject-matter of the amendment, and which political actors would need to consent to which particular changes? Canadian political actors tried but failed to reach agreement in 1927, one year after the Balfour Declaration. In that intergovernmental conference among first ministers, the sticking point had been a concern that amendment under the proposed formula would be too easy, rendering the Constitution too malleable. A cautious preference emerged for keeping the status quo of constitutional amendment by the Parliament of the United Kingdom rather than going with a suboptimal and untested procedure.[27]

Canadian political actors tried once more in 1931 in anticipation of the passage of the Statute of Westminster. And again they failed to reach agreement on a domestic amendment formula that would give Canada the power to amend its own Constitution without relying on the Parliament of the United Kingdom. Knowing that Parliament would soon pass the Statute of Westminster, Canadian political actors agreed on a course of action: they would make a formal request for an exception to the devolution of powers upon Canada that would exclude the power to amend the *British North America Act, 1867* and its subsequent amendments.[28] Canada's request was granted, and the exception was written into the Statute of Westminster, leaving the power to amend Canada's Constitution in the hands of the Parliament of the United Kingdom.[29]

In the midst of the decolonization of Canada,[30] what should have been an assertion of independence became a resumption of dependence. The failure of Canadian political actors to agree on a domestic amending formula led to Canada's request that the United Kingdom continue to exercise its constitution-level decision-making authority for Canada. Yet simple formality or not, this arrangement undermined the claim that Canada had finally become independent. It would take over one dozen failed efforts before Canadian political actors finally agreed on an amending formula.[31] It was ultimately enacted in the *Constitution Act, 1982*.[32]

27 James Ross Hurley, *Amending Canada's Constitution: History, Processes, Problems and Prospects* (Ottawa: Minister of Supply and Services Canada 1996) at 26.
28 *Ibid* at 26.
29 *Ibid* at 26–27.
30 Statute of Westminster (n 23) s 11 (stating that 'the expression 'Colony' shall not, in Act of the Parliament of the United Kingdom passed after the commencement of this Act, include a Dominion…').
31 *See* Hurley (n 27) at 23–67.
32 *See* Procedure for Amending Constitution of Canada, Part V of the *Constitution Act, 1982*, being Schedule B to the *Canada Act 1982*, 1982, c. 11 (U.K.) (hereinafter 'Constitution Act, 1982').

Grenada and the Judicial Committee of the Privy Council

A constitution can be imposed with consent also when a state invites an external actor to adjudicate conflicts arising under its constitution. This is unusual because domestic constitutional interpretation is commonly understood to be an exercise of sovereign law-making authority, bounded by limits drawn by local political actors according to their own norms and preferences. And yet as Rosalind Dixon and Vicki Jackson have shown, "outsider interpretation" of national constitutions is not uncommon, particularly in our day as the world shrinks, globalism takes root and borders become more permeable than they once were.[33] The case of Grenada is illustrative here; it shows that a country could willingly invite a foreign actor to exercise the ordinarily domestic but here externally-seated power to interpret its constitution.

Constitutional reform in Grenada

The countries of the Caribbean are currently living an extraordinary period of transformative constitutional change. These last twenty years or so have seen virtually every Caribbean country engage in a serious process of national self-reflection about whether, and if yes how radically, to reform their constitution.[34] Some of the subjects for reform are unique to particular countries, for instance, whether to adopt plurality voting in the Bahamas,[35] how to regulate campaign finance in St. Lucia,[36] or what to name the Office of the Opposition in Trinidad and Tobago.[37] But a significant part of the reform debate cuts across the region, concerning specifically whether and how to sever ties with the British monarchy. This question has arisen in connection with two issues: whether to become a republic and whether to end legal appeals to the United Kingdom.

Legal appeals were at the center of a major effort at constitutional reform in Grenada, completed recently in 2016, albeit unsuccessfully. This was the third time a blue-ribbon commission had studied and suggested how to modernize the Grenadian Constitution,[38] only later to see its recommendations fail to win passage. Grenadians voted no in a seven-question referendum in November 2016 on various matters of constitutional reform: whether to create an Elections and

33 Rosalind Dixon & Vicki C. Jackson, 'Constitutions Inside Out: Outsider Interventions in Domestic Constitutional Contests' (2013) 48 *Wake Forest Law Review* 149.

34 *See* Derek O'Brien, *The Constitutional Systems of the Commonwealth Caribbean: A Contextual Analysis* (Oxford: Hart Publishing 2014) at 267–68.

35 *See Constitutional Commission Report of the Constitutional Commission into a Review of The Bahamas Constitution* (2013) at 165.

36 *See Constitutional Reform Commission Report of the Constitutional Reform Commission of Saint Lucia* (2011) at 227–28.

37 *See Trinidad and Tobago Constitutional Reform Commission, National Consultation on Constitutional Reform* (2013) at 21–22.

38 Francis Alexis, *Recommendations by Grenada Constitution Review Commissions* (6 February 2014).

Boundaries Commission; whether to ensure the appointment of a Leader of the Opposition even if one party wins all of the seats in general elections; whether to set fixed general election dates; whether to change the name of the state to recognize the two other islands that make up the country; whether to codify new rights and freedoms in the Constitution; whether to establish term limitations on the Office of Prime Minister and whether Grenada should end appeals to the Judicial Committee of the Privy Council and accede to the final appellate jurisdiction of the Caribbean Court of Justice. Each of these seven referendum questions failed by a wide margin.[39]

The Judicial Committee of the Privy Council is a relic of the Imperial Parliament but it continues to exercise the power of appellate review in many countries today, including Grenada. Section 104 of the Grenadian Constitution mandates that appeals from the Court of Appeal must be heard by the Judicial Committee of the Privy Council for "final decisions in any civil or criminal proceedings which involve a question as to the interpretation of this Constitution."[40] This means that Grenada's final court of appeal is not its own domestic court but rather a court located in London, staffed by non-Grenadians and interpreted from a non-Grenadian perspective, despite London's honest efforts to resolve local Grenadian disputes fairly. The court has brought some measure of stability, reality and protection from local corruption. History, however, shows that the Judicial Committee of the Privy Council has been a tool of British imperial policy, issuing decisions to serve the Empire above all, to retain for London oversight over economic policy in its colonies and territories, to keep order among the many peoples across its possessions and to further "the values of an enlightened metropolis to the peripheries of Empire."[41] Appeals from the Caribbean Community form a large portion of the court's case law; the Judicial Committee of the Privy Council therefore exercises real authority in the region.[42]

But Grenada is not without alternative options should it wish to cast off this vestige of British colonialism. In February 2001, twelve Caribbean states agreed to create a Caribbean Court of Justice. The Court, with both original and appellate jurisdiction, is intended to deepen regional integration but is also committed

39 Linda Straker, 'Low Voter Turnout, as Grenadians Snub Changes to the Constitution' in *The Montserrat Reporter*, 25 November 2016, online: https://www.themontserratreporter.com/low-voter-turnout-as-grenadians-snub-changes-to-constitution (last accessed 1 February 2017).

40 The Grenada Constitution Order 1973, s 104 (1973 No 2155). There are other instances where appeals from the Grenadian Court of Appeal are available as of right to the Judicial Committee of the Privy Council.

41 Thomas Mohr, 'The Privy Council Appeal and British Imperial Policy, 1833–1939' (2016) UCD Working Papers in Law, Criminology & Socio-Legal Studies Research Paper No 13/2016, at 3–4.

42 *See* Andrew Le Sueur, 'What Is the Future for the Judicial Committee of the Privy Council?' Working Paper at 7, online: http://www.ucl.ac.uk/political-science/publications/unit-publications/72.pdf (last accessed 1 February 2017) (reporting that 90 out of 193 appeals in the years 1996-99 came from the Caribbean Community).

to respect the boundaries of national sovereignty.[43] The Caribbean Court of Justice's appellate jurisdiction makes it the court of final appeal for those countries that accede to it and abolish appeals to the Judicial Committee of the Privy Council. At its creation, the Caribbean Court of Justice was seen, and rightly so, as an important symbol of national sovereignty and regional solidarity.[44] The Judicial Committee of the Privy Council itself was seen as "an inhibiting factor to the development of an indigenous jurisprudence which is more responsive to the values within our society and or aims and aspirations as independent Caribbean nations."[45] The Court of Caribbean Justice offered a new path for the countries of the region—a road to formal and functional independence. And yet fifteen years later, only four countries had acceded to the appellate jurisdiction of the Court of Caribbean Justice; the others had chosen to retain the Judicial Committee of the Privy Council as their final court of appeal.[46]

Choosing foreign over local authority

In the November 2016 referendum on constitutional reform, Grenadians made the conscious choice to keep the Judicial Committee of the Privy Council as their final court of appeal. In the vocabulary of heteronomy, Grenadians self-consciously ceded control over the development of their domestic constitutional law and traditions by choosing to continue delegating constitution-level decision-making authority to an external actor, here to a court. This arrangement of course differs substantially from a militarily imposed constitution where the locals are denied any real choice. This delegation nonetheless amounts to an alienation, voluntary though it may be, of a central aspect of self-governance. As Simon McIntosh once decried, "the continuing *presence* of the Crown and its Judicial Committee in the post-independence Commonwealth Caribbean political order represents a vestigial incongruity, a contradiction in the constitutional symbolism of a politically independent sovereign order."[47] Grenadians made an extraordinary choice that many others might not have. But their decision is not without explanation.

There are four major arguments against the abolition of final appeals to London.[48] First, the Judicial Committee of the Privy Council is thought to have

43 Agreement Establishing the Caribbean Court of Justice, prmbl (14 February 2001).

44 *See* Hugh Salmon, 'The Caribbean Court of Justice: A March with Destiny' (2000) 2 *Florida Coastal Law Journal* 231 at 231.

45 *Ibid* at 234.

46 Salvatore Caserta & Mikael Rask Madsen, 'Between Continuity Law and Common Law: The Rise of the Caribbean Court of Justice at the Intersection of Regional Integration and Post-Colonial Legacies' (2016) *79 Law & Contemporary Problems* 89 at 90.

47 Simeon CR McIntosh, *Caribbean Constitutional Reform: Rethinking the West Indian Polity* (Kingston: The Caribbean Law Publishing Company Ltd, 2002) at 265.

48 *See* Michael Anthony Lilla, 'Promoting the Caribbean Court of Justice as the Final Court of Appeal for States of the Caribbean Community' (May 2008) Institute for Court Management, at 12–13, online: http://www.ncsc.org/~/media/files/pdf/education%20and%20careers/cedp%20papers/2008/lilla_caribjustasfinalctappeal.ashx (last accessed 1 February 2017).

a greater capacity to take an objective and detached view of local constitutional disagreements.[49] Second, some fear that Caribbean jurisprudence is not yet sufficiently developed to give a foundation for high-quality judgments.[50] Third, there is a concern that political actors might interfere with the work of the Caribbean Court of Justice.[51] And, fourth, because of the different views on the death penalty in the Caribbean and London—the countries of the Commonwealth Caribbean authorizing capital punishment and the Privy Council having ruled against the death penalty[52]—some worry that the Caribbean Court of Justice would become a "hanging court."[53]

Not everyone accepts these criticisms. For example, Duke Pollard has described many of the arguments for retaining the Judicial Committee of the Privy Council as "dubious and unworthy."[54] Cheryl Thompson-Barrow has suggested that modern norms of access to justice require delinking of the Commonwealth Caribbean from the London court, not only for symbolic reasons but very practical ones like the costs of retaining counsel for hearings—costs that include travel and accommodation as well as entry visas.[55] Most importantly, Rose-Marie Belle Antoine has shown that the jurisprudence of the Privy Council demonstrates that it is not "equipped to determine and assess social norms and reflect them in legal policy"[56]—a serious indictment of London's capacity to be an effective arbiter of the constitutional law of those Caribbean countries that continue to rely on London to resolve their deepest questions of public law. Yet for now, Grenadians have chosen to keep the Privy Council as its final court of appeal.

49 Ezekiel Rediker, 'Courts of Appeal and Colonialism in the British Caribbean: A Case for the Caribbean Court of Justice' (2013) 35 *Michigan Journal of International Law* 213 at 247–50.

50 David Simmons, 'The Caribbean Court of Justice: A Unique Institution of Caribbean Creativity' (2005) 29 *Nova Law Review* 171 at 183–85.

51 Cynthia Barrow-Giles, 'Regional Trends in Constitutional Developments in the Commonwealth Caribbean' (January 2010) Conflict Prevention and Peace Forum, at 17, online: http://www.cpahq.org/cpahq/cpadocs/cynthia%20barrow.pdf (last accessed 1 February 2017).

52 Dennis Morison, 'The Judicial Committee of the Privy Council and the Death Penalty in the Commonwealth Caribbean: Studies in Judicial Activism' (2006) 30 *Nova Law Review* 403 at 406–08.

53 Lilla, *supra* note 48, at 12.

54 Duke E. Pollard, *The Caribbean Court of Justice: Closing the Circle of Independence* (Kingston: The Caribbean Law Publishing Company Ltd, 2004) at 207.

55 Cheryl Thompson-Barrow, *Bringing Justice Home: The Road to Final Appellate and Regional Court Establishment* (London: Commonwealth Secretariat, 2008) at 32; *see also* Andrew N. Maharajh, 'The Caribbean Court of Justice: A Horizontally and Vertically Comparative Study of the Caribbean's First Independent and Interdependent Court' (2014) 47 *Cornell International Law Journal* 735 at 742–46.

56 Rose-Marie Belle Antoine, *Commonwealth Caribbean Law and Legal Systems* (Abington: Routledge-Cavendish Publishing Ltd, 2d ed 2008) at 317–18.

International law in the South African Bill of Rights

A third variation on the idea of a heteronomous constitution imposed with consent is a constitution whose interpretation is controlled functionally by local actors but formally constrained by external sources of law. Ordinarily, local actors interpret their own domestic constitution constrained only by local sources of law. Here, however, the meaning of the domestic constitution is shaped by external rules. One example that illustrates this third model of heteronomy is the Swiss Constitution, which in all cases of constitutional amendment or replacement must respect "mandatory provisions of international law."[57] Another example, which I discuss below, is South Africa's 1996 Constitution, although it demonstrates only the weak-form of this third model of heteronomy since the Constitution has so far been interpreted with more deference to domestic norms than its textual commands otherwise suggest.

Peremptory rules of constitutional interpretation

International law is explicitly incorporated into the South African Constitution in many ways. First, treaties negotiated and signed by the executive ordinarily become part of domestic law when they are ratified by Parliament.[58] Second, a self-executing treaty provision, even if ratified by Parliament, does not become effective if it is inconsistent with the Constitution or an Act of Parliament.[59] Third, customary international law applies in South Africa unless it is inconsistent with the Constitution or an Act of Parliament.[60] Fourth, when interpreting domestic legislation, courts must privilege any "reasonable interpretation" that conforms to international law over all other interpretations that would conflict or otherwise fail to align with international law.[61]

The South African Constitution also requires the Constitutional Court to look to international law when it interprets the country's domestic Bill of Rights: "When interpreting the Bill of Rights, a court, tribunal or forum ... must consider international law."[62] The word "must" is peremptory, both in its plain meaning and in contrast to a related provision in the same section of the Constitution, which instead only invites the Constitutional Court to look to foreign law when interpreting the Bill of Rights: "When interpreting the Bill of Rights, a court, tribunal or forum ... may consider foreign law."[63] The critical difference lies in the use of the words *must* and *may*: the former suggests that the interpretation of the Bill of Rights should necessarily track international law.

57 Switzerland Constitution, arts 193(4), 194(2) (1999).
58 South Africa Constitution, s 231(1)–(2) (1996).
59 *Ibid* s 231(4).
60 *Ibid* s 232.
61 *Ibid* s 233.
62 *Ibid* s 39(1)(b).
63 *Ibid* s 39(1)(c).

Yet as Devika Hovell and George Williams have shown in their empirical study of the first decade of the South African Constitution, the Constitutional Court has made "limited use" of international law in its interpretation of the Bill of Rights.[64] In the 137 cases at the Constitutional Court involving the Bill of Rights from 1995 to 2004, only 33 percent referred expressly to international law and 22 percent gave it detailed consideration.[65] These findings have led Hovell and Williams to conclude that "judges seem to consider international law on an ad hoc basis rather than having thorough regard to international law in each case. In some cases, this suggests a failure to pay due regard to the constitutional injunction to consider international law."[66]

Of course, a requirement merely to consider international law does not entail an obligation to import it into domestic law.[67] The Constitution's peremptory rules on international law are best understood as guidelines for the Court as to the kinds of interpretative methodologies to deploy and how to evaluate the relevance of available sources of authority. As Constitutional Court Justice Zakeria Yacoob wrote in a judgment invoking international law in connection with the right to housing, "the relevant international law can be a guide to interpretation but the weight to be attached to any particular principle or rule of international law will vary."[68] The Court had earlier put the point more directly and indeed more clearly in one of its first cases:

> In dealing with comparative law, we must bear in mind that we are required to construe the South African Constitution, and not an international instrument or the constitution of some foreign country, and that this has to be done with due regard to our legal system, our history and circumstances, and the structure and language of our own Constitution. We can derive assistance from public international law and foreign case law, but we are in no way bound to follow it.[69]

The Constitutional Court has therefore been unequivocal from the very beginning that its task is to interpret its own constitution, "not an international instrument" written in a different "language," rooted in a different "history and circumstances," and by and for other peoples.

64 Devika Hovell & George Williams, 'A Tale of Two Systems: The Use of International Law in Constitutional Interpretation in Australia and South Africa' (2005) 29 *Melbourne Law Review* 95 at 114.

65 *Ibid* at 114–115.

66 *Ibid* at 119.

67 *See* Stu Woolman & Michael Bishop, *Constitutional Law of South Africa* (Cape Town: Juta & Co Ltd, 2d ed 2013) at 30–12 and 30–13.

68 Government of the Republic of South Africa v Grootboom (CCT 11/00) [2000] ZACC 19; 2001 (1) SA 46, 2000 (11) BCLR 1169 (4 October 2000) at para 26.

69 S v Makwanyane and Another (CCT3/94) [1995] ZACC 3; 1995 (6) BCLR 665; 1995 (3) SA 391; [1996] 2 CHRLD 164; 1995 (2) SACR 1 (6 June 1995) at para 39.

The aspirations of global constitutionalism

Hovell and Williams note in their study that some have argued that the Constitutional Court has not fulfilled its obligation to consider international law when interpreting the Bill of Rights: "the relatively limited use of international law in constitutional interpretation has led to criticism of the Constitutional Court for failing to have greater regard to such material."[70] The data show that the Court has looked to international law in fewer than half of the relevant cases. Yet we must appreciate that the Court has confronted competing pressures when interpreting the Constitution: it has had to balance respect for the mandatory requirement to consider international law in its interpretation of the Bill of Rights with the reality that the act of interpreting a national charter of rights is a distinctly localist enterprise that must speak to local norms, values and lived experiences. The Constitutional Court has thus far struck the right balance given the constitutional, social and political constraints on its function as the authoritative interpreter of the young Constitution. If the Court were to yield to the criticisms highlighted by Hovell and Williams, the Constitution would run the risk of becoming considerably more heteronomous than indigenous.

When the meaning of a national constitution is keyed to an external standard, in this case a standard set by international ideational norms of the scope of rights and freedoms, the people subject to that national constitution are both functionally and formally under the rule of another. The South African case is different even though the Constitution, on a particularly strict reading of section 39(1)(b), may seem to formally bind the Constitutional Court to conform its interpretation of domestic law to an external source of law. We know, however, that as a matter of practice the Court makes its own choice not only whether to refer to international law but also whether to apply it to the national context. Were the Court to take the strictest reading of section 39(1)(b), the meaning of the Constitution would still be functionally decided by local judges but its content would be governed formally and in reality by the actors who make international law.

Seeding the "world's law"[71] in South Africa may well have been the aspiration for its Constitution. The preamble identifies its purposes, two of which are to "heal the divisions of the past and establish a society based on democratic values, social justice and fundamental human rights" and to "build a united and democratic South Africa able to take its rightful place as a sovereign state in the family of nations."[72] At the country's new beginning after apartheid, John Dugard remarked that the new Constitution "seeks to ensure that South African law will evolve in accordance with international law."[73] Dugard observed also that the

70 Hovell & Williams, *supra* note 64, at 116.

71 Richard Cameron Blake, 'The World's Law in One Country: The South African Constitutional Court's Use of Public International Law' (1998) 115 *South African Law Journal* 668 at 668.

72 South Africa Constitution, prmbl.

73 John Dugard, 'International Law and the South African Constitution' (1997) 1 *European Journal of International Law* 77 at 92.

provision requiring the Constitutional Court to look to international law when it interprets the country's domestic Bill of Rights was intended to "inform the international community of South Africa's new commitment to international law and give notice of the manner in which South Africa will bind itself in its future relations with states."[74]

Having been isolated from the global community of nations for more than two generations, the new Constitution was written strategically to help "bring[] South African law into harmony with international human rights norms."[75] The new South Africa made international law one of "the pillars of the new democracy," in contrast with the South Africa of old that had been "in conflict with both the international community and international law," and had "bec[o]me a pariah state within the international community," and a "delinquent state in the context of the 'new' international law of human rights."[76] South Africa's new international constitution would help rehabilitate the country with a measure of "international legitimacy after decades of isolation of the apartheid regime, which had ignored international standards on fundamental rights."[77] To put it another way, South Africa needed to show that it was building a new regime based on standards that "were not drawn from the same well, but from purer waters."[78]

The admiration of the South African Constitution around the world suggests that the idea of constitutionalism may have "escaped its territorial bounds."[79] It is no longer unusual to read scholars arguing for "an international constitutional order," one that rejects the traditional understanding of a constitution as a tool for domestic ordering.[80] Yet lost amid the success of the South African model—today more constitutions resemble it than they do the United States Constitution[81]—is the normative question whether a national constitution should be anything but localist in its authoritative sources of law and in the actors authorized to change and interpret it.

A people can of course choose to cede constitution-level decision-making to an external actor, as appears to have been the case at least to some degree in South Africa, whether or not the Constitutional Court has adequately fulfilled

74 John Dugard, 'International Law and the Final Constitution' (1995) 11 *South African Journal of Human Rights* 241 at 241.
75 Dugard, *supra* n 73, at 84.
76 *Ibid* at 77.
77 Andrea Lollini, 'Legal Argumentation Based on Foreign Law: An Example from Case Law of the South African Constitutional Court' (2007) 3 *Utrecht Law Review* 60 at 63.
78 Hoyt Webb, 'The Constitutional Court of South Africa: Rights Interpretation and Comparative Constitutional Law' (1998) 1 *University of Pennsylvania Journal of Constitutional Law* 205 at 219.
79 *See* Larry Catá Backer, 'From Constitution to Constitutionalism: A Global Framework for Legitimate Public Power Systems' (2009) 113 *Pennsylania State Law Review* 101 at 172.
80 *See* Erika de Wet, 'The International Constitutional Order' (2006) 55 *International & Comparative Law Quarterly* 51 at 51.
81 *See* David S. Law & Mila Versteeg, 'The Declining Influence of the United States Constitution' (2012) 87 *New York University Law Review* 762 at 828–29.

the expectations of section 39(1)(b). Any informed and deliberative choice of the people and their representatives must be respected as an expression of their consent. Yet there is often overwhelming pressure from the outside to take advice or follow trends in constitution-making—options that may not represent the first choice of local actors. It would be incorrect to describe these choices as freely made. Indeed the global convergence around liberal democratic constitutional government makes those options look more like requirements, particularly if a state, like South Africa in its transition from official apartheid to formal democracy, wishes to join the international community of liberal democratic nations.

Conclusion—Indigeneity in constitution-making and -changing

The concept of heteronomy is useful to define what we mean by an imposed constitution. Beyond imposition in the context of war or conquest, constitutions can be imposed with consent if we define an imposed constitution as heteronomous—created, governed or adapted directly or indirectly by an external actor. I have identified three categories of heteronomous constitutions imposed with consent: constitutions that are amended by an external actor, for instance the Canadian Constitution until patriation; constitutions that rely on an external actor to adjudicate disputes under it, namely the Grenadian Constitution still today and indeed many constitutions in the Commonwealth Caribbean; and constitutions whose meaning is keyed to an external source of law, for example the South African Constitution and its relationship with international law. It is worth observing, though, that the choice to self-bind to the rule of others in both the Canadian and Grenadian cases was made by constituted powers, not the constituent power. In the South African case it was the constituent power. This has implications for the variable legitimacy of the self-imposition, though in all cases there exists a non-trivial measure of constraint.

Defining an imposed constitution this broadly, though, raises the question whether all new constitutions today are in fact in some way externally imposed. Constitution-makers often turn to foreign advisers for help in designing their basic constitutional arrangements and they cannot help but be influenced directly or indirectly by global models of democratic constitutional success. Even where constitutions may not be designed with an eye to the external world, they may be reformed under constraint of either continuing or aspiring membership in regional or multilateral organizations. For example, the Venice Commission in the Council of Europe advises its 47 member states on whether their domestic constitutional law—including amendments, emergency powers, rights and freedoms—conform to the Council's expectations. Though this may be a soft form of constraint, it nonetheless amounts to coercive pressure to conform to what are becoming increasingly regional if not global standards of constitutional law.

And yet there is something distinctive about the categories of heteronomy I have identified. Each of them reflects what I understand to be the estrangement or alienation of a central feature of self-governance and self-determination.

Amending, adjudicating or interpreting a national constitution is an incidence of sovereignty that belongs to the people bound by the constitution. Where those choices are made by persons or bodies external to the state, it is right to ask whether the state is sovereign. Even where local political actors and the people have made an informed decision to cede this constitution-making and -changing power to an external actor, we should probe the reasons why. In the case of Canada, internal discord made it impossible to agree on a domestic amending procedure, and so the chosen solution—not the preferred route—was to invite London to retain amendment authority over the Canadian Constitution. In Grenada as in other countries of the Commonwealth Caribbean, the choice to retain the Judicial Committee of the Privy Council as the court of final appeal is a common but troubling vestige of colonialism and perhaps a function of a taught and now unconscious self-construction of external validation. Similar forces are evident in the case of South Africa, whose new democracy, in order to succeed, must be recognized and supported by the international community. The point is that all of these choices, though nominally made locally, have external forces at their root.

Will a people ever again write an indigenous constitution of their own? We could ask the same question of major constitutional amendments that are used to remake constitutions beyond introducing simple housekeeping changes. On one view, the rise of global constitutionalism suggests the answer may well be no. Mounting regional or international pressures to codify in new constitutions a standard menu of rights and liberties, to adopt what are described as democratic norms of power-division in law-making, and also to write and ratify a constitution according to what are thought to be best practices for constitution-making are threatening to standardize what one might argue should remain anything but standard.

Constitutions, on this particular view, should necessarily differ across peoples because no two peoples are alike, whether in their origins, their internal divisions, their geographic distribution, their aspirations and their lived histories. To expect peoples to harmonize their constitutions under one dominant vision of social and political organization therefore seems not only to ask too much, but to ask the impossible according to this view of constitutions as purely domestic undertakings. To require such conformity in constitution-making and -changing, whether by hard or soft forms of coercion, yields a heteronomous constitution that may be conceptually indistinguishable from a constitution imposed by force. The strongest claim from this view is that the peoples of the world should resist the globalizing pressures of constitutionalism as it is currently promoted by the power centers in the international order, and that they should instead look deep within themselves and their own local history to settle on the best answers for themselves quite apart from what those answers may be for others. That view may be best suited for a time long past in which the world was smaller, borders were less permeable and Westphalian rules prevailed. Today the world is much different.

6 Are 'octroyed constitutions' of the 19th century to be considered as imposed constitutions?

*Jörg Gerkrath**

The following contribution contemplates so-called 'octroyed', 'conceded' or 'granted' constitutions of 19th century Europe whose common roots are to be found in the French *Charte constitutionnelle* of 1814. Strongly influenced by the spirit of Restoration and based on the monarchical principle, as reaffirmed by the Congress of Vienna (1814–1815) and the founding act of the German Confederation (1820),[1] these Charters stem from a paternalistic process of domestic constitution-making without any direct involvement of (a body representing) the people.

The terminology employed in legal literature to examine the phenomenon is not entirely fixed. Although English-speaking scholars refer predominantly to '*conceded*' or '*granted*' constitutions, it appears to be more adequate to speak of 'octroyed' constitutions. The term 'octroyed' is commonly used in its different linguistic expressions in those countries which experienced significant periods of octroyed constitutions: in German, *oktroyierte Verfassung*, in French, *constitution octroyée*, in Italian, *costituzione ottriata* and in Portuguese, *constituição outorgada*.

The French Charter of 1814, the archetype of all octroyed constitutions, contains the following royal statement at the very end of its preamble: '*Nous avons volontairement et par le libre exercice de notre autorité royale accordé, et accordons, fait concession et octroi à nos sujets, tant pour nous que pour nos successeurs et à toujours, de la charte constitutionnelle qui suit*'.[2] Clearly the three terms are used together in that occasion. Hence, from a linguistic, as well as from a legal-historical perspective, the adjectives 'granted' and 'conceded' might be used as synonyms of 'octroyed'. But as we are dealing here with a matter of constitutional law and theory where language matters and as we are striving to develop convincing elements of a theory of octroi in constitution-making, this contribution will

* Professor of Public and European Law at the University of Luxembourg, jorg.gerkrath@uni.lu.

1 Final Act of the Ministerial Conference to Complete and Consolidate the Organization of the German Confederation, signed by the parties May 15, 1820.

2 Which may be traduced as: 'We have voluntarily and by the free exercise of our royal authority granted, and grant, made concession and octroi to our subjects, both for us and for our successors and forever, the constitutional charter that follows'.

therefore promote the corresponding vocabulary, even though the above quoted final sentence of the preamble of the French Charter of 1814 contains the only explicit mention of the term octroi in a constitutional document of the considered period. Regarding all the other constitutional documents, the designation 'octroyed' was introduced later by literature.

The paper intends to fill a gap in the legal literature. Besides a stimulating contribution of Luigi Lacchè, Professor in Legal History at the University of Macerata, on the very theory of octroi,[3] and a synthetic Encyclopedia entry authored by Yasuo Hasebe,[4] the lack of comprehensive comparative literature on the technique of constitutional octroi is obvious.[5] All other relevant works (known by the author) are based on the study of one single charter or an analysis of constitutions from a single country.[6]

This study does not pretend to constitute a fully-fledged comparative work. It is more of an essay aiming at defining criteria allowing us a) to better understand the concept of an octroyed constitution and b) to find out whether an octroyed constitution is equivalent to an imposed one. Nevertheless, the inquiry faces some of the same challenges and has to comply with the methodology of comparative law, as far as possible.[7] In the first place the *tertium comparationis*, that is the common quality of the charters and constitutions to be compared, needs to be properly defined.

An octroyed constitution can be described as resulting from an authoritarian or paternalistic process of constitution-making engaged unilaterally by a monarch possessing the *de facto* constituent power and exercising it without the direct involvement of a body representing the people. By this act, the formerly absolute sovereign renounces – in theory spontaneously and irrevocably – to a part of his

3 Published in three different language versions: Luigi Lacchè, 'Granted Constitutions: The Theory of Octroy and Constitutional Experiments in Europe in the Aftermath of the French Revolution' (2013) 9 EuConst, 285; 'Las Cartas otorgadas. La teoría de l'octroi y las experiencias constitucionales en Europa post-revolucionaria' (2010) 6 Fundamentos 269; 'Le carte ottriate, La teoria dell'octroi e le esperienze costituzionali nell'Europa post-rivoluzionaria' (2009) 18 Giornale di storia costituzionale 229.

4 Yasuo Hasebe, 'Imposed Constitutions (constitutions octroyées)', *Max Planck Encyclopedia of Comparative Constitutional Law* (2016) http://oxcon.ouplaw.com/view/10.1093/law-mpeccol/law-mpeccol-e21 accessed on 10 September 2017.

5 cf also Oscar Ferreira, 'Les équivoques du „constitutionnalisme octroyé: un débat transatlantique I' (2015) 16 Historia Constitucional 67. The author focused on the French Charter of 1814 and unfortunately didn't publish yet the second part of his work, intended to deal with octroyed constitutionalism in Portugal and Brazil.

6 cf notably Philippe Lauvaux, 'La technique de l'octroi et la nature de la Charte' (2014) 13 Jus politicum 1.

7 As exposed by Léontin-Jean Constantinesco, *Rechtsvergleichung. Die vergleichende Methode*, vol 2 (Carl Heymanns Verlag 1972). Regarding the methodology of comparative constitutional law cp Vicki C. Jackson, 'Comparative Constitutional Law: Methodologies' in Michel Rosenfeld, András Sajó (eds), *The Oxford Handbook of Comparative Constitutional Law* (OUP 2012).

own exclusive authority.[8] In reality, such acts of constitutional voluntarism were intended to conceal the need to compromise with social reality.[9]

Jon Elster distinguishes two forms of constitution-making by a single founder: 'In one, a wise man writes a constitution for his community and then withdraws from politics. Plutarch tells us that Solon and Lycurgus (if he existed) took this path. It has never been followed again'. One could, however, object that the Brazilian Emperor and King of Portugal, Don Pedro IV, precisely followed this example when he octroyed the Portuguese *Carta constitucional* in 1926 and abdicated from the Portuguese throne a few days later.[10] In the other case, Elster pursues, 'a ruler, presumably assisted by advisors, imposes an "octroyed" constitution on his people. The French Charter of 1814 and Prussian constitution of 1850 are often cited as examples'.[11]

As an 'octroyed constitution' is evidently enacted top-down by a monarch, there is some confusion to be found in the legal literature regarding the concept of an 'imposed constitution' and the 'technique of constitutional octroi'. In their contribution to the *Oxford Handbook of Comparative Constitutional Law*, devoted to 'Process' and within their developments about 'constitution-making as an international effort', Claude Klein and András Sajó consider for instance that 'the involvement (of the occupying power) may reach the level of imposition (constitutional octroy)' and refer in a footnote to 'various forms of colonization'.[12]

Yasuo Hasebe applies the same inaccuracy considering: 'Inherent in this concept of imposed constitution is the assumption that constituent power belongs to the people. Therefore, a constitution which the monarch concedes to his subjects (*constitution octroyée*) is also a kind of imposed constitution'.[13] His affirmation contains a striking anachronism as, at the time when constitutions could legitimately be octroyed by a monarch holding the *plenitudo potestatis,* the democratic principle had not yet successfully superseded the monarchical principle.

A similar misunderstanding can be found regarding Cyprus. As well known, the Constitution of Cyprus did not emanate from the free will of its people but was in fact imposed on the population by the London and Zürich Agreements of 1959, concluded between representatives of the two Cypriot communities of the one part, and Greece, Turkey and the United Kingdom of the other part. Considering, as Tornaritis does: 'It is, therefore (…) of the nature of a granted

8 cf Paolo Biscaretti di Ruffia, Stefan Rozmaryn, *La Constitution comme loi fondamentale dans les Etats de l'Europe occidentale et dans les Etats socialistes* (LGDJ 1966) 29.

9 Lauvaux (n 6) 2.

10 cf Jorge Miranda, *Manual de direito constitucional. O sistema constitucional* português vol 1 (10th edn, Coimbra Editora 2014) 40.

11 cf Jon Elster, 'Constitutions and Constitution-Making' http://www.ccpds.fudan.edu.cn accessed on 10 September 2017.

12 Claude Klein, András Sajó, 'Constitution-Making: Process and Substance' in Michel Rosenfeld, András Sajó (eds), *The Oxford Handbook of Comparative Constitutional Law* (OUP 2012) 432.

13 Hasebe (n 4) para 2.

Constitution – *constitution octroyée*, which in the monarchical times of the past centuries the monarch condescended to grant to his people, but is not consistent with the new prevailing democratic principles under which the constituent power vests in, and is exercised by, the people', isn't helping to understand the true nature of the Constitution of Cyprus.[14]

At first glance, it does not seem accurate to use the same terminology for such different realities as constitutional charters granted by monarchs of the early 19th century and a Constitution imposed by means of an international agreement in 1959. But could it be as simple as to distinguish 'domestically octroyed' constitutions on the one side and 'internationally imposed' constitutions of the other side? Or, in other words, would the main question be whether external or internal patrons put a given constitution in place? In this event, however, how should we deal with constitutional charters octroyed by a monarch ruling on two countries which are linked through his person in a so-called personal or real union? This was precisely the case in Poland (1815), Portugal (1826) and Luxembourg (1841).

It goes without saying that in my opinion octroyed constitutions can never be seen as 'democratically established constitutions'. One could consider them as a subdivision of 'imposed constitutions', even though they show a number of specific characteristics which distinguish them clearly from imposed constitutions in the usual sense. The expression 'constitutional octroi' should not be used as a synonym for any process leading to an 'imposed Constitution'. This paper aims to develop and to validate or invalidate the value of a series of distinctive criteria and possible elements of a definition of 'octroyed' constitutions in order to underline their specificity.

In order to avoid any kind of anachronism, the different charters need to be understood within their historical as well as their political context.[15] Before starting to discuss the criteria that I consider to be distinctive of octroyed constitutions, it seems indicated to give some preliminary consideration to the dissemination of the phenomenon and to define the scope of this study.

I Dissemination of the phenomenon and scope of the study

The constitutions of a given country certainly are 'the product of historical circumstances and the reflection of certain political, economic, social and cultural elements'.[16] In order to compare the comparable, this contribution will only consider octroyed constitutions enacted in 19th century Europe.

The golden age of octroyed constitutions is the first half of the 19th century and more precisely the period from 1814 to 1850. This period can be identified

14 cf Criton G. Tornaritis, *Cyprus and Its Constitutional and Other Legal Problems* (2nd ed, Nicosia 1980) 54.

15 All mentioned documents have been studied in their original linguistic versions and the relevant literature in English, French, German and Portuguese has been taken into account.

16 cf Miranda (n 10) 9, considering the characteristics of Portuguese constitutionalism.

as an own 'cycle' of constitution-making. We can call it the 'restoration cycle'.[17] Each of the octroyed constitutions is indeed a historical product linked to the specific transitional period called Restoration or the restorative period. They stand as necessary first or intermediate acts of constitutionalism and transitional steps towards the emergence of parliamentarism and the final victory of the idea of the people as the only legitimate constituent power. German authors generally refer to the constitutions of this period as inspired by the principle of dualism (*Dualismus*). In the German constitutional monarchies of the early 19th century it was indeed possible to observe what Carl Schmitt called a 'dualistic intermediate status' (*dualistischer Zwischenzustand*).[18]

Nevertheless, not all constitutional documents adopted during this period have been octroyed unilaterally by a monarch. Amongst the main exceptions to be mentioned is the Dutch *Grondwet* from 1814. Adopted by an Assembly of six-hundred notables convened in Amsterdam in March 1814, its preamble nevertheless opened with the words: 'We, William, by the grace of God'. Despite not technically being a *charte octroyée*, the Fundamental Law was indeed 'a typical product of Restoration constitutionalism'.[19] So is the Dutch *Grondwet* of August 24, 1815 which results from a revision of the *Grondwet* 1814 and is still in place. The Norwegian *Grunnloven* of May 17, 1814 likewise was elaborated within a Constitutional Imperial Assembly.[20] Furthermore, several member states of the German Confederation adopted constitutions in the 1830s in the form of constitutional pacts. The Kingdom of Württemberg reached this stage pre-eminently in 1819.

Finally, a specific case to be mentioned is the *Estatuto de Bayona* of July 6, 1808, the first written Spanish constitution, even though it had no practical significance because it never entered into force. The *Estatuto* was an octroyed constitution by which Napoleon wanted to impose an autocratic system in Spain. In the preamble, the constitution is presented as a pact between the king and his people. In reality, it was more like a constitutional octroi by Napoleon who previously had presented a draft to an assembly of Spanish notables, and only 75 (91 at the final session) out of 175 appeared when asked to do so.[21]

During the considered period of Restoration more or less influential constitutional documents have been octroyed in about a dozen European countries. Some of them

17 cf José Joaquim Gomes Canotilho, *Direito Constitucional e Teoria da Constituição* (7th edn, Coimbra Editora 2003) 134, who speaks of restoration constitutionalism (*o constitucionalismo da Restauração*).

18 Carl Schmitt, *Verfassungslehre* (8th edn, Duncker & Humblot 1993) 54.

19 Boris Mirkine-Guetzévitch, 'L'histoire constitutionnelle comparée' (1936) Annales de l'Institut de Droit comparé de l'Université de Paris II 86, 93.

20 cf Ulrike Müßig, 'Juridification by Constitution. National Sovereignty in Eighteenth and Nineteenth Century Europe' in Ulrike Müßig (ed) *Reconsidering Constitutional Formation I, National Sovereignty, A Comparative Analysis of the Juridification by Constitution* (Springer Open 2016) 56.

21 cf Müßig (n 20) 36 : 'This constitutional octroi of July 6, 1808 based on monarchical prerogatives of the intruder king (*rey intruso*) was widely rejected by the people as a sign of French foreign rule'.

broke records in terms of longevity, others had a rather ephemeral lifespan. When on June 4, 1814 Louis XVIII granted the French '*Charte constitutionnelle*', often referred to by scholars as the prototype of an octroyed Constitution, he incidentally launched at the same time the restoration cycle. The Charte became for numerous years one of the most influential constitutional documents in continental Europe.

It inspired notably the '*Charte constitutionnelle du Royaume de Pologne*', the constitution granted by Tsar Alexander I in his role as King of Poland on November 27, 1815, executing an obligation laid down in article I of the Final Act of the Congress of Vienna. The Charter was proclaimed by the Tsar both in its original French and a translated Polish version.[22] Transfer and reception of the French *Charte* model could also be observed in the southern German states during the period termed early constitutionalism (*Frühkonstitutionalismus*).[23] The constitutions (*Verfassungsurkunden*) of Nassau (September 2, 1814), Württemberg (*Landständische Verfassung* of March 15, 1815), Sachsen-Weimar-Eisenach (May 5, 1816), Bayern (May 26, 1818) and Baden (August 22, 1818) have indeed all been octroyed by reigning monarchs who wanted to secure their authority by granting rights and freedoms to their subjects and sharing the legislative power with an elected Parliament.

Portugal experienced actually the longest period of octroyed constitutionalism (*constitucionalismo outorgado*) during the 19th century.[24] The *Carta Constitucional da Monarquia* granted by Emperor Don Pedro IV from Brazil on April 29, 1826, remained in place, beside two interludes, for seventy-two years between 1826 and 1910.[25] Influenced by the French Charter and the thinking of Benjamin Constant, it also contained many aspects copied from the Brazilian Constitution of 1824. In Spain, on the contrary, the *Estatuto real* of 1834 only had an ephemeral existence. The Royal Statute was put into effect on April 10, 1834 by the Regent Maria Christina in the name of her daughter Isabella II in absence of any democratic consent. After a short and troubled period, Regina Maria Christina re-established the constitution of *Cádiz* on August 13, 1836.

Luxembourg's constitutional history displays two cases of octroi. The first occurred in 1841, when William II, King of the Netherlands and Grand-Duke of Luxembourg, in order to comply with the provisions of the German Confederation, of which the Grand Duchy was a member, granted the *Constitution d'Etats pour le Grand-Duché de Luxembourg*.[26] The second happened in 1856 when William III, who succeeded his father in 1849 and proved to be a militant defender of the

22 cf Markus J. Prutsch, *Making Sense of Constitutional Monarchism in Post-Napoleonic France and Germany* (Palgrave Macmillan 2013) 61.

23 cf Jacky Hummel, 'La Charte française de 1814 et le deutscher Konstitutionalismus : les inflexions d'une réception durable' (2014) 13 Jus Politicum 1.

24 Expression borrowed from José Miguel Sardica, 'A Carta Constitucional portuguesa de 1826' (2012) 13 Historia Constitucional 527, 530.

25 cf Gomes Canotilho (n 17) 147.

26 The royal grand-ducal ordinance of October 12, 1841, establishing the Constitution of Estates (*landständische Verfassung*), was published in German and French in the Legislative and Administrative Memorial no 51 (1841) 425.

royal prerogatives, staged a coup d'état and octroyed a constitutional revision.[27] He dissolved the Chamber on his own authority and promulgated a revised text of the liberal Constitution of 1848. The new Constitution restored monarchy and abolished the parliamentary system. Though clearly adopted in breach of the formal requirements of revision of the 1848 constitution, it was published by a royal ordinance of November 27, 1856, 'carrying revision of the Constitution'.[28]

Similar to the southern German states, the Italian monarchies of the 19th century also came across the technique of constitutional octroi. The most significant document was the so-called *Statuto Albertino,* officially named *Statuto del regno di Sardegna,* granted to the kingdom of Sardinia by King Carlo Alberto on March 4, 1848. The *Statuto* is not an oeuvre of a parliamentary assembly. Its octroi rather points to strong parallels with the French Charter in 1814 and the constitutions of Bavaria and Baden in 1818. Their common aim was to protect royal authority by an 'eternal and irrevocable fundamental law of the monarchy'.[29]

The Albertine Statute was also consistent with other Italian constitutions of 1848, which drew inspiration from the French Charter. Such were the Constitution of the Kingdom of the Two Sicilies (February 10, 1848) and the Statute of the Grand Duchy of Tuscany (February 15, 1848). Being written in order to subdue popular uprisings, they were brief and laconic and left a lot to constitutional practice. But these charters had a very brief lifespan and were unable to translate their goals into practice.[30] In contrast to the *Statuto Albertino*, which later became the constitution of the unified Kingdom of Italy and remained in force, with changes, until 1948.

At the end of the Restoration cycle of constitution-making by octroi, we finally encounter the experiences of Prussia and Austria. The Constitution of Prussia (*Verfassungsurkunde für den preußischen Staat*) was octroyed by Friedrich Wilhelm, King of Prussia by the grace of God, on December 5, 1848, after having dissolved a constitutional convention previously convened. It was definitively confirmed by the King on January 31, 1850, once revised and accepted by both chambers according to the reservation stated in the preamble of 1848 and according to the amendment procedure laid down in article 112. Thus, this specimen of an *oktroyierte Verfassung* was in fact octroyed, revised, accepted by Parliament and finally proclaimed by the King in an unprecedented four-step procedure.

Concerning Austria, the Empire constitution of March 4, 1849, the so-called '*oktroyierte Märzverfassung*', is similarly a result of a sequence of four

27 cf Raymond Fuselier, *Les Monarches parlementaires* (Les éditions ouvrières 1960) 558 who mentions the 'revision octroyée'.

28 cf Paul Eyschen, *Das Staatsrecht des Grossherzogtums* (Paul Siebeck 1890) 10, Pierre Majerus, *L'Etat luxembourgeois* (Saint.Paul 1990) 26, and Luc Hommel, *Les étapes constitutionnelles du Grand-Duché de Luxembourg* (L'édition universelle 1935) 11.

29 As states the final line oft the Statuto's preambel: '(...) abbiamo ordinato ed ordiniamo in forza di Statuto e Legge fondamentale, perpetua ed irrevocabile della Monarchia, quanto segue: (...)'.

30 Müßig (n 20) 175.

imperial patents proclaimed by Ferdinand I. It is also known as 'Count Stadion constitution', Count Franz Stadion being the Interior Minister who drafted it, while the constitutional committee of the Parliament was preparing a rival draft constitution.[31]

The phenomenon of constitutional octroi did not fully disappear with the end of the Restoration period. There are still some examples of 20th-century octroyed constitutions to be discovered in the Eastern part of the European continent as for instance: The Serbian Constitution of 1901, granted by Alexander I of Serbia; the Russian Fundamental Laws of 1906, conceded by Tsar Nicholas II; the constitution of Lithuania of May 15, 1928[32]; and the Constitution of Yugoslavia of September 3, 1931, proclaimed by Alexander I. But even in the heart of western Europe the Principality of Monaco received a first '*Acte constitutionnel*' by octroy in 1911. The more recent Monegasque Constitution of December 17, 1962 – even though prepared consensually – is still considered being a *charte octroyée*, according to an opinion of the Venice Commission.[33]

As we have seen, octroyed constitutions were adopted primarily in continental Europe. However, the phenomenon has never been limited to the 'triangle consisting primarily, but not exclusively, of France from 1814 until 1830; secondly of the German lands from the Congress of Vienna; and thirdly, of the Italian states, in particular the Kingdom of Sardinia', as suggested by Luigi Lacchè.[34] Geographically speaking, it could also be observed outside of Europe. A first example is the Ottoman Basic Law (*Ḳānūn-ı Esāsī*), promulgated by Sultan Abdülhamit II on December 23, 1876. The Constitution was prepared by a commission directly assigned by the Sultan and published in Turkish with an official translation in French.[35] As a unilateral declaration of the Sultan, it is to be considered as an octroyed constitution.[36] A second example is the well-known Japanese Meiji constitution of February 11, 1889; and a third one is the 'Fundamental

31 cf on this interesting period Eric Voegelin, Ruth Hein (tr), Gilbert Weiss (ed), *The Authoritarian State: An Essay on the Problem of the Austrian State. Collected Works of Eric Voegelin* vol 4 (University of Missouri Press 1999) 130.

32 This dictatorial constitution had been octroyed by the President of the Republic, Anton Smetona. It was repealed in 1938 and remained widely unapplied. cf Wolfgang Ismayr, *Die politischen Systeme Osteuropas* (2nd ed, Leske+Budrich 2013) 156.

33 Commission européenne pour la démocratie par le droit, CDL-AD(2013)018, avis no. 695/2012 sur l'équilibre des pouvoirs dans la constitution et la legislation de la Principauté de Monaco, Strasbourg 18 June 2013, 9.

34 Lacchè (n 3) 286.

35 Abdolonyme Ubicini, *La Constitution ottomane du 7 zilhidjé 1293 (23 décembre 1876). Expliquée et annotée* (Cotillon 1877).

36 Ergun Özbudun, 'The Ottoman Constitution of 1876', *Max Planck Encyclopedia of Comparative Constitutional Law*, (2016) http://oxcon.ouplaw.com/view/10.1093/law-mpeccol/law-mpeccol-e639 accessed on 10 September 2017; Aslı Topukcu, 'The processes and the principles of constitutional design in Turkey. Historical and legal perspective', Paper presented to the World Congress of Constitutional Law, Oslo 2014, https://www.jus.uio.no/english/research/news-and-events/events/conferences/2014/wccl-cmdc/wccl/papers/ws11/w11-topukcu.pdf accessed on 10 September 2017.

State Laws of the Russian Empire' of April 23, 1906, granted by Tsar Nicholas II and preceded by the 'October Manifesto' of October 17, 1905 forming 'a typical act of octroyed constitutionalism'.[37]

I have only taken into account the octroyed constitutions adopted in European monarchies between1814 and 1850. In order to illustrate their distinctive patterns, I will mainly refer to the following six historical exemplars: France 1814, Portugal 1826, Luxembourg 1841, Italy 1848, Austria 1849 and Prussia 1848/1850. Although there are of course many differences to be observed, these constitutions have sufficient elements in common to illustrate what makes the category of octroyed constitutions (the *tertium comparationis*) unique. I will elaborate on five elements or criteria, which are all classical criteria in constitutional thought, and which I consider decisive for the understanding of octroyed constitutions: Process (II), Form (III), Legitimacy (IV), Substance (V) and Amendment (VI).

II Process: The technique of octroi, a constitutional bluff?

An octroi is a monarchical proceeding to establish a constitution (*oktroyierte Verfassung*). It is classically opposed to a second proceeding, which is the pact concluded between the monarch and the people, represented by Parliament (*paktierte Verfassung*). Octroyed constitutions are, in theory, voluntary concessions of absolute rulers. In practice, however, it was simply and only under the pressure of events that monarchs abandoned a fraction of their sovereignty.[38] Accordingly, there are some prejudices to get rid of. As we will see, the constitutional octroi never resulted from the monarch's free will alone, mostly it wasn't even a true unilateral act, nor a product of the monarch's sole authorship and it has often to be considered within a sequence of several royal acts. Altogether this points to the direction that the performance of octroying a constitutional charter has to be seen as what it really is: a royal ruse and a constitutional bluff.

Rather than acting of their free will, monarchs deciding to proceed to a constitutional octroi did regularly believe to fulfil a moral obligation towards their subjects or even to execute a legal obligation laid down in a superior document. The historical circumstances created by the Parisian peace treaties of 1814 and 1815, the course of the Vienna Congress and the establishment of the German Confederation strongly promoted this development.

In France, Louis XVIII was pushed by his counsellors to 'concede rather than receive' a constitution. And at the same time, the allied powers had made clear during the conclusion of the first peace treaty of Paris on May 30, 1814, that they wouldn't leave the French territory unless a government was established on constitutional foundations.[39] The preamble of the second peace treaty of Paris,

37 cf Andrei Medushevsky, *Russian Constitutionalism: Historical and Contemporary Development* (Routledge 2006) 124.

38 cf Joseph Barthélemy, *Précis de droit constitutionnel* (4th edn, Dalloz 1938) 110.

39 cf Hummel (n 23) 6.

concluded after Napoleon's return and the so-called '100 days' on November 22, 1815, refers consequently to the octroyed charter of 1814.[40]

The Congress of Vienna had also a noteworthy influence. According to article I of the Final Act of June 8, 1815, Tsar Alexander I of Russia was obliged to give a constitution to the newly recreated Poland, the so-called 'Congress-Poland'. In addition, article XIII of the founding Act of the German Confederation (*Deutsche Bundesakte*), adopted during the Congress of Vienna, founded a duty to establish a 'constitution of Estates' in all of the member states, but without prejudicing the procedure to follow.[41] Article XIII of the Federal Act was largely responsible for the German early constitutionalism, especially in the southern German states. Some of the member states' constitutions referred explicitly to this duty. The preamble of Luxembourg's constitution of Estates of 1841 did so, and the octroyed revision of 1856 was also explicitly motivated by the obligation of the king-grand duke to comply with the federal duty to respect the principles of the German Confederation. The octroyed constitution of Württemberg of 1815 also contains the expression.[42] Beyond this legal duty, most certainly other underlying motivations of an octroi prevailed: the unification of territorial gains, the consolidation of finances and the demonstration of the new state's sovereignty.[43]

Regarding the unilateral nature of an octroi, things aren't by far as clear as they seem. German scholars started in the 19th century to oppose constitutional octrois and constitutional pacts as two different models, the former uni-, the latter bilateral. But still, an octroi can be understood as the fulfilment of a promise by a monarch, who sacrifices some of his powers in establishing a constitutionally limited monarchy and in doing so makes a gift to his subjects who accept it. In this sense the octroi results from a kind of dialogue, which is different than a joint and bilateral constitution-making procedure involving a ruler and an assembly. But it isn't truly unilateral either.

The octroi appears as a kind of transactional measure, even though the degree of popular consent varies naturally. The strongest case was to be found in Prussia in 1848/1850 where the octroyed constitution required a revision to be voted by the two chambers in order to become effective. But also in Austria the imperial patent (constitutional act) that introduced the Pillersdorff Constitution on April 25, 1848 'appears as the fulfilment of a fundamental obligation toward the

40 'Participating at present with his Most Christian Majesty in the desire to consolidate, by maintaining inviolate the Royal Authority, and by restoring the operation of the Constitutional Charter, the order of things which had been happily re-established in France, as also in the object of restoring between France and her Neighbours those relations of reciprocal confidence and goodwill which the fatal effects of the Revolution and of the system of conquest had for so long a time disturbed (…)'.

41 Article XIII : 'In allen Bundesstaaten wird eine landständische Verfassung stattfinden'.

42 cf Ernst Rudolf Huber, *Deutsche Verfassungsgeschichte seit 1789. Band I: Reform und Restauration 1789 bis 1830* (2nd edn, W. Kohlhammer 1967) 640.

43 cf Hummel (n 23) 5–6; Ulrike Müßig, *Die europäische Verfassungsdiskussion des 18. Jahrhundert* (Mohr Siebeck 2008) 91.

contractual partner, the people'.[44] In one case, as in Bohemia in October 1871, a nation of the Austrian Empire considered an octroi by the shared dynast to be a satisfaction of their own demands rather than a unilateral absolute action. Such a 'requested octroi' was 'understood as something to be granted or bestowed, not as something to be imposed'.[45] In this understanding the people relied on a virtual (moral) compact between the monarch and itself.

Taking a closer look at the drafting procedure of the constitution, which usually precedes its formal octroi, a distinction between the author (*auteur*) and the writer (*écrivain*) of the constitution is suggested in the literature. Some go as far as to consider the king being only the writer, writing down what the true author, the nation, accepted.[46] In any case, the monarch assisted by advisors, counsellors and drafting committees, is always more or less actively involved in the editing of the text. In some cases, like in Bavaria, he would nominate a constitutional committee charged to prepare a draft.[47] In others, like in Prussia, a reluctant Monarch who wanted to keep his promise of a constitution to be agreed upon with an elected Parliament, had to be convinced by his ministry to proceed by octroi.[48] The drafting of the Portuguese Charter in 1826 constitutes another interesting example. Don Pedro IV, emperor of Brazil, assisted by his counsellor, Francisco Gomes da Silva, prepared this text in a few days by working on a draft of the Brasilian Constitution from 1823. Each of the two worked on a paper copy, which was revised and annotated and then switched between them.[49]

Frequently the octroi wasn't an isolated act but resulted from a sequence of acts adopted in a step-by-step process as the constitution was announced by preceding declarations or statements, for instance. The Declaration of *Saint-Ouen*, made by the future Louis XVIII on May 2, 1814, may illustrate this. Upon landing in France, the future king rejected the provisional constitution proposed by the Senate but promised to adopt a new 'liberal constitution'. This promised constitution was eventually adopted in the Charter of 1814. He later sought to eradicate the legal effects of the initial compromise in a third step by establishing the offence of criticising the octroi by a statute of March 22, 1822.[50] The Austrian Empire faced a similar sequence of several constitutional *patents* between April 1848 and March 1849. A first patent of March 15, 1848 promised a constitutional charter, which was octroyed on April 25, 1848, the so-called *Pillersdorffsche Verfassung*. It was declared provisional in May 16, 1848,

44 Voegelin (n 31) 131.
45 Ibid.
46 cf Ferreira (n 5) 115.
47 On the constitutional committee nominated in the Kingdom of Bavaria by a royal edict of September 17, 1814, see Hummel (n 23) 6; Eberhard Weis, ‚Zur Entstehungsgeschichte der bayerischen Verfassung von 1818. Die Debatten in der Verfassungskommission von 1814/15' (1976) 39 ZBLG 414.
48 cf Michael Kotulla, *Das konstitutionelle Verfassungswerk Preußens 1848–1918* (Springer 2012) 13.
49 On the drafting process cf Miranda (n 10) 39.
50 cf Ferreira (n 5) 114.

withdrawn in July by the Emperor and replaced by the '*oktroyierte Märzverfassung*' of March 4, 1849, which itself was repealed by the New Year's Eve Patent (*Silvesterpatent*) of Emperor Franz Joseph I on December 31, 1851.

III Form: How to avoid any reference to revolutionary constitutionalism

As in architecture, one could assume as well in constitutional theory that 'form follows function'. Octroyed constitutions were intended to restore the belief in the monarchical principle, but at the same time had to conceal with social reality and could not possibly ignore all revolutionary achievements and liberal demands. Their function was to restore the authority of a monarch by absorbing parts of the revolutionary acquis.[51] Or, as Eric Voegelin phrased it: 'The authoritarian gesture of the monarch, appointed by the grace of God to see to the welfare of his subjects, captures the revolutionary element of the movement for a constitution and transforms it into an act by the monarch'.[52]

This function could only be assumed by presenting the octroi as a gift of the enlightened monarch and thereby avoiding any reference to the constitutional theory, vocabulary and proceedings invented during the preceding revolutionary periods in Europe. Formal elements of octroyed constitutions, such as their title, wording, style, preambles, and the legal form chosen for enactment, reveal this specific function. The compromise consists of making concessions with regard to the substance but remaining firm on the form of the octroi.

This becomes most visible with the denomination chosen for the constitutional document. In France the expression '*charte constitutionnelle*' was deliberately picked after having discussed other solutions such as 'constitutional act', 'ordinance' and 'edict'.[53] The choice denotes a strong reverence to the Magna Carta of 1215. Already the naming of the Charter as 'constitutional' was a compromise. The decision to name some of the octroyed constitutions in Italy and Spain *Statuto* (*Estatuto*) rather than Charter proceeded from similar considerations.

Following the terminology chosen by the German Federal Act of 1815,[54] referring in its article 13 to the duty of each member state to establish a constitution of estates (*Landständische Verfassung*), several member states employed this expression in the title of their constitutions. Notably Würtemberg and Luxemburg did so respectively in 1815 and 1841. However, the term *Landständische Verfassung* has never been properly defined. In theory, it would have meant a system of corporative representation of the estates, impossible to restore within constitutional monarchies of that time. It wasn't even very clear whether the term refers to a

51 cf Lacchè (n 3) 291.

52 cf Eric Voegelin (n 31) 132.

53 cf Lauvaux (n 6) 3 quoting the memories of count Beugnot.

54 The 65 articles were unanimously approved by the Frankfurt Confederal Assembly on June 8, 1820.

type of constitution or rather to a form of representation. In some English versions the term has thus been translated as 'a constitutionally guaranteed assembly of the estates of the land'. And although some octroyed documents were simply named 'constitution', as in Bavaria in 1818, the choice of the name should not be overrated.

The wording used in the corpus as well as and especially in the preambles of the octroyed charters is probably more significant. Most of the charters are undeniably preceded by preambles, or followed by a 'postamble' as in the case of the Polish Charter. The preambles are sometimes rather lengthy with up to 724 words (France 1814) or even 988 words (Austria 1849). Written in a paternalistic style the preambles insist on the monarchic principle and the generosity of the conceding monarch. They also contain hints to the expectations of the people and to preceding promises of the monarch.

In analyzing the formal instrument used to proclaim the constitutional octroi, it is possible to detect in most of the cases the classical distinction between the *instrumentum* and the *negotium*. In all examined cases the octroy takes the form of a royal act.[55] Luxembourg's constitution of estates of 1841 was published in the form of a royal ordinance establishing the constitution.[56] The constitution is, however, at the same time called a statute ('loi') for the purpose of its amendment (art. 52).

The form taken by the different charters and their denominations does not deprive them of the recognition as genuine constitutions. The voices of those who completely denied all constitutional nature to octroyed documents remained in the minority during the period of their greatest spread.[57] The definition of the notion of constitution according to the usual functional, formal and material criteria clearly embraces the octroyed specimen.

Of course, we are confronted here with monarchical constitutionalism, and not yet representative constitutionalism. The notions and concepts to describe this movement had to be developed successively. In Portuguese literature the term 'Chartism' (*cartismo*) was coined to describe the peculiarities of octroyed constitutionalism. It can be understood as an effort to develop its own constitutional concepts. In a number of respects, Chartism definitely rethought and reworked its own liberal vocabulary, redefining basic concepts such as legitimacy, representation, nature of government or extension of suffrage (indirect and census and non-direct and extended).[58]

Call it octroyed constitutionalism,[59] restoration constitutionalism, chartism or monarchic constitutionalism, all of these suggestions can be considered an effort to ally both constitutionalism ancient and modern. But it has to be born in mind

55 cf Schmitt (n 18) 52: 'ein vom König erlassenes Gesetz'.

56 cf the official journal, Mémorial n° 51, 1841, p. 425, orig: *ordonnance*, *Verordnung*.

57 cf Lacchè (n 3) 286 quoting Karl Theodor Welcker, who considered: '*eine bloss oktroyierte Verfassung ist gar keine Verfassung*'.

58 cf notably Sardica (n 24) 529.

59 Though 'octroyed constitutionalism' can be taken for an oxymoron, cf Ferreira (n 5) 70.

that there are strong differences in the meaning of 'constitutionalism' in general, with a narrow meaning in German compared to a much wider meaning in France, for instance.[60]

IV Legitimacy: Reconciling conflicting sources

The concept of legitimacy can be understood in the divine, meta-legal or sociological 'Weberian' sense. According to German sociologist Max Weber, a political regime being legitimate means, in a descriptive sense, that its participants have certain beliefs or faith (*Legitimitätsglaube*) in regard to it: 'The basis of every system of authority, and correspondingly of every kind of willingness to obey, is a belief, a belief by virtue of which persons exercising authority are lent prestige'.[61] The three types of political legitimacy labelled by Weber are: traditional, charismatic and rational-legal. Constitutional legitimacy, in a normative sense, implies a justification of the constitution that must be found beyond the constitution itself. According to Matthias Hartwig, the sources of constitutional legitimacy can be found in forms of justification as: religion, consent, minimal substantive requirements and standards developed on an international level.[62]

Surprisingly, octroyed constitutions do not draw their legitimacy from religion alone. Once enacted, they combine two opposing sources of legitimacy: religion and consent. The latter is on the rise, the first declining. We will see in the next part of the contribution to what extent they obtain additional legitimacy by fulfilling substantive requirements and early international standards. I do not share the conclusion of Yasuo Hasebe that 'how a constitution was made, or in whose name, is not so relevant to its legitimacy'.[63] This aspect remains important, even though it has to be considered in conjunction with the other foundations of its legitimacy. An octroyed constitution unavoidably conceals a strong ambiguity resulting from the contradiction of two antithetic legitimacy doctrines: the monarchic principle, personified by the donor, and the representative principle, embodied by Parliament.

The divine legitimacy of the donor's power to concede the constitution was generally referred to in the preambles of the different Charters, describing the source of legitimacy as 'the grace of God' or 'the divine Providence'. In the sense of this line of reasoning, an octroyed constitution was 'legitimately imposed'.

60 cf on the notion of 'monarchischer Konstitutionalismus' notably Martin Kirsch, *Monarch und Parlament im 19. Jahrhundert. Der monarchische Konstitutionalismus als europäischer Verfassungstyp – Frankreich im Vergleich* (Vandenhoeck & Ruprecht 1999) 40; Hummel (n 23) 1, who both point out these differences.

61 Max Weber, *The Theory of Social and Economic Organization* (orig. *Wirtschaft und Gesellschaft*, Tübingen 1922, Free Press 1997) 382.

62 Matthias Hartwig, 'What Legitimises a National Constitution? On the Importance of International Embedding' in Armin von Bogdandy, Pál Sonnevend (eds), *Constitutional Crisis in the European Constitutional Area* (Nomos 2015) 322.

63 Hasebe (n 4) para 41.

According to the monarchical principle, the king, holding the *pouvoir constituant*, was entitled to give a constitution by a unilateral act.[64] However, as if the donation of the constitution needed additional justifications, some preambles went further and stated reasons like the request for peace, promises that had been made and even the 'expectations of enlightened Europe'.[65]

Because of the nature of the *Charte octroyée*, granted constitutions were naturally weak in regard to their (democratic) legitimization. But at a subsequent stage, they were able to achieve some popular adherence or at least implicit consent through the election of representative bodies and the active participation of elected assemblies in the implementation of the constitution. In the case of Prussia (1848/1850), one could even observe an act of explicit consent. According to the transitional rule of article 112, a compulsory revision of the document octroyed in 1848 had to take place to let the constitution become definitive.[66] In the case of the *Statuto Albertino*, contemporaneous observers immediately attempted to re-interpret the *Statuto* into a convention between king and parliament.[67] In such a vision an octroyed constitution could come with consent.[68]

Another indication for the existence of at least implicit consent is the durability of some of the octroyed charters. For memory: The *Statuto Albertino* remained formally in force after the Italian unification until 1946, and the Portuguese *Carta* of 1826 still holds the record of longevity amongst the six Portuguese constitutions adopted since 1822. We can definitely identify a kind of de facto legitimacy, in the descriptive sense, through effectivity and longevity of a constitution.

V Substance: 'Absorbing the Revolution into the monarchy'[69]

In terms of constitutional substance, octroyed charters have to be evaluated by their degree of consistency with the ideals of constitutionalism (limited government, representation, separation of powers, protection of human rights, etc.). Consequently, this degree is rather low as the spirit of restoration prevails. The ruse consisted of capturing some elements of the revolutionary and liberal achievements within a monarchical system.

The octroyed charters therefore re-affirmed the monarchical principle but established at the same time what German literature rapidly called the principle of

64 cf Schmitt (n 18) 52. On the monarchical principle see Friedrich Julius Stahl, *Das monarchische Prinzip, eine staatsrechtlich-politische Abhandlung* (Weltgeist 1845).

65 Preamble of the French *Charte constitutionnelle* : '*l'attente de l'Europe éclairée*'.

66 cf art. 112: The present Constitution is to be made subject to a revision by (ordinary) legislation (Articles 60 and 106) immediately after the first meeting of the chambers.

67 cf Giuseppe Mecca, 'The Omnipotence of Parliamentin the Legitimisation Process of 'Representative Government' under the Albertine Statute (1848–1861)' in Müßig (n 20) 183.

68 cf Richard Albert, 'Constitutions imposed with consent?', Chapter 5 in this volume.

69 Formula borrowed from Lacchè (n 3) 291.

dualism (*Dualismus*).[70] Predictably, the monarch retains the executive power and cedes parts of the legislative power to an assembly, justice remaining exercised in the name of the king. The transfer of competences to a parliament, consisting typically of two chambers, entails a self-limitation of the former absolute monarch and contributed to establish the first practices of parliamentarism.

The Portuguese *Carta* innovated insofar as it introduced a fourth power, named 'Moderating Power' (*Poder moderador*). It attributed inter alia an absolute veto to the monarch over legislation emanating from parliament. This moderating power was the exclusive competence of the King, as supreme head of the Nation, to watch over its independence, as well as for balance and harmony among the other political powers. As the holder of this power, the King was called furthermore to convene the Cortes; to appoint the Kingdom Peers; to dissolve the Chamber of Deputies; to appoint and dismiss the Government; to suspend magistrates and to grant amnesties and pardons.

In addition, some rights are granted to the citizens. The French Charter of 1814 thus contains a chapter dedicated to the 'Public Law of the French' reaffirming liberal fundamental rights as permanent achievements of the Revolution. As the octroyed charters always strictly limited the right to vote by strict rules on censitary vote and indirect suffrage, they belong to the liberal non-democratic type of Constitutions.[71] In the German monarchies of the 19th-century electorate was for instance limited to less than 1% of the population for the election of the lower house.

Compared to the previous situation, however, they still do appear in a number of cases as improvements. The constitution of Prussia 1848/1850 guaranteed for instance the 'Rights of the Prussians' as citizens' rights comprising equality, personal freedom, inviolability of residence, freedom of opinion and of the press and freedom of assembly.

Some observers underline the 'incompleteness' of octroyed constitutions as one of their specific features.[72] The French Charter of 1814 obviously lacks a rule of devolution of the crown and a procedure of amendment. This must be understood as an inevitable consequence of the fact that the king's sovereignty remains exterior to the granted constitution. Regarding the absence of rules of devolution of the crown, the same is true for the Constitution of Luxembourg from 1841 and even for the current constitution dating back to 1868.

As a natural effect of the mentioned incompleteness, octroyed constitutions left a broad margin for interpretation. Their exact meaning was often disputed because of ambiguous formulations, leaving place for both a royalist and a liberal

70 Regarding the influence of dualism in Luxembourg, see Luc Heuschling, *Le citoyen monarque. Réflexions sur le Grand-Duc, la famille grand-ducale et le droit de vote* (Larcier 2013) 117.

71 cf Dieter Grimm, 'Types of constitutions' in Michel Rosenfeld, András Sajó (eds), *The Oxford Handbook of Comparative Constitutional Law* (OUP 2012) 119.

72 cf with regard to the French Charter : Stefan Rials, 'Essai sur le concept de monarchie limitée (autour de la Charte de 1814)' in Stefan Rials (ed), *Revolution et Contre-Révolution au XIXè siècle* (Albatros 1987) 96.

lecture. Flexibility was thus a common feature of the granted charters. As judicial review was regarded as incompatible with the monarchical principle, there was no 'authentic interpreter' but the king himself.

VI Amendment: Who is entitled to revise the octroi?

The question of amendment of octroyed constitutions leads to interesting but divergent outcomes regarding existence, nature and practice of an amendment power. As a consequence of the inherent ambiguity of octroyed constitutions, many discussions took place regarding the question of the constitution's binding character on the conceding monarch. Within the German constitutional monarchies, the prevailing position was that the constitution, once granted by the king, could no longer be modified or withdrawn unilaterally. A revision had to be decided jointly by the Monarch and the people's representatives, as with ordinary laws. When, for example, the King of Hanover unilaterally abolished the constitution in 1837, this was regarded as a breach of the law, and was proclaimed as such on September 18, 1837 by seven professors of the University of Göttingen.[73] For the first time in German history, they postulated the continued validity of the constitution (one of the constitutions of estates under the Federal Act) by risking their own existence.[74]

Their position was consistent with articles 54 and 56 of the Vienna Final Act. Article 54 reaffirmed the duty of the States to establish a constitution. The Confederal Assembly had to monitor that this regulation did not remain unfulfilled in any Confederal state. In theory, subjects were able to file a complaint if this did not happen. In practice, this meant little as long as the leading states of Austria and Prussia refrained to adopt constitutions. According to Article 56, 'the constitutions of estates standing in recognized validity can only be changed by constitutional means'. Therefore, monarchs could not lawfully change or abolish the constitution, not even in a coup d'état. The terms 'recognized validity' referred to the fact that a constitution was actually applied. The expression was meant to exclude attempts to restore ancient constitutional law, theoretically valid, which had not been applied since absolutism.

The donor's de facto power to revoke the Constitution unilaterally did not disappear completely. The Austrian Empire created the precedent. First the *Pillersdorffsche Verfassung* was repealed in July 1848 and later replaced by the octroyed Constitution of March 1849. But the latter was once more retracted by the imperial patent of 31 December 1851, the so-called *Silvesterpatent*.[75] So, a process of neo-absolutist reorganization of the state, announced since the defeat of the Vienna uprising in October 1848, took place in the Austrian Empire.

73 cf Wilhelm Bleek, Bernhard Lauer, 'Protestation des Gewissens. Die Rechtfertigungsschriften der Göttinger Sieben' (2012) 36 Schriften der Brüder Grimm-Gesellschaft.

74 In fact all of them were dismissed and three even banished from the country.

75 Published in the imperial official journal, RGBl. no 3, 1852, 27.

During the Restoration period it wasn't evident at all how to establish a '*pouvoir constituant dérivé*' distinct from the monarch's '*pouvoir constituant originaire*'. In some cases, the question was therefore simply left open. The French Charter of 1814 gave the example. In absence of an explicit amendment procedure, it was in fact amended either following the ordinary legislative procedure or, in case of necessity acknowledged by the king, by royal ordinances.[76] The only tangible obstacle to amendments was the promise made by Louis XVIII at the end of the preamble octroying the Charter 'both for him and his successors and forever'.[77] But this promise could easily be modified by agreement between the King, holding the monopoly of legislative initiative, and the two houses of Parliament. Some important amendments were adopted by the houses upon royal proposal in the form of ordinary legislation.[78] The Italian *Statuto albertino*, as well, did not provide for an amendment procedure. However, in practice, it was later amended by ordinary laws and consequently qualified as flexible constitution.

Within the member states of the German Confederation the situation was different. Most of their constitutions contained precise rules on amendment. In Luxembourg, article 52 of the 1841 constitution of estates, required, for instance, the election of a Chamber with twice the number of members, a procedure respected in 1848 but violated by the coup d'état of 1856. The German constitutions, established by octroi in the period of the early constitutionalism, also recognized the necessity of special rules for amendment. A two-thirds majority in both chambers was commonly required to revise the constitutional act. Yet, in spite of the shared exercise of the amendment power, the monarch retained the right to sanction all legislative acts and held a veto right.[79] The constitution of Prussia of 1848/1850 established a flexible procedure. Amendments were to be adopted by the king and both chambers through the procedure applicable for ordinary legislation (art. 60 and 106).

Portugal's *Carta* of 1826 knew the most detailed procedure as described in its articles 140–143. Any proposal of revision had to be supported by a third of the members of the chamber of deputies and the first amendment being allowed only after the end of an initial four-year period. A proposal had to go through three readings in the Chamber and to be submitted for final approval to the Chamber in the following legislature. This procedure was only required for 'constitutional provisions', defined by article 144 as 'those who concern the limits and respective powers of the Political Powers, and the individual and political rights of the Citizens'. Everything 'not constitutional' in this sense could be amended according to the formalities applying for ordinary legislation. Four additional acts were

76 cf Lauvaux (n 6) 5 who quotes two ordinances of July 13, 1815 and August 19, 1815.

77 Orig: '*tant pour lui que pour ses successeurs et à toujours*'.

78 cf Georg Jellinek, *Allgemeine Staatslehre* (3rd edn, Häring 1914), 527, mentioning the legislative act of June 9, 1824, modifying the rules on the renewal of the house of deputies from partial to integral renewal; Adhémar Esmein, *Eléments de droit constitutionnel français et compare* (6th edn, repr. Editions Panthéon-Assas 2008) 575.

79 cf Hummel (n 23) 7 quoting the amendment procedures in Bavaria and Baden.

published in 1852, 1885, 1895–1896 and 1907, but only the second one strictly observed the detailed rules on amendment.[80]

In absence of specific rules on amendment the development of some octroyed constitutions materialized naturally through informal constitutional change. This was, for instance, the case of the *Statuto albertino* that remained in force for almost a century. According to its wording, the government was responsible to the king only. Originally, it was understood as a rather conservative document that set up a strong constitutional monarchy. But its spirit was subsequently altered, at first in a liberal way, to adapt it to the parliamentary government of the late 19th and early 20th centuries, and then in an authoritarian direction under Benito Mussolini's Fascist regime (1922–1943).

Having examined process, form, legitimacy, substance and amendment of octroyed constitutions in 19th-century Europe, a clearer picture emerges as to what they really were. To answer the question raised in the title of this contribution: No, octroyed constitutions should not be considered as imposed constitutions. They form a category of their own. Moreover, it should be avoided to equate imposed constitutions with octroyed constitutions or to use the term octroi in a general manner to describe imposed constitutions.

Our Japanese colleague, Yasuo Hasebe, said that 'whether a constitution is imposed is a question of degree, not a question of kind'.[81] In my opinion, an octroyed constitution is a kind of its own. It is decreed by a monarch claiming to hold the '*pouvoir constituant*' through divine providence. It is in most cases domestically enacted and it is also self-imposed by a, more or less, enlightened monarch who sacrifices, more or less, voluntarily parts of his absolute power to share their exercise with a parliamentary body. As these charters commonly confirmed some of the liberal achievements of post-revolutionary constitutionalism they encountered tacit approval or passive tolerance of the peoples considering the substantive achievements resulting from the monarch's 'gift'.

Bibliography

Bastid Paul, 'La théorie juridique des Chartes' (1953) 11 Rev. int. d'histoire politique et constitutionnelle 163

Fernandes Paulo Jorge, 'Os Actos Adicionais à Carta Constitucional de 1826' (2012) 13 Historia Constitucional 563

Ferreira Oscar, 'Les équivoques du "constitutionnalisme octroyé": un débat transatlantique I' (2015) 16 Historia Constitucional 67

Hartwig Matthias, 'What Legitimises a National Constitution. On the Importance of International Embedding', in Armin von Bogdandy, Pal Sonnevend (eds) *Constitutional Crisis in the European Constitutional Area,: Theory, Law and Politics in Hungary and Romania* (Bloomsbury Publishing 2015)

80 cf Miranda (n 10) 50; Paulo Jorge Fernandes, 'Os Actos Adicionais à Carta Constitucional de 1826' (2012) 13 Historia Constitucional 563.

81 Hasebe (n 4) para 1.

Hasebe Yasuo, 'Imposed Constitutions (constitutions octroyées)', *Max Planck Encyclopedia of Comparative Constitutional Law*, 2016

Hummel Jacky, 'La Charte française de 1814 et le deutscher Konstitutionalismus : les inflexions d'une réception durable' (2014) 13 *Jus Politicum* 1

Kirsch Martin, *Monarch und Parlament im 19. Jahrhundert. Der monarchische Konstitutionalismus als europäischer Verfassungstyp – Frankreich im Vergleich* (Vandenhoeck & Ruprecht 1999)

Kotulla Michael, *Das konstitutionelle Verfassungswerk Preußens 1848–1918* (Springer 2012)

Lacchè Luigi, 'Granted Constitutions: The Theory of Octroy and Constitutional Experiments in Europe in the Aftermath of the French Revolution' (2013) 9 EuConst 285

Lacchè Luigi, 'Las Cartas otorgadas. La teoría de l'octroi y las experiencias constitucionales en Europa post-revolucionaria' (2010) 6 Fundamentos 269

Lacchè Luigi, 'Le carte ottriate, La teoria dell'octroi e le esperienze costituzionali nell'Europa post-rivoluzionaria' (2009) 18 Giornale di storia costituzionale 229

Lauvaux Philippe, 'La technique de l'octroi et la nature de la Charte' (2014) 13 Jus Politicum 1

Müßig Ulrike, 'Juridification by Constitution. National Sovereignty in Eighteenth and Nineteenth Century Europe' in Ulrike Müßig (ed.), *Reconsidering Constitutional Formation I National Sovereignty, A Comparative Analysis of the Juridification by Constitution* (Springer Open 2016)

Prutsch Markus J., *Making Sense of Constitutional Monarchism in Post-Napoleonic France and Germany* (Palgrave Macmillan 2013)

Sardica José Miguel, 'A Carta Constitucional portuguesa de 1826' (2012) 13 Historia Constitucional 530

Stolleis Michael, 'Oktroi, oktroyierte Verfassung', in *Handwörterbuch zur deutschen Rechtsgeschichte*, HRG III (Erich Schmidt 1984) 1230

Voegelin Eric, Ruth Hein (tr.) and Gilbert Weiss (ed.), *The Authoritarian State: An Essay on the Problem of the Austrian State*, *Collected Works of Eric Voegelin* vol 4 (University of Missouri Press 1999)

7 Inter-venire, sed ubi ire?

'Imposed' constitutions, the 'will' of 'the people', and the eye of the beholder

*Zoran Oklopcic**

Introduction: The 'imposed constitution' as an artefact of the theoretical imagination

Though many have prognosticated its demise, the concept of a sovereign people continues to exist as the privileged arbiter, warden, and manager of our political expectations. What sustains its hegemonic grip over our social imaginary is not only our willingness to take it for granted, but also the cumulative work of all those who, as professional thinkers, help keep it alive as a perceptually credible, politically sensible, and ethically imperative political concept. What allows them to portray it as such are the conceptual templates in which 'the people' appears either as the predicate, or, more often, as the subject across different propositions of peoplehood: the *bearer* of constituent power; the *holder* of the right to self-determination; the *source* of ultimate constitutional authority; the *subject* of constitutional self-government; and the *equal*, among equally sovereign peoples. Together, these propositions lend theoretical dignity to the social imaginary of popular sovereignty. Together, they also shape folk imaginations of scenes that evoke that people as the author of its constitution and the source of its authority—the only agent vested with constituent power, the right to self-determination, and control over the institutions of its self-government. From that perspective, everything else—authoring a constitution by *someone other* than 'the people'; locating the source of constitutional authority *someplace else* than in the inextinguishable will of the people; exercising *pouvoir constituant* by those who, unlike the people, won't end up being governed by the resultant *pouvoir constituée*; frustrating legitimate claims to popular self-determination; or restricting the scope of popular self-government—must count as illegitimate violations of the ideal of popular sovereignty. From that perspective, all imposed constitutions are *normative oxymorons*—even when

* Please do not quote or cite—comments welcome oklopcic@gmail.com

they are regrettably accepted as the lesser of two evils or as the devices that sometimes facilitate the transition towards popular self-government.[1]

Until quite recently, constitutional theorists remained silent on the phenomenon of constitutional imposition, irrespective of their longstanding preoccupation with the ontological status and normative implications of the mythical narratives of founding, constitutional moments, original contracts, irruptions of constituent power, and other scenic representations of the act of constitution-making. Implicitly, however, their attitudes towards imposed constitutions gravitate either towards the template of 'normative oxymoron', or—much more rarely, but with increasing frequency—towards the template of 'ontological pleonasm'. While the former draws normative implications from the imagination of scenes in which a popular sovereign establishes a constitutional order for itself without interruption from the outside, the latter proclaims these scenes unintelligible. From the perspective of the latter, all constitutions are in some sense 'imposed' in real life, hence ontological pleonasm.[2] For the most part, however, both camps recoil from drawing links between their implicit imaginations of the scenes of constitution-making and the increasingly important real-life phenomenon of imposed constitutionalism.

To an important extent, their reticence stems from their disciplinary attachments, theoretical vocabularies, professional self-images, and scenic imaginations. If you are, for example, a constitutional theorist preoccupied with the ontological nature of the acts of constitution-making (which your discipline traditionally envisioned as localized consequences of constituent power) you will be less likely to devote your attention to the normative framework that ought to govern the behavior of external actors in regional conflicts over territorial self-determination. What will solidify your disciplinary gaze, however, is not only your belief that tackling those phenomena is someone else's disciplinary 'job', but also a chastened sense of the nature of the social practice in which you participate as a theorist, jurist, philosopher, or a political scientist. Oftentimes envisioned as a 'conversation', that practice presumes conformity with its disciplining template, which compels the participants to converse by exchanging statements such as:

1 The *X* of *Y* in the context of *W*, from the perspective *Z* is ABC
2 ABC is DEF than … (1)'

where *X* stands for the meaning, structure, function, importance, promise, or peril; *Y* for the 'will', 'constituent power', 'sovereignty', or 'right to self-determination'

1 cf Simon Chesterman, 'Imposed Constitutions, Imposed Constitutionalism and Ownership' (2005) Conn L Rev 947, 954. ('The job, then, of … international actors must be to create not just a constitutional space but a political space in which a population can begin a conversation about what kind of country they want theirs to be'.)

2 For the most forceful expression of this position among constitutional lawyers, see David S. Law, 'The Myth of the Imposed Constitution' (2013) Legal Studies Research Paper No. 13-05 (1 May 2013). For a less radical vision of the 'pleonastic' perspective on imposed constitutionalism, see Richard Albert, infra note 48.

of a 'people'; *W* for a historical era, geographical location, or particular arena of struggle, or nothing in particular; Z for a particular discipline (constitutional theory, international legal theory, normative political theory, democratic theory) or a particular 'approach' (ontological, normative, systems-theoretical, historical-sociological, and so on); ABC for the substance of the contribution; DEF for *more* 'coherent', 'attractive', 'productive', 'comprehensive', 'accurate', and so on; and, finally, (1) for the argument of one's opponent. But Kenneth Burke reminds us, every such disciplinarily disciplined utterance is an act of imagination, which, whether intended or not, carries imaginative consequences: in every such case, the chosen terminology 'establish[es] a circumference [and] mark[s] the outer boundaries of the ground that is to be covered'.[3] In turn, every 'choice of circumference [will always have] a corresponding effect upon the interpretation of the act itself'.[4]

For the purposes of this essay it is irrelevant whether those who theorize acts of constitution-making ignore the imaginative character of their theoretical practice or whether they refuse to exercise their imaginative freedom by transcending the traditional frame of the scene of constitution-making (spatially narrow and temporally brief). Had they expanded their view, they would have had a harder time ignoring *everyone else*—before, during, and after the act of constitution—as potential external constituent powers.

At this point, it is more important to pause and take notice of *two scenic choices* that unite those who do and those who do not attribute the act of constitution-making *exclusively* to the agent(s) that will end up living under the authority of that constitution.

First, even when they recognize the constitutive agency of agents other than those above, the latter never choose to *keep* them on the stage of constitution-making. In that regard, they resemble the former. Second, even when they recognize that the agency of external constituent powers (co-)determines the spatial, temporal, material, and personal aspects of the constitutive act, their imaginations end up compulsively affirming the constitutive agency of a wilful, self-determining, popular, or people-like political community.

I emphasize these commonalities for three reasons. On the one hand, they give us a clear sense of two ways in which it is possible to deviate from the prevailing imaginations of imposed constitutionalism: first, without retouching external others from the scene of constitution-making; and second, without reconciling ourselves with the performative contradiction implicit in the image of a self-constituting peoplehood. On the other hand, the two commonalities also allow us to get a better sense of the registers of theoretical imagination, whose work makes the idea of imposed constitutionalism intelligible. That imagination is scopic, scenic, *and* dramatistic. Its practitioners are not simply cameramen, stage-setters, and screen-writers; they are also dramatists, the creators of

3 Kenneth Burke, *A Grammar of Motives* (first published 1945, University of California Press 1968).

4 ibid.

'representative anecdotes', which in most cases represent one constitutive protagonist to the exclusion of all others and which always end with a successful act of constitution-making. Finally, the two commonalities discourage us from imputing scopic naïveté or dramatistic timidity to those who gaze at the scenes of constitution-making from their disciplinarily self-disciplined vantage points. For example, it is perfectly possible to be keenly attuned, as are Chaihark Hahm and Sung Ho Kim, to the way in which the 'artificial freezing' of our mental frame contributes to 'our habit of thinking that the constitution is an inanimate object created by a single, pre-existing, and readily identifiable agent', *and still not allow* other agents—now visible after the act of un-freezing—to figure in the scene of foundation as co-constitutive. In this case, it is obvious that an embrace of the paradox of constitution-making as Hahn and Kim demonstrate has nothing to do with their scopic naiveté and everything to do with hopes they harbor about the ethico-political productivity of concealing constitutive others under the picture of a chicken-and-egg dilemma. Or, in their words:

> [a] successful founding is one that establishes a framework within which conversation continues to take place among the people. By enabling the ongoing conversation, that is, the constitutional structure set up at founding allows the people to engage in the endless activity of self-constitution.[5]

Notice, however, that the clause, 'allows … to engage in the endless activity of self-constitution'[6] can function as part of Hahm and Kim's argument only if we understand it as the communication of the content of their expectations and expectant emotions, not as the expectation-free description of a state of affairs. Put differently: (one of) the reason(s) why Hahm and Kim refuse to inscribe external *pouvoirs constituants* onto the scene of constitution-making in Korea and Japan is that they either *worry* that the ongoing 'endless activity' might become meaningless without the picture of self-constitution, *hope* that this picture might stimulate citizens to take part in such an activity in the future, or *bet* that the chances of that occurring are higher with the visual aid of 'self-constitution' than without it. If so, their imagination of the scene of constitution-making is not only scopic, scenic, and dramatistic. It is also *prognostic* (in that it imagines pros and cons of different future scenes of constitution-making); *affective* (in that it is shaped by their hopes, anxieties, and political desires); and, last but not least, *polemical* (intent on shoring up the perceptual credibility of liberal-democratic constitutionalism). In the context of this essay, this means that the new scene of constitution-making I begin to sketch in section 2 cannot hope to attract sympathy without the complementary effort to identify the reasons that speak against the two-fold choreographic move on which it relies in section 3.

5 Chaihark Hahm and Sung Ho Kim, *Making We the People: Democratic Constitutional Founding in Postwar Japan and South Korea* (Cambridge University Press 2015).
6 ibid.

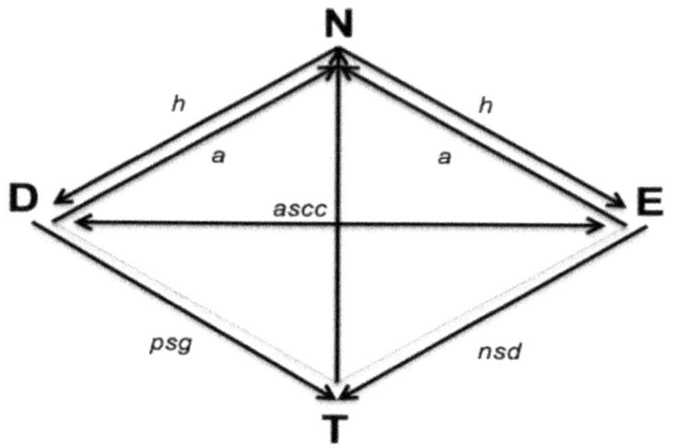

Figure 7.1

In the eye of the beholder: *demos*, *ethnos*, *nomos*, *telos*... *xenos*

The 'experimental' scene of constitution-making developed in this paper hinges on a two-fold act of imagination: first, it 'agentifies' part of the 'scenic environment' of constitution-making in the figure of *xenos*; second, it 'de-agentifies' the figures of *demos* and *ethnos*—which in most of our folk imaginations still exist as the exclusive protagonists in the drama of constitution-making. Doing is destined to disrupt the web of conceptual relationships among N (*nomos*), D (*demos*), T (*telos*), and E (*ethnos*)—summarized in the TEND parallelogram in Figure 7.1.

From the perspective of the TEND diagram, *demos* and *ethnos* may be seen in two ways. On the one hand, they may be seen as the competing interpretations of the identity of the holder (h) of the right to self-determination—the norm whose validity depends on its membership in *nomos*, best described with reference to what Christian Reus-Smit called a 'justificatory framework'[7]: the system of 'deep constitutional norms which define certain units of authority as legitimate, specify the scope of their respective authority, and define how they stand in relation to one another'.[8] On the other hand, *demos* and *ethnos* may be seen as the *authors* (*a*), not the products, of the overarching normative frame. In contrast to the first understanding—which will more likely be embraced by international lawyers—the second one will follow more naturally from the perspective of constitutional theorists who envision peoples as self-constituting (*demos*), or as pre-existing,

7 Christian Reus-Smit, *The Moral Purpose of the State: Culture, Social Identity, and Institutional Rationality in International Relations* (Princeton University Press 1999) 10.

8 Christian Reus-Smit, 'The Concept of Intervention' (2013) 39 Review of International Studies 1057.

institution-independent, collective political subjects (*ethnos*). Either way, the interplay between *demos*, *ethnos*, and *nomos* will make the *telos* of constitution-making appear self-evident, and, as a result, uninteresting from both theoretical and polemical perspectives.

Seen from the side of *nomos*, the *telos* of popular constitution-making must be seen as derivative (d) of whatever happens to be our understanding of the *telos* of those deep constitutional norms. Seen from the side of *demos*, the act of constitution-making presents itself as an exceptional moment of democratic self-government. From that perspective, the purpose of that act exhausts itself in the creation of an institutional framework that will perpetuate that practice in the 'normal' mode, as well as to create the possibilities for its occasional change via constitutional amendment. Seen from the side of *ethnos*, the purpose of the act of constitution-making must be viewed through the lens of national self-determination. From that perspective, *ethnoi* establish new constitutional orders with an aim of establishing an institutional environment capable of protecting and promoting historically crystallized attributes of nationhood. From the perspective of its members, every act of constitution-making is an act of their self-determination. Finally, Figure 7.1 allows us to see *demos* and *ethnos* not just as competing understandings of constitutional authorship or the meaning of the right to self-determination, but also as poles in the conceptual architecture of a sovereign people, which, from the perspective of the *demos/ethnos* binary, reveals itself not just as polemical, but also as an asymmetric counter-concept. As was the case with other similar concepts in history, the left side in the dichotomy Greek/Barbarian, Christian/Heathen, or *demos/ethnos* incarnates 'the claim to universality' that enables those who invoke its name to 'discriminate against those who have been defined as the "other"'.[9]

As will soon become apparent, emplacing *xenos* on to the scene of constitution-making is destined to have a two-fold effect. On the one hand, *xenos* will keep reminding us of three external dimensions of constituent power that are ignored by mainstream constitutional theory. The first is the manifest constituent power implicit in the acts of persuading, seducing, cajoling, or forcing relevant antagonists—otherwise captured by the labels of '*demos*' or '*ethnos*'—to engage in the act of constitution-making on terms that are, in most cases, only marginally theirs. The second is the elusive constituent power of *hospitable environment*. As Edward Casey argued, 'to be emplaced is not just to be cozily contained by an encircling surface but to be sustained by powers that ensure that what is in place will be inherently stronger for having been there'.[10] Finally, the third dimension of external constituent power manifests itself in the capacity of *xenos* to act as an agent of symbolic empowerment by elevating the dignity of some struggles by

9 Reinhart Koselleck, *Futures Past: On the Semantics of Historical Time* (Keith Tribe tr, first published 1979, Columbia University Press 2004) 156–157.

10 Edward Casey, *The Fate of Place: A Philosophical History* (University of California Press, 1998) 89.

associating them with *demos*, and in doing so diminishing the symbolical capital of others relegated to the inferior position in the *demos/ethnos* polemical binary.

On the other hand, introducing *xenos* to the scene of constitution-making will also have the effect of diminishing the intelligibility of the conceptual scheme summarized in Figure 7.1. Without a *demos* or an *ethnos* to single-handedly *will* a new constitutional order into existence, we also must rethink the web of meanings these two figures otherwise make possible:

- the character of the right to self-determination without the holders to claim them (*h*),
- the meaning of popular self-government without the subjects to exercise them (*psg*),
- the meaning of national self-determination without the subject to enjoy them (*nsd*) and,
- the *telos* of *nomos* (now without the 'wills' of the 'peoples', which thus far allowed us to satisfy ourselves with the image of a peaceful co-existence of sovereign states, as its pre-eminent objective).

The answers to these questions will emerge gradually at different points in this essay and will be diagrammatically summarized in its conclusion. At this point, however, it is critical to stress the importance of one additional imaginative variation without which we would not be able to approach the diagram with new eyes. In order to look beyond *demoi* and *ethnoi* as the peoples that author them, we must do the same with the *xenoi* whose constituent power puts them in shape. To do so, we must move beyond our contemporary *nomos*, whose deep constitutional norms of sovereign equality and self-determination make such a move inconceivable. Instead, we need to imagine *xenos* less parochially: still as a figure of external intervention—which may or may not culminate in the exercise of its constituent power—but not as a figure exclusively related to a historical *nomos* in which intervention exists as the other of (popular) sovereignty.[11] Following Reus-Smit,

> the idea of intervention assumes an initial realm of differentiation: it assumes the extraneous and the intrinsic, the exogenous and the endogenous. Without this assumption of initial differentiation, the idea of coming in as something extraneous makes no sense. Second, intervention is an act of transgression, a crossing or violation of lines of differentiation. To intervene is to enter from the outside as an outsider. Third, intervention is purposive, it is to transgress with intent. … Finally, [a]ctors intervene to alter

11 For the most influential argument along these lines in 'constructivist' IR scholarship, see Cynthia Weber, *Simulating Sovereignty: Intervention, the State and Symbolic Exchange* (Cambridge University Press, 1995) 128. See similarly, Helle Malmvig, *State Sovereignty and Intervention: A Discourse Analysis of Interventionary and Non-Interventionary Practices in Kosovo and Algeria* (Routledge 2006).

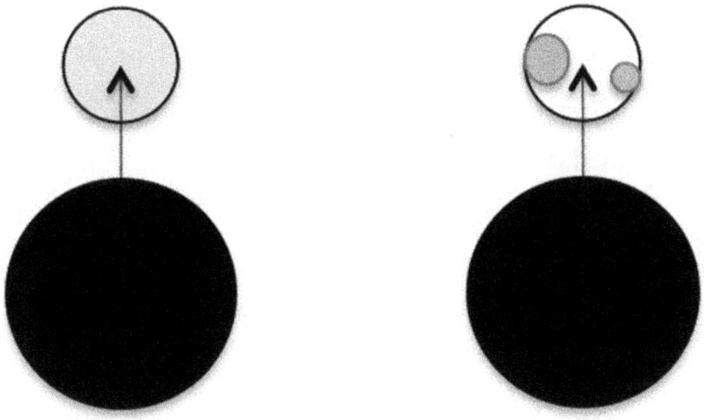

Figure 7.2

> endogenous processes and to bring about outcomes that would otherwise not have occurred. Interventions often have unintended instead of intended consequences, but transformative intentions animate them nonetheless.[12]

Notice, however, that when Reus-Smit says that 'to come *between* so as to prevent or modify a result', this must presuppose not one, but two 'initial realm[s] of differentiation'— two 'exogenous' and 'endogenous' realms, not one. Put differently, to *inter-vene*, the intervener must operate in the context of two outsides: the first one presupposed in the verb *venire*—arrive (in)to something and not something else (*i*); and the other, presupposed in the preposition *inter*: to position oneself, after having arrived, in 'between' those who are already within (*ii*) (Figure 7.2).

So in order to intervene, the intervener must transgress the boundaries of both inside/outsides, and in doing so, determine for himself the meaning of both: first, when he decides to transgress the authority of units predefined by *nomos*—or what Reus-Smit called 'deep constitutional norms, which define certain units of authority as legitimate, specify the scope of their respective authority, and define how they stand in relation to one another'; and second, when he decides how to act transgressively, which involves imagining the identity of relevant agents in the conflict. However, in failing to represent *xenos* as an agent in constitutive anecdotes, contemporary dramatizations of constitution-making also fail to reveal the choice that every *xenos* confronts in making those determinations. On the one hand, *xenos* can approach those determinations hermeneutically—as a matter of interpreting extant, governing *nomos*. In that case, the interpretation of *nomos* would determine

12 Christian Reus-Smit, 'The Concept of Intervention' (2013) 39 Review of International Studies 1057, 1065.

the identity of both inside/outsides at the same time. On the other hand, *xenos* can approach these determinations aspirationally—as a matter of conformity with its vision of the *telos* of the world. In that case, the determination of the existence, shape, and location of insides and outsides will also be shaped by the way in which *xenos* exercises its scopic imagination—by the way in which it frames the conflict. As Martti Koskenniemi argued in the context of self-determination conflicts in the former Yugoslavia, '[w]hat appear as "minorities" from an extensive gaze (when focusing on "Yugoslavia") will turn themselves into majority populations once one's focus is closer (on "Croatia", say)'.[13]

Like all accounts that evoke the figure of external interveners, this is an act of imagination that privileges some constitutive anecdotes at the expense of others. By way of example, consider the way in which your sense of 'intervention' changes from Scene 1 to Scene 2. In Scene 1, after a relaxing walk in the forest, you suddenly encounter a scene of a fistfight between two boys. Coming closer, you realize that the older one—tall, fat, and strong—is actually savagely beating the younger one. In Scene 2, instead of two little boys you encounter two groups in a dark alley, whose members are armed and ready to start shooting at each other. Now ask yourself: how would you react in each case? Would you intervene and stop the fight? How would you do so: by beating the older one, or by taking the younger one by his hand and taking him home? If you did neither, but attempted to separate them on the spot, how long would you linger around? Would you try to reconcile them and impose on them the commitment to resolve their differences peacefully from now on? Or would you just force them to stop and quickly move on?

For Reus-Smit, interventions are marked by transformative intentions. But even if you 'intervened' on the second scene, how reasonable would it be to call you an intervener? Equally, how sensible would it be to treat your decision not to get involved as an act of 'non-intervention', which 'means about the same as intervention', as famously claimed by Marquis de Talleyrand? In Scene 1, your failure to act intervened on the side of one party. In Scene 2, your failure to act cannot do so because it cannot even register as potentially transformative. I emphasize this because it provides us with the first attribute of *xenos*, as a figure of external intervention and constitutional imposition. That attribute is neither subjective nor objective, but relational: to qualify as *xenos*, his constituent power must be comparatively overwhelming—sufficient enough to make his chances of affecting the outcome of a conflict worth inscribing into the scene of constitution-making. Only in that case it is possible to agree with Frederick Schauer's remark that

> non-involvement is not an option, not only because of their influence and pervasive reach, but also because, even nominal non-involvement sends out

13 Marrti Koskenniemi, 'National Self-Determination Today: Problems of Legal Theory and Practice' (1994) 43 ICLQ 241, 260.

> signals and thus has influence. These entities must decide how to exercise their influence, and to what substantive end. But there is no not deciding.[14]

Notice also that the intentions of *xenos* must not only be 'transformative', as Reus-Smit rightly observed, but must also be presumed as, in principle, ambivalent, existing somewhere in the middle of the spectrums of *predictability*, *reasonability*, and *other-regard*. First, in order to make sense as an exercise by an agent, 'intervention' (or 'imposition') must not be imagined as an act of nature, which means neither as fully unpredictable (tsunamis, earthquakes) or fully predictable (sunrises, sunsets, high and low tides). Second, in order to be meaningfully attributed to an agent, intervention must be performed by someone who is, in principle, amenable to persuasion, which—third—means that such agent must not be imagined as always and exclusively being driven by self-regarding considerations.

While implicit in Reus-Smit's account of intervention, *xenos* is a figure that is nowhere to be found in constitutional theory: a body of thought most explicitly and directly preoccupied with the acts of constitution-making. The only exception is Carl Schmitt's *The Theory of the Partisan*, which evokes the scene of political struggle in a way that deviates not only from most of modern and contemporary dramatizations of constitutional subjects and their agency, but also from most of Schmitt's own constitutional thought. In that work, the scene is populated not by sovereign peoples, but rather by 'partisans' and 'interested third parties', who belong to their 'situation'—the actual protagonists whose struggle set the stage for the act of constitution-making in the name of one or another 'people'.[15] While not actively participating in the activity of constitution-making, Schmitt is clear that the *Interessierte Dritte* performs an 'essential function' that is, for all intents and purposes, constitutive. By 'providing the link for the irregularity of the partisan to a regular so that he remains within the realm of the political', the *Interssierte Dritte* keeps his constituent power alive, preventing him from 'falling like the thief and the pirate into the unpolitical, ... criminal sphere'.[16]

Before moving on, it is important to take notice of a subtle scopic choice that allowed Schmitt to envision the interested third party this way, because we must rely on the same approach if we want to keep the figure of *xenos* intelligible for the purposes of this essay. In order to inscribe *xenos* as one of the protagonists in the scene of constitution-making, *demos* must appear not just as the name for the 'product' of that act, but also as the figure that conceals *etairos*: the figure of a partisan, whose identity is something that *xenos* determines for itself every time it joins the scene of constitutional struggle. Earlier in this section we saw that *xenos* may (but also may not) do so by interpreting the ruling *nomos*. That has its reverse side, which Schmitt's account makes manifest: partisans stand on

14 Frederick Schauer, 'On the Migration of Constitutional Ideas' (2005) Conn L Rev 905, 917.

15 Carl Schmitt, *The Theory of the Partisan: A Commentary/Remark on the Concept of the Political* (AC Goodson tr, Michigan State University Press 2004) 61.

16 ibid.

an equal plane with those whom they resist, even when they struggle against the authorities of recognized states. As a matter of scopic imagination, this requires an oscillating gaze capable of inhabiting the minds of those who appear on the scene. The partisan '*knows, and accepts*'—writes Schmitt, reporting the partisan's inner thoughts—'that the enemy places him outside law, statute, and honour'.[17] But instead of judging him prudentially or morally, Schmitt simply concludes that 'the revolutionary fighter does this too, and declares the enemy a criminal and all concepts of law, statute, and honor an ideological fraud'.[18] Instead of dismissing partisans on moral or prudential grounds—a move that would enable us to more confidently proclaim the spatiotemporal integrity of a sovereign state—Schmitt detects the objective political symmetry in mutual recriminations, which can be identified *only* if we continue oscillating between two antagonistic perspectives. The perspective that shapes that scene, as one commentator noted, is 'prior to, and outside, the assumptions of state and sovereignty', and does not 'axiomatically seek[] to defend the existing order'.[19] In the context of such scene, the partisan is not the protagonist of constitution-making but a figure of 'conceptual danger'. As such, it sets us on a trajectory of 'radical and accelerating political dissolution' within which a state can only be imagined as a 'parody' of political order.[20]

Constitutive anecdotes and their scenic environment

While the aim of this essay is not to problematize or critique such verdicts, they do alert us to the work of other dimensions of constitutional imagination, which also shape the way in which we think of popular sovereignty, constitution-making, and, in special cases, the phenomenon of imposed constitutionalism. To get a sense of their influence, however, we need look no further than Schmitt himself, and his more widely discussed figurations of political agency in which there is no room for *xenos* as a figure of external constitutional agency. Instead, his *Concept of the Political* evokes either enemies or tutors. The former wish 'destroy our way of life', while the latter will 'protect[] [us] against foreign enemies and thereby tak[e] over political rule', if we, as 'a people' are too 'afraid of the trials and risks implied by existing in the sphere of politics'.[21] Notice that in both cases, speaking of 'intervention', 'imposition', or external 'participation' makes no sense, even though the consequences of the behavior of the enemies and tutors is, in both cases, constitutionally consequential. What makes both figures unworthy of dramatization is not the absence of drama surrounding their acts, but rather

17 ibid 20.
18 ibid.
19 William Hooker, *Carl Schmitt's International Thought: Order and Orientation* (CUP 2009) 165.
20 ibid 193.
21 Carl Schmitt, *The Concept of the Political* (Georg Schwab tr, first published 1932, The University of Chicago Press 1996) 30.

the pointlessness of treating them as reminders of something problematic that may elicit a creative response from those who confront them on the scene of constitutional struggle. As 'enemies', they are there to be defeated and nothing else. As 'tutors', they are there to draw consequences from our failure to act and are in that regard similar to Rousseau's *Lawgiver* (another external agent whose constitutive agency is not intrusive but selfless, nurturing, and indispensable—in the best interest of those subject to his constitutive intervention).

I mention this because here we see one of the dramatistic 'tricks' that prevent *xenos* from appearing on the scene: the trick, in this case, is not to evoke an undifferentiated environment of the state of nature, or 'isolation', but rather to portray other agents as unworthy of special attention by portraying them in black and white: either as existentially threatening or as existentially nurturing, and as nothing in between. What informs this choice? Schmitt, for one, is very clear about a myriad of ways in which we can exercise our visual imagination by selecting, mixing, and matching a number of diverse images. In that way,

> The king can appear as God, and God as a king. But God can also be imagined as the world's electric motor, and the electric motor as a kind of machine that moves the world. Finally, human beings all refer to such images for their own self-understanding and they comprehend themselves through their psycho-physiological apparatus scientifically, as if through a kind of space-shuttle. All of this can be expressed in polymorphic metaphors. The huge Leviathan, Thomas Hobbes' state, is tetramorphic: as well as being the great but mortal god, he is a huge animal, and, furthermore, a large man and a big machine.[22]

A better sense of what informed his dramatistic choices can be gleaned from his private postwar correspondence, in which the work of other aspects of the affective dimension of his imagination becomes more apparent:

> The indeterminacy of the enemy evokes anxiety (there is no other kind of anxiety, and it is the essence of angst to sense an indeterminate enemy); by contrast, it is a matter of reason … to determine who is the enemy (which is always the same as self-determination), and with this determination, the anxiety stops and at most fear remains.[23]

From this perspective, Schmitt's friend/enemy distinction presents itself not as an accurate description of the logic of the formation of political 'entities' but as a visual therapy for his own anxieties. Without the requisite 'contrast', as the one represented in Rubin's vase on the left (Figure 7.3) there would be no way—Schmitt

22 Carl Schmitt, *Political Theology II: The Myth of the Closure of any Political Theology* (Michael Hoetzl and Graham Ward tr, first published 1970, Polity 2008) 57.

23 Quoted from Gopal Balakrishnan, *The Enemy: An Intellectual Portrait of Carl Schmitt* (Verso 2000) 113.

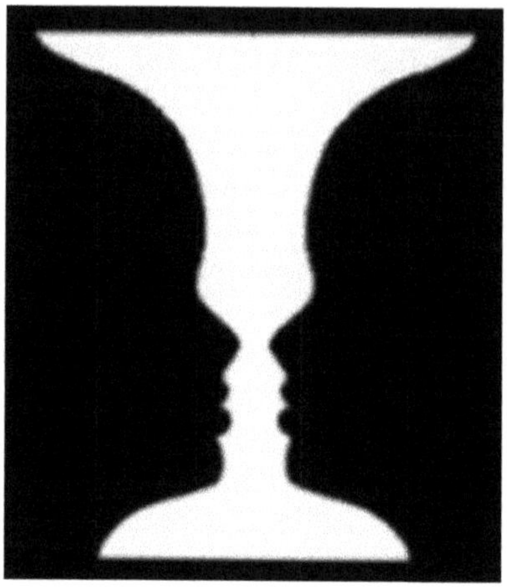

Figure 7.3

Figure 7.4

seems to suggest—in which we could imagine ourselves as politically meaningful ('vase') without the stark background. Without it, we would disappear into a thin air of political meaninglessness (Figure 7.4).

On closer inspection, Rubin's vase is somewhat misleading, as a metaphorical representation of Schmitt's anxiety. What endows political meaning to white and black surfaces as political 'entities'—from Schmitt's perspective—is the *sharpness* of contrast between them, not any particular configuration in which they present themselves as 'silhouettes' or the 'vase'. And this, it should be noted, has an implication that Schmitt was unwilling to accept: if the intensity of contrast *alone*

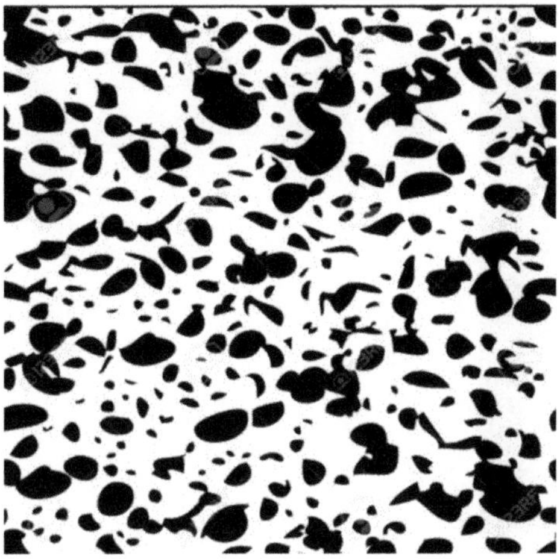

Figure 7.5

is the criterion of the political, we need not rely on any particular arrangement of the relationship between the black and the white, nor do we need to remain committed to the preservation of their distribution. Instead of Rubin's vase, the mental image informing such understanding of the political might as well be any black spotted coat of a Dalmatian dog, whose spots may or may not have faded away. Within this image, no one 'constitutes' anyone: what plays the constitutive function is the genetic code of our Dalmatian canine friend, the genetic algorithm that prefigures this pattern.

Schmitt eventually came to this conclusion in *The Nomos of the Earth*, where he attributed constitutive agency not to a flesh-and-blood agent, but to a mythical *nomos*, as the name for someone's (it does not matter whose) 'constitutive *act*' of land appropriation, which, from a broader, global perspective, presents itself as a comprehensive normative framework comprised of 'public and private principles and procedures for territorial changes'.[24] Though such *nomos* justifies the creation of new polities and shapes global territorial changes, its continuing operation critically relies on a global constellation of political power. In such a constellation, great powers serve as 'agents and guarantors' of global territorial order, tasked with the role of 'adjudicating territorial changes'.[25] That is the second dramatistic 'trick' that keeps *xenos* from appearing on the scene of constitution-making: rendering it politically unproblematic by portraying its constitutive involvement as juridical in nature.

24 Carl Schmitt, *Nomos of the Earth in International Law and Jus Publicum Europaeum* (Telos Press 2003) [emphases added].
25 ibid 191.

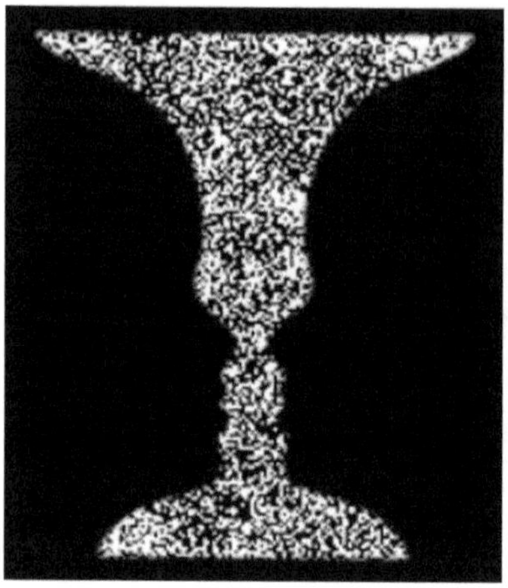

Figure 7.6

The third 'trick' can be gleaned from the work of the most influential contemporary Schmittian, Chantal Mouffe. It consists of hiding *xenos* in plain sight, on the scene in which political identities must always be constituted against a 'constitutive outside'. From the perspective of political ontology, that 'outside' must be understood as a necessary, but not sufficient, condition of every constitutive act, broadly understood. From the perspective of dramatistic imagination, however, the 'constitutive outside' is the result of a choice of how to view the scenic environment of such an act without representing concrete agents as constitutive. That choice is not forced by ontological necessity, but rather the other way around: a 'constitutive outside' is chosen to represent ontological necessity in order to make an ethical message of that vision of constitution-making more evocative. For this reason, 'outside' is 'not simply the outside of a concrete content but something which puts into question "concreteness" as such'.[26] Thus understood, the constitutive outside is 'a content, which, by showing the radical undecidability of the tension of its constitution, makes its very positivity a function of the symbol of something exceeding it: the possibility/impossibility of positivity as such'.[27] From Mouffe's perspective, the constitutive role of black silhouettes establishes the white space as a politically meaningful subject-vase, *but*, at the same time, estranges us from fully believing in that subject's political identity (Figure 7.6).

The elements in that inner diversity may be seen as political subjects during, and for the purposes of, political *struggle*, but are not political subjects for the purposes of its *outcome*. A constitutional subject is not the partisan; it is the

26 Chantal Mouffe, *The Challenge of Carl Schmitt* (Verso 1999) 12.
27 ibid.

people. By putting its identity in perpetual doubt, Mouffe's interpretation of the constitutive outside accommodates the fact that there is no homology between the actual subjects and the imagined collective beneficiary of constitutional struggle. Ignoring the spatial aspect of that struggle, however, allows her to ignore the *distributional* question that presents itself once we allow more diversity into the picture of the constitutive inside and outside.

The next scenic 'trick' can be gleaned from another contemporary adaptation of Schmitt's constitutional theory, which, instead of the friend/enemy distinction, takes as its starting point Schmitt's account of constituent power. That power, as Andreas Kalyvas argues, belongs not to a 'commanding', but to a 'founding' sovereign, and is the manifestation of the capacity of a sovereign to create a new political order 'ex nihilo'. Thus understood,

> instead of stressing the discretionary power of a superior command emanating from the *top*, the notion of the constituent sovereign redirects our attention to the underlying sources of the instituted reality located at the *bottom*.[28]

At this point, we must pause and ask: *where* is everyone else? If constitution-making occurs 'at the bottom', where is everyone else *around*? Kalyvas doesn't consider this question. In fact, his etymological argument, which associates the Latin '*constituere*' with *con-statuere*, with the prescriptive meaning of '[c]onstituent power'—as a 'demand[ ] that those *who are subject* to a constitutional order co-institute it'—distracts us from questioning the identity of agents involved in the act of constituting.[29] But what enables Kalyvas to do this is not simply his focus on the etymology of 'constituting', but rather its specific dramatistic character of a 'stance word', uniquely capable of 'merging intrinsic and extrinsic reference',[30] so that Casey's point—that '*statuere*' in *con-statuere*, 'is not just to be cozily contained by an encircling surface but to be sustained by powers that ensure that what is in place will be inherently stronger for having been there'—never occurs to us as a challenge to our idea of constitution-making.

What helps that 'trick' succeed is not simply the stance character of constitutionalist vocabulary that makes us indifferent to the agents within 'an encircling surface' of the act of constitution-making, but also Kalyvas' strategic use of the present tense—his claim that constituent power 'demands that those *who are subject* to a constitutional order co-institute it'—which can only be made if Kalyvas presupposes the 'encircling surface' *and its other*: *the surface which it encircles*, whose role is to serve as the territorial referent of the act of constitution-making. In other words, in order to be able to say 'those who are subject', Kalyvas must smuggle onto the scene of co-institution, before it actually occurs, a common

28 Andreas Kalyvas, 'Popular Sovereignty, Democracy, and the Constituent Power' (2005) 12[2] Constellations 223.

29 ibid.

30 Burke (note 3) 51.

referent that establishes the *fact* of their subjection. With the help of Rubin's vase, we can see the difference between Schmitt's own, and Kalyvas's neo-Schmittian, dramatistic 'tricks'. While Schmitt relied on the allegedly inevitable ontological character of antagonism (Figure 7.3) and, later, on the prefigurative power of *nomos* (Figure 7.5) to conceal the external constituent agency of external agents, Kalyvas relies on the help of stance words to predefine the location of the act of constitution-making and in that way render irrelevant the constituent power of those who inhabit its surrounding environment. That way, the act of co-institution may be portrayed as fully voluntary—as in Figure 7.7—even if, for all intents and purposes, it is critically predetermined by those who have defined the spatial shape of the 'vase'—the territorial referent of constitution-making.

At this point, a Burkean dramatistic perspective allows us to ask a scholarly 'inconsiderate', even pointless question: what is the point of issuing normative prescription in the form of an etymological argument if Kalyvas could make that point independently? Likewise, if Kalyvas only wanted to dignify the spontaneity of constitution-making outside constitutionally prescribed procedures, he could have done so without the anecdote where a number of individuals embark upon the project of 'co-instituting'. However, Kalyvas' argument *is* necessary in the form in which he makes it (including his reliance on the visual 'tricks' of stance words) if one wants to have it both ways, lending political dignity to popular uprisings outside of the prescriptive frame of liberal-democratic constitutionalism *and* postulating a normative frame for evaluating the legitimacy of an act of constitution-making as the culmination of a successful popular insurgency.

This is why *xenos* must never appear on the scene of constitution-making, though for reasons radically different from those that animated Schmitt's own constitutional theory, where the 'Other' appeared either as an enemy, a protector,

Figure 7.7

or an arbiter, and when it appeared as an *Interessierte Dritte*—someone who directly belonged to 'the situation of the partisan'—in a materially, not formally constitutive role. Before moving on, it is important to notice that the exclusion of *xenos*—the figure of the other, co-constitutive, external agent—is not just a defining feature of those constitutional theories, such as Schmittian ones, which privilege antagonism and spontaneous outbursts of popular 'will' as the defining features of constitution-making. In fact, most contemporary constitutional theory, including the markedly anti-Schmittian, banishes other agents from the scenes of popular decision-making, some of which, like Claude Lefort's, do so explicitly. For Lefort, the 'Other' must be 'abolished' for the sake of evoking a vision of democracy in which 'power belongs to no one'[31] and which allows for a 'controlled challenge' of political authority and its 'creat[ion] and re-creat[ion]' in the name of the people.[32] Or, to put it in terms of Rubin's vase from Figure 7.3, perceiving the dark silhouettes as the figures of the Other—and not abolishing them—would cause the white space to lose its intelligibility as the site of collective self-government. Instead of being an object invested with meaning—a 'vase'—it would return to existing as a *meaningless*, not meaningful, empty space between the silhouettes. To perpetuate the idea of a people as a collective, willing agent, silhouettes must therefore retreat into nothingness. Moreover, if we did not abolish the Other,

> the authority of those who make public decisions [would vanish], leaving only the spectacle of individuals or clans whose only concern is to satisfy their appetite for power [and] [s]ociety [would be] put to the test of a collapse of legitimacy … by all the signs of the *fragmentation* of the social space, of heterogeneity.[33]

And even worse: were the figure of the Other not abolished, 'an index of social unity and identity [would] become invested with fantastic power and the totalitarian adventure [would be] under way'.[34] 'The question is, also and above all', as Slavoj Žižek noted in a different context, 'which secret privileging and inclusions/exclusions had to occur for this empty place as such to emerge in the first place'? While Lefort never confronted this question, he did make a cryptic remark that brings us to the theme of the section that follows: 'the ultimate reference to the identity of the People *as the instituting Subject*, proves to mask the enigmatic arbitration of Number'.[35]

31 Claude Lefort, *Democracy and Political Theory* (Polity 1988) 225.
32 ibid 230.
33 ibid 233 [emphasis mine].
34 ibid.
35 ibid [emphasis mine].

From Lefort's *demos* to Kelsen's *nomos: Xenos* and its reverse side

What is meant by this 'arbitration'? Why is it enigmatic? How does the 'reference to the identity of the People' mask it? While attributing the constitutive act to 'the people' and its will may mask a swarming plurality of individual aspirations—and in so doing tone down our Schmittian anxiety, as we saw in the preceding section—none of the scenes of constitution-making so far have evoked the 'arbitrating' function alluded to by Lefort. The best sense of its content and the way in which it is masked by 'the people' comes not from the representative anecdotes in the canon of constitutional theory, but rather from a legal positivist, Hans Kelsen, and his quasi-psychoanalytical account of the 'essence and value of democracy'. Because our 'basic instincts' cannot stand the image of an 'alien will that subjugates one's own', Kelsen argued that we conjure the image of a sovereign people: a 'mystical general person' that allows us to imagine ourselves as both norm-takers and norm-makers.[36] On Kelsen's view, the 'will' of 'the people' is not simply a metaphor that is divorced from individual aspirations to escape the torment of heteronomy, but rather a mechanism that actually helps them to do so. In contrast to other forms of political decision-making, the majority vote requires 'fewer ... individual wills ... for changing the will of the state' and in that way makes the '[a]ccord between the individual will and the will of the state ... easier'.[37] Thus, '[a]s many people as possible shall be free, that is, as few people as possible should find their wills in opposition to the general will of the social order'.[38] Put differently: when it manifests itself in a majoritarian democracy, the so-called will of the so-called people is a manifestation of 'the tendency to unanimity in the formation of the will of the community' and embodies the aspiration to achieve 'maximum possible [individual] freedom'.[39] Notice, however, that to be imagined as a technique that makes '[a]ccord between the individual will and the will of the state ... easier',[40] the majority vote can only be intelligible if we re-imagine the act of constitution-making in three mutually compatible ways. First, we must imagine it as an act of heteronomy—an act belonging not to the people, but to someone else. Second, we must imagine this act as neither good nor bad, but rather as a condition of social order. Finally, in order to be able to imagine the function of the majority vote in such a way, we must move beyond the images of a collective self-constituting wilful agent that prevent us from imagining a never-ending oscillation in the content of individual political aspirations over time. As a result, 'the people' cannot be a collective person, but rather one among many 'provisional entities', which 'rise like waves in the sea and after

36 Hans Kelsen, 'On the Essence and Value of Democracy' in Arthur J Jacobson and Bernhard Schlink (eds), *Weimar: A Jurisprudence of Crisis* (University of California Press 2000) 84, 88-89.

37 ibid 87.

38 ibid.

39 ibid 101.

40 ibid 87.

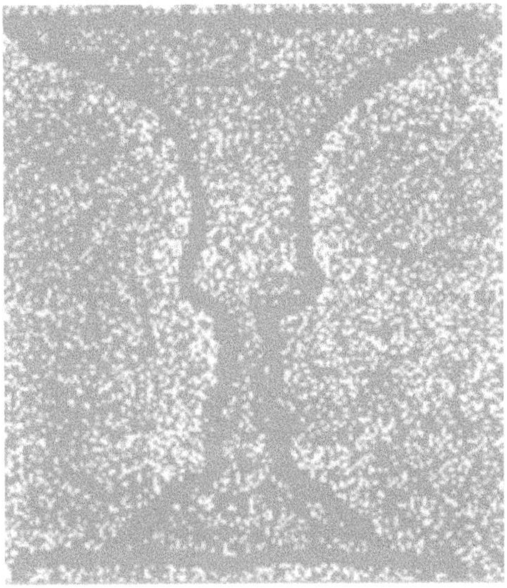

Figure 7.8

a brief space [are] lost again in an ever-changing ebb and flow' in a wider 'ocean of psychic happenings'.[41] In such a scene, there are no external constituent powers ('silhouettes'), and no internal peoples ('vases') whose identity they prefigure. Instead, both are—if they are democratic—subject to the ideal of 'maximum possible [individual] freedom'[42] (Figure 7.8).

In *On the Essence and Value of Democracy*, however, the operation of this imperative is still local, not *yet* crystallizing into a criterion of state-formation. The first reason for its absence in that essay has to do with the Rousseauvian road that Kelsen takes to arrive at it, essentially noticing that the same charge Rousseau makes against the English—who are famously said to only be free at the moment of parliamentary elections—can be raised against the alternative Rousseau himself prefers (direct but still *occasional* democracy). From this, Kelsen concludes that

> even if the governing will of the state arises directly from referendum, the individual is free only at one moment, only while voting, and only if he votes with the majority and not with the outvoted minority. Therefore, the democratic principle of freedom appears to demand that the possibility of being outvoted be kept to a minimum.[43]

41 Hans Kelsen, 'The Conception of the State and Social Psychology—With Special Reference to Freud's Group Theory' (1924) 5 International Journal of Psycho-Analysis 1, 9–10.

42 Kelsen (note 36) 101.

43 ibid 86.

The second reason has to do with preserving the intelligibility of the ideas of the state, law, and order, which must logically presuppose the discrepancy between the individual wills and the corporate wills that rule them. We cannot pursue the tendency towards unanimity *openly* and to the *extreme* because this would render it impossible for the state to tell us *not to*. Finally, the third reason why Kelsen did not treat the tendency towards unanimity as the content of Framework in his 1928 essay has to do with his claim that the 'majority vote' as a technique of approaching unanimity is a 'democratic ideology', not a principle operative in reality. Instead, Kelsen makes clear (though not unequivocally) that, in reality, the majority vote exists as a technique of social compromise, which, instead of *serving* individual 'basic instincts', *demands* from them a compromise-friendly 'relativist *Weltanschauung*'.[44]

A decade and a half later, however, Kelsen drew global and real-life political implications from the logic behind the majority vote, which he previously insisted must be seen as localized and, for all intents and purposes, inoperative. Unlike in 1928, in imagining a potential world federation in 1942, Kelsen abandons his earlier idea that 'democracy contents itself' with approaching unanimity only domestically:

> [I]f one assumes as the fundamental principle of democracy not only equality but freedom, freedom in the sense of self-determination, and if one takes as the unit, from a collectivistic viewpoint, national communities, not human individuals, then one must admit self-determination of peoples as a democratic requirement; and one must also admit that a community of states approaches the democratic ideal more closely by way of decentralization than by way of centralization. The problem is to unite a number of states whose nationals differ from one another in language, culture, and history, and who feel themselves different. If matters that the people of a member state regard as their own are regulated by norms are created by a central organ in which these people are not represented or are represented inadequately, then these people will feel themselves injured in their right to self-determination. They will then demand decentralization in the name of the democratic right of self-determination, and will prefer a purely international organization of the community of states to a federal one. The principle of international law that binding decisions can be reached only by unanimity, that no full member of the community can be obligated against its will, corresponds to the idea of self-determination.[45]

To grasp the significance of these remarks, it is important to underscore what Kelsen means by 'decentralization': *not* the decentralization from a somehow

44 ibid 108.

45 Hans Kelsen, *Law and Peace in International Relations: The Oliver Wendell Holmes Lectures, 1940–41* (first published 1942, William S Hein & Co 1997) 141–42.

more abstractly centralized international order of sovereign states, but rather *the secession from his imaginary world federation*, which would help us approach 'the democratic ideal' on the world stage—unanimity.[46] Put differently: a local (domestic) majority vote in favour of 'secession' from an imagined world federation would be a move towards unanimity globally. While Kelsen quickly retreated from this conclusion, in his *Holmes Lectures* he considered it not simply as prudential, but also ethically imperative.

> A satisfactory solution of the territorial problem is, therefore, possible only on the basis of the principle of self-determination. We must try to realize the right of self-determination of the peoples as extensively and honestly as possible. Where minorities are unavoidable they are to be organized as entities with constitutional rights.[47]

Apart from the fact that Kelsen himself soon abandoned this argument, several other things prevent us from envisioning 'the people' and its 'will' along the lines he suggests. At a more superficial level, what prevents us from envisioning popular sovereignty as a device that contributes to the maximization of satisfied allegiances—not only *locally* (within an existing polity) but also *regionally* (within the space of conflict over territorial sovereignty) as well as *globally* (within the world organized in conformity with the principles of sovereign equality and self-determination)—is the perspective and the frame we assume when we gaze at the situations in which the people exercises its 'will'. For the most part, our gaze approaches these situations sideways, looking only at the spatiotemporal referent, whose destiny is being decided by a 'wilful' popular sovereign. That act of scenic imagination is described in Scheme (2) in Figure 7.9.

From the perspective assumed in Scheme (2), the 'will' of 'the people' must be imagined as a force that rightfully changes the jurisdictional 'position' of a pre-existing unit (described as a cylinder above) between two moments: t1 (before it became manifest) and t2 (after the moment of its manifestation). In that sense, the 'will' is the power that operates the juridical elevator: it 'lifts' the designated units up (towards sovereign statehood), or down (towards extinguishment). Imagining the effects of the popular 'will' through the lens of Scheme (2) prevents us from ever comparing the effects of t1 and t2. In contrast, had our mind's eye been gazing at the same scene from above—as depicted in Schemes (1) and (3)—we would have immediately realized that heeding the will of the people of one segment of a constitutional space reconstitutes it in its *entirety*. It is only

46 This homology between domestic and international tendency towards unanimity—something, which, in my mind, also suggests that Kelsen considered this aspiration an operational ideal in real life—is absent from rare contemporary theoretical interpretations of Kelsen's account of democracy. For the most recent 'Habermasian' reading of Kelsen, see for example Nadia Urbinati, *Democracy Disfigured: Opinion, Truth and the People* (Harvard University Press 2014) 76 *passim*.

47 Kelsen (note 45) 160.

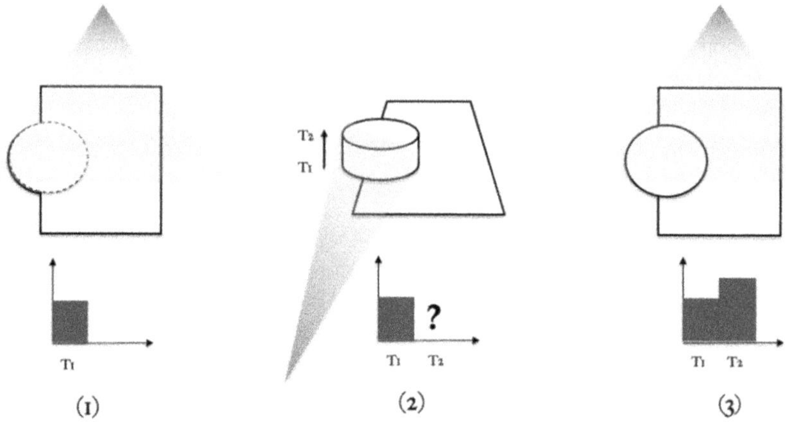

Figure 7.9

against the backdrop of these two schemes that the question of what happens to the overall consent between t1 and t2 becomes intelligible. From the perspective entailed in Schemes (1) and (3), 'the people' and its 'will' are juridical constructs intended to contribute to the approximation of the ideal, implicit in the ways in which we think about the spatiotemporal reconfiguration of democratic constitutional orders. That ideal is not 'self-determination', but rather the overall increase in constituent allegiances, understood as satisfied identifications with a particular constitutional order. Seen in that light, every manifestation of the 'will' of the people is intended to indicate which constellation contributes to that ideal better: the status quo (Scheme (1)) or its reconfiguration (Scheme (3)). The purpose of mediating that judgment via the vocabulary of the will of the people is to diminish the anxieties that inadvertently follow such judgments. Without the vocabulary of peoplehood, such judgments would reveal themselves as what they are: inconclusive and therefore contestable verdicts about what degree of increase in satisfied constitutive attachments is good enough. The vocabulary of peoplehood prevents this, potentially paralyzing contestation by mobilizing the secular-theological aura of incontestability to such essentially contestable judgments. This does not mean that the vocabulary of popular sovereignty is 'secularly theological', as Schmitt claimed, but rather that it must appear as such in order to serve the Kelsenian 'tendency' of 'maximization' *effectively*. Put differently: serving that tendency *furtively*—hiding the aggregative effects behind the imagery of popular 'will' and its binary choices—is what keeps it operative.

Beyond *demos*: Symbolical advantage and the configuration of responsiveness

Though it confronts us with an uncomfortable vision of the world—in which everyone ideally gets everything he or she wants, everywhere, all the time—following

Kelsen down the rabbit hole of popular sovereignty is productive, as it allows us to reimagine the *nomos* that aspires to regulate conflicts over territorial sovereignty beyond the inflaming vocabulary of the right to national self-determination. Without Kelsen's help, that vocabulary was destined to remain apodictic and incommensurable: if you think that your *demos* has a right to self-determination in a particular location, you will be destined to reject as illegitimate or unintelligible similar claims made in the name of an *ethnos* and its right to self-determination, and vice versa. With Kelsen's help, we see these incommensurable claims for what they are: competing assertions about what level of satisfied constitutive identifications is good enough. With Kelsen's help, such conflicts transform themselves from categorical to distributional, without any party having to abdicate the substance of its claim first as the price of seeing the point of their antagonist. From that perspective, *demos* and *ethnos*—as the most popular images of 'holders' of the right to self-determination—present themselves not only as the contingent predictions of what degree of aggregate satisfaction is enough within the space-time of a particular constitutional order, but also as the symptoms of the degree of satisfied attachments that *xenos* thinks is good enough, from the perspective of its own self-interest.

This claim sounds opaque until we remind ourselves of the polemical character of all political concepts like 'the people', including its more specific figurations such as *demos* (a territorial 'people') and *ethnos* (non-territorial 'nation'). From the perspective of these two figures, 'the people' reveals itself as an *asymmetric counter-concept*, with *demos* as a rhetorically superior pole within a *demos-ethnos* binary. When we invoke it to justify a particular outcome, 'the will of a *demos*' allows us not only to claim that the *nomos* that pre-approved it is on our side, but also to cast our opponents as the other-of-*demos*: the partisans of *ethnos*. In presenting ourselves as forward-looking, rational, and civic-minded citizens, we also present our opponents as passionate, resentful, atavistic, or petty ethnic nationalists; religious fundamentalists; or, more broadly, dangerous political radicals. While amply critiqued in the scholarship on nationalism and popular sovereignty, one thing about this binary escaped the attention of contemporary political theorists. Those who invoke the will of *demos* do so not because they schematically embrace a territorial receptacle that most obviously serves their purpose, but because they *bet* that it is *that* receptacle that enjoys the constitutive support of *xenos*—all those on the outside, who have the capacity to affect the success of our struggle.

This has additional implications. By deferring to *demos*—in hope that doing so will enhance the perceptual credibility of the ideal of equal concern and respect—we agree not to challenge the way in which *xenos* calibrates the scale of its constitutive involvement by selectively dignifying some agents as '*demoi*' and devaluing the symbolical capital of others by identifying them as '*ethnoi*'. To remain silent before the way in which *xenos* uses the symbolical power of the *demos-ethnos* binary as a tool in calibrating the scope and scale of its involvement is to allow it to use moralistic subterfuge to discourage the consideration of other imaginable constitutional outcomes that might require *xenos* to exercise its external *pouvoir constituant* in ways that would be inferior from the perspective of its own interests, but superior from the perspective of those who will end up living under new *pouvoirs constituées*. Finally, from a theoretical perspective, seeing *xenos* as an agent that uses '*demos*' and '*ethnos*' as labels that allow it to distribute symbolical capital in the field of struggle—according to what it thinks is good enough—challenges the way in which we generally think about imposed constitutions: either as oxymoronic and illegitimate, as exceptionally legitimate if constitutive of the capacity of a people to govern itself, or as inevitable and thus unworthy of critical scrutiny.

Set against the scene that makes the *xenos-demos-ethnos* dynamic manifest, the first approach presents itself as too critical: it neglects the element of truth in Talleyrand's claim. In environments marked by gross power differentials, an act of non-intervention will be an act of intervention, which contributes to a constitutional imposition that favours someone over someone else. Set against the same scene, the second approach presents itself as too *unimaginative*: while it makes *xenos* accountable for the way in which it behaves during and after the period of post-conflict constitution-making, it lets it 'of the hook' when it comes to the character and scope of its constitutive involvement. Finally, the same perspective (with Kelsen's help) allows us to see the third approach to imposed constitutions as too indifferent towards the *attitude* of their institutions. Put differently, even if it is true that all constitutions are in some way 'imposed', this still leaves open questions about their responsiveness to the sentiments that Kelsen identifies as the 'torments' of heteronomy.

To dispense with this question by treating it as a matter of institutional output legitimacy (representative democracy) or sociological output legitimacy (popular support) hinges on a chastened sense of their relationship with *constitutional responsiveness*: the imperative of government inscribed into 'imposed' and non-'imposed' constitutions alike. In addition to helping us reframe apodictic conflicts over the right to self-determination in distributional terms, Kelsen's approach to popular sovereignty also allows us to detect a misleading lack of granularity involved in liberal-democratic descriptions of representative democracy as a regime that 'ensure[s] some measure of responsiveness to the people by representatives and political parties who speak and act in their name'. Following Kelsen, representative democracies entail not simply 'some measure' of responsiveness, but also a forthcoming *attitude*—on display in 'the tendency towards unanimity', served by every act of majority voting. While Kelsen argues that such acts make escape from the torment of heteronomy 'easier', his claim can be further refined once we realize that the criterion of 'ease' can be interpreted as a stand-in for several other, not necessarily mutually compatible, dimensions of responsiveness encoded in the constitutional provisions that regulate the process of popular self-government.[48] By way of example, consider the following four.

48 cf Richard Albert, 'Imposed Constitutions with Consent?' (2017) Boston College School of Law Research Paper 434, 1, 2. ('Imposed constitutions … sit along a scale of heteronomy'.)

First, depending on its *sensitivity* towards the amount of expressed political aspirations, a constitutional order may be more or less responsive in triggering the occasion of democratic decision-making. From the perspective of sensitivity, constitutional orders that allow for a constitutional referendum or a constituent assembly to be triggered by popular initiative, or those that entail the possibility of recalling elected officials, are more responsive than those without such provisions. Next, depending on its attitude towards the number of political preferences it aims to satisfy, the responsiveness of constitutional orders can be distinguished along the dimension of *plenty*. Modern constitutional orders calibrate the degree to which they satisfy the imperative of plenty through a combination of different devices. From the perspective of contemporary constitutional theory, these devices—from the recognition of 'creed' as a ground of discrimination in human rights legislation in Ontario to the cascading referendums used to carve out new cantons in Switzerland—appear incomparable. What they have in common is service to an underlying constitutional ideal: the more satisfied political preferences, the better, whether it is the case of vegetarian meal options in Canada, or belonging to the canton of one's choice in Switzerland. Finally, in addition to sensitivity and plenty, the final two imperatives—*agility* and *reliability*—shape the content of constitutional responsiveness that hides under the concepts of popular will, collective self-government, and representative democracy.

On the one hand, agility denotes the speed with which a constitutional order reacts to the impulse for democratic change. On the other, reliability denotes the likelihood of translating the option chosen by a majority vote into government policy without distortions. For the most part, our imaginations of popular self-government as representative democracy blindside us not only to the existence of more specific imperatives of responsiveness, but also to their specific spatial and substantive distribution within a particular constitutional order, and may exist at different scales and across the public/private divide, which we take for granted. Though this quasi-geological morphology of constitutional responsiveness is in principle conceivable in isolation from our imaginations of the scenes of constitution-making, what increases our chances of doing so are the scenes which do not feature the peoples as the agents that exercise their 'wills' in the exceptional moments of their self-government, but rather those in which the constituent power of another agent—*xenos*—makes the very idea of popular 'will' dubious from the start.

Beyond *demos*: From constitutional self-government to 'empowered' democracy

Another cursory glance at Rubin's vase allows us to see what must be kept suppressed for the sake of the perceptual credibility of such proposals. As we can see from the image in Figure 7.10, an empty place of power cannot serve as the receptacle for every imaginable purpose: the 'vase' can be filled with wine, grain, or even sand—but not with bricks.

Figure 7.10

As Schmitt argued long ago, '[t]he external territorial form with its linear boundaries [is] guaranteed, but not its substance, i.e., not the social and economic content of territorial integrity'.[49] While Schmitt made that point in the context of the Monroe Doctrine, it is still valid today—long after the Monroe Doctrine ceased to be the hallmark of American hegemony, the conceptual point behind it still stands: by entertaining ourselves with visions of ongoing conversations and endless activities, we recoil from the truth that stares us in the face: that international 'markets', military alliances, and regimes of international finance, trade, and migration render some conversations and activities impossible from the very outset.

As I suggested a moment ago, the choice between a scene that foregrounds this 'scandal' and a scene that keeps it suppressed will depend not only on what one considers to be scandalous enough, but also on one's imagination of the practical advantages of focusing on one scandal over another.[50] In most cases, this background calculus will shape a theorist's sense of worthy and unworthy ways of looking at things. Every now and then, the contours of that background judgment will present themselves more clearly. 'Staring obsessively', says Gunther Teubner, 'at power struggles in the global political arena of international politics where legal globalization takes place only partially at best, they will overlook

49 Schmitt (note 22).

50 For sympathetic critiques of Lefort's dichotomy between the people as the 'empty place of power' and the totalitarian People-as-One, see Andrew Arato, 'Political Theology and Populism' (2013) 80[1] Social Research 143, 168. For a *prudential* critique of that binary, see Ernesto Laclau and Chantal Mouffe, *Hegemony and Socialist Strategy* (first published 1986, Verso 2001) 188.

dynamic processes in other arenas where global legal phenomena are emerging in relative insulation from politics'.[51] The attempts to de-paradoxify the paradox would only result in 'temporary postponement, concealment, invisibilisation, suppression, repression', '*pensiero debole*', or 'blind experimentalism'.[52] Notice, however, that what makes Teubner's conclusion problematic is not that inescapable judgment of which way of looking at things is productive and which is not, but rather his refusal to acknowledge the element of *care* implicit in every selection of issues as 'problematic' enough.

Against Teubner, we may ask: *who cares* about 'dynamic processes in other arenas where global phenomena emerge in insulation form politics'? What if staring obsessively elsewhere provides us with an advantage, which, from Teubner's perspective, may be neither imaginable nor relevant? Why should anyone—before even exploring that possibility—take Teubner's word for granted and accept that the only kind of thinking that would result from that is *pensiero debole*? In fact, what if '*pensiero debole*' is exactly what is needed in some arenas of political struggle, such as in the nationalist conflicts over territorial sovereignty? What if the stark choice that Teubner presents us with is a matter of 'false necessity' that prevents us from imagining a different kind of political order beyond those that hinge on accepting the paradox of self-constitution?

As Kelsen helped us realize, moving beyond this paradox and envisioning the people not as an agent whose 'willing' results in an act of (self-)constitution, but rather as a device of anxiety- and allegiance-management, need not result in 'surrendering the idea of democracy'. In fact, it can provide us with new analytical devices—such as the constellation of tendential responsiveness—which give dignity to 'experimentalism', and which raise the profile of a different kind of 'empowered' democracy. The vision of such democracy is future-oriented, and 'emphasizes whatever in the experience of the individual enables him to treat others and himself as an original'. 'Addressed to the unconverted', however, such a vision must proceed from the picture they already find *familiar*: 'a regime in which the basic arrangements of social life are chosen by the wills of free and equal citizens'. In such a regime,

> no majoritarian choice destroys the framework that enables new majorities to emerge and to change or reverse earlier decisions. It is also one in which majorities do not choose to abandon individuals to a circumstance of dependence or subjugation that mocks the claim of the abandoned to be the free coauthors of the social worlds they inhabit.[53]

51 Gunther Teubner, 'Global Bukowina: Legal Pluralism in the World Society' in Gunther Teubner (ed), *Global Law Without a State* (Dartmouth 1997).

52 Gunther Teubner, 'Dealing with Paradoxes of Law: Derrida, Luhmann, Wiethölter' in Oren Perez and Gunther Teubner (eds), *Paradoxes and Inconsistencies in the Law* (Hart 2006) 60–1.

53 Roberto Mangabeira Unger, *False Necessity: Anti-Necessitarian Social Theory in the Service of Radical Democracy* (Cambridge University Press 1987) 374.

To reach the ideal of an 'empowered democracy', the 'unconverted' must 'enlarge' this understanding of democratic political order, which, for Unger, also requires 'a new democratic theory'. The figure of *xenos* contributes to that goal indirectly: it does so via a Kelsenian detour that establishes the link between founding heteronomy and the practice of collective autonomy through a majority vote. Interpreted not only as the manifestation of a binary collective choice but also as the technique of maximizing the satisfaction of individual desires, Kelsen's explanation may also be seen as an exemplar of the democratic theory Unger wished for: an account that 'weaken[s] the practical and imaginative force of the contrast between the pursuit of private interests within a framework and the self-conscious fighting over the content of this framework'.[54] Empowered democracies are purposeful in a way that is different from those that describe themselves as regimes of constitutional government in which a collective people governs 'itself'. In contrast, 'empowered democracy' is another name for a purposeful effort

> to identify and to realize arrangements exploiting the area of potential overlap between the conditions of material progress and the conditions of individual emancipation [and] moves toward the generalization of experimentalism in social life. It subjects the institutional forms of representative democracy and of regulated market economy to this same experimentalism. ... It refuses to sacrifice the plurality of human interests to a single-minded egalitarianism.[55]

With an eye on Figure 7.10, such democracies are also more and less than that: they are always constitutional enterprises devoted to the pursuit of political projects beyond their abstract commitments to the common good of 'the people'. Our current fascination with paradoxes of self-constitution is just a manifestation of a more enduring style of constitutional thought that discourages us from considering the question of constitutional *telos* more straightforwardly: without the mediation of figures such as *demos* and *ethnos*, which give us a chastened account of possible constitutional purposes, and without the mediation of legitimizing scenes of constitution-making, which help make those chastened accounts of constitutional *telos* obvious and incontestable. In order to do so, we must move beyond both the folk imaginary and the theoretical imaginations of popular sovereignty and popular constitution-making.

Conclusion: *nomos*, *demos*, *ethnos*... *telos*

While contemporary constitutional theories do not explicitly lend support either to a *demos*-based imagination of popular self-government or to *ethnos*-based imaginations of national self-determination, they build on the tradition of the

54 Ibid 376–77.

55 Roberto Mangabeira Unger, *Democracy Realized: The Progressive Alternative* (Verso 1998) 276.

scenes of constitution-making that help preserve the dual hegemony of civic and nationalistic understandings of constitutional *telos*. For our purposes, three such scenes are particularly important: first, where an act of constitution represents the moment of existential triumph over an enemy; second, where an act of constitution represents the moment of birth, which inevitably involves an expert midwife; and third, where an act of constitution represents the moment of immaculate conception, untarnished by *xenos*—an agent that (co-)constitutes, but which is not (co-)constituted in turn. In the first case, the *telos* of that act is concrete and backward-looking: by defeating an enemy, the people affirms its constitution, and in that way assures the survival of its specific 'way of life'. In the second case, the *telos* of the act of constitution is abstract and forward-looking: in exercising its constituent power, an external agent aims to shape the spirit of civic-mindedness among those who are about to exercise it in the future. The *telos* of that exercise remains unaffected by the constitutive agency of the external 'Lawgiver'. In that case, as in the case where a new constitutional order results from an act of immaculate (self-)conception, we can only get the sense of the *telos* of constitution-making from the identity of the agent, the nature of its agency, and the content of its act. In all such cases, the purpose of the act of constitution-making is to *perpetuate* nothing but the ideals already inscribed in its scenes.

Dramatized as intimately associated with the identity of the constitution-making agent, the character of its agency, or the content of its act, the purposes evoked in such scenes are formal and hollow: the purpose of self-constitution is self-government; the purpose of co-institution is the institution of a government of co-equals. Seen as the attempts to legitimize a constitutional order, they establish the source of legitimacy either in the past act of foundation, or in an atemporal connection with the constituent power of the people—as the ever-available opportunity to renew the legitimacy of the order from below—or with the atemporal *nomos* that prefigures the identity of the constitutional subject, and its autonomy, from *above*. The figure of *xenos* disrupts this theoretical imagination, and with it the web of meaning that accompanies the ideal of popular sovereignty, summarized in the diagrammatic representation of the TEND parallelogram in Figure 7.1 at the beginning of this essay. The changes which *xenos* introduces in this regard can be summarized in the adapted version of that parallelogram (Figure 7.11).

First, in comparison with the first version, represented in Figure 7.1, *demos* and *ethnos* present themselves neither as the holders (h) of the right to self-determination, nor as the authors (a) of *nomos*. In estranging us from their image of willing collectivities, the figure of *xenos* has nonetheless allowed us to reinterpret *demoi* and *ethnoi* without having to abandon them in favour of a different collective political phenomenon (e.g. 'multitude') or in the name of another comprehensive political ideal (e.g. cosmopolitan federation or global constitutionalism). Instead, following the Kelsenian logic from section 5, *demos* and *ethnos* present themselves as names for the competing regimes of cognitive economy serving, in both cases, the algorithm of allegiance (A) which conforms, in both cases, to Kelsen's 'tendency towards unanimity', this time—as Kelsen explained in his

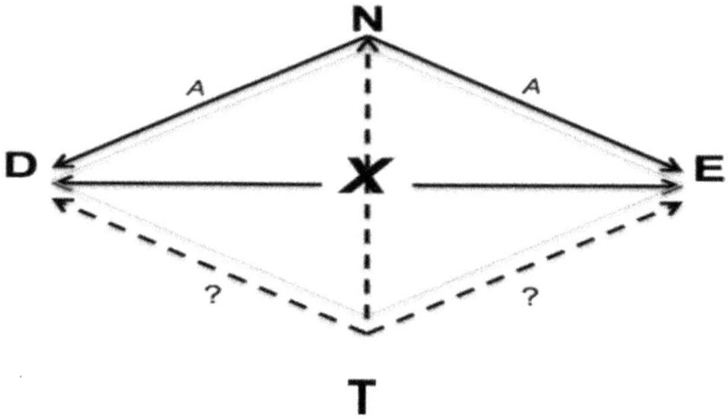

Figure 7.11

Holmes Lectures—on a global scale. Put in simplest terms: irrespective of which 'people' in whose name we reallocate territorial sovereignty, the result will be an increase in the satisfaction of constituent allegiances, not only among those who invoked their 'right', but also among those who have denied the legality or legitimacy to such invocation.

Second, allowing *xenos* to disturb the web of meaning described in Figure 7.1 also renders us more sensitive to the way in which *demos* and *ethnos* exist not simply as descriptions of two types of nationalism (good, 'civic'; vs. bad 'ethnic') or as the superior and inferior poles in an asymmetric counter-concept of sovereign peoplehood, but also as the tools used to redistribute symbolical capital among those who participate in a political struggle from *the outside*. Today, for the most part, *xenoi* rely on 'will', 'interests', or the ideal of a '*demos*' as their figures of choice, which allow them to justify the amount of political energy they are willing to spend in exercising their external constituent power. That, however, can change. Inscribing *xenos* on to the scene of constitutional imposition prevents us from forgetting that, or, to be more precise, prevents us from naively embracing *demos* as the most natural and unproblematic way of evoking the ideals of political equality and democratic government.

Finally, the figure of *xenos* disrupts our understanding of the purpose of *demoi* as the subjects of constitutional self-government and of *ethnoi* as the holders of the right to national self-determination. In the first case—on the view implicit in Figure 7.1–constitutional order must be seen as a *vehicle*, which allows *demos*, as its 'pilot', to pursue whatever goals it sets before itself in the process of democratic deliberation. In the second case, constitutional order must also be seen as a *receptacle*: it seeks to ensure the survival of whatever crystallized itself as precious enough in the life of an *ethnos* to deserve institutional protection in the future—from an elusive 'way of life' to national language, culture, and shared memories. From the perspective of Figure 7.1, such constitutional orders in both cases remain instrumental to projects that are essentially self-, not other-regarding: they are intended to serve the *telos* of the agents that established them, not the

T	Forward-looking	Backward-looking
abstract	**D**	**n/a**
concrete	**?**	**E**

Figure 7.12

teloi of others or the world. What remains beyond the ambit of our imagination is described in Figure 7.12.

That is, *teloi* which are concrete and forward-looking (described in Figure 7.12) and which may be not only self-, but other-regarding as well. Put differently, what is absent is a possibility to derive part of its legitimacy from *the future*: the anticipated capacity of a constitution to serve as a vehicle for bringing about *something tangibly better* ahead.

Contemporary constitutional theorists don't like thinking about it this way. Instead of the morphology of constituent struggles, their theories evoke abstract, austere, and hollow topologies of their outcomes. Perhaps this stylistic preference for hollow spaces—sharply at odds with the way in which early-modern thinkers evoked allegorical, but naturalistic scenes of the social contract in the state of war—is just a random variation in the way in which contemporary theorists exercise their imagination. If Ernst Bloch was right, however, that preference is symptomatic of something else: a more profound and pervasive 'nihilism of theoretical hopelessness'—indicative perhaps of an enduring post-socialist post-traumatic stress disorder of theoretical imagination—evinced in the 'aversion to the penetrating glance forwards' that keeps constitutional and other theorists in the state of 'interested dreamlessness'.[56] Oscillating between an oxymoron and a pleonasm, the concept of an imposed constitution ought to be seen in that light. It ought to be seen not just as a *problematic phenomenon*—closely related to post-conflict constitution-making—but also as *the moment for reckoning*: an occasion to step back, take Bloch's allegation seriously, and reflect on the extent of our 'nihilism', the intensity of our 'aversion', and the asking price of our 'dreamlessness'.

56 Ernst Bloch, *The Principle of Hope: Volume 3* (translated by Neville Plaice, Stephen Plaice and Paul Knight, first published in German 1959, The MIT Press 1986) 1199.

Part III

Applications

8 On the priority that Publius gives to national security in constitutional design

Reflections on the longevity of Article 9 of the Japanese Constitution

*Sanford Levinson**

Introduction: War and peace in constitutions

Perhaps the central constitutional controversy in contemporary Japan concerns the maintenance (or modification or outright repeal) of Article 9 of the Japanese Constitution that was adopted by Japan in the immediate aftermath of World War II. It has been described as "one of the three non-negotiable demands imposed on the Japanese by General Douglas MacArthur" when MacArthur in effect became the suzerain over Japan following the September 1945 surrender by Japan.[1] Under the general heading in the English-language translation of "Renunciation of War," it begins with the announcement of an aspiration to join an international community "based on justice and order," which seemingly entails that "the Japanese people forever renounce war as a sovereign right of the nation and the threat or use of force as means of settling international disputes." That is the overall aspiration. Section 2 of Article 9 provides a more specific guarantee: "In order to accomplish the aim of the preceding paragraph, land, sea, and air forces, as well as other war potential, will never be maintained."[2]

Americans often speak of "American exceptionalism." But surely Article 9 is a truly exceptional—even if not literally unique—feature of any national constitution, particularly with respect to what may be regarded as a truly "major" nation within the international geo-political community. Moreover, it has survived for what is approaching 75 years. It is interesting to compare Japan and Germany in this context, given that the German Basic Law of 1949 was also

* This chapter is drawn from remarks made at an international conference in Tokyo, Japan, in December 2016.

1 See J. Patrick Boyd and Richard J. Samuels, Nine Lives?: The Politics of Constitutional Reform in Japan, Policy Studies 19 (East-West Center, Washington, D.C. 2005), p. 2, http://www.eastwestcenter.org/publications/nine-lives-politics-constitutional-reform-japan.

2 Constitution of Japan.

the product of the utter defeat in World War II of a notably militaristic regime and the insistence by the victors that Germany take a decidedly different path in the future. Donald Kommers, the leading American authority on the German Constitution, has described the 1949 Basic Law as "a peace constitution," as "required by the Allies in the aftermath of demilitarization and fully supported by the Germans."[3] Although Article 24 of the Basic Law allowed the new constitutional regime "to enter into a system of mutual collective security (but only for peaceful purposes),"[4] the Basic Law was silent with regard to "the armed services, a commander in chief, or a military affairs power."

However, these sentiments, at least on the part of the victors, scarcely outlasted the beginning of the Cold War. Within a decade, by the mid-1950s, "Germany was being pressed, by the US in particular, to join the European Defense Community and later NATO. (The EDC went down to defeat in the French parliament.)" Joining NATO was highly controversial, "strongly supported by Adenauer and his Christian Democrats but adamantly opposed by the SPD and," says Kommers, "public opinion more generally." However Adenauer prevailed, and the Basic Law was amended "to establish the armed forces, to create a defense establishment, and to vest the command of the military in the Federal Minister of Defense." Just as important, another Amendment adopted about the same time required "compulsory military service along with a generous program of conscientious objection. A second major wave of constitutional change on these matters was the introduction of emergency powers in a new multi-paragraph section called the 'State of Defense'." Still, Kommers goes on to suggest that German society as a whole remained "very much committed to pacifism, in many cases militantly so. This culture of pacifism, especially among the young, was supported by an array of constitutional court decisions requiring parliament to approve any deployment of German troops abroad." The German court was far less deferential in the area of military affairs than the United States Supreme Court. Quite obviously, Japan was not immune to some of the same pressures by the United States to enlist in the Cold War and to engage in forms of remilitarization, but that did not happen. That fact provides much grist for the political scientist's mill.

Costa Rica is also famous for its constitutional renunciation of an armed force or, at the very least, as spelled out in Article XII of its constitution, "[t]he Army as a permanent institution is abolished. There shall be the necessary police forces for surveillance and the preservation of the public order."[5] But "Military forces may only be organized under a continental agreement or for the national defense; in either case, they shall always be subordinate to the civil power: they may not deliberate or make statements or representations individually or collectively."[6]

3 References to Kommers are drawn from an email from Donald Kommers to Sanford Levinson, 11/20/2016 4:26 PM.

4 As will be seen below, this in itself is an interesting contrast to the reading of Article 9.

5 Constitution of Costa Rica.

6 Online: http://www.therealcostarica.com/government_costa_rica/constitution_costa_rica.html#1.

It is as if Costa Ricans absorbed fully the 18th-century critiques of "standing armies." Comparative constitutional lawyers should certainly be familiar with Costa Rica, but one must acknowledge that this country, whose 2016 population remains under five million people, roughly half the population of Tokyo alone, obviously does not play the same role that Japan does in international politics.

The central point is that even those countries that subscribe to the United Nations Charter and its own renunciation of aggressive war nonetheless certainly maintain vigorous militaries with much "war potential" in order to defend themselves. Moreover, several countries, including but not limited to, Great Britain, France, Russia, Pakistan, India, China, Israel, and now North Korea, maintain nuclear arsenals in order, they claim, to credibly threaten external enemies with the prospect of retaliation as a response to attack. It is glaringly obvious that the so-called "Great Powers," for all of their opposition to nuclear proliferation, have never been willing even to consider renunciation of their own possession of nuclear weapons and of military strategies that depend on the possibility of their use.

The argument, of course, is that maintenance of such a capability helps to maintain the peace by deterring attacks in the first place. This is the basis of the slogan "Peace Through Strength." I presume that maintenance of Article 9 has been aided at least to some extent by the reality, for better or worse, of the presence of American armed forces, including the "nuclear umbrella." The "potential" for the most extreme kinds of war exists on Okinawa and other U.S. bases or, for that matter, in the promised use by the United States of intercontinental missiles should Japan come under direct attack from, say, North Korea. Whether Japan can continue any longer to trust American promises in that regard is, of course, an issue posed by the recent election in the United States and subsequent statements by President Trump. I suspect that the answer to that question will affect one's views on the continued viability of Article 9 as a constitutive feature of the Japanese state.

The creation of a standing army in the United States

My own expertise is about the United States Constitution, not the Japanese counterpart. It is highly relevant, I believe, that one of the most important decisions made by those who drafted the 1787 Constitution in Philadelphia was to endorse the possibility of what in 18th-century political discourse was called a "standing army." No one should underestimate the importance, both ideological and practical, of that decision. A "standing army" refers basically to an army or navy composed more or less of professionally trained personnel, many of whom—i.e., the officer class—would likely make a career of military service. The alternative to a "standing army" was a "citizens militia," composed of ordinary men (at least until the late 20th century), trained in the use of arms who, it was thought, could be mobilized on those specific occasions when defense of the state was necessary.

The notion of a "citizen militia" is an enduring icon within segments of American political thought and, just as importantly, political mythology.

However, whatever the appeal of a citizen militia to that part of the American consciousness that is deeply suspicious of the organized state and cherishes the Minuteman statue in Concord, Massachusetts, it was firmly rejected by those actually drafting the Constitution. The President of the Convention—and, of course, the first President of the United States under the new Constitution—was George Washington, who had gained his pre-eminence by being the commanding general of the insurrectionary forces who successfully forced Great Britain to recognize American independence. He had little regard for amateur armies and strongly supported the creation of a standing army. That was true also of Alexander Hamilton, perhaps his primary aide during much of the War.

It is no coincidence that the first "national university" in the United States was the United States Military Academy, located in West Point, New York, founded in 1804 during the administration of Thomas Jefferson, who was scarcely a general devotee of national power. To this day, the only "national universities" run by the United States government itself are the service academies that train officers for the army, navy, air force, and coast guard. Attempts in the early 19th century to found civilian national universities devoted to transmitting, say, a humanistic culture appropriate to what the Constitution calls a "Republican Form of Government" were always rejected by Jeffersonians on the grounds that the national government had only limited powers. Running universities was not one of them, but training a national officer corps most certainly was. The Constitution recognized that the United States might well find itself at war, and Congress was given the power to create standing armed forces that would, presumably, allow the United States to prevail in any such encounters. There have, of course, been often bitter debates about how big (and expensive) the armed forces should be, but that is entirely different from arguing that Congress was without authority to build up, as well as limit, the military.

Publius and the Federalist Papers

The Constitution drafted in Philadelphia was, of course, subject to much debate. The most famous defense of the new Constitution is surely *The Federalist*, a set of 85 essays published in New York newspapers between October 27, 1787 and May 28, 1788, under the pen name "Publius."[7] They were motivated, after all, by the necessity to persuade delegates to state constitutional conventions who might be strongly tempted to vote against the Philadelphia draft. In such circumstances, there are more important things than absolute candor. The authors were politicians, not academic political theorists. In any event, although the historical questions are no doubt interesting, they are not the ones that provoked my recent book *An Argument Open to All: Reading the Federalist in the 21st*

7 There are literally dozens of editions of *The Federalist* both in print and online. One useful source is the site maintained by Yale University, http://avalon.law.yale.edu/subject_menus/fed.asp. All subsequent quotations from the Federalist are taken from this site.

Century.[8] Instead, I was interested exclusively in whether these essays published over 225 years ago really need be read by anyone in the 21st century who does not have a deep interest in the particularities of American history. And the reference to "anyone" goes well beyond an American audience.

I believe that the American Bar Association (ABA) and the United States Department of State often send copies of *The Federalist* to people around the world, particularly when a given country is involved in drafting a new constitution or significantly revising an old one. "Constitutional design" has become a major project since the end of World War II. The Japanese and German constitutions were famously designed—and some would say "imposed"—after the catastrophe that was World War II and the defeats suffered by those two nations. Almost all constitutions can link their origins, or radical redesigns, to transformational political events, whether losing a war, dismantling a repressive regime, as in Spain, Portugal, or South Africa, or, quite commonly, to resolve or forestall that particular and almost uniquely threatening form of conflict called "civil war." In any event, the ABA and the State Department appear to believe that what Publius said long ago might still be relevant to readers today. Is that the case? Just as importantly, to the extent that it *is* the case, might the ways in which *The Federalist* continues to be relevant be quite surprising, and perhaps even dismaying, to the State Department or ABA?

Let me emphasize that I do not in the least view *The Federalist* as a necessary fount of wisdom or guidance. There are many things in the essays that are problematic and that we might well wish to reject. The point is that the authors who came together as Publius were unusually able and literate politicians who had an ability to set out some extraordinarily important questions with which we are still wrestling over two centuries later.

"The" or "These" United States?

So let me summarize my overall argument before turning to the specifics of Publius's arguments in many of the essays. What the authors of the new Constitution did was in effect to engage in what Harvard professor Michael Klarman, in a recently published book, has called a "coup" against the government established only six years before by the Articles of Confederation. That government was ruthlessly dismissed as ineffectual and even "imbecilic."[9] Part of the reason was the degree to which the Articles had not in fact created a national government strong enough to pass some necessary laws regarding commerce, including the simple ability to collect tariffs on goods entering the United States. But what is most striking is the overriding concern for what we have come to call "national security."

8 Yale University Press, 2015 (pb. edition 2017).

9 See, e.g., Federalist No. 15.

The early essays especially are all written against the background of threats to the new nation. It had formally won its independence in the Treaty of Paris of 1783, but Great Britain was scarcely eager to comply with provisions that required removal of all of its forces along the border, and there were many other potential enemies as well, including France, Spain, Portugal, and many American Indian tribes who were justifiably opposed to the westward expansion of the United States. It is no coincidence that many tribes had in fact supported the British during the secession of the English colonies from the British Empire because they expected the London government to be more sympathetic to tribal claims than would American settlers seeking new and cheap land. Moreover, it should be recognized that the "it" that begins the second sentence in this paragraph is what grammarians call an "indefinite antecedent." Was there a single country—the United States of America—or, instead, was the entity called the "United States" in fact only a collection of independent "sovereign" states coming together in a decidedly limited "confederation," as might be suggested by the very name of the first "American constitution," the Articles of Confederation? After all, the very first Article of the September 1783 Treaty of Paris acknowledges each of the named thirteen former colonies "to be free sovereign and independent states,"[10] not yet, presumably, amalgamated into a singular entity treating them merely as subnational units.

Great clarity on the basic thrust of Publius's argument is provided early on in *Federalist* No. 6. He is arguing against those who would accept the prospect of the United States ultimately fragmenting into two or perhaps three separate countries along the Atlantic Ocean. Anyone with such views "must be far gone in Utopian speculations" if he or she believes that those separate countries would in fact live together in harmony. Such utopians would require "forget[ting] that men are ambitious, vindictive and rapacious. To look for a continuation of harmony between a number of independent unconnected sovereignties, situated in the same neighborhood, would be to disregard the uniform course of human events, and to set at defiance the accumulated experience of ages." His vision might even be described as basically Hobbesian. He denounces as idle "reveries" and intellectual "seductions" the belief that "peace and cordiality" rather than "discord and hostility" will be the reality should the United States reject the unity (and far stronger government) promised by the new Constitution.

One of the most interesting essays in this regard is the almost never-read *Federalist* 11, which argues against the United States remaining what Publius calls an "insignificant" state that would simply remain "a prey to the wanton intermeddlings of all nations at war with each other." Only countries with "adequate power" can expect to be respected, even if all they wish to do is to remain neutral in the struggles among larger and more powerful countries. Thus he strongly advocates the building up of a navy as a means of defense. Obviously, however, navies originally built for such purposes can later be used more aggressively.

10 Online: http://avalon.law.yale.edu/18th_century/paris.asp.

A seminal event in Japanese history was Admiral Perry's aggressive "visit" to Japan in 1853 demanding that Japan open its trade to American products, an issue that has not fully been resolved between the two countries to this day. In my book, I suggest that Chinese readers of *Federalist* 11 may well feel encouraged to build up their forces in the South China Sea in part as a defense against future American attack (or, of course, service as potential bases for aggressive war against Japan or the Philippines). Perhaps North Korean readers would also find *Federalist* 11 of unusual relevance, substituting the development of a nuclear capacity for building a navy.

The ABA might wish to confine interest in *The Federalist* to No. 78; other essays, however, might have at least as much relevance for foreign readers. This possibility is one of the things that makes reading *The Federalist* in the 21st century potentially interesting. Although written at the time for an American audience contemplating the virtues of the newly drafted U.S. Constitution, its arguments can scarcely be confined to the American experience. At no time, for example, does Publius truly treat the United States as "exceptional." Instead, those contemplating the future of the new country must take account of all political experience dating back to ancient times.

War in the Federalist Papers

By *Federalist* 23, Publius has turned from his harsh criticisms of the "imbecilic" and weak government under the Articles of Confederation to the virtues of the new government established by the new Constitution. Those who believe that the United States Constitution necessarily establishes a limited government devoted simply to achieving what the Preamble calls the "blessings of liberty" or even "establishing justice" should realize as well that one of the announced purposes of the Constitution is to assure an effective "common Defence." According to Publius, "The circumstances that endanger the safety of nations are infinite." This means, as a practical matter, that "no constitutional shackles can wisely be imposed on the power to which the care of [that safety] is committed." One can, if one wishes, read this as discussing the power of Congress and not, for example, the unilateral power of the President, but the major point should obviously be the critique of what he calls "constitutional shackles" against full protection of public safety. Devotees of "limited government" scarcely find an unequivocal ally in Publius.

Perhaps it is telling that both the Japanese and German constitutions, however influenced by the United States in the aftermath of 1945, firmly rejected the U.S. model of presidential government in favor of a somewhat complex form of parliamentarianism (given the bicameralism present in both countries). Recent events in the United States might underscore both the wisdom of that decision and the costs of what political scientists call "path dependence," whereby decisions made at time X become entrenched and impossible, as a practical matter, to undo. In any event, *Federalist* 23 in effect defends an all-powerful state with regard to matters of national defense.

Perhaps the most illuminating essay, and at the same time most troubling, is *Federalist* 41. Early on we read that "[s]ecurity against foreign danger is one of the primitive objects of civil society" and, presumably, of any well-designed constitution. This entails that the national government be given "an INDEFINITE POWER of raising TROOPS, as well as providing fleets; and of maintaining both in PEACE, as well as in WAR" (capitalization in original). The reason for such a basically unlimited power is all too simple: only if a country can "prohibit in like manner the preparations and establishments" of potential means of aggression on the part of other countries in the international system would it make sense to impose rigid limits on one's own military potential. It is at that point in the argument that we read what is perhaps the most chilling sentence in all of the 85 essays: "It is in vain to oppose constitutional barriers to the impulse of self-preservation. It is worse than in vain; because it plants in the Constitution itself necessary usurpations of power…"

It is, I think, telling that the author of this last passage is James Madison and not Alexander Hamilton. Those familiar with American constitutional history know that Madison is often somewhat sentimentally described as the father of the Bill of Rights and champion of liberty (though at the same time a slaveowner). Whatever his undoubted commitments to such rights, though, we see here the overarching commitment to national security as perhaps the central feature of any constitution that is designed truly to endure.

There is therefore good reason that many opponents of the Constitution described it as creating a "consolidated government" that would sooner or later become all-powerful and break free of any purported limitations established by the Constitution itself. Indeed, Publius famously dismissed as "parchment barriers" limitations on governmental power. The imperatives of realpolitik would inevitably take priority. We in the United States may have occasion over the next several years to find out exactly how much our vaunted protections in the Bill of Rights will really stand up against determined opposition by a Trump Administration seemingly organized around the notion that the United States faces an existential threat from what it will insist on calling "Islamic terrorism" or even "Islam" itself. Similar questions, of course, may be raised in such countries as the United Kingdom and France, both of which seem under the thrall of invocations of "emergency powers" that justify suspension of what some had viewed as "traditional" civil liberties.

Publius and Article 9

I trust that the relevance of this overview to the future of Article 9 is obvious. The great question hovering over Japan at present is whether or not this remarkable feature of the national constitution is to be limited by clever exercises in what law professors call "constitutional interpretation" or even repealed and replaced by language explicitly allowing the full remilitarization of Japan. That possibility is attributed, no doubt correctly, to the rise of a more nationalistic ruling elite, exemplified by Prime Minister Shinzo Abe, that, in effect, wishes firmly to treat World War II as more-or-less ancient history with regard to Japan's role and behavior in the international system 75 years later. As an American liberal, I am upset by some of what I have read about the Abe government and feel solidarity with those that are opposing it, but as a political scientist/lawyer those political sympathies are nearly irrelevant with regard to analyzing the concrete realities of contemporary Japan (and the United States).

Given the kinds of arguments set out in *The Federalist*—and thinking of their relevance for 21st-century readers—I find myself increasingly asking why it has taken so comparatively long, well over 60 years, for Article 9 to come under such sustained attack. After all, as noted earlier, it took less than a decade for similar provisions in the German Basic Law to be significantly limited. But Japan presents a very different historical and political tale. The significant limitation on what was traditionally viewed as a central "aspect of sovereignty" has remained a constitutive, albeit highly controversial, aspect of Japanese political and constitutional identity. Is Japan a useful case study for the proposition that a great country really can in effect become significantly demilitarized and renounce the development of a military capacity that might be thought required to provide a full defense to potential threats? (I put to one side that another practical "aspect of sovereignty" is the willingness to use such military forces as mechanisms of aggressive expansion, a regrettable part of both American and Japanese history.)

Sovereignty and military

Perhaps it is worth noting the implications of these reflections for another issue that I also often reflect upon, the future of Israeli and Palestinian communities in the Middle East. Like most American liberals (and Jews), I support the "two-state solution" in spite of justifiably increasing concerns that its time may have passed as a genuine possibility. Many two-state proposals have adopted one-or-another version of a militarily disarmed Palestinian entity (in stark contrast to the Israeli state that is universally believed to possess nuclear weapons and is ranked by most observers as within the world's top-ten military powers). One can easily understand why Israel and its supporters would attempt to impose such a condition on the creation of an ostensibly "sovereign" Palestinian state, just as one can easily understand why Article 9 in 1946 made such good sense to Americans working to draft (or "impose") a new constitution on the completely-defeated Japan. But the radical understanding of Article 9 did not survive even a decade; instead, Article 9 was interpreted by the Cabinet Legislative Bureau, which is, as a matter of fact, far more important than the Japanese Supreme Court, to allow "self-defense" forces. Other interpretations further expanded the ostensible meaning of Article 9; one alternative to highly contentious formal amendment is, of course, to continue further "amendment-by-interpretation," which is arguably a staple of American constitutional development.[11] It is now decidedly unclear, given developments in both the United States and Japan, whether Article 9 will reach its 80th birthday.

In any event, this history gives one cause to wonder about the endurance of any purported agreement by the founders of a Palestinian state to accept a basically neutered status as a country without a significant military capacity. Would any such clause inevitably turn into a mere "parchment barrier" that would be ignored at the earliest possible opportunity? Perhaps one might reflect in this context on German renunciation in the 1930s, after the Nazi takeover, of the demilitarization required by the Versailles Treaty. One must obviously be appalled by the Nazi regime. But why would one realistically have expected the Versailles promises to endure beyond the point that other countries were willing to restrain German re-armament by force?

Pressures to rearm and to create an independent military capacity are obviously most compelling when they can be justified in the name of "self-defense," and it is completely understandable that the initial modification-by-interpretation of Article 9 allowed the development of a Japanese Self Defense Force. To be sure, this was accompanied by a strong ban against the foreign use of the Japanese military, which meant, most importantly, the illegitimacy of Japan endorsing genuine "mutual defense" pacts that would require Japan, for example, to join its ally the United States in fighting those viewed as threats to peace by the hegemon. As Boyd and Samuels emphasize in their own overview of the first 60 years of Article 9, what they call "pragmatists" within the Japanese ruling parties were quite happy to join with "pacifists" on the left to limit being overly entangled in what might be viewed as American adventurism abroad. As was the case with Germany, Japan was placed under great pressure by President Dwight Eisenhower's Secretary of State John Foster Dulles to become a full-scale partner within a mutual defense arrangement. Konrad Adenauer agreed; Japanese political leaders did not, and they were able to invoke the American-imposed Article 9 as the reason (or excuse) for doing so. Japanese public opinion was highly supportive of this degree of a non-entangling alliance. It allowed Japan to escape participation in the Korean and Vietnam Wars, much to its advantage.

Responsibility to protect

It is worth noting, however, that one of the most important, and controversial, elements of contemporary international law is the so-called "responsibility" shared by states within the international community "to protect" the residents of what

11 See, e.g., Sanford Levinson, "Accounting for Constitutional Change (or, How Many Times Has the United States Constitution Been Amended? (a) <26; (b) 26; (c) >26; (d) all of the above)," 8 *Constitutional Commentary* 395 (1991); reprinted in revised form as Sanford Levinson, "How Many Times Has the United States Constitution Been Amended? (A) <26; (B) 26; (C) 27; (D) >27: Accounting for Constitutional Change," in Sanford Levinson, ed., *Responding to Imperfection: The Theory and Practice of Constitutional Amendment* 13 (1995).

might be deemed rogue states against the oppressions of their own government. To put it mildly, it is difficult to set out with any great clarity the way the "R2P" system works, save that it may well involve the introduction of foreign troops or other military personnel in countries undergoing civil wars or experiencing other forms of oppressive and inhumane treatment of a country's own populations. Japan also faced pressure to participate in such interventions, and in 1992 Japan legalized, again through what might be viewed creative interpretation of Article 9, its participation in peacekeeping operations by the United Nations, though at the same time the nature of the participation was apparently limited in order to recognize the limits imposed by Article 9. Japanese soldiers could not, for example, take part in military operations against those deemed threats to the peace in a "peacekeeping" operation. It is altogether relevant to note that Japanese politics in July 2017 were being roiled by accusations that high-level officials covered up the degree to which Japanese "peacekeepers" in the South Sudan were in fact exposed to harm and engaging in combat. Both the Japanese Defense Minister and the head of army resigned after they were accused of dissembling about the actual realities.[12] For this as well as other reasons, support for Prime Minister Abe, an avid supporter of both the peacekeeping missions and revision of Article 9, has seemingly plummeted, and it is unclear whether he can summon the parliamentary (and then public) support necessary for explicit revision or repeal.

The Japanese experience underlines the fact that "humanitarian intervention" based on a "responsibility to protect," however, is not so pleasant in all of its associations. Today we might well think of Libya, Iraq, or Syria, to name only the three most notable examples from an American perspective. The forces sent to such countries are expected to kill and to risk being killed in return. The states doing the intervention in an ongoing civil war must inevitably take sides. Can one describe the existing government as tyrannical in the same way that, for example, the English King George III was described as being so in the American Revolution (or civil war within the British Empire)?

What should be clear in the modern world is that "sovereign states" are now expected to act *against* the sovereign claims of other states in at least certain circumstances when the state that is the object of intervention poses no plausible threat, in any standard sense, to the intervening state. What is at issue is maintenance of ostensible international standards of decency and humanitarian treatment—or adherence to international law—rather than any classic notion of self-defense.

12 Online: https://www.nytimes.com/2017/07/27/world/asia/japan-south-sudan-shinzo-abe.html?_r=0.

The paradoxes of Article 9

So Article 9 in the modern world has two perhaps paradoxical aspects. The most obvious is its limitation of Japan, an ostensibly sovereign state, with regard to developing the kind of military resources its leaders, perhaps backed by public opinion, might believe necessary to provide a sufficient defense in the modern world against any and all external threats, including those coming, for example, from the truly rogue state of North Korea, let alone China. At the extreme, of course, this could ultimately include the development by Japan of an independent nuclear capacity justified by its ability to deter those countries. Publius, as I've already suggested, might wonder why it has taken Japan so long.

There are, of course, several different possibilities, and I am certainly without sufficient knowledge to know which, if any, might get close to the truth of the matter. But my insufficient knowledge does not prevent me from suggesting three hypotheses.

I have already offered the first hypothesis, which is, to oversimplify, that Japan was content to live under American guarantees of defense of the Japanese homeland, including even the potential use of nuclear weapons. At least so long as that promise is believed, and Japan has no appetite for aggression, that should be completely satisfactory, especially inasmuch as it frees the country from having to pay the full cost for its defense. Although those described by Boyd and Samuels as "revisionists" wished to reinvigorate Japan's military capacity, they have always, at least up to the present, been counterbalanced by "pragmatists" and "pacifists" who wished, on grounds either of principle or prudence, to emphasize economic and not military development.

To be sure, I have been informed that roughly 54% of the expenses—approximately $7 billion U.S.—incurred by the placement of United States military forces in Japan is in fact paid by the Japanese government (and, therefore, Japanese taxpayers). This apparently is considerably more than the share paid by Germany and South Korea. One can only wonder if this was brought up in a 2016 meeting in New York between Prime Minister Abe and Donald Trump, especially since the meeting apparently occurred without Trump's being briefed by the State Department even though he is notably ignorant of the basics of American foreign policy. Unfortunately, there is reason to believe that he would welcome the expansion of Japanese military potential, especially if it led to reduced expenditures by the United States.

The second hypothesis focuses on political culture far more than on the formalities of law. Since I entered graduate school over a half-century ago, political scientists interested in constitutionalism have been sharply divided over the importance of formal institutions and structures. Instead, many argued, as typified in a famous book by Gabriel Almond and Sidney Verba, *The Civic Culture,* that the key to understanding differences between countries lay far more in their underlying cultures than in the formal institutions that might be found on the surface of their constitutional texts. If, as in Germany, one lesson of World War II for Japan was the popular renunciation of war as an extension of politics, then the relative degree of pacifism of the two countries would have almost literally nothing to do with the actual text of the constitution and everything to do with public opinion and the successful inculcation especially in the young of a decidedly non-militaristic culture. The recent interest in amending Article 9 may be a sign that that cultural moment may have run its course, for whatever reason, and that Japan is reverting to what might be termed "normalcy" within the international state system. However, the inspiring resistance to its repeal (or what might be called "imaginative reinterpretation") may be a strong indication of a *disjunction* between what continues to be a strong Japanese cultural norm and the more specific desire of a nationalist political class, led by a vigorous prime minister willing to exercise the considerably enhanced powers of his office, in comparison to prime ministers of earlier decades, to transform the culture. (Again, one can see ominous reflections of the same tension in the United States as a result of the 2016 presidential election.) In any event, Publius might wonder about the degree to which Article 9 is simply a "parchment barrier," waiting to be breached when the political culture changes, or whether its presence in the Constitution can be used effectively as a means of reinforcing the underlying culture and making it more difficult for ruling elites to prevail, especially if that included the necessity of gaining approval from at least semi-independent judges with their own professional norms.

Still, an interesting question for a political scientist is to what extent the existence of Article 9 genuinely hindered any earlier development of a more militaristic disposition in the wider culture. At the very least, it provided an extraordinarily important rhetorical resource, whether or not it was an effective tool in litigation. Were Japanese children, for example, taught of its existence in school and encouraged to cherish it as part of what constituted one of the most admirable aspects of contemporary Japanese identity? And has public education with regard to Article 9 changed in recent years as political leaders have increasingly been antagonistic to it?

There is also a linked question, which involves the practical importance of military resources. Many American analysts have emphasized the priority of "soft power" over its "stronger" varieties in explaining such success as the United States might have had in the international domain. Indeed, its use of its military forces is scarcely inspiring, not only from a normative perspective, but also, and just as importantly, from a consequentialist one. Many can remember when books were written in the United States about the coming Japanese takeover of the world economy because of the innovations created by Toyota and other major corporations and the omniscient cleverness ascribed to MITI. It did not work out that way, of course, but the point is that no one during that time was speaking about fears of Japanese militarism. Nor, I suspect, for all of the attention being paid to the Chinese expansion of their navy, is there real fear of overt military aggression. Instead, the emphasis is more likely to be placed on an ever-increasing Chinese presence in Latin America and Africa with regard to building roads and other infrastructure and gaining, along the way, political influence. It should be clear, though, that such arguments against military buildups, including those apparently envisaged by a Trump Administration, rest far more on what might be called "practical" considerations and empirical argument than recourse to high philosophic principle.

Finally, as already suggested, one can wonder about the extent to which Article 9 was used to resist efforts by the United States and others that Japan in fact play a greater role in the international arena especially with regard to joining such efforts as the wars in Afghanistan, Iraq, or elsewhere. It is clearer than ever that most American interventions, beginning with Vietnam, have been disastrous both for the United States and for the countries that we were ostensibly trying to help. "Humanitarian intervention" may be thought to offer a certain guarantee, at least to the speaker, of the purity of one's motives. It does not, however, guarantee that the ensuing policy will be effective in achieving the high-minded goals. Nevertheless, as a worldwide movement has emphasized the "responsibility to protect" victimized populations even by "humanitarian" military intervention, there may be a desire to enlist more countries in that project and, therefore, to encourage amendment of the Constitution inasmuch as that is thought to stand in the way.

Against the repeal of Article 9

These questions—and the approaches to constitutional analysis underlying them—obviously are evidence of my own distance from Japan and its problems. I am very definitely an American lawyer and political scientist trying to understand a fascinating aspect of contemporary Japanese constitutional politics. But let me end by saying that I admire greatly those who are resisting the repeal of Article 9. It does enunciate an important vision of a more enlightened, less warlike international system that I am afraid appears to most people as nearly Utopian. And, to return to my central argument, it is doubtful that Publius, with his own rather depressing analysis of international politics and the need for overwhelming state power, would be very sympathetic.

In my book, I suggest that a paradoxical implication of Publius's argument is in fact the desirability of some kind of genuine world government. Only such a universally "consolidated" government could control the predatory impulses of states or, for that matter, non-state actors like the Islamic State of Iraq and the Levant (ISIL), that threaten both national and international security around the world. Some, of course, had the hope that that would turn out to be the role played by the United Nations. Alas, that is not the case. We continue to live within the international state system that, however modified by the United Nations and international alliance systems, is nonetheless all too recognizable in Publian terms. That is nothing to be proud of, but it is the world we sadly inhabit and feel constrained to act within.

9 The constituent power of the 'imposed' Constitution of Japan

An amalgam of internationalised revolutionary power and nationalist devolutionary power

*Yota Negishi**

Introduction

The Constitution of Japan [憲法*Kenpo*] is often labelled as an 'imposed' [押しつけ*oshitsuke*] constitution,[1] which is the pioneer case of the modern constitution-making process based on 'internationalised *pouvoir constituant*'.[2] In accordance with the August Revolution theory, the most influential post-war constitutional doctrine, the acceptance of the Potsdam Declaration in August 1945 had been interpreted as a legal revolution in that the fundamental principle of the pre-war *Meiji* [明治] Constitution was totally reshaped in accordance with *international* law.[3] The *internationalised revolutionary* power to change the internal sovereignty has persistently contoured the discourse under the post-war *Showa* [昭和] Constitution.

In parallel, the so-called '*Imposed Constitution*' discourse has repeatedly arisen as the nationalist public contestation. It says that the *Showa Kenpo* should be comprehensively revised because it was not enacted on the basis of the free

* At the time of writing, the Author was Research Fellow of the Japan Society for the Promotion of Science; and Guest Researcher of the Max Planck Institute for Comparative Public Law and International Law (Heidelberg). Email: ynegishi@seinan-gu.a.jp.

1 See in general, David Law, 'The Myth of the Imposed Constitution' in Denis J Galligan and Mila Versteeg (eds), *Social and Political Foundations of Constitutions* (Cambridge University Press 2013).

2 Philipp Dann and Zaid Al-Ali, 'The Internationalized *Pouvoir Constituant*: Constitution-Making Under External Influence in Iraq, Sudan and East Timor' (2006) 10 *Max Planck Yearbook of United Nations Law* 423; Michael Riegner, 'The Two Faces of the Internationalized *pouvoir constituant*: Independence and Constitution-Making Under External Influence in Kosovo' (2010) 2 *Göttingen Journal of International Law* 1035.

3 Hajime Yamamoto and Yota Negishi, 'From International Revolution to Constitutional (R)Evolution: The Interplay between International and Japanese Constitutional Principles' in Fulvio M Palombino (ed), *Supremacy of International vs National Fundamental Principles: A Comparative Law Perspective* (Cambridge University Press, forthcoming).

will of the Japanese people but 'imposed' by the occupying authority General Headquarters.[4] Indeed, the post-war *Showa* Constitution embraces a deep contradiction: while it established *popular sovereignty* defined in the Potsdam Declaration, the text written mainly by the international occupying authority was not directly connected to the will of the people. The 'Imposed Constitution' discourse often advocates atavistic, or in the biological sense *devolutionary*, exercise of constituent power to resurrect the historically accumulated *nationalist* values sanctified in the *Meiji Kenpo*.

Due to its coherent significance through the entire history of constitutionalism, the author believes that the concept of *constituent power* [憲法制定権力 *Kenpo Seitei Kenryoku*] has still a contemporaneous meaning in Japan. In addition, the history of Japanese constitutionalism, albeit its unique context, provides implications for other cases of 'imposed' constitution that by its nature involves the conflict of different values. To show its virtue beyond time and space, this paper makes a legal account for the 'imposed' Constitution of Japan, which is an amalgam between *internationalised revolutionary* power and *nationalist devolutionary* power. Before entering the analysis of the post-war *Showa* Constitution, this paper starts with the pre-war *Meiji* Constitution since it is quite important to examine whether the national traditional values were completely disconnected by the international 'imposed' values through the constitutional change after the War (I). Then the article moves to the main issue of constituent power under the 'imposed' Constitution of Japan. The liberation of such a revolutionary authority has been prevented, at least superficially, by the international and/or national normative values (II). In the final part, the paper extracts more general lessons from the experiences in the *Meiji* and *Showa* Constitutions. Concretely speaking, we may observe therefrom three tensions of imposed constitutionalism: internationalism *versus* nationalism, discontinuity *versus* continuity, and constituent power versus constituted power (III).

The constituent power of the pre-war *Meiji* Constitution

The first section aims to make a preliminary analysis to bridge the different conceptualisation of the constituent power between the pre- and post-war eras. In order to understand the *revolutionary* aspect of the post-war *Showa* Constitution, we need to firstly trace the *devolutionary* origin of the constituent power, namely, imperial sovereignty under the pre-war *Meiji* Constitution (1). Furthermore, to contrast with the *Showa Kenpo*'s internationalisation process, we should confirm the nationalist *Kokutai* concept enshrined in the *Meiji Kenpo*, which has jealously haunted the politico-legal discourse even after the constitutional change (2).

4 Isao Sato, '"Oshitsuke Kenpo" Rongi no Sainen [*The Resurgent of the "Imposed Constitution" Discourse*'] (1964) 221 *Sekai* 173; '"Oshitsuke Kenpo" Rongi no Kiketsu [*The Consequence of the "Imposed Constitution" Discourse*'] (1964) 222 *Sekai* 98.

Imperial sovereignty as the constituent power

The legal order created under the *Meiji* Constitution was anchored by the principle of *imperial sovereignty*. The First Chapter of the Constitution started with the provisions that stipulated the Empire's spirits. Article 1 proclaimed that '[t]he Empire of Japan shall be reigned over and governed by a line of Emperors unbroken for ages eternal'. This sacred provision was often considered as embodying not only the historically 'intrinsic and unchangeable principle of governing structure' but also the 'principle of *constituent power* in the sense that the Constitution has its ground therein'.[5] In accordance with the ultimate basis, Article 4 provided that '[t]he Emperor is the head of the Empire, combining in Himself the rights of sovereignty, and exercises them, according to the provisions of the present Constitution'. Put differently, the Emperor as the present ruler was entitled to exert the constituted power which was conferred to Himself by the constituent power, i.e. 'a line of Emperors unbroken for ages eternal'. In practice, however, the Emperor was expected to behave as 'static supervisor' over the actual exercise of His powers by State organs in light of the general will.[6] Indeed, the nominal reign by the Emperor was complemented by the *Shogunate* [幕府*Bakufu*] elements that technically assumed the actual governance.[7]

Against the gap between constitutional wording and practice as a backdrop, the academic mainstream in the field of public law at the pre-war era circumvented the theoretical question of *constituent* power, and instead focused on the practical management of *constituted* powers. More precisely, the main purpose was to *formalise* the Emperor's extraordinary power to make the ultimate decision as the subject of the constituent power that would lead to the destruction of the current constitutional order. As the leading scholar representing the governmental position, Tatsukichi Minobe [美濃部達吉] elaborated the Emperor Organ theory [天皇機関説*Tenno Kikan Setsu*] in light of the German public law concept *juristische Staatsperson* [国家法人説*Kokka Hojin Setsu*]. By regarding the Emperor as an institution under the constitutional system, the theory could artfully lay the conundrums of sovereignty, particularly the legitimacy of public authority, on the shelf.[8]

5 Toshiyoshi Miyazawa, '*Kenpo Ryakusetsu*' [*The Outline of the Constitution*] (Iwanami Syoten 1942) 73–74 (emphasis added).

6 Yoshiyasu Ebara, '*Hachigatsu Kakumei Setsu Saiko no tame no Oboegaki* [*Memorandum for Reconsideration on Toshiyoshi Miyazawa's Theory of August Revolution*]' (2012) 97 *Memoirs of the Research Institute of the Cultural Sciences of Ritsumeikan University* 37, 46.

7 Taichiro Mitani, '*Seitou Naikaku Ki no Joken* [*The Condition During the Term of the Party Cabinet*]' in Takahusa Nakamura and Takshi Ito (eds), *Kindai Nihon Kenkyu Nyumon* [*The Introduction to the Research of Modern Japan] (University of Tokyo Press 1977)* 68, 71.

8 Naoyuki Hayashi, '*Syuken Huzai no Teikoku: Kenpo to Hougai naru Mono wo Meguru Rekishigaku* [*The Empire with Sovereignty in Absence: The Study of History Regarding Constitution and Extra-Legality*]' (Yushisya 2012) Chaps 2 and 4 (explaining that Minobe's constitutional theory has been consistent throughout the pre-war and post-war eras).

As the totalitarian idea gradually obsessed the society during the 1930s, the Emperor's constituted powers were frequently invoked to create the state of emergency. A typical example is the 1938 National Mobilization Law [国家総動員法*Kokka Sodoin Ho*] that directly controlled the entire economy of Japan including the distribution of capital, labour, production, and daily materials on wartime footing after the start of the Sino-Japanese War. The legislation was intended to expand the scope of Article 31 of the *Meiji* Constitution, according to which '[t]he provisions contained in the Chapter [II regarding Right and Duties of Subjects] shall not affect the exercise of the powers appertaining to the Emperor, in times of war or in cases of a national emergency'.

In the politically exceptional situation, the essence of imperial sovereignty came to the central issue for constitutional lawyers. The academic mission was particularly pressing after Minobe's *Tenno Kikan* theory was impeached, which once tactfully sidestepped the issue of the legitimacy of public authority. The doctrinal hole was filled by Satoru Kuroda [黒田覺], who squarely engaged in the theorisation of constituent power for the first time in Japanese constitutionalism.[9] Kuroda justified the National Mobilization Law within the constitutional framework by extending the 'spirits of the Imperial Constitution' allegedly reflected in the Emperor's emergency powers under Article 31 from wartime to peacetime.[10] The logic was completely in line with the concept of constituent power for reconstructing the confused constitutional order. To theorise the constituent power of the *Meiji* Constitution, Kuroda started with pointing out the limits of Japanese versions of *juristische Staatsperson* that purposefully escaped from the problem of legitimacy of public authority.[11] Kuroda also questioned the validity of Kelseninan *Normativismus* [規範主義*Kihan-syugi*], where 'what determines the contents of *Grundnorm* is at every moment the facts that were adopted from the factual power relation'.[12] In seeking an alternative framework, Kuroda made reference to the concept of *pouvoir constituant* developed by Emmanuel Joseph Sieyès in the era of the *Révolution Française*, and later revived by Carl Schmitt in the tumultuous interwar period towards the *Nazi-Deutsch*.[13] In his masterpiece *Verfassungslehre*, Schmitt defines *Verfassungsgebende Gewalt* (constituent power) as 'the political will, whose power or authority is capable of making the concrete,

9 Masaki Minagawa, '*Tenno Kikan Setsu Go no Rikken Syugi: Kuroda Satoru no Kokubo Kokka Ron* [*Constitutionalism after the Emperor Organ Incident: Satoru Kuroda's Theory of National Defense State*]' (2003) 183 *Historia* 219, 228–229.

10 Satoru Kuroda, '*Kokka Soudouin Hou to Hijo Taiken* [*The National Mobilization Law and the Emperor's Emergency Powers*]' in '*Kokubo Kokka no Riron* [*The Theory of National Defense State*]' (Kobundo 1941) 179.

11 Satoru Kuroda, '*Nihon Kenpo Ron* [*The Theory of the Constitution*]' (Kobundo 1937) 185–186.

12 Satoru Kuroda, '*Hou Dankai Setsu to Shizenhou* [*The Legal Hierarchy Doctrine and Natural Law*]' (1937) 17 *Hogaku Ronso* 437.

13 Satoru Kuroda, '*Kenpo Seitei Kenryoku Ron* [*The Theory of Constituent Power*]' in Tokuji Tamura (ed), '*Kenpo Oyobi Gyoseiho no Syo Mondai* [*Issues of Constitutional and Administrative Law*]' (Yuhikaku 1938) 27–33.

comprehensive decision over the type and form of its own political existence'.[14] While appreciating the conceptual *renaissance* of constituent power by Schmittian *Dezisionismus* [決断主義 *Ketsudan Syugi*], Kuroda criticised this understanding as the *existenzielle Wille* without *Legitimitätsgrundlage*. By lacking the legitimacy aspect, Kuroda argued, Schmitt's theory failed to reconcile the relationship between *Sein* and *Sollen*, as pointed out from the Kelsenian perspective as well.[15]

In order to overcome the conundrum *normative Kraft des Faktischen* (normative power of the factual), Kuroda made an important revision to Schmitt's theory by juxtaposing *Legitimitätsmoment* [正当性的契機 *Seitosei-teki Keiki*] with *Machtsmoment* [権力的契機 *Kenryoku-teki Keiki*] within the concept of constituent power. Through the former legitimacy notion, according to Kuroda, the normative would be interconnected with the factual.[16] Regrettably, despite this insightful attempt, Kuroda did not provide a sufficient elucidation regarding the *Legitimitätsmoment* of constituent power. Accordingly, Kuroda took a similar way with Minobe in the sense that both scholars refrained from committing directly to the ideology under the Imperial System, though giving an indirect answer to the problem of legitimacy against the political backgrounds.[17] By roughly noting that all foundations for legitimacy existed in the Emperor and Himself was the subject of constituent power, Kuroda's theory, against his original purpose, blurred the distinction between *Machtsmoment* and *Legitimitätsmoment* in this concept, which unfortunately made the *Meiji* constitutional order even more distracted.[18]

Kokutai (national entity) as *Grundnorm*

In order to accurately evaluate the possibility and limit of the constituent power of the *Meiji* Constitution, it is necessary to comprehend the concept of National Entity [国体 *Kokutai*]. The *Kokutai* presupposes that Japan is based on the history of 'line of Emperors unbroken for ages eternal' as sacred in the Constitution (Article 1). The most original notion developed in Japan served as an inspiring and unifying ideology and accommodated the national political framework with the system of constitutional monarchy.[19] The historiography revealed that

14 Carl Schmitt, *Verfassungslehre* (Duncker & Humbolt, 1928) 75; Carl Schmitt, *Constitutional Theory* (Jeffrey Seitzer tr and ed, Duke University Press 2008) 125.

15 Kuroda (n 18) 30–31.

16 ibid 31.

17 Hiroshi Suga, '*Kenpo Seitei Kenryoku Ron no Nihon Teki Henyo: Kuroda Satoru ni Sokusite* [*Eine Wandlung von der Lehre von der verfassunggebende Gewalt ins Japanischen (2): Satoru Kuroda und Carl Schmitt*]' (1999) 145 *Hogakuronso* 39, 51.

18 Satoru Kuroda, '*Syowa 11 Nendo Teikoku Kenpo Kougi An* [*Lecture Draft of the Constitution of the Empire in 1936*]' (Kobundo 1937) 268.

19 John S Brownlee, 'Four Stages of the Japanese Kokutai [*National Essence*]' available at http://www.adilegian.com/PDF/brownlee.pdf. (accessed 5 April 2017).

Yatsuka Hozumi [穂積八束] imported the German *Staatsform* and customised the Western concept to the Japanese context.[20]

In the constitutional legal discourse, scholars debated over the question of whether the *National Entity* [国体*Kokutai*] should be conceptually discerned from the National Polity [政体*Seitai*]. As a dualistic view, Hozumi distinguished the whereabouts of sovereignty corresponding to the *Kokutai* (Article 1) from its behavioural pattern as the *Seitai* (Article 4). The former denotes the fact that the Emperor is the subject of sovereignty sustained by 'a line of Emperors unbroken for ages eternal', whereas the latter supposes the actual form of governance that is changeable over time.[21] His pupil Shinkichi Uesugi [上杉慎吉] succeeded the dualism between the 'hard' *Kokutai* law that constituted the fundamental of the nation and the 'soft' *Seitai* law that only regulated the means and system of governance.[22] These views attaching both legal and historical aspects to the *Kokutai* concept were categorised as the Emperor Subject theory [天皇主体説*Tenno Syutai Setsu*] that regarded the Emperor as the subject to which the sovereign will directly attribute.

Contrastingly, Tatsukichi Minobe took the monistic position as regards the relationship between the National Entity and Polity. In circumventing the whereabouts of sovereignty under his *Tenno Kikan* theory, Minobe expounded that the *Kokutai* is 'not a legal notion but principally historical and ethical notion'.[23] In his understanding, the unwritten custom as the normative 'power of the factual' performs as the most important reference point for complementing constitutional provisions.[24] The custom denotes for him 'the attribute of the historical State that constitutes the foundation of legal systems', in short, the meta-legal *Kokutai* concept.[25]

Even though the *Tenno Syutai* theory and the *Tenno Kikan* theory were concerned with the *Kokutai*, another constitutional law school espousing the nationalist concept ironically criticised both theories as unconstitutional. The so-called *Kokutai* constitutional school prioritised the *Kokutai* as the *Grundnorm* [根本建前（規範）*Konpon Tatemae* (*Kihan*)] limiting any possibilities to damage the National Entity. As a representative, Kishio Satomi [里見岸雄] blamed the *Tenno Syutai* theory that, from the school's viewpoint, not only disrespectfully confused the Japanese original *Kokutai* with the Western sovereignty, but also implied

20 Yuichi Nishimura, '*Nihon Kenpo Gaku ni okeru Kokutai Gainen no Donyu ni Tsuite* [*The Introduction of the Kokutai Concept in the Study of Japanese Constitution*]' in Kazuyuki Takahashi (ed), '*Nichi-Chu ni okeru Seiou Rikken Syugi no Keiju to Juyo* [*The Inheritance and Acceptance of Western Constitutionalism*]' (Iwanami Syoten 2014) 53.

21 Hozumi Yatsuka, '*Kenpo Teiyo* [*The Elements of the Constitution*]' (Yuhikaku 1910) 30.

22 Shinkichi Uesugi, '*Shinko Kenpo Jutsugi* [*New Constitutional Law Description*]' (Yuhikaku 1924) 165.

23 Tatsukichi Minobe, '*Chikujo Kenpo Seigi* [*Constitutional Law Lecture Clause by Clause*]' (Yuhikaku 1927) 73.

24 Tatsukichi Minobe, '*Kenpo Satsuyo* [*The Compendium of Constitutional Law*]' (Yuhikaku 1923) 121.

25 Minobe, *Chikujo Kenpo Seigi*, (n 30) 34.

the potential to transform the National Entity by characterising it as a transformable legal concept rather than an unchangeable historical notion.[26] Satomi also blamed the *Tenno Kikan* theory in that Minobe deliberately refrained from ascertaining the meaning of the National Entity under Article 1 but rather technically utilised the historical concept for managing the National Polity under Article 4.[27]

Admittedly, the *Kokutai*-oriented normative argument was to some extent valuable to counter the extra-legal dynamism of the constituent power fused with the Emperor's emergency power. In order to mitigate the *Machtsmoment* of constituent power, Tomoo Otaka [尾高朝雄] put a normative caveat with the motto: 'Law is the "ruler of politics"'.[28] It is noteworthy in this context that Kuroda got inspirations from Otaka's teachings in incorporating *Legitimitätsmoment* into his theory of constituent power, even though Kuroda's failure to clarify the legitimacy issue became the target of criticism by Otaka.[29] In this sense, the historical and cultural concept *Kokutai* that was legally posited as the *Grundnorm* in the *Meiji* Constitution could serve as the meta-legal limitation on the extra-legal nature of the constituent power.[30]

At the end of the day, however, the *Kokutai* was unsuccessful to put the breaks to the total destruction of the *Meiji* constitutional order. During the 1920s and 1930s, gathering momentum of warfare, the *Kokutai* had been invoked as a politicised legal tool rather than a historical or cultural notion for the purpose of destroying the parliamentary government. As a prominent example, the 1925 Maintenance of Public Order Act [治安維持法*Chian Iji Ho*], aiming at controlling and repressing political dissidents including communists and anarchists, criminalised the intentional acts to overthrow the *Kokutai*.[31] In 1935, Minobe's constitutional teachings were completely driven out for the reason that his *Tenno Kikan* theory emphasised the custom as *normative Kraft des Faktischen* carrying the risk to radically destroy the *Kokutai* itself.[32] The distended *Kokutai* concept

26 Kishio Satomi, '*Kikan Setsu Utsu bekunba Syutai Setsu Tomoni Utsu beshi* [*If the Emperor Organ Theory Should Be Criticised, the Emperor Subject Theory Should Also Be Criticised*]' (1935) 155 *Syakai to Kokutai* 2.

27 Kishio Satomi, '*Kokutai Hou no Kenkyu* [*Research on the Kokutai Law*]' (Kinseisya 1935) 453.

28 Tomoo Otaka, '*Hou ni Okeru Seiji no Keiki* [*The Momentum of Politics in Law*]' (1943) 15 *Horitsu Jiho* 757–758.

29 Kenji Ishikawa, '*Kokka, Kokumin Syuken to Tagenteki Syakai* [*State, Popular Sovereignty and Pluralistic Society*]' in Yoichi Higuchi (ed), *Koza Kenpo Gaku, vol 2: Syuken to Kokusai Syakai* [*Lecture on the Study of Constitutional Law, vol 2: Sovereignty and International Society*] (Nihon Hyoron Sya 1994) 71, 81.

30 Hayashi (n 8) 102–104.

31 'Anyone who has formed an association with the aim of altering the *Kokutai* or the system of private property, and anyone who has joined such an association with full knowledge of its object, shall be liable to imprisonment with or without hard labour, for a term not exceeding ten years'.

32 Muneki Minoda, *Minobe Hakase 'Kenpo Teiyo' no Kiben Sajutu-teki 'Kokutai Henkaku' Sisho* [*The Sophistic Idea of 'Transformation of the Kokutai' in Dr Minobe's The Compendium of Constitutional Law*]' (Shikishima no Michi Kai Genri Nihon Sya 1933) 4–5.

was codified as the Corporeal Principles [国体の本義*Kokutai no Hongi*] in 1937 that contributed to the ideology edification of the nationals.[33] Through these several steps crowning the nationalist *Kokutai* ideology, the state of permanent emergency was frequently reproduced by the individual Emperor's emergency authority (constituted power) on behalf of the collective line of Emperors (constituent power).

As an ironical consequence, the overly divinised *Kokutai* concept hindered any subject to appear in the permanent emergency. The Emperor, who was originally entitled to make the final determination to re-create the collapsing constitutional system, was blocked by the nationalist concept itself to behave as the sovereign in the meaning of Schmitt's *Politische theologie*: 'sovereign is he who decides on the exception'.[34] Only after the Empire reached the critical limit of self-destruction, the external powerful actor, i.e. the United Nations, especially the United States of America, as the factual sovereign in Schmitt's sense, triggered the constituent power of the people of Japan to reconstruct the *Meiji* constitutional order.

The constituent power of the post-war *Showa* Constitution

We now turn to investigating the transformation from the pre-war Constitution to post-war Constitution with regard to the concept of constituent power. The post-war constitutional discourse formulated the discontinuity between the *Meiji* and *Showa* constitutional orders in that the constituent power shifted from the Emperor to the population (1) and that the *Grundnorm* has changed from the collective *Kokutai* to individual human rights (2).

Popular sovereignty as the constituent power

As the Great East Asia War was coming to the end, the United Nations worked out the Potsdam Declaration defining the terms for Surrender. Article 12 of the Declaration is remarkable for the present purpose. The victorious nations emphasised there that [t]he occupying forces of the Allies shall be withdrawn from Japan as soon as these objectives have been accomplished and there has been established in accordance with the freely expressed will of the Japanese people a peacefully inclined and responsible government. In addition, Article 10 of the Declaration required the Japanese Government to 'remove all obstacles to the revival and strengthening of democratic tendencies among the Japanese people'.

The most controversial issue was whether the *Kokutai* could survive unscathed, the answer for which was not literally guaranteed in the conditions of Surrender.

33 Yutaka Nagahara, 'The Corporeal Principles of the National Polity: The Rhetoric of the Body of the Nation, or the State as Memory-Apparatus' in Nina Cornyetz and J. Keith Vincent (eds), *Perversion and Modern Japan: Psychoanalysis, Literature, Culture* (Routledge 2010) 61.

34 Carl Schmitt, *Politische Theologie: Vier Kapitel zur Lehre von der Souveränität* (Duncker & Humblot 1922) 2.

After the shocking incidents such as the atomic bombings in Hiroshima and Nagasaki and the Soviet Union's participation, the Japanese Government was forced to prepare for accepting the Potsdam Declaration. As the primary mission for that objective, the Government requested the United Nations to clarify their position with regard to this crucial National Entity issue. To address the serious concern expressed by the Japanese Government, James Byrnes in the status of the Secretary of State of the United States repeated the words in Article 12 of the Potsdam Declaration. Although the Byrnes Reply did not eliminate all doubts of governmental officials, the Emperor finally made the Divine Decision to accept the Potsdam Declaration, and announced the defeat in the War to nationals with the famous phrase: 'having been able to safeguard and maintain the *Kokutai*'.[35]

The next challenging question was the practical way to reconcile the nationalist idea and the international agreement within the new constitutional wording. The Government originally intended to keep imperial sovereignty under Article 1 of the *Meiji* Constitution in believing that the Imperial System was compatible with the promotion of democracy in terms of Article 10 of the Potsdam Declaration.[36] The General Headquarters resolutely declined the conservative proposal, and instead, 'imposed' the more revolutionary expression that '[t]he Emperor shall be the symbol of the State and of the Unity of the People, deriving his position from the sovereign will of the People, and from no other source'. After tough negotiations, the occupying and occupied authorities reached the conclusion on a new Article 1, with superficially slight (but potentially significant) changes: 'the Emperor shall be the symbol of the State and of the unity of the People, deriving his position from the will of the people with whom resides sovereign power'.

Facing the end of the seemingly ever-lasting Imperial System based on the Devine Revelation, Toshiyoshi Miyazawa [宮澤俊義] dared to put forward the *August Revolution* theory [八月革命説*Hachigatsu Kakumei Setsu*] as the justification for the principle of *popular sovereignty* [国民主権*Kokumin Syuken*].[37] The August Revolution theory presupposes three conditions, all of which have been subject to criticism.[38] The first is to adopt a specific interpretation of the Potsdam Declaration and the Byrnes Reply. Compared to the Government's original proposal aiming at reconciling imperial sovereignty and democracy under Article 10 of the Potsdam Declaration, Miyazawa interpreted Article 12 of the Declaration repeated in the Byrnes Reply as requiring the transformation of sovereignty from

35 Imperial Rescript, 14 August 1945.

36 Jun Eto (ed), '*Senryo Shiroku* [*The Historical Record of the Occupation*]' (New ed, Kodansya 1995) 163.

37 Toshiyoshi Miyazawa, '*Hachigatsu Kakumei to Kokumin Shuken Shugi* [*The August Revolution and the Principle of Popular Sovereignty*]' (1946) *Sekai Bunka* 61, 68. For the final version, Toshiyoshi Miyazawa, *Nihon Koku Kenpo Tanjo no Houri* [*Legal Logic of the Birth of the Constitution of Japan*] (Iwanami Syoten 1967).

38 For criticism of each condition, see Tsutomu Hibino, '*Genko Kenpo Seiritsu no Hori* [*Theory for the Establishment of the Current Constitution*]' in Kazuyuki Takahashi and Makoto Oishi (eds), '*Kenpo no Soten* [*Issues of the Constitution*]' (3rd ed, Yuhikaku 1999) 10.

the Emperor to the population. The second is to accept the primacy of international legal values over national legal values.[39] During the occupation after the War, the doctrine of the supremacy of international law in line with international democracy bestowed legitimacy sources on the national authorities for embedding the Potsdam commitments into the new Constitution.[40] The third is to recognise the limits of constitutional amendment. The theory explains that the fundamental change of the whereabouts of sovereignty transcended the constitutional limitation, and therefore, could not be achieved except for a revolutionary momentum.

Miyazawa's August Revolution theory provoked a fierce debate with Tomoo Otaka, one of the most famous discussions in the post-war academia of Japan.[41] To counter the revolutionary theory, Otaka elaborated the *Nomos Sovereignty* theory, according to which sovereignty is permanently subject to the *Nomos* as the ultimate *idea* of governance regardless of the change of its whereabouts from the Emperor to the population.[42] In terms of the normative position, Miyazawa's theory was criticised as the 'sophist Meritocraticism' in that the latter leaves the theoretical possibility of abandoning popular sovereignty through another revolution with the factual *kratos* (power) of the *demos* (people).[43] In response, Otaka's criticism was cynically called as the 'Apologia of the Imperial System',[44] which from Miyazawa's eyes seemed like persistence to the infamously abused *Kokutai* idea.[45] Though the academia in general acclaims Miyazawa the victor in

39 Koji Sato, '*Kenpo* [*Constitution*]' (Seirin Syoin 1995) 76 (explaining from dualistic point of view that Japan simply assumed the international obligation as 'claim' to reform the *Kokutai* for implementing the Potsdam Declaration, in contrast with the August Revolution theory implying the 'real right' character).

40 Kaoru Obata, 'Historical Function of Monism with Primacy of International Law: A View Based on the Japanese Experience during the Early Period of the Allied Occupation' (2006) 49 *Japanese Annual of International Law* 1, 27–31.

41 It was indeed succeeded by other two intellectual giants, Souichi Sasaki [佐々木惣一] and Tetsuro Watsuji [和辻哲郎]. See Munenori Kaneko, '*Nihon Koku Kenpo to "Kokutai": Sasaki Souichi to Watsuji Tetsuro no Ronso* [*The Constitution of Japan and "National Body": The Debate between Souichi Sasaki and Tetsuro Watsuji*]' (2015) 1096 *Kokutai Bunka* 2.

42 Tomoo Otaka, '*Nomos no Syuken ni Tsuite* [The *Nomos* Sovereignty]' (1948) 62 *Kokka Gakkai Zasshi* 577.

43 Asao Otaka, 'Jijitsu to Site no Syuken to Toui to Shite no Syuken [Sovereignty as *Sein* and Sovereignty as *Sollen*]' (1950) 64 *Kokka Gakkai Zasshi* 201.

44 In the debate with Sasaki, Watsuji inherited Otaka's understanding of the relationship between the individual and the collective to characterise the symbolic role of the Emperor under the post-war *Showa* Constitution. See Kenji Ishikawa, '*Syocho, Daihyo, Kikan* [*Symbol, Representation, Organ*]' in Zenkoku Kenpo Kenkyukai (ed.), *Nihonkoku Kenpo no Keisyo to Hatten* [The Inheritance and Development of the Constitution of Japan] (Sanseido 2015) 179–182. For an affinity between Watsuji's ethics and Jean-Luc Nancy's ideas of 'singularity', see Anton L Sevilla, *Watsuji Tetsurô's Global Ethics of Emptiness: A Contemporary Look at a Modern Japanese Philosopher* (Springer 2017) Chapter 2.

45 Toshiyoshi Miyazawa, '*Kokumin Syuken to Tenno Sei to ni tuite no Oboegaki: Otaka Kyoju no Riron wo Megutte* [Memorandum on Popular Sovereignty and the Imperial System: Around the Theory of Professor Otaka]' (1948) 62 *Kokka Gakkai Zasshi* 289.

the debate, we should not carelessly overlook a variety of essential issues that were illuminated from their different angles.

Above all, in relation to the adoption of popular sovereignty, the intellectual debate between Miyazawa and Otaka sheds light on the (dis-)continuity of the *Kokutai* concept between the pre-war and post-war eras. Despite the labelling 'Apologia of the Imperial System' on Otaka's theory, Miyazawa himself admitted the double meaning of the *Kokutai*: while the Imperial System in the 'theocratic' meaning where the Emperor reined based on the Devine Revelation was rejected by the August Revolution, the Imperial System in the 'simplistic' meaning was not abolished thereby.[46] Otaka supported the maintenance of the Imperial System as the complementary element for the Japanese version of popular sovereignty that still remained at the embryotic stage. Under the new principle characterised as a 'responsibility', the governance ideal *Nomos* would be achieved not by relying solely on the Emperor but by the co-operation among the people themselves.[47]

Human rights as *Grundnorm*

The Miyazawa-Otaka debate also insightfully demonstrated the dual aspect of sovereignty and constituent power, i.e. *Machtsmoment* and *Legitimitätsmoment*. Although Miyazawa was deeply influenced by Kelsenian *Normativismus*, his August Revolution theory certainly incorporated Schmittian *Dezisionismus* when defining sovereignty as the 'power to ultimately decide the way of politics in the nation'.[48] Otaka critically named the revolutionary theory as the 'sophist Meritocraticism' because he was fully aware of Schmitt's *normative Kraft des Faktischen* doctrine, as well as the paradox of Kelsenian *Grundnorm*, which ironically implied the transformation of factual power into law.[49] To overcome such *Machtsmoment*, Otaka adhered not simply to the Imperial System but more essentially to his own motto 'law is the "ruler of politics"', according to which the constituent power shall be legally limited by the eternally unchangeable *Nomos* corresponding to *Legitimitätsmoment*.

In his academic masterpiece titled *Constituent Power*, Nobuyoshi Ashibe [芦部信喜] puts the emphasis on the aspect of *Machtsmoment* rather than *Legitimitätsmoment*.[50] Remarkably, Ashibe reintroduced Kuroda's insight beyond generations that once tried to juxtapose the couple of moments to

46 ibid 385.

47 Otaka (n 42) 595–596.

48 Kenji Ishikawa, '*Hachigatsu Kakumei, 70 Nengo: Miyazawa Toshiyoshi no 8.15* [*The August Revolution, After 70 Years: 8.15 of Toshiyoshi Miyazawa*]' (2015) 87 *Horitsu Jiho* 80, 85.

49 Tomoo Otaka, '*Jittei Hou Chitsujo Ron* [*The Theory of Positive Legal Order*]' (Iwanami Syoten 1942) 164.

50 Nobuyoshi Ashibe, '*Kenpo Seitei Kenryoku* [*Constituent Power*]' (University of Tokyo Press 1983) 43.

balance Kelsenian *Normativismus* and Schmittian *Dezisionismus*.[51] In practice, as a member of the Commission of the Constitution that was founded for a fundamental constitutional reform after the recovery of sovereignty, Ashibe relied on the *normative Kraft des Faktischen* doctrine to defend the August Revolution in that the originally unlawful factual was transformed into the legally validated norm through the acceptance of the people.[52] In spite of this logic, Ashibe does not uncritically approve Schmitt's doctrine that the constituent power may be permanently invoked without legal limitations.[53] Situating constituent power at the crossroad of law and politics, Ashibe reserves the existence of the constituent power that might be invoked only in the very exceptional case.[54]

Contrastingly, Yoichi Higuchi [樋口陽一] concentrates on the aspect of *Legitimitätsmoment* to confine the liberation of *Machtsmoment* of constituent power as, according to his theory, sovereignty/constituent power in its own terms concerns the whereabouts of legitimacy of authority rather than that of actual powers.[55] Higuchi views that the original 'constituent power of the people' is in the *rivalité* with the finally established constitutional order, while the transformed power is in the *complémentarité* with that order.[56] His legitimacy-oriented doctrine leads to the conclusion that constituent power must be eternally frozen after its original invocation.[57]

Albeit the difference in their conclusions, these two intellectual giants come to an agreement that the individual as the subject of human rights [人権*Jinken*] impose the ultimate limitation on the *kratos* of the *demos* (constituent power). Ashibe's theory presupposes that the constituent power is conceptually demarcated by the meta-legal Basic Norm, in particular the principle of the 'inviolability of human personality' that constitutes the core contents of human rights.[58] In this formula, Ashibe considers the principle as neither a Kelsenian hypothetical and

51 Hiroshi Okamoto, '*Kenpo Seitei Kenryoku Ron no Keifu: Kuroda Satoru to Sengo Kenpo Riron* [*The Theory of Constituent Power: Satoru Kuroda and Postwar Japanese Constitutional Doctrine*]' (2015) 58 *Law Journal of Shimane University* 111, 121–125.

52 The Commission on the Constitution, *Report on the Doctrine of Constitutional Nullity* (1964) 52.

53 Ashibe (n 50) 39. Meanwhile, referencing Otaka's insight, Ashibe is also aware of the paradox of Kelsen who ironically implied the *normative Kraft des Faktischen* by explaining that the *Grundnorm* means the transformation of power into law.

54 ibid 324.

55 Yoichi Higuchi, '*Kindai Rikken Syugi to Gendai Kokka* [*Modern Constitutional and Contemporary State*]' (Keiso Syobo 1973) 301–302.

56 Yoichi Higuchi, 'Constitutionnalisme et pouvoir constituant: rivalité et complémentarité entre eux: A propos des arguments récents en Europe et au Japon' (2015) 69 *Transactions of the Japan Academy* 105.

57 Higuchi (n 55) 301–302. See also, Yasuo Hasebe, '*Kenpo Seitei Kenryoku no Syokyo Kanousei ni Tsuite* [*The Possibility to Erase the Concept of Constituent Power*]' in Yashuo Hasebe (ed), '*Kenpo to Jikan* [*The Constitution and Time*]' (Iwanami Syoten 2007) 51, 57 (proposing the possibility to erase the concept of constituent power by focusing on the ethical foundation of the Constitution, namely, the compatibility with extra-legal political morality).

58 Ashibe (n 50) 39–40.

value-neutral *Grundnorm* nor a pure-naturalist substantive value, but the 'legally posited meta-legal' principle that is actually valid in the existing national constitutions in Western Europe as well as the Constitution of Japan.[59]

In a similar direction, Higuchi remarkably argues that human rights are based on 'the tension where the people have held the State's authority in control by their will, and then see even the national authority = their own will as "Other"'.[60] Accordingly, the essential function of the individual as the subject of human rights is to constantly keep the distance between constituted and constituent powers. Accepting to the August Revolution theory, Kuroda explained the dual aspect of the new fundamental principle of popular sovereignty: while the positive people or *Aktivbürger* correspond to the subject of actual politics, the integral people are the foundation for justifying the exercise of such powers. Kuroda gave a warning that the scope of each definition of people should not be equated.[61] A prominent political theorist Akira Nakamura also regards popular sovereignty not as the issue of 'domination' but as the legitimacy source of such authorities. Nakamura advocated that the people as the subject of constituent power is always 'Other' for national authorities as constituted power.[62] The human rights of the people hinder constituted power ('Other') from behaving as if representing the constituent power ('Self').

Notwithstanding the ontological change from the collective *Kokutai* to individual human rights, we should not naïvely espouse the latter as the absolute ideology. It is undeniable that crowning the metaphysic of the individual as the subject of human rights as the *Grundnorm* is a kind of value judgment, or a value 'imposition' in the case of Japan, under the strong influence of Western-centrism.[63] The qualification of the principle of the inviolability of human personality as the meta-legal Basic Norm with substantive values potentially carries, at least at the theoretical level, the risk to 'absolutise' or 'ideologise' the *Showa Kenpo*, as is the case of the *Meiji Kenpo* where the *Kokutai* was excessively hallowed.[64]

Three tensions of imposed constitutionalism: Japanese lessons

Based on the examinations above regarding the constituent power in Japanese constitutionalism, the final part purports to draw some lessons that may be generalised to other cases of imposed constitution. We may point out three, mutually

59 ibid 321–324.

60 Yoichi Higuchi, '*Kindai Kokumin Kokka no Kenpo Kozo* [*The Constitutional Structure of Modern National State*]' (University of Tokyo Press 1994) 48.

61 Satoru Kuroda, '*Kenpo ni okeru Syotyo to Syuken* [*The Symbol and Sovereignty in the Constitution*]' (Yuhikaku 1946) 44.

62 Akira Nakamura, '*Syuken: Kokunai Hou Jou no Gainen to Shite no* [*Sovereignty: As the National Legal Concept*]' (Nihon Hyoron Sya 1951) 67–68.

63 Atsushi Naito, '*Kenpo Gaku ha Rikkenteki Kenpo wo Seitouka dekiruka?* [*Justifying Constitutional Laws in Japanese Constitutional Theories*]' (1)' (2013) 12 *Hitotsubashi Journal of Law and International Studies.*

64 Suga (n 17) 54.

interrelated tensions inherent in imposed constitutionalism: internationalism *versus* nationalism (1), discontinuity versus continuity (2), and constituent power and constituted power (3).

Internationalism *versus* nationalism

The first lesson that Japanese history can provide to imposed constitutionalism is the tension between *internationalism* and *nationalism*. On the one hand, the constituent power of the post-war *Showa* Constitution was factually triggered by the intervention of the international actors, particularly the United States of America. The Potsdam Declaration, an international legal document, was the fundamental base to reconstruct the constitutional order that was totally upset by the excessive inflation of the Emperor's emergency power. In the post-war era, the 'internationalised *pouvoir constituant*' has been cryptically extracted to convert the constitutional order in favour of the *author* who turned the trigger of such a revolutionary power. Particularly, the most significant timing was September 1951, in which the San Francisco Peace Treaty and the Security Treaty with the United States of America was signed. This momentum may be rephrased as the *September Revolution* restoring the external aspect of sovereignty, which should be comparable with the August Revolution regarding the internal transformation of sovereignty.[65]

Such parallel revolutions produced by international legal documents incontestably contoured the post-war *Kokutai*, namely the diplomatic subservience to the United States, which have prompted alleged constitutional changes.[66] First, the Government of Japan has gradually pushed the policy of remilitarisation such as the creation of the Self-Defence Force in 1954, which has been criticised as the first '*de facto* constitutional change through interpretation'.[67] Second, the current Cabinet of Prime Minister Shinzo Abe forcefully modified the traditional negative interpretation, which is allegedly equivalent to the second '*de facto* constitutional change through interpretation'.[68]

On the other hand, the internationalised revolutionary power did not completely eliminate the theories and practices influenced by the pre-war nationalist *Kokutai* concept. Among the *Kokutai* constitutional scholars, Toyoo Ogushi elaborated the most radical argument on the basis of the Emperor's emergency

65 Hideaki Shinoda, '*Syudanteki Jieiken no Shiso Shi: Kenpo 9 Jyo to Nichi-Bei Anpo* [*The History of Thoughts on Collective Self-Defence: Article 9 of the Constitution and the Security Treaty between Japan and the United States*]' (Fukosya 2016), 82–86.

66 ibid.

67 Diet Records, the House of Representatives, 21st Session, the Committee on Budget, 22 December 1954, No 2, 1. For a comprehensive criticism, Siro Kiyomiya, '*Kokka Sayo no Ronri* [*The Logic of State Operation*]' (Yuhikaku 1968), 194 et seq.

68 Cabinet Decision on Development of Seamless Security Legislation to Ensure Japan's Survival and Protect its People July 1, 2014. See Hajime Yamamoto, 'Interpretation of the Pacifist Article of the Constitution by the Bureau of Cabinet Legislation: A New Source of Constitutional Law?' (2017) 26 *Washington International Law Journal* 99, 117–121.

authority stipulated in Article 31 of the *Meiji* Constitution.[69] His *Emergency Power* theory regarded the acceptance of the Potsdam Declaration as the emergent Devine Decision to temporarily suspend the *Meiji* constitutional system that should be restored when the occupation was finalised.[70] As a minor opinion among international lawyers, Hikomatsu Kamikawa questioned the legal status of the Potsdam Declaration because its forceful imposition on Japan allegedly violated the classical international principles such as self-determination and non-intervention. Kamikawa argued that the *Showa Kenpo* should be null and void since its enactment process lacking the formal amendment procedure enshrined in Article 73 of the *Meiji Kenpo* contradicted those international basic principles.[71]

In practice, against the background of the emergence of 'Imposed Constitution' discourse after the restoration of sovereignty, the leading Liberal Democratic Party (LDP) established the Commission on the Constitution in 1956 to propose the amendment of the Supreme law of the nation including its fundamental principles, though it failed because of the political opposition at that time.[72] In the contemporary scene, the leading LDP suggests an amendment proposal of the Supreme law of the nation including re-crowning of the Emperor as the Head of the State, codification of nationals' obligations regarding national defence, legal compliance and loyalty to the State, modification of the wording '[t]he Diet shall be the highest organ of state power', and reconsideration of the family concept.[73]

Discontinuity *versus* continuity

In close relation to the first lesson, the history of Japanese constitutionalism represents the tension between *discontinuity* and *continuity* of imposed constitution.[74] The August Revolution theory presupposes a certain break between the *Meiji* and *Showa* constitutional orders. Miyazawa's radical theory emphasised the fictitious invocation of the constituent power by the people themselves, aiming at eliminating the *Kokutai* ideas that were infamously inflated in the wartime ('sophist Meritocraticism'). Meanwhile, Otaka elucidated the permanency of sovereign governance by the ideal Nomos irrespective of its whereabouts from the Emperor to the population. His Nomos Sovereignty theory tried to defend the legitimising function of the *Kokutai* concept to compensate the immaturity of popular sovereignty at that time ('Apologia of the Imperial System').

69 See in general, Akifumi Kanda, '*Hijyo Jitai to Teikoku Kenpo: Ogushi Toyoo no Hijyo Taiken Hatsudo Ron* [The *Meiji* Constitution and National Emergency: The Views of Ogushi Toyoo]' (2011) 120 *Shigaku Zasshi* 290.

70 Toyoo Ogushi, '*Kenpo no Koryoku* [*The Effect of the Constitution*]' (1965) *Kenpo Kenkyu* 6.

71 The Commission on the Constitution (n 52), 34–35.

72 See in general, John M Maki, *Japan's Commission on the Constitution: The Final Report* (University of Washington Press 1980).

73 Carl F Goodman, 'Contemplated Amendments to Japan's 1947 Constitution: A Return to *Iye*, *Kokutai* and the *Meiji* State' (2016) 26 *Washington International Law Journal* 17.

74 See in general, Tomoya Yamazaki, '*Kakumei to Kokka no Keizokusei* [*Revolution and the Continuity of State*]' in Hasebe (ed), (n 57) 51.

Otaka's criticism against Miyazawa admonish us not to simply suppose that the *Kokutai* no longer exerts any influence under the *Showa* constitutional order established by *international revolutionary* power. We should rather be conscious of the potential that the *Kokutai* would continuingly perform over ages as the driving force affecting the constituent power for the opposite direction, namely, *national devolution* dating back to the *Meiji* era. Indeed, recent excellent historiographies more cautiously view the nationalist concept's persisting effect throughout the pre-war and post-war stages. They venture to re-examine the forgotten *Kokutai* constitutional school, for the purpose of inspecting their structural influence in the post-war discourse, rather than unrepentantly worshipping the pre-war illegitimately sanctified ideas.

Naoyuki Hayashi beautifully illustrates the contrast between the orthodox Miyazawa's August Revolution theory indicating constitutional discontinuity and the heterodox Ogushi's *Emergency Power* theory advocating the constitutional continuity. The first revolutionary theory, which underlines the discontinuity between the pre-war and post-war constitutional orders, has exerted the influence as the authentic constitutional logic to defend the newly introduced principles in terms of international legal documents. In the meantime, the latter devolutionary theory, which highlights the continuity between them, uses the unconstitutional logics to nullify the current principles. According to Hayashi analysis, such an unconstitutional *Kokutai*-driven theory explains the reason why the post-war 'Imposed Constitution' discourse has involved unconstitutional logics that focus on resurrecting the pre-war National Entity by nullifying the post-war Constitution.[75]

Shinji Otani also well explicates that the school attempted to reconcile the *Kokutai* with democracy, which we nowadays consider as mutually contradicting. He points out the limits of Hayashi's analytical framework that still remain in the dichotomy between the positive evaluation of the August Revolution theory and the negative labelling on Ogushi's theory.[76] Instead, Otani re-appraises the latter that incorporated an element close to republicanism in his proposal of a constitutional amendment. His work well tells us that the *Kokutai* constitutional school explored the third way, different from either a return to the traditional manner or a compromise to the Western style; the hybrid way directly was connected to our post-war democratic trend.[77]

75 Naoyuki Hayashi, '*Senji Kokutai Ron no Naka no Kenpo Seitei Kenryoku to Kaiken Shiso* [*An Outline of "Constituent Power and the Idea of Constitutional Revision within the Theories of the National Body (Kokutai-ron) during the War"*]' (2015) 643 *Journal of Cultural Sciences (Ritsumeikan)* 1.

76 Shinji Otani, '*Haisen Tyokugo ni okeru Ogushi Toyoo no Kenpo Kaisei Ron* [*Ogushi Toyoo's Theory on Constitutional Amendment Just After the Loss in the War*]' (2017) 126 *Shigaku Zasshi* 161.

77 Shinji Otani, '*Showa Sen Zenki no Kokutai Ron to Democracy: Yabe Teiji, Satomi Kishio, Ogushi Toyoo no Hikaku kara* [*The Kokutai Doctrine and Democracy in the Prior Period of the Showa War: Comparison among Teiji Yabe, Kishio Satomi and Toyoo Ogushi*]' (2014) 777 *Japanese History* 73.

Constituent power *versus* constituted power

The two lessons from Japanese constitutionalism, ***internationalised revolutionary discontinuity*** and ***nationalist devolutionary continuity***, tell us the third tension between ***constituent power*** and ***constituted power***. Here we should remember that the concept of constituent power is implicitly lodged in the current movement of fundamental constitutional amendments by constituted powers.[78] The value of pacifism, which the people as the subject of constituent power sanctified as one of the three pillars of the post-war *Showa Kenpo*, has been manipulated by the Government, executive constituted power. Moreover, as the presently governing party of legislative constituted power, LDP implies an atavistic attempt to fundamentally reverse the subject of constituent power by re-crowning the Emperor as the Head of the State and by modifying the wording '[t]he Diet shall be the highest organ of state power'.[79]

To comprehend such a conflation between national authorities (constituted power) and their origins (constituent power), we borrow great legal-philosophical insights. In his celebrated work *Force de loi*, Jacques Derrida distinguished the two different kinds of violence that are categorised in Benjamin's masterpiece *Zur Kritik der Gewalt*: first, ***position du droit*** (*Rechtsetzende Gewalt*) corresponding to constituent power, and second, ***conservation du droit*** (*Rechtserhaltende Gewalt*) corresponding to constituted power.[80] Derrida coined the term ***contamination différantielle*** between the dual violence to express the ***itérabilité*** or ***répétition auto-conservatrice*** of the former by the latter.[81] With referring to Carl Schmitt, Giorgio Agamben also explicates that such a confusion between the constituent power and constituted powers creates the state of permanent emergency in which the sovereign makes a decision as described in Carl Schmitt's *Politische Theologie*.[82] Agamben certainly recognises the difficulty to completely separate the Aristotelian nexus between potentiality (***dynamis***) and act(-uality) (***energeia***). He then uncovers the pure potentiality (***adynamia***), namely '[w]hat is potential can pass over into actuality only at the point at which it sets aside its own potential not to be'.[83]

Such an implicit vicarious exercise of constituent power by constituted power shows the theoretical function of *Grundnorm* that prevents the *Machtsmoment*

78 Higuchi, (n 56), 106–107.

79 For a comprehensive criticism, Toshihiro Yamauchi, *'Anzen Hosyo' Hosei to Kaiken wo Tou* [*Questioning the 'National Security' Legislation and Constitutional Amendment*]' (Horitsu Bunka Sya 2015) 169–216. See also for the re-introduction of emergency Carl Goodman, 'The Threat to Japanese Democracy: The LDP Plan for Constitution Introduce Emergency Powers' (2017) 15 *Asia Pacific Journal*.

80 Jacques Derrida, *Force de loi* (Galilée 1994) 92–93.

81 ibid.

82 Giorgio Agamben, State of Exception (Kevin Attell tr, the University of Chicago Press 2003) 37–39.

83 Giorgio Agamben, *Homo Sacer: Sovereign Power and Bare Life* (Daniel Heller-Roazen tr, Stanford University Press 1998) 45–46.

of constituent power. Within the *Meiji* constitutional order, the *Kokutai* concept was situated in the co-operative relationship between the Emperor and His subjects for the purpose of sustaining and evolving the society under the *Meiji* constitutional legal order.[84] As a result, the *Kokutai* as the pre-war *Konpon Tatemae* (*Grundnorm*) functioned to contain both the sovereign Emperor as the subject of sovereignty and the individual as the subject of human rights.[85] Ironically, however, the concept was rather dilated as a nationalist ideology by abusing the Emperor's emergency authority (constituted power) to radically overcome the constitutional limits for the sake of totalitarian regime (constituent power).

In a similar vein, we may reasonably doubt whether the constituent power has been inactivated as a mere symbol under the current Constitution by means of individual human rights. As described with the radical concept of *Human Righting*, 'human rights have often been used as a means of generating democratic movements more focused on the power of the people (the constituent power) than on the limitation of that power'.[86] A prominent example is the Government's attempt to change the essence of pacifism that constitutes one of the pillars of the Constitution of Japan.[87] It should be noticeable in the context that the executive body (constituted power) has ventured on alleged amendments of the constitutional core value through interpretation in the name of the people (constituent power) to address the cases of 'pos[ing] a clear danger to fundamentally overturn people's right to life, liberty and pursuit of happiness' as well as to 'ensure Japan's survival'.[88]

Conclusion

The paper started with chronologically explaining the process of hybridising 'internationalised revolutionary power' and 'nationalist devolutionary power'. Under the pre-war *Meiji* Constitution, imperial sovereignty as the constituent power was structurally limited by the *Kokutai* concept that was also invoked to create the permanent state of emergency restricting human rights. Under the post-war *Showa* Constitution, the *Kokutai* concept in the *Meiji* Constitution is alleged to persist between the two constitutional systems and has indeed affected the public discourse supporting a national devolutionary change of the 'imposed' Constitution. However, the most accepted August Revolution theory endorsed

84 Hayashi (n 8) Chap 3.

85 ibid 259.

86 Illan rua Wall, *Human Rights and Constituent Power: Without Model or Warranty* (Routledge 2012) Chapter 9 (referring to Costas Douzinas, *The End of Human Rights* (Hart 2000) 215–216). Human right-ing 'is a process of creation, an exercise of constituent power, a process of being-with which struggles for the in-common rather than merely reducing it to the bland monotony of everyday politics'. ibid 141–146.

87 Koji Sato, 'The Pursuit of the Principle of International Cooperation in the Constitution of Japan' (1993) 36 Japanese Annual of International Law 5.

88 Cabinet Decision (n 68), para. 3(3).

the internationally 'imposed' principle of popular sovereignty as the constituent power that is put under the ultimate limitation by the individual as the subject of human rights.

This article's arguments are clearly differentiated from the dogmatically influential August Revolution theory in the following three points. The August Revolution theory emphasised the internal change of sovereignty, the discontinuity of constitutional history, and the static understanding of constituent power. In contrast, the present study takes into account the restoration of 'external' sovereignty through international law, explores the possibility of historical 'continuity', based on which we may observe the persistent influence of the *Kokutai* concept over ages, and understands the dynamism of the constituent power that may be implicitly represented by constituted powers to produce substantive changes of constitutional values. These features experienced in Japanese constitutionalism deserve to be generalised to other cases of 'imposed' constitutions.

10 The legitimacy of internationally imposed constitution-making in the context of state building

*Manon Bonnet**

The paradigm of the sovereignty of people is central to most classical constitutional legal theory. However, contemporary practices such as an imposition of the Constitution tend to question this foundational imagery.[1] This phenomenon leads to a paradox between the traditional idea that people are the *pouvoir constituant* and the involvement of the international community in constitution-making processes. Moreover, the *pouvoir constituant* is considered the instance or force that gives the constitution its legitimation and legitimacy.[2]

The participation of the international community in constitution-making processes has taken different forms over the years. Interventions were previously prompted by imperialist and militaristic motives.[3] Maintaining international peace and security was later on invoked as a justification for military interventions. In particular, the creation of the United Nations (UN) system made peacebuilding operations a key element of the international peace and security architecture. The end of the Cold War and the urge to deal with breakdowns in governmental systems of many states previously belonging to the socialist bloc necessitated the creation of new means of actions to ensure peace and security. Moreover, globalization, by bringing about unprecedented interconnectedness among states, turned some domestic issues, traditionally considered as purely national affairs, into international ones; therefore involving the implication of other states. Thus, in the past fifty or so years the western powers have intervened in other states with a declared purpose of state building and peace making.[4] In this view, peacebuilding operations are developed as a civilian

* PhD Student, Aix-Marseille Univ, Université de Toulon, Univ. Pau & Pays Adour, CNRS, DICE, ILF, Aix-en-Provence, France.

1 Z Oklopcic, 'Constitutional (Re)Vision: Sovereign Peoples, New Constituent Powers, and the Formation of Constitutional Orders in the Balkans' (2012) 19 *Constellations* 81, 81.

2 E-W Böckenförde, *Le droit, l'état et la constitution démocratique essais de théorie juridique, politique et constitutionnelle* (LGDJ 2000) 207.

3 R Caplan and B Pouligny, 'Histoire et contradictions du state building' (2005) 28 *Critique internationale* 123.

4 F Polet, 'State Building Au Sud : De La Doctrine À La Réalité', *(Re)-construire les États, nouvelles frontières de l'ingérence*, vol 19 (Syllepse, 2012) 7.

component of international interventions[5] and are meant to help fragile states to stand on their feet and re-emerge as 'responsible' members of the international community.[6] Different measures are employed to this end, one of which is constitution-making.

The international community participates in various ways in state-building processes including the imposition of constitution-making processes. Imposed constitutions may refer to different concepts[7] but always refer to cases where people did not choose either the whole constitution or part of it. For the purpose of this study, I will consider that constitution-making processes are imposed when the decision of making a new constitution is initiated by international actors. This definition means that cases where national actors decided to adopt a new constitution and then called upon the international community for legal expertise are excluded from the present study. In my view, there is a difference in the nature of a nationally initiated process, one that is encouraged by the international community and a process that was imposed from its beginning by international actors. Though there might be some sort of imposition through political pressure in constitutional assistance, the imposition by international actors of a constitution-making process should be studied in itself as a different legal instrument. From a legal point of view, the process of imposition is characterized by the existence of an international norm that regulates either the design of the constitution-making process, the content of the constitution or both. Indeed, international actors may interfere with the constitution-making process at different levels. Some processes, such as the latest Tunisian one, are national processes seeking international assistance. The latter largely differ from processes imposed by external actors, and are therefore excluded from the field of the present research. Therefore I consider that the specific criterion of imposition is the initiative of the constitution-making process by external actors. Translated in legal terms this means that the pre-constituent act is a binding international legal instrument.

Legitimacy is used in various contexts. For example, in its political comprehension, legitimacy might be understood as the material identification of the rule to the expectation of the people.[8] Quoting the Penguin Macquarie dictionary, Andrew Coleman refers to legitimacy as 'in accordance with established rules, principles or standards'.[9] For the purpose of this study, I will use a normative sense

5 T Tardy, 'Le bilan de dix années d'opérations de maintien de la paix' (2000) 65 *Politique étrangère* 389, 393.

6 SL Woodward, 'Construire l'État: légitimité internationale contre légitimité nationale?' (2005) 28 *Critique internationale* 139, 146.

7 N Feldman, 'Imposed Constitutionalism' (2005) 37 *Connecticut Law Review* 857 s.; S Chesterman, 'Imposed Constitutions, Imposed Constitutionalism, and Ownership' (2005) 37 *Connecticut Law Review* 947 s.; DS Law, 'The Myth of Imposed Constitution' in DJ Galligan and Mila Versteeg (eds), *Social and Political Foundations of Constitutions* (Cambridge University Press 2013).

8 P Rosanvallon, *La légitimité démocratique impartialité, réflexivité, proximité* (Éd du Seuil 2010).

9 A Coleman, *Resolving Claims to Self-Determination: Is There a Role for the International Court of Justice?* (Routledge 2013) 35.

of the concept of legitimacy. The legitimacy of a norm may then be understood as 'whether that norm [...] satisfies certain specified conditions for possessing legitimacy'.[10] Now remains the question of the reference standard of legitimacy. It easily appears that the reference varies in accordance with the situation to be analyzed and the legal order it belongs to. In the case of constitution-making, the rules or conditions for possessing legitimacy refer to democratic standards. The legitimacy of a constitution lies in the recognition of the constituent power as such.[11] Thus, the normative legitimacy of a constitution-making process mainly relies on the entity who holds the pen during the process. Under the classical theory of popular sovereignty, the legitimate 'holder of the pen' is the people. Thus, a constitution-making process should be considered legitimate if it is a moment of expression of the will of the people.

Furthermore, democratic legitimacy will be understood here in its procedural understanding. The legitimacy test relies hence in the satisfaction of a procedural democratic standard measurable via the level of participation of the people through the process. Thus, to appreciate the legitimacy of a constitution-making process, the means of participation of the people and the way their concerns are taken into account shall be analyzed.

The success of a constitutional transition largely depends on legitimacy;[12] the consistency of the imposition of a constitution-making process should be questioned. To deal with this issue, the legitimacy of each step of the process will be analyzed. This analysis will be conducted chronologically, starting from the context of these processes, i.e. state-building operations, to the adoption of the constitution resulting from it.

This study is based on a comparative law approach along with public policy analyses and only the process of making the constitution will be discussed here. It compares seven cases of international constitution-making processes, which can be divided into three types: internationally provided process framework (Timor Lest [2002] and Afghanistan [2004]), internationally framed process and content of the constitution (Namibia [1990], Cambodia [1993], Sudan [2005] and Iraq [2005]) and heteronomous constitutions (Bosnia and Herzegovina [1995]).

As an attempt to determine whether and to what extent those processes are legitimate, the study discusses two types of legitimacy: inherent legitimacy and built legitimacy. Inherent legitimacy refers to the legitimacy of the constitution-making process resulting from its original parameters (such as the design of the process and its context). Built legitimacy can be identified through legal instruments seeking to improve the level of legitimacy of the process.

10 ibid.

11 C Schmitt, *Théorie de La Constitution, Préface d'Olivier Beaud* (Presses Universitaire de France 1993) 225.

12 K Samuels, 'Post-Conflict Peace-Building and Constitution-Making' (2006) 6 *Chicago Journal of International Law* 663 s., 664.

The inherent lack of legitimacy of imposed constitution-making processes

Imposed constitution-making results from interventions of the international community in internal affairs, namely the reconstruction of the state after an armed conflict. In order to discuss the legitimacy of internationally imposed constitution-making, the legal standards of international law and internal law must be determined.

Paradoxes of international state-building: Political and legal aspects

Even though each internationally imposed constitution-making process is specific, commonalities between the cases studied may be identified. First of all, they result from three different types of context:[13] shift in power (Afghanistan, Iraq), civil war context (Cambodia, Bosnia and Herzegovina, Sudan, Namibia) or uncertainties on the statute of a territory (Timor-Lest). These contexts refer to cases of 'deconstruction' of the state; the international community will then decide to reconstruct. To analyze the legitimacy of such a reconstruction, the ideological basis of state-building operations will be highlighted along with the legal instruments used to do so.

Ideological basis and political impacts of international state-building

Over time, international reconstruction of states has had different ideological basis. They firstly relied on an imperialist ideology. During decolonization, they were mostly used by the colonialist states to withdraw from their colonies *via* the mandate and tutelage system.[14] This mechanism was based on the idea that the local populations were not able to govern themselves and, thus, they needed help from more 'advanced' states.[15] The UN Charter includes a similar system, the trusteeship system,[16] that led to questioning the sovereignty of post-decolonization states.

In parallel, the end of WW2 led to a radical change in the perception of the role of the international community in state-building processes. The German and

13 M Guimezanes, 'Les Transitions Constitutionnelles "Internationalisées": Étude de Droit Interne' [2014] *Annuaire Français de Droit Constitutionnel* 11.

14 Caplan and Pouligny (n 3) 128.

15 *Covenant of the League of Nation*, 29 April 1919 (Paris), Art. 22.

16 'The basic objectives of the trusteeship system, in accordance with the United Nations laid down in Article 1 of the present Charter, shall be:

a. to further international peace and security;

b. to promote the political, economic, social, and educational advancement of the inhabitants of the trust territories, and their progressive development towards self-government or independence as may be appropriate to the particular circumstances of each territory and its peoples and the freely expressed wishes of the peoples concerned, and as may be provided by the terms of each trusteeship agreement'.

United Nations, *Charter of the United Nations*, 24 October 1945 (San Francisco), 1 UNTS XVI, Art. 76.

the Japanese reconstruction processes were marked by the imposition of the law of victorious powers.[17] They were mostly aimed at ensuring that Germany and Japan would comply with the Allies' standards. It should be noted here that, though those cases are very significant cases of imposition, they are not included in this study. Indeed, they result from an international armed conflict to which the 'imposer' engaged directly. In this way, the imposition occurred by the victors on the losers of the war, on actors who were unable to undertake combat operation. Those two elements, the fact that the imposers were directly involved in the war and the inability to undertake fighting at the end of the conflict, certainly changed the reconstruction process.[18]

During the Cold War, state reconstruction became at stake in the battle for influence. The intervention of each block was meant to reinforce the ruling power and thus ensure the loyalty of the state to the block.[19]

The last evolution of the ideological basis of international state-building is the rise of security challenges. The end of the Cold War marked a significant change in the nature of armed conflicts. The peace and security architecture designed to address international conflict was faced with the increasing number of civil conflicts.[20] In a highly interconnected context, the failure of a state threatens all the actors of the system:

> The rise and fall of nation-states is not new, but in a modern era when national states constitute the building blocks of legitimate world order the violent disintegration and palpable weakness of selected African, Asian, Oceanic, and Latin American states threaten the very foundation of that system.[21]

Thus, most of international state-building operations are nowadays based on the purpose of protecting 'international security'. Even though this concept is not legally defined, its 'general objective is to build states [...] that do not constitute a threat neither to their direct neighbours, nor to their regional sub-systems, nor to the whole international system'.[22] Thus, contemporary international state-building, especially in the cases studied here, is meant to build a state that will not threaten the rest of the international community.

17 N Maziau, 'L'internationalisation du pouvoir constituant. Essai de typologie : le point de vue hétérodoxe du constitutionnaliste' (2002) 3 *Revue Générale de Droit International Public* 549, 565.

18 See M Duffy Toft, 'Ending Civil Wars: A Case for Rebel Victory?' (2010) 34 *International Security* 7; J Widner, 'Constitution Writing in Post-Conflict Settings: An Overview' (2008) 49 1513.

19 Woodward (n 6) 145.

20 Polet (n 4) 9.

21 RI Rotberg, 'Failed States, Collapsed States, Weak States: Causes and Indicators' in RI Rotberg (ed), *When States Fail: Causes and Consequences* (Princeton University Press 2004) 1.

22 Woodward (n 6) 146. 'objectif général est de construire des Etats [...] qui ne constituent une menace ni pour leurs voisins immédiats, ni pour les Etats appartenant à leur sous-système régional ni pour l'ensemble du système international'.

At the same time, the creation of a state is often considered as the gathering of three elements: financial resources, exclusive coercive power and legitimacy resources. Normally, states are created through negotiation between citizens and political actors who seek to gain legitimacy, to be able to control financial resources and exercise coercive power with the view of protecting the public from external threats. On the contrary, when international actors are involved within the constitution-making process, political actors seek international legitimacy to obtain financial resources to fight against internal threats.[23] This fundamental change in the reconstruction of the state leads to the prevalence of international concerns over internal issues. There is then a paradox of international state-building. Based on the willingness to create more stable and responsible states, the international community interferes with the reconstruction of states in a way that seems to be counterproductive.

Sovereignty and self-determination: A legal framework of international state-building

International state-building includes a very large rank of tools used by the international community in order to participate in the reconstruction of states. Based on the idea that democracy participates to stability and thus to security, tools to create democracy have been used in peacebuilding strategies. Constitutionalism hence appears as an adequate tool. Constitutions are then seen as 'a liberal democratic transition-promoting device'.[24]

However, the intervention of the international community in constitution-making should be questioned on the ground of international law, especially regarding two central principles of international law, namely sovereignty and self-determination.

> Sovereignty is the cornerstone of international rhetoric about state independence and freedom of action, and the most common response to initiatives which seek to limit a state's action in any way is that such initiative constitute an impermissible limitation on that state's sovereignty.[25]

The concept of sovereignty finds many definitions and corollaries, however, as Antonio Cassese points out, the essence of the notion is the independence of the state understood as its 'fundamental authority [...] to exercise its powers without being subservient to any outside authority'.[26] The constitution-making

23 BR Rubin, 'Afghanistan, la souveraineté comme condition de la sécurité' (2005) 28 *Critique Internationale* 169, 173.

24 C Bell, 'Introduction: Bargaining on Constitutions – Political Settlements and Constitutional State-Building' (2017) 6 *Global Constitutionalism* 13, 18; Samuels (n 12).

25 H Hannum, *Autonomy, Sovereignty, and Self-Determination: The Accommodation of Conflicting Rights* (Rev ed, University of Pennsylvania Press 1996) 14.

26 ibid 15.

process, traditionally understood as a national process and the exercise of the sovereign internal power,[27] should thus be protected from international intervention. However, the possibility for a state to intervene on the sovereign territory of another state is framed by international law. Binding legal instruments such as peace agreements[28] or United Nation Security Council (UNSC) resolutions may indeed enable a state to delegate part of its sovereignty. Those instruments rely on the purported consent of the state to delegate part of its sovereignty.

Regarding the cases studied here, peace agreements were used in four cases (Afghanistan, Cambodia, Sudan and Bosnia and Herzegovina) and UNSC resolution in three cases (either directly or through the establishment of a transitional administration in Namibia, Iraq and Timor-Leste). It should be noted that the use of peace agreements or UNSC resolutions is not exclusive, and in cases where peace agreements were signed, UNSC resolutions were also used to implement transitional measures. However, if the consent of a state is given either through the signature of the peace agreement or based on the principle of consent concerning peace-keeping operations[29], the validity (or at least the legitimacy) of this consent can be questioned. Indeed, as recent cases show,[30] the legal capacity of an entity to internationally bind a state in transitional periods is hard to determine. Still, international constitution-making might be understood as a classical delegation of sovereignty of a state *via* a legal instrument.

The possibility to leave the very design of the political system to international actors is questionable regarding the right to self-determination. The right of peoples to self-determination is recognized in various instruments of international law.[31] However, its understanding depends on the context and might be understood through internal or external aspects.[32] External aspects refer to

27 M Riegner, 'The Two Faces of the Internationalized Pouvoir Constituant: Independence and Constitution-Making under External Influence in Kosovo Current Developments in International Law' (2010) 2 *Goettingen Journal of International Law* 1035, 1039.

28 On the binding nature of peace agreements, see C Bell, 'Peace Agreements: Their Nature and Legal Status' (2006) 100 *The American Journal of International Law* 373.

29 On the issue of consent in peacebuilding and peacekeeping operations see R Higgins, 'A General Assessment Pf United Nations Peace-Keeping' in Antonio Cassese (ed), *United Nations Peace-Keeping: Legal Essays* (Sijthoff & Noordhoff [International Publishers] 1978); A Di Blase, 'The Role of the Host State's Consent with Regard to Non-Coercive Actions by the United Nations' in Antonio Cassese (ed), *United Nations Peace-Keeping: Legal Essays* (Sijthoff & Noordhoff [International Publishers] 1978); H Nasu, *International Law on Peacekeeping: A Study of Article 40 of the UN Charter* (Martinus Nijhoff Publishers 2009).

30 ICC, Office of the Prosecutor, The determination of the Office of the Prosecutor on the communication received in relation to Egypt (2014) ICC-OTP-20140508-PR1003.

31 For instance: United Nations, *Charter of the United Nations*, 24 October 1945 (San Francisco), 1 UNTS XVI. For a complete list of international instruments referring to Self-Determination see A Cassese, *Self-Determination of Peoples: A Legal Reappraisal* (Reprinted, Cambridge University Press 1996).

32 J Summers, 'The Internal and External Aspects of Self-Determination Reconsidered' in Duncan French (ed), *Statehood and Self-Determination: Reconciling Tradition and Modernity in International Law* (Cambridge University Press 2013) 229.

the horizontal relation between peoples or states whereas the internal aspect of self-determination refers to the relation between the people and the state.[33] In its internal understanding, self-determination means 'granting the peoples of all sovereign states the right to internal self-determination, that is, the right freely to choose their rulers'[34]. Like in the case of Kosovo[35], the issue of external self-determination may be at stake in cases of international constitution-making, however, it appears that the main interference between such process and international law relies on the internal aspect of self-determination. The principle of constitutional autonomy, reaffirmed by the International Court of Justice (ICJ) in its decision in the case of Nicaragua,[36] is counterbalanced by the general consensus of western countries around the democratic ideal.[37] However, as Antonio Cassese highlights, 'the existence of many authoritarian or despotic regimes in the world community has so far prevented the emergence of a fully fledged customary rule of international law [granting internal self-determination]'.[38]

Even though no legal ground prevents a state from delegating its constituent power through an international treaty or the UNSC from helping the constitutional transition of a state, imposed constitution-making presents a paradox. Indeed, under the guise of providing a stable foundation to a failing state, the international community contravenes to a fundamental principle of international law, which is sovereignty. However, by using the legal fiction of the consent, internationally imposed constitution-making processes appear consistent with international law.

Externally initiated constitutional transition: International pre-constituent act and legitimacy

From the internal point of view, the issue of legitimacy of internationally imposed constitution-making might be analyzed by questioning the *pouvoir constituant*. Following Sieyès, it might be understood through two aspects: the *pouvoir*

33 P Thornberry, 'The Democratic or Internal Aspect of Self-Determination with Some Remarks on Federalism' in Christian Tomuschat (ed), *Modern Law of Self-Determination* (M Nijhoff Publishers 1993).

34 Cassese (n 31) 319.

35 M Pertile, 'Self-Determination Reduced to Silence: Some Critical Remarks on the ICJ's Advisory Opinion on Kosovo' in Maurizio Arcari and Louis Balmond (eds), *Questions de droit international autour de l'avis consultatif de la Cour internationale de justice sur le Kosovo* (Giuffrè 2011); Riegner (n 27).

36 *Military and Paramilitary activities in and against Nicaragua (Nicaragua v. United States of America)*, Merits, Judgment, ICJ, *Reports 1986*, p.14.

37 R Déchaux, 'La légitimation des transitions constitutionnelles' in N Danelciuc-Colodrovschi and X Philippe (eds), *Transitions constitutionnelles et constitutions transitionnelles: quelles solutions pour une meilleure gestion des fins de conflit?; [actes de la journée d'études organisée à Aix-en-Provence, le 29 juin 2012]* (Institut universitaire Varenne, Institut Louis Favoreu 2014) 173.

38 Cassese (n 31) 319.

déconstituant, meaning the power to rupture with the anterior constitution, and the *pouvoir reconstituant*, meaning the power to write the new constitution.[39] I will not discuss the theoretical aspect of the constituent power but rather identify who exercises this power, and determine direct or indirect participation of the people in the constitution-making process. The first expression of the constituent power is the decision to engage into a constitution-making process. This decision, called the pre-constituent act, is the cornerstone of international constitution-making as it is the legal instrument of imposition. Its legitimacy must be analyzed from two perspectives: the actors drafting the pre-constituent act and its content.

International drafting of a pre-constituent act

International constitution-making processes are framed by a legal act belonging to the international legal order. It defines, in a more or less precise manner, the process of constitution-making and the content of the constitution. The legitimacy of a pre-constituent act relies on the identity of its authors.[40] Indeed, the legitimacy of the legal instrument depends here on the level of representativeness of the authors. Two different situations may be identified: cases where the pre-constituent act is a peace agreement (Afghanistan, Sudan and Bosnia and Herzegovina) and cases where it results from a UNSC resolution (either directly or through the establishment of a temporary administration as it was the case in Namibia, Iraq and Timor-Leste).

In the first case, the negotiation of the process takes place between international actors and the parties engaged in the armed conflict. As stated earlier, the identity of those able to internationally bind the state remains unclear in the transition period. From an international humanitarian law perspective, ex-combatants have the power to negotiate settlement.[41] International public law seems to rely on the criteria of effective control. In either case, the representatives of the state cannot rely on any democratic legitimacy. Thus, their capacity to carry the voice of the people in the constitution-making process is highly questionable. Concerning representativeness, the table of negotiation of the international pre-constituent act does not necessarily include all political forces of the time. In cases where the pre-constituent act is a peace agreement, the existing political forces include parties to the conflict and international powers taking part to the peace process. If, in the case of Cambodia and Bosnia and Herzegovina, all the parties to the conflict were present, the negotiations of both the Bonn Agreement

39 O Beaud, *La Puissance de l'Etat* (1 éd, Presses universitaires de France 1994) 224.

40 X Philippe, 'Tours et contours des transitions constitutionnelles...Essai de typologie des transitions' in N Danelciuc-Colodrovschi and X Philippe (eds), *Transitions constitutionnelles et constitutions transitionnelles: quelles solutions pour une meilleure gestion des fins de conflit?; [actes de la journée d'études organisée à Aix-en-Provence, le 29 juin 2012]* (Institut universitaire Varenne, Institut Louis Favoreu 2014) 18.

41 Guimezanes (n 13) 13.

(in the case of Afghanistan) and the Comprehensive Peace Agreement (in the case of Sudan) did not include all the protagonists of the conflict.[42]

Moreover, in those cases where the pre-constituent act is a peace agreement, the role played by the internal actors can be questioned. A case study shows that, with the exception of Sudan, where international organizations only managed the negotiations without truly influencing its content,[43] international actors play a prominent role in the drafting of such a pre-constituent act. In the case of Bosnia and Herzegovina, for instance, to cope with the humanitarian situation in ex-Yugoslavia, the European community and the United States of America (USA) were at the origin of the peace negotiations. It was mostly the United States that monitored the process, especially by organizing, on their own territory, the peace conference.[44] Even though the parties to the conflict physically took part in the negotiation of the pre-constituent act, they were not in any way in a position to impose their positions. Thus, participation of internal actors in the drafting of the pre-constituent act does not guarantee that the outcome of the negotiation will be focused on internal concerns. The legitimacy brought by the participation of internal actors to the negotiation might then be considered as a legitimacy *de façade*.

In cases where the imposition of the constitution-making process results from the UN body's decisions, they directly (as it was the case in Iraq) or indirectly (through interim international administration) derive from UNSC resolution. Thus, the decision-making process of this UN body in terms of legitimacy shall be appreciated. UNSC resolutions are not based on the expression of the will of the people. Concerning state-building operations, the decision-making process of the UNSC admittedly involves the consent of the state, but seldom the consent of the people.[45] Thus, internationally sponsored state-building processes do not often rely on any form of public participation. When the pre-constituent act results from a UN resolution, the concerned state and thereby its people are not represented during the negotiation of the pre-constituent act.[46] The absence of national actors around the table of pre-constituent negotiation reveals an inherent lack of legitimacy of such a process.

42 M Brandt, 'Constitutional Assistance in Post-Conflict Countries, the UN Experience: Cambodia, East Timor and Afghanistan', (Programme des Nations Unies pour le Développement 2005) 9.

43 P Dann and Z Al-Ali, 'The Internationalized Pouvoir Constituant – Constitution-Making Under External Influence in Iraq, Sudan and East Timor' (2006) 10 *Max Planck Yearbook of United Nations Law* 423 s.

44 J Cottrel and others, *Constitution-Making and Reform: Options for the Process* (Interpeace 2011) 335.

45 Tardy (n 5) 395.

46 This finding results from Article 27 of the UN Charter, which defines the mode of adoption of UNSC's resolutions.

Content of international pre-constituent act

The pre-constituent act 'provides the legal framework, defining principles and parameters for the exercise and mandates most post-conflict constitutional exercise'[47] and depends largely on the context of the transition in question. Two types of constraints might be identified during the constitution-making process: upstream and downstream constraints. 'Upstream constraints are imposed on the assembly before it starts to deliberate. Downstream constraints are created by the need for ratification of the document the assembly produces'.[48] The pre-constituent act defines upstream constraints and, in some cases, part of the downstream constraints. In cases of imposed constitution-making processes, the pre-constituent act is an international law instrument. I will now argue that the content of those acts influences the level of legitimacy of the constitution-making process by setting a tight timeframe for the process and predetermining the actors of the transition, even though the pre-constituent principles seem to have little influence on legitimacy.

Each pre-constituent act is defined by external elements which influence the parameters it sets, such as its degree of accuracy and flexibility or its material content.[49] However, regardless of its nature, the pre-constituent act commonly sets a timeframe for the constitution-making process, the mandate of the constitutional body, the process of adoption of the constitution and the role assigned to each actor of the process. Two types of elements shall thus be separated: those relating to the design of the transition and those, referred to as pre-constituent principles, which concern the content of the final constitution. The pre-constituent act defines the constitution-making process with a greater or lesser degree of flexibility.[50]

Among the elements related to the design of the process, its timeframe is an important issue. In terms of legitimacy, time setting is an important issue because it highly influences the choice of the future political actors, and, as public consultation is a long process, the level of participation of the people. A brief analysis of the timeframes established by the pre-constituent act in the case of Cambodia, Timor-Lest, Afghanistan and Iraq[51] shows a will to accelerate constitution-making processes.

47 Brandt (n 42) 2.

48 J Elster, 'Forces and Mechanisms in the Constitution-Making Process' (1995) 45 *Duke Law Journal* 364 s., 373.

49 Brandt (n 42) 9.

50 A distinction is usually made between strict and flexible frameworks. The first ones tend to define in a very precise manner all the parameters of the constitution-making process (as it was the case in Timor-Lest, Cambodia, Iraq and in the second part of the Sudanese process). Flexible frameworks, for its part, only define the guidelines of the transition (it was the case in Namibia, and for the first part of the Sudanese process). The Afghan case seem to be an intermediate case as the Bonn Agreement defined the constitutional body but did not determine its mode of election. See ibid 10.

51 Only those 4 cases are relevant here: in Bosnia the constitution was imposed through the Dayton Peace agreement, so no timeframe was set, likewise, in Sudan and in Namibia, no timeframe was set by the pre-constituent act.

Tight timeframes are thus defined,[52] often based on political considerations of the international actors, including as a quick exit strategy (as was the case in Iraq) or as 'a clear indicator of a successful political transition in the form of a constitution',[53] like in the case of Timor.

Another element defined by the pre-constituent act and related to the design of the process is the choice of the actors of the coming transition. The exclusion from the process of some political actors is an important issue in the context of imposed constitution-making. Indeed, because the choice of who participates in the process falls under the international protagonist, it is not always guided by internal political considerations. Moreover, the exclusion, whether voluntary or not, of some political actors from the drafting of the pre-constituent act predetermines the representativeness of the process. For instance, in the case of Iraq, despite an attempt to involve the Sunnis in the process after the adoption of the pre-constituent act, they largely stayed excluded from it.[54]

Concerning the material elements provided by the pre-constituent act, the content of pre-constituent principle can be questioned. The case of Bosnia and Herzegovina shall here be treated separately as the whole constitution was included in the Dayton Peace Agreement. Pre-constituent principles were used in the case of Namibia, Sudan and Cambodia, concerning mostly human rights and democratic elections.[55] The legitimacy of those principles is hard to appreciate as they are quite general. In each of the three cases, references to international declarations of human rights, independent judiciary and elections are made. A comparative analysis of the pre-constituent principles also shows that they tend to respond to the roots of the finishing conflict. However, some principles seem to respond more to the international agenda than to internal considerations. For instance, the reference to 'liberal democracy' in the case of Cambodia[56] seems to result from international standards more than from national considerations.[57]

The case of Bosnia and Herzegovina is very specific on this point. 'The constitution-making process is entrusted to the international order, the constitution is itself inserted in an international treaty'.[58] The same legal instrument thus defines

52 International constitution-making processes have an average timeframe of 17,35 months. As a comparison, the South African process, which is considered as a model, took around 5 years to be completed.

53 Brandt (n 42) 9.

54 Dann and Al-Ali (n 43).

55 In each of the 3 cases, references to international declarations of human rights, independent judiciary and elections are made. A comparative analysis of the pre-constituent principles also shows that they tend to respond to the roots of the conflict. However, some principles seem to respond more to the international agenda than internal consideration. For instance, the reference to 'liberal democracy' in the case of Cambodia seem to result from international standards more than from national considerations.

56 Agreement on a Comprehensive Political Settlement of the Cambodia Conflict, Paris, 23 October 1991, Annex 5, art. 4.

57 LM Konan, 'Le Transfert Du Pouvoir Constituant Originaire À Une Autorité Internationale' (Thèse en vue de l'obtention du grade de docteur en droit, Nancy II 2007) 94.

58 Maziau (n 17) 566.

the constitution-making process (as it defines the way the constitution shall enter into force) and the constitutional text. In this case, referred to as heteronomous constitution,[59] there is no more distinction between upstream and downstream constraints. The constitution is negotiated as an international treaty and the constitution-making process is self-defined by the legal instrument itself. This specific situation finds really little legitimacy.

Even though international state-building is based on laudable intentions, it does not provide imposed constitution-making processes with inherent legitimacy. Rather, the legal framework of such processes is established out of the internal concerns. Even if international pre-constituent principles are not necessarily in conflict with the people's will,[60] the core of such a process surely lacks legitimacy. It is therefore necessary to analyze the design of the process to establish the degree of legitimacy of those transitions.

Attempts to build legitimacy of imposed constitution-making processes

The design of constitution-making processes influences its outcome. As legitimacy is built on the participation of the people, one of the major issues in the designing of constitutional transitions is how to involve the public. Four guiding principles to ensure the legitimacy of the process have emerged from the practice of constitution-making: inclusiveness, representation, transparency and national ownership.[61] It shall be now discussed whether or not imposed constitutional transition are designed in accordance with these principles. On the one hand, the design of the processes reflects a lesser or greater willingness to involve the public, including the composition and the election of the constitutional body. On the other hand, other means of public participation can be used in order to involve the people.

The design of international constitution-making processes

> Given the nature of the foreign intervention that typically provides the impetus for [international constitutional-making], ownership through democratic institutions and processes may well be the end of the intervention, but by definition it is not the mean.[62]

However, imposed constitution-making processes have mostly attempted to involve the public in some ways. This willingness is reflected in both the choice of the body in charge of drafting the constitution and the way the same body is nominated.

59 ibid.
60 Konan (n 57) 138.
61 Cottrel and others (n 44).
62 Chesterman (n 7) 947.

The choice of the constitutional body

Traditionally, two forms of constitution-making processes are considered as democratic: constituent assemblies and convention. Contemporary practice added a third possibility: round table.[63] Each of these processes presents comparative advantages and it is not possible to objectively determine which approach allows the highest degree of public participation.

The decision over the form of the constitutional body depends on contextual considerations. In the case of Namibia, Cambodia and Timor-Lest, decision-makers used constituent assemblies to write and adopt a constitution. Round table processes were used in Afghanistan and Iraq. In Sudan the constitution was written by a convention.

One may determine elements that define the degree of legitimacy of the process: the choice of the constitution-making body and the selection of its representatives, the rules of procedure of the debate, the public consultation, the adoption process and the implementation of the constitution.

The selection of representatives of the constitutional body

The way delegates are selected impacts all four elements of credible constitution-making. The design of elections in constitutional transition can help in setting a legitimate basis for the entire process. So far, all international constitution-making processes have used a proportional representation electoral system. It allows the representation of almost all national forces in accordance with their popular support. However, it does not necessarily fit with the context of transition.

The transitional context impacts the political spectrum. On the one hand, as an armed conflict recently ended, political parties may not have the organizational structure, financial resources and experience to engage in a peaceful political game. On the other hand, political forces that fought for the independence or the liberation of the state are likely to be in a position of gaining a large majority of the seats in the constitutional body and thereby play a leading role in the constitution-making process. Thus, in the cases of Timor-Lest, the FRETILIN (*Frente Revolucionara do Timor-Leste Independante*), which led the fight against Indonesia, gained over 50% of the seats in the constituent assembly.[64] One may argue that as long as the dominance of such a political force results from a popular support, the representativeness of the assembly should be assumed. However, in the case of Timor-Leste, surveys showed that barely 5% of the population understood what they were voting for, and most of the people did not know that Xanana Gusmao, the charismatic leader of the revolution, had split from the

63 A Arato, 'Conventions, Constituent Assemblies, and Round Tables: Models, Principles and Elements of Democratic Constitution-Making' (2012) 1 *Global Constitutionalism* 173 s., 175.

64 Brandt (n 42) 15.

party.[65] This lack of knowledge of the population over the elections remained unaddressed by international decision-makers.

Ensuring the descriptive representation[66] of the elected assembly is a key criterion for its legitimacy. In the case of Afghanistan, quotas have been imposed to ensure the representation of women and ethnic minorities.[67] It is important for decision-makers to take into account those two groups, since without special procedures, it is likely that they will be marginalized in the process.

The level of descriptive representation of constituent assemblies varies among the cases of international constitution-making processes. Concerning inclusiveness, all of the political actors have not always been involved in the process of constitution-making. In Iraq, for example, Sunnis refused to take part in the process even though the Transitional National Administration (TNA) tried to involve them.[68] Likewise, in Cambodia the *Khmers Rouges* refused to take part in the process as they felt it was not politically neutral. The Taliban did not participate in the constitutional transition of Afghanistan.[69] The exclusion of ex-combatant groups increases the possibility that they will later become spoilers of the process. The boycotts described above are evidence of the failure of international actors to ensure an ostensible political neutrality of the process and its national ownership. One of the factors of this failure is the lack of objective criterion for choosing local interlocutors. This decision mostly appears to be linked to the interest of international decision-makers and the willingness of local actors to comply with the demands of the former.[70]

The level of representation, inclusiveness and national ownership of processes are influenced by the choice of the constitution-writing body and the way its delegates are selected. However, even a truly representative assembly, for instance the Afghan's *Loya Jorga*, may lack legitimacy due to the way debates are conducted.

The rules of procedures of constitution-writing bodies

Policy-makers need to ensure that each point of view is taken into account as it 'affect[s] who has a say in choosing substantive terms, which in turn shapes willingness to comply with agreement'.[71] This is largely impacted by rules of procedures.

65 ibid 18.

66 Descriptive representation '*means that parliament is composed in a way that accurately reflects the demographic characteristic of a society*', S Dreef and W Wagner, *Designing Elections in Conflict-Prone Divided Societies: The Case of South Sudan* (PRIF 2013) 4.

67 Brandt (n 42) 19.

68 Dann and Al-Ali (n 43).

69 Brandt (n 42).

70 Woodward (n 6) 114.

71 J Widner, *Constitution Writing and Conflict Resolution* (UNU WIDER 2005) 3 http://www.wider.unu.edu/publications/rps/rps2005/rp200551.pdf accessed 11 May 2015.

Rules of procedure have an impact on the transparency of the process. For example, publicity of the debates may be an issue in the design of the process. While publicizing the debates increases popular accountability of the delegates, it may however create an opportunity for spoilers to intimidate delegates and undermine the quality of the debates.[72] In Afghanistan, for example, even though women were adequately represented in the constitutional *Loya Jorga*, the presence of warlords during the debate undermined their ability to express their claims.[73] Furthermore, the choices over the working language of the assembly and voting rules may be an issue directly linked to representation and inclusiveness. Most of the international constitution-making processes had rules of procedures that, in one way or another, sought to ensure the participation of all the delegates, but overall none of them succeeded to create a balance between political forces.

Designs of international constitution-making processes did not succeed to create their legitimacy. The post-apartheid South African constitution-making process brought a conceptual shift on constitutional transitions through the use of public consultation. However, international actors failed to take this opportunity to legitimate constitution-making processes.

Public participation in imposed constitution-making processes

> The constitution-making process is a unique moment – an opportunity to build consensus, a shared sense of identity, values, and purpose, and to resolve major differences. To have any realistic hope of achieving such outcomes, constitution-makers must be committed to a credible and transparent process where the concerns of the people are central and where the people know that choices on constitutional issues take account of their views.[74]

It has already been established that the very nature of imposed constitution-making processes does not really take into consideration the concerns of the people. The conceptual shift brought by the South-African constitution-making process was a first attempt to include more widely the population through public consultation and the mode of adoption of the constitution.

The failed attempts in public consultation

From a legal point of view, public consultation appears to be subject to soft law. Even though there is no binding norm providing a legal obligation of a state to consult its people to draft a constitution, international law recognizes a series of rights that may be linked to constitution-making, such as the right to participate

72 Elster (n 48) 370.
73 Brandt (n 42) 21.
74 Cottrel and others (n 44) 108.

in public affairs[75] or the right to self-determination.[76] It seems there is a consensus on the existence of a right of people to participate in the choices on their own government[77] from which derives a right to participate in the constitution-making process. However, legal frameworks of imposed constitution-making processes include various levels of public participation and consultation.

In Sudan, Namibia, Cambodia and Bosnia and Herzegovina the public was not consulted in the constitution-making process. On the other hand, in Afghanistan, Timor-Leste and Iraq policy-makers tried to implement some kind of direct participation.

In Iraq, the constitution-making process had some level of public consultation through the use of public conferences on constitutional matters. The debates took place only during the three months of the writing process and before the High Council led by US representative took over the process.[78]

In Timor-Leste, the Regulation 2001/2 of the United Nations Transitional Administration in East Timor (UNTAET)[79] referred to public consultation as an option for the process. Following public demonstration, policy-makers decided to create constitutional commissions. However, the process was extremely hasty as the commissions created in each district had only 45 days to educate the people and collect their propositions.[80] The final report of the Commissions was not taken in consideration by the Constituent Assembly. The population felt like the consultation process was entirely made by the UN officials, undermining its credibility.

The case of consultation in Afghanistan is the most extensive one. It used a constitutional commission, which was specially created for the purpose of public consultation. Representatives of the commission were sent to each region (including refugee camps in Pakistan and Iran) to educate the people over constitutional issues and gather propositions. The consultation process managed to overcome the lack of security in some areas and raised a high enthusiasm among the population as 15,000 citizens gave suggestions.[81] However, the Bonn Agreement did not provide any insurance for the independence of the Constitutional Review Commission and President Karzaï controlled the entire process. Moreover, the draft constitution, which was written by a nine-member committee behind a closed door, was released to the public only one month before the Constitutional *Loya Jorga* adopted it.

75 *International Covenant on Civil and Political Rights*, Adopted by the General Assembly of the United Nations on 19 December 1966, Art. 25.
76 United Nations, *Charter of the United Nations*, 24 October 1945 (San Francisco), 1 UNTS XVI, Art.1§2.
77 Cottrel and others (n 44) 80.
78 Dann and Al-Ali (n 43).
79 UNTAET, Regulation 2001/2 on the Election of a Constituent Assembly to Prepare a Constitution for an Independent and Democratic East Timor (2001) UNTAET/REG/2001/2.
80 Brandt (n 42) 14.
81 ibid 20.

International actors failed in creating public consultation processes in constitution-making. This failure is closely linked to the tight agendas of the processes and the lack of political will to involve the population in the writing process.

Adoption and implementation of the constitution

Two major ways have been used to adopt constitutions in imposed constitution-making: adoption by an assembly or through referendum. All but the Iraqi and the Bosnian processes used adoption by an assembly. Even though referendum is a way of directly involving the people in the process and gives some legitimacy to it,[82] its outcome is limited by the level of polarization it creates and by the risks of political manipulation of the process.[83] An overview of the different processes shows that the means of adoption of the constitution did not make any major difference in its legitimacy.[84] Even a highly representative and inclusive referendum failed to legitimize a closed and secretive process.

Furthermore, concerning the implementation of the constitution, a comparison of international constitution-making processes shows that international actors had little interest to be involved in the implementation of the constitution. Thus, in Cambodia and Timor-Leste the international administration left the territory a few days after the adoption of the draft. In Iraq, the American army stayed a few years after the adoption of the draft constitution, but its mandate was limited to maintaining security and not ensuring the implementation of the constitution. Bosnia and Herzegovina was the exception to this trend as the constitution brought by the Dayton agreement relied so heavily on international administration that international forces never withdrew.

Conclusion: Outcomes of international constitution-making processes

International constitution-making processes are not designed based on public participation. They are rather grounded in the will of the international community to create responsible states in accordance with international standards. Above all, they are undertaken within a tight timetable, which undermines attempts to give the people a voice. This finding of a lack of legitimacy of internationally imposed constitution-making does not involve the idea that any imposed process is meant to fail. Some counter-examples, such as the case of Japan, show that even the most externally imposed processes might happen to succeed. However, the lack of legitimacy is patently an obstacle to success.

82 J Blount, Z Elkins and T Ginsburg, 'Does the Process of Constitution-Making Matter?' in T Ginsburg (ed), *Comparative Constitutional Design* (Cambridge University Press 2012) 54.
83 Cottrel and others (n 44) 296.
84 ibid.

> To endure, constitutions must be self-enforcing, meaning they must give rise to an equilibrium from which no party has an incentive to deviate. Even though constitutions may produce relative winners and relative losers, they will endure to the extent that the losers believe they are better off within the constitutional bargain than in taking a chance on negotiating a new one.[85]

Constitutions that are adopted through the intervention of international actors repeatedly fail to be self-enforcing since international actors – who often fail to take into account the preferences of the public that is to be governed by the constitution – control the processes of their adoption.[86] This finding doesn't mean that international constitution-making *cannot* lead to self-enforcing constitution, but rather that it undermines the construction of a constitutional culture. Indeed, the exclusion of some local political actors coupled with the little participation and consultation of the people tend to create rather unstable systems.

85 Z Elkins, T Ginsburg and J Melton, 'Baghdad, Tokyo, Kabul…Constitution Making in Occupied States' (2008) 49 *William & Mary Law Review* 1139 s., 1144.
86 ibid 1145.

11 A post-national legal order

Does the European Union have an imposed constitution?

*Graham Butler**

I Introduction

Constitutionalism is notionally focused around the law of nation states. Beyond that, there is international law, which also has historically focused on the laws that govern the relationship between states. Yet, Europe today sees a special relationship between states on a regional basis where powers are held by states unilaterally, as well as through an advanced international organisation multilaterally. With Europe's drive from coexistence to cooperation,[1] a form of post-national constitutionalism sprung in the latter half of the twentieth century. The emergence and growth of supranational law-making has been occurring in Europe in the highly-developed European Union—an international organisation—playing a leading role in shaping the societies of twenty-eight Member States through a defined multi-institutional procedure involving executives, civil servants, parliamentarians, citizens, and jurists. Given the historical and foundational steps in forming the European Union, from an economic entity starting with coal and steel,[2] to a fully-fledged constitutional system, can it be considered a form of imposed constitutionalism?

Membership of the Union was and continues to be an expression of integration-minded actors delving into a larger community of like-minded states. Regionally, this exercise of internal integration occurred through various means. Legally, the signing of treaties between European states that founded the Union was a fine balance between constitutionalism that was imposed, or rather, self-imposed. Whether this constitutionalising process stemmed from necessity or

* Support from the *Aarhus University Research Foundation* and the *Professor dr. jur. Max Sørensens Mindefond* is gratefully acknowledged. The author wishes to thank all the participants at the Imposed Constitutions conference at the University of Nicosia, Cyprus, 5–6 May 2017 for their comments and input. The usual author disclaimer applies.

1 For early sentiments, see Wolfgang Friedmann, *The Changing Structure of International Law* (Columbia University Press 1964); Eric Stein and Peter Hay, *Cases and Materials on the Law and Institutions of the Atlantic Area* (Overbeck Company 1963).

2 Gerhard Bebr, 'The European Coal and Steel Community: A Political and Legal Innovation' (1953) 63 *Yale Law Journal* 1.

otherwise is relevant, given that the nature of European constitutionalism, and how it has manifested itself throughout the decades, is a continuously evolving process. Thus, the existence of the EU, and its legal effects on Member States provokes the need to ask the following overarching questions in the context of study on imposed constitutions—can constitutionalism in the EU be considered imposed?

Other chapters in this volume have expressed sceptical views on the very existence of an imposed constitution.[3] This chapter explores the constitutionalising process of European integration through a supranational organisation model, putting supranationalism and imposed constitutionalism, when they meet, into perspective, arguing that some degree of soft imposition is evident in a post-national legal order—in the form of the European Union. The chapter is structured in that Section II discusses Europe and its Member States as a post-national legal order. Following this in Section III, supranationalism in the form of the European Union is analysed, in search of signs, however faint, of constitutionalism that has been impositioned. Section IV debates whether the principled understanding an imposed constitutional is in fitting with the European Union, before Sections V and VI round off the inquiry, with an understanding of imposed constitutionalism that may have to be expanded further, beyond the current normative outlook, to accommodate post-national legal orders. Through an understanding of the European Union as having an imposed constitution,[4] it can be seen with a level of concerted pressure in the post-war environment, and the imposed nature of the EU constitution can be viewed as both an internal and external construction.

II A post-national legal order

Constitutionalism is notionally focused around the international legal principle of nation states as prime actors within the global sphere of law. Post-national and supranational constitutional orders are relatively rare concepts, and they are even more scarce when supranationalism of any real significance is looked for, or one that works in a demonstrable, functional manner. Yet, the emergence of a post-national and supranational law-making order has occurred, most notably in Europe, with the highly-developed European Union playing a leading role in shaping the societies covering twenty-eight Member States. This has continued to the present day, despite recent turbulence times that has

3 See in particular, the contributions of David S. Law ('Imposed Constitutions and Romantic Constitutions', Chapter 2) and Yaniv Roznai ('Internally imposed constitutions', Chapter 3) in this volume.

4 For the distinction between imposed constitutions and imposed constitutionalism, see, Xenophon Contiades and Alkmene Fotiadou ('Imposed constitutions: Heteronomy and (un)amendability', Chapter 1) in this volume.

espoused crises in law-making,[5] from the financial sector,[6] to migration from non-EU Member States,[7] which have all demonstrated the resilient nature of European constitutionalism.

The Union's existence covers a relatively short period of time over the latter half of the twentieth century. The type of Union that the original six Member States wanted to create was, for all intents and purposes, collaboration on a formal footing. Membership of the Union for the original states was a voluntary exercise on the face of it. For these original states, looking beyond the voluntary actions of forming international treaties came as a result of indirect need (internal) and international pressure (external) to ensure long-lasting peace and harmony on a continent that, many times over, had been stricken with conflict and violence. In the aftermath of the Second World War, cooperation between Member States was to be based on international treaties. This was the era of newly formed international institutions to guide peace, prosperity, and economic development across the world, and the beginning of an age of globalisation for the masses.

However, the Union was not created just to see intergovernmental cooperation thrive. It also established supranational institutions, in what we know today as the European Commission (the Union's executive arm) and the Court of Justice (the Union's judicial branch).[8] Whilst the EU's initial institutions were weak, it was revolutionary for the time to establish international bodies to handle matters flowing from the founding treaties, which eventually led to a framework for the adoption of legal acts. Behind this was the good faith, or *bona fides*, to formally bind European cooperation, and ensure the recent ills of the early twentieth century were not repeated. Regionally for the EU, this necessitation of internal integration for the continent occurred through various means. In turn, this created problems given that regional integration of Europe was by no means absolutely politically appetising. To successfully integrate, actions had to be done on an intergovernmental model, or alternatively, the Union would have to chart a new supranational course that previously had not been truly attempted in any real formation, in Europe, or elsewhere. Even though the latter would involve '*deep*

5 Anca D Chirita, 'The Impact of the European Union Current Crisis on Law, Policy and Society' (2014) 16 *Cambridge Yearbook of European Legal Studies* 255.

6 See, Thomas Beukers, Bruno De Witte and Claire Kilpatrick, *Constitutional Change through Euro-Crisis Law* (Cambridge University Press 2017); Alicia Hinarejos, *The Euro Area Crisis in Constitutional Perspective* (Oxford University Press 2015).

7 Marco Scipioni, 'Failing Forward in EU Migration Policy? EU Integration after the 2015 Asylum and Migration Crisis' (2018) 25 *Journal of European Public Policy* 1357.

8 For seminal work on the role of the Commission enforcing Union law, see, Stine Andersen, *The Enforcement of EU Law: The Role of the European Commission* (Oxford University Press 2012). For the most comprehensive work on the institution of the Court of Justice, see, Anthony Arnull, *The European Union and Its Court of Justice* (Second Edition, Oxford University Press 2006).

incursion into domestic jurisdiction',[9] the EU did evolve as a unique supranational setting that still today has not been replicated as successfully elsewhere.

Whereas there was a need and unfastened obligation for the major continental powers in Europe to integrate in some manner, the opposite can be said for states joining the Union later during enlargement actions. The nature of European constitutionalism and its convolution by no means put off what were previously peripheral states to the Union. Thus, the Union expanded in all directions—to the north, south, and extensively to the east. Rather than shying away from the constitutionalising features of a post-national and supranational setting, states were queuing up in order to accede, to bring themselves into line of being western democracies.[10] Many states, noting the economic success of the Union, were all too keen to join. With the signing of treaties between fellow European states that blossomed from six to twenty-eight states in a few mere decades, it is demonstrative of a fine balance that exists between constitutionalism that was imposed, compared to constitutionalism that was self-imposed.

The EU is a constantly gradualising process of imposed constitutionalism where multiple influences shape the constitutionalism and legalism of the European Union, including the legal services of the institutions.[11] The Union's construction has developed along the lines of the intentions of the initiating Member States, but also as a result of encapsulating a view shared beyond the governmental level, stretching down to the citizenry more directly. Whether this constitutionalising process has stemmed from the Union's judicial arm,[12] or political actions consequent to establishing the Union, the imposed nature of European Union constitutionalism appears evident. With this in mind, the intertwined nature of supranationalism and constitutional imposition have never been fully addressed in academic scholarship. Standard texts on the European Union, from the dominating legal or political science perspectives, rarely if ever discuss the Union as a form of imposed constitutionalism, despite some elements of what this entails being present.

With the European Union being the most advanced international organisation known to date, it has gone beyond a straightforward multilateral body and extended itself to being a supranational entity with large legal ramifications. Supranationalism, as seen over recent decades in the EU, has brought up questions about how the unity of law can be reconciled with European diversity, leading to the rise of constitutional pluralism. The practice of pluralism has never

9 Harold Hongju Koh, 'Why Do Nations Obey International Law?' (1997) 106 *Yale Law Journal* 2599. p. 2615.

10 For essential works, see, Christophe Hillion (ed), *EU Enlargement: A Legal Approach* (Hart Publishing 2004); Marise Cremona, 'EU Enlargement: Solidarity and Conditionality' (2005) 30 *European Law Review* 3.

11 Albeit they being small in nature. See, Jean Paul Jacqué, 'The Role of Legal Services in the Elaboration of European Legislation' in Antoine Vauchez and Bruno De Witte (eds), *Lawyering Europe: European Law as a Transnational Social Field* (Hart Publishing 2013).

12 See, Alec Stone Sweet, *The Judicial Construction of Europe* (Oxford University Press 2004).

had an easy ride in Europe, however. Historically,[13] or more contemporarily,[14] the ultimate source of law differs depending on the legal question being asked. Was this what was in mind when the Union was formulated, and under what circumstances were such foundational plans for the Union laid? Looking beyond the voluntary actions of forming international treaties, sentiment about post-national constitutionalism through imposition in the EU, post-war, is evident. Thus, the very existence of the European Union can broaden the understanding of what an imposed constitution is, and that it must take into account post-national legal orders.

III European supranationalism

The supranational setting of the European Union is an advanced example of supranationalism at its most sophisticated level seen in practice to date. The integration of Europe takes place in a number of domains; economically, politically, and legally; and the desire to unify Europe, whilst respecting the parameters and scope of nation states powers in the context of international law was to draft treaties which, at their heart, was to form the basis for strengthened cooperation and dialogue. In law, the EU's own treaties do not specifically refer to the term 'supranational' or 'supranationalism' anywhere. In the unity of knowing the existence of good faith behind the need to come together as a precursor for formalised cooperation, the commitment to entering international treaties would guarantee that previous acts of aggression and dominance would be prevented. Economic institutions have been at the heart of reconstructing previously-powerful states, albeit in such a way that each state was successfully interconnected through global institutions in a way that they previously weren't. Europe has and continues to be a diverse continent, but still it has and still is possible to espouse notions of common European values.

The boundaries of Member State jurisdiction as were previously known have lost much of their previous significance. As it is known today, the Union is a cohesive set of treaties, with an array of institutions across the legal and political spectrum, with each serving an individual purpose. Supranationalism is an extremely broad-reaching context. The term in and of itself is difficult to define, but was evoked as early as the foundation of the Union's precursor, the European Coal and Steel Community.[15] Today, it is accepted that much of Union law and its

13 See, Matej Avbelj and Jan Komárek (eds), *Constitutional Pluralism in the European Union and Beyond* (Hart Publishing 2012); Matej Avbelj, *The European Union under Transnational Law: A Pluralist Appraisal* (Hart Publishing 2018).

14 On a recent struggle between the Supreme Court on Denmark, and the Court of Justice of the European Union, see, Ulla Neergaard and Karsten Engsig Sørensen, 'Activist Infighting among Courts and Breakdown of Mutual Trust? The Danish Supreme Court, the CJEU, and the Ajos Case' (2017) 36 *Yearbook of European Law* 275.

15 See, Henry L Mason, *The European Coal and Steel Community: Experiment in Supranationalism* (Martinus Nijhoff Publishers 1955).

law-making framework constitutes a supranational environment, if not a transnational environment. Some qualifications must be made, however, when discussing supranationalism and law in Europe. Constitutionalism does not unequivocally extend beyond each Member State in the European Union. Whilst framing the Union as a supranational actor, it is not, *per se*, a fully supranational body.

One of the great hallmarks of the Union and its legal framework has been the ability to adapt every number of years, with amendments being proposed at Intergovernmental Conferences for textual changes to the primary law; materially and symbolically. The treaties, amended every number of years in recent memory,[16] still cater for differing levels of distinction along different paths, with some still largely on intergovernmental paths, such as the Common Foreign and Security Policy (CFSP).[17] The full acceptance of a multispeed Europe in legal term has been accepted, with some reluctance, but yet, a fully 'two-speed' Europe with categories of membership has yet to be fully embraced.[18] However, European constitutionalism is far more entrenched than intergovernmentalism, where the absolute law-making powers of Member States within the Union curtailed, recognising the role that the EU legislative process and Union law plays. Indeed, Europeanism has never truly been about developing a state,[19] and yet, its aspirations at times clearly represent such inclinations. Whether it is the existence of the phrase such as 'ever closer Union' in the preamble of the Treaty on European Union (TEU), as well as Article 1 TEU, or the admiral external vision of the Union set down in Article 21 TEU,[20] the integrationist agenda leading to

16 For discussing the treaty revision process and the intervals between amendment, see, Bruno De Witte, 'The Closest Thing to a Constitutional Conversation in Europe: The Semi-Permanent Treaty Revision Process' in Paul Beaumont, Carole Lyons and Neil Walker (eds), *Convergence and Divergence in European Public Law* (Hart Publishing 2002).

17 On the special nature of CFSP, see, Graham Butler, 'The Coming of Age of the Court's Jurisdiction in the Common Foreign and Security Policy' (2017) 13 *European Constitutional Law Review* 673. Also, Panos Koutrakos, 'Foreign Policy between Opt-Outs and Closer Cooperation' in Andrea Ott, Bruno De Witte and Ellen Vos (eds), *Between Flexibility and Disintegration: The Trajectory of Differentiation in EU Law* (Edward Elgar 2017); Geert De Baere, *Constitutional Principles of EU External Relations* (Oxford University Press 2008); Graham Butler, *Constitutional Law of the EU's Common Foreign and Security Policy: Competence and Institutions in External Relations* (Hart Publishing 2019).

18 This is discussed in Jean-Claude Piris, *The Future of Europe: Towards a Two-Speed EU?* (Cambridge University Press 2012).

19 Joseph HH Weiler, 'The Reformation of European Constitutionalism' (1997) 35 *Journal of Common Market Studies* 97. p. 120. That is not to say that one has been wanted. See, Giuseppe Federico Mancini, 'Europe: The Case for Statehood' (1998) 4 *European Law Journal* 29. The Court of Justice of the European Union only confirmed in 2014 that the European Union is not a state. '*…the EU is, under international law, precluded by its very nature from being considered a State*'. Opinion 2/13 of the Court, *Accession of the European Union to the European Convention for the Protection of Human Rights and Fundamental Freedoms*, ECLI:EU:C:2014:2454, paragraph 156.

20 For example, Article 21 TEU: '*[the Union] shall be guided by the principles which have inspired its own creation…*'

supranationalism within EU primary law has been, and to a large extent continues to be alive and kicking.

Integration through supranationalism has been a gradual process. Earlier writers, and judges,[21] created a key role in elucidating the true meaning of European constitutionalism. Although next-to-few described the Union as imposed, there was certainly elements of it there. Its early years mainly involved chipping away on the barriers to inter-state trade, and also saw the introduction of revolutionary doctrines from the Union judiciary. Progress on what constituted a supranational legal setting can be identified in the Court of Justice of the European Union's own case law. Much of the early case law of the Court of Justice reflected legal change,[22] as traditional barriers to inter-state trade were removed. The Court of Justice had taken a bold step in creating what is now informally referred to the European or EU Constitution. The case of *Van Gend en Loos*,[23] seen as one of the defining judgments in the primitive days of the Court, declared the Union was a 'new legal order', and thus marked the notion of the EU treaties as a defining understanding to set the new creation of the Communities apart from other international relationships that existed in treaty format up to that point. The caveat to the 'new legal order' in *Van Gend en Loos* was followed by an often-forgotten phrase, in that the Member States 'limited their sovereign rights, *albeit within limited fields*'.[24] This is a common judicial technique in the Court of Justice's jurisprudence to make a groundbreaking statement, only to compliment it with a qualification.[25] It took another twenty-eight years for the Court of Justice to revise this small constraint, to blowing open the gate to recognising that the Member States, by the treaties, 'limited their sovereign rights, *in ever wider fields…*'.[26]

The Court, as a largely dominant institution in the development of Union law, has had the sufficient legal space in order to construct constitutionalism,

21 Pierre Pescatore, *The Law of Integration: Emergence of a New Phenomenon in International Relations, Based on the Experience of the European Communities* (A W Sijthoff 1974); André M Donner, *The Role of the Lawyer in the European Communities* (Northwestern University Press 1968).

22 For work on contemporary legal history, see, Morten Rasmussen, 'The Origins of a Legal Revolution—The Early History of the European Court of Justice' (2008) 14 *Journal of European Integration History* 77.

23 Case 26/62, *NV Algemene Transport- en Expeditie Onderneming van Gend & Loos v. Netherlands Inland Revenue Administration*, ECLI:EU:C:1963:1.

24 *Ibid.*, page 12.

25 This could be called 'judicial minimalism'. For the situation in Union law, see, Daniel Sarmiento, 'Half a Case at a Time: Dealing with Judicial Minimalism at the European Court of Justice' in Monica Claes and others (eds), *Constitutional Conversations in Europe: Actors, Topics and Procedures* (Intersentia 2012), which has largely been inspired by the doctrine seen in US law. See, Cass R Sunstein, *One Case at a Time: Judicial Minimalism on the Supreme Court* (Harvard University Press 2001).

26 Opinion 1/91 of the Court, *Draft agreement between the Community, on the one hand, and the countries of the European Free Trade Association, on the other, relating to the creation of the European Economic Area*, ECLI:EU:C:1991:490, paragraph 21.

reinforcing constitutionalism that sought to be imposed in the first place. The very existence of judicial review within the EU legal order itself has brought with it many changes to how national courts operated in Member States. It can even be said that changes have been of an 'imposing nature',[27] with unparalleled changes to how Member States functioned. The natural growth and ever-expanding influence of the Union would suggest that areas of national competence were being eroded due to the opening up of Member States to an ever-more integrated region with the liberalisation of marketplaces. As the Court of Justice continues to adapt what a market is, which historically has been interpreted very broadly, the very acts of the Court of Justice, broadening the basis for where Union law can be applied, underpins the constitutionalising process of the Union.

With the Union being born under the ashes of the Second World War, the main belligerents and their opponents were the first to formulate the EU project which, by its very scope, was the antithesis to war, would eventually extend in all directions outwards to all the parameters of Europe. The Union, while fulfilling a clear purpose within the public sphere of law,[28] has been a constitutional creation, not necessarily by actions of European citizens as a group, but rather, conducted by governments acting on behalf of citizens whose origins lay in an intergovernmental setting from the 1950s.

Like any system of forging an inter-state treaty arrangement, the explicit inclusion of the subjects of what would become European constitutionalism was absent. That is not to say, however, that such actions were against such subjects' interests. Their involvement was originally more marginal, but in times of late, has reached a greater critical mass. The six original Member States that forged the Coal and Steel Community in Paris in 1951, and later the wider European Communities in Rome in 1957, were national governments acting under the democratic will of their respective states. However, referenda throughout Europe are a more common feature of European democratic expression today than when the Union's treaties were first ratified. Given this historical backdrop to the Union's founding constitution, and the resulting glimpses of supranationalism, the Union can fit the traditional category of possessing a mild form of an imposed constitution.

IV Imposed constitutionalism

The study of imposed constitutions, or imposed constitutionalism, has traditionally been associated with constitutions of nation states, as prime actors within the field of international law. Whether it is historically the Japanese scenario,[29] or the more

27 Mauro Cappelletti, 'The Expanding Role of Judicial Review in Modern Societies' in Shimon Shetreet (ed), *The Role of Courts in Society* (Martinus Nijhoff Publishers 1988). p. 83.

28 See Chapter 2, '*The Theory of Functional Constitutionalism*', in Turkuler Isiksel, *Europe's Functional Constitution: A Theory of Constitutionalism Beyond the State* (Oxford University Press 2016).

29 See, Justin Williams, 'Making the Japanese Constitution: A Further Look' (1965) 59 *American Political Science Review* 665.

recent study of Iraq,[30] this dominant focus on traditional forms of the nation state must adapt when focus turns to the continent of Europe. The Union, whilst not a state,[31] has carved its way through the system of being a pioneering constitutional project, which is by no means an average situation for where an imposed constitution exists. Despite Europe not being an occupied place by non-European actors, attempts have been made by states from within the continent to take over other states. Thus, the constitutionalising process of European integration through an international organisation model has been no accident, with deliberate attempts on a number of fronts, in order to achieve a workable framework to come into being. Such undertakings thus provoke the need to sustain constitutionalism, and ensure long-lasting harmony between European states and peoples.

An imposed constitution has been described as an entity in which the constituent power is rested squarely with the people.[32] Yet contrastingly, the notion in its very existence can be challenged altogether.[33] For the EU, this is a more problematic feature of its imposed constitutional nature, given the Union is founded upon international treaties, consented to by the parties as opposed to peoples. The Union's construction has developed along the lines of the intentions of the initiating Member States, but also as a result of encapsulating a view shared beyond the governmental level, stretching down to the citizenry more directly. The individual constitutions of EU Member States, where applicable, mostly predate the very existence of the founding European bodies that later assembled as the European Union.

The national spheres of law and the intertwined nature of Union law inherently espouse the notion of legal conflict at different junctures. Law-making and its implicit implications means the laws of Member States have to change to accommodate the supranational law-making process. This involves run-of-the-mill law-making, but can also extend all the way up to necessitating amendments to national constitutional texts, where applicable. The manner in which membership of the Union is embedded within the constitutional structures of Member States varies considerably. Enlargement first became a reality in 1973 with the accession of Denmark, Ireland, and the United Kingdom.[34] As each Member State accedes,

30 See, Andrew Arato, *Constitution Making Under Occupation: The Politics of Imposed Revolution in Iraq* (Columbia University Press 2009).

31 Discussed in, Graham Butler, 'The European Union and Diplomatic Law: An Emerging Actor in Twenty-First Century Diplomacy' in Paul Behrens (ed), *Diplomatic Law in a New Millennium* (Oxford University Press 2017).

32 Yasuo Hasebe, 'Imposed Constitutions (Constitutions Octroyées)' in Rainer Grote, Frauke Lachenmann and Rüdiger Wolfrum (eds), *Max Planck Encyclopedia of Comparative Constitutional Law* (Oxford University Press 2016), paragraph 2.

33 See, David S Law, 'The Myth of the Imposed Constitution' in Denis J Galligan and Mila Versteeg (eds), *Social and Political Foundations of Constitutions* (Cambridge University Press 2013).

34 Jean-Pierre Puissochet, *The Enlargement of the European Communities: A Commentary on the Treaty and the Acts Concerning the Accession of Denmark, Ireland, and the United Kingdom* (A W Sijthoff 1975).

it has to ensure that membership is adopted 'in accordance with their respective constitutional requirements'. For Denmark and the United Kingdom, this meant an Act of Parliament,[35] and for Ireland,[36] an amendment to the national constitution which could only have been done by referendum. Given the Union had no particular constitutional moment,[37] but instead had a process of continuous constitutionalising through practice and jurisprudence, *prima facie*, the Union could be considered an imposed constitution.

Yet, if the Union itself is not specifically an imposed constitutional system, then the very effect of the Union has a wider legal effect in the region through the Court of Justice's jurisprudence. In addition to *Van Gend en Loos*, thereafter shortly followed an equally revolutionary doctrine that emerged—the doctrine of primacy—in the *Costa v. ENEL* case,[38] further cementing the shift of moving the Union's legal system away from a mere casual international arrangement, but interpreting the treaties as if they were a formative constitutional text. In *Les Vert*,[39] the Court of Justice said the Union and actions therein must be 'in conformity with the basic constitutional charter, the Treaty',[40] demonstrating the revolutionary doctrines of Union law were not confined to the 1960s, but continued well on into the 1980s.

Whether the EU's constitutionalism has been internally or externally imposed is a musing worthy of reflection. Stating that the internal nature to how the Communities were first espoused through a declaration, leading to binding treaties with accompanying institutions to further their ends, it would accordingly be insufficient to claim that the EU's own constitutional framework has been internally imposed. External pressure to forge together greater European cooperation was pressed for, but heading down a road of economic integration was one of a

35 Albeit the former held a plebiscite to approve membership of the then Communities. See, Ole Due and Claus Gulmann, 'Constitutional Implications of the Danish Accession to the European Communities' (1972) 9 *Common Market Law Review* 256.

36 John Temple Lang, 'Legal and Constitutional Implications for Ireland of Adhesion to the EEC Treaty' (1972) 9 *Common Market Law Review* 167; Mary T Robinson, 'Recent Legal Developments in Ireland in Relation to the European Communities' (1973) 10 *Common Market Law Review* 467.

37 Although, the Treaty on European Union (TEU) introduced by the Treaty of Maastricht has been considered such. Discussed extensively in, Joseph HH Weiler, *The Constitution of Europe: 'Do the New Clothes Have an Emperor?' And Other Essays on European Integration* (Cambridge University Press 1999).

38 The doctrine is also sometimes referred to as supremacy. Case 6/64, *Flaminio Costa v E.N.E.L.*, ECLI:EU:C:1964:66.

39 This judgment has been considered so critical that the current President of the Court of Justice has stated that '*[i]ts significance is multi-faceted and it is indeed striking so many fundamental points of European law can be found in one case*'. Koen Lenaerts, 'The Basic Constitutional Charter of a Community Based on the Rule of Law' in Miguel Poiares Maduro and Loïc Azoulai (eds), *The Past and Future of EU Law: The Classics of EU Law Revisited on the 50th Anniversary of the Rome Treaty* (Hart Publishing 2010). p. 295.

40 Case C-294/93, *Parti écologiste 'Les Verts' v. European Parliament*, ECLI:EU:C:1986:166, paragraph 23.

chosen number of paths. Acceding to the European Union for some states could have been presented as merely becoming a party to an international treaty in the same way that states are themselves a party to hundreds of treaties on everything, from foreign relations to matters of internal taxation. Having constitutionalism in Europe, therefore, with sophisticated autonomous institutions capable of having significant effects on national legal systems, was not immediately presented as such at the time of accession.

Whether this development was the scheming of states or citizens remains a subjective question, given that such constitutionalism was largely in fitting with their interests. As noted by the current version of the treaties themselves, they 'respect the equality of Member States before the Treaties, as well as their national identities, inherent in their fundamental structures, political and constitutional, inclusive of regional and local self-government'.[41] In whatever form this may be dispatched on how true the process of European integration has proceeded, the analysis can continue recognising the competing claims to what European integration through law has meant. Yet still, as before as it is now, the Union has a continuing problem of perception. Often it is seen through a national lens, as an instrument of state powers. Constitutionalism takes time to embed, develop, and ultimately, to be legitimately accepted. Thus, the roots of European constitutionalism and all that it entails has needed tools in order for it to develop in a way that was seen fit. Sustaining constitutionalism in supranationalism requires legal tools—the Union's treaties themselves.

V A continuing constitutional affair

The writings on Europe more than a century ago today still bear resemblances to the hidden backdrop of Europe today. In 1914, Stefan Zweig spoke of a people's 'educated and disciplined solely with a view to waging war and with blatant cynicism the whole economic structure...is galvanised with this single aim in mind'.[42] Thus, it has always been necessary to have pacific tools within a polities grasp to stem the tide of rampant nationalism that shattered Europe twice in a single half-century. The reason for the existence beyond the establishment of the Union has been economic integration, and thus coupled with this, has been the need to further an internal market, itself, a legal concept.[43] For the Union, constitution-making is one element, but constitutional amendment is quite another. Each treaty amendment can be considered an amending form of constitutionalism. A constitutional treaty to underpin the Union was for a long time under discussion,

41 Article 4(2) TEU.

42 Stefan Zweig, '1914 and Today (1936)' in Will Stone (tr), *Messages from a Lost World: Europe on the Brink* (Pushkin Press 2016). p. 131. Originally published in, Stefan Zweig, '1914 und heute (1936)' in Richard Friedenthal (ed), *Zeut und Welt. Gesammelte Aufsätze und Voträge 1904–1940* (Bermann-Fischer 1943).

43 Effectively argued in, Stephen Weatherill, *The Internal Market as a Legal Concept* (Oxford University Press 2017).

and subject to much debate.[44] An explicit attempt at forging a Constitution for Europe was considering a real, palpable option in the early part of the twenty-first century. Matters finally came to a head, and one overt attempt at forming a textually significant 'constitution', the *Constitution for Europe*, was drafted.[45] After two Member State referendum hurdles, the proposition was abandoned after an overwhelming rejection by two national electorates. Thus, the fallback to the standard option of multiple treaties providing for the European Union continued. The significant attempt of forming an explicit regime of constitutionalism in a supranational setting was an offer that certain citizens were not quite ready to accept. Instead, what resulted was a continued entrenchment of EU constitutionalism in the form of an amending treaty, the *Treaty of Lisbon*, which contained much of what the *Constitution for Europe* had to offer, and was of similar character, albeit with a different title.

What did this constitutional saga tell us about Europe, when specific proposals to form a defined constitutional framework are abandoned following rejections in two Member States? One fear was similar pushbacks in other Member States, and instead, an easier route was opted, with continued churning away of the imposition of implicit supranational constitutionalism. The halting of a textually significant 'constitution' effectively scuppered the overtly federalist vision for how an enhanced supranational organisation such as the EU would function. Whereas the proposed renamed primary law framework of the Union constitution could have been charged as being deliberately provocative, it can also be characterised as an accurate attempt of naming what the Union finds itself to be; a largely successful supranational integration project that does have a constitutional system, just without a correspondingly suitable name.

Yet citizens are not alone in feeling discontent with change.[46] National courts and Member States can have equally questioning roles, as the continuing role of national constitutional orders still peeks above the parapet from time to time. The German Constitutional Court in its 1993 *Maastricht* judgment[47] said '[i]f the

44 For example, see, Joseph HH Weiler, 'A Constitution for Europe? Some Hard Choices' (2002) 40 *Journal of Common Market Studies* 563.

45 'C 310. Treaty Establishing a Constitution for Europe'. *Official Journal*, 16 December 2004.

46 As argued, through referenda and direct democracy initiatives, EU citizens have a stronger voice in European affairs than they have previously. See, Helle Krunke, 'Sovereignty, Constitutional Identity, Direct Democracy? Direct Democracy as a National Strategy for Upholding the Nation State in EU Integration' in Xenophon Contiades and Alkmene Fotiadou (eds), *Participatory Constitutional Change: The People as Amenders of the Constitution* (Routledge 2016).

47 BVerfG 89, 155. For a variety of analysis and views, see, Joseph HH Weiler, 'Does Europe Need a Constitution? Demos, Telos and the German Maastricht Decision' (1995) 1 *European Law Journal* 219; Ulrich Everling, 'The Maastricht Judgment of the German Federal Constitutional Court and Its Significance for the Development of the European Union' (1994) 14 *Yearbook of European Law* 1; Dieter Grimm, 'The European Court of Justice and National Courts: The German Constitutional Perspective after the Maastricht Decision' (1997) 3 *Columbia Journal of European Law* 229.

peoples of the individual states (as is true at present) convey democratic legitimation...then limits are *imposed*, by the principle of democracy, on the extension of the [EU's] functions and powers'.[48] More recently, the imposition and evolutionary tale of European constitutionalism over a drawn-out period of time is beginning to show its character when a Member State from within the Union is gearing up to withdraw itself from a Union, for which it has been a member for over four decades.[49] Notwithstanding temporal change, twenty-seven states remain committed to membership of the Union, which will survive and exit crisis-mode at some juncture. Challenges still stands for the constitutionalising effect of the Union, however. For it can be claimed that it is structurally 'impossible for a federal system of a democratic nature to have members with basically different constitutional systems'.[50] Beneath the surface, the Union has been keen to shake-off the feeling that its status as an enhanced international organisation is encroaching upon national prerogatives, stoking a political backlash. More recently, given the highlighted issues with democracy in the specific context of the Eurozone,[51] new proposals are coming forward to reform the various essential components of the Union to make it more functional and responsive to contemporary demands, from the Euro crisis,[52] to the migration crisis,[53] and rule of law crisis.[54]

There is the implicit temptation to draw varying distinctions in what ultimately constitutes a wide definition of an imposed constitution. If a wide view is drawn, then it could be captured that all constitutional frameworks are imposed,[55] one way or another. This is as a result of the definition of what is 'imposed' is not fully settled. Accordingly, there is the understanding that the Union is some way along the theoretical spectrum. In the same manner in which nation states and constitutional scholars cling to their national constitutional orders and underpinning legal texts, EU Member States in an alternative manner implicitly have acquainted

48 Emphasis added. Translation from Christian Joerges, 'Taking the Law Seriously: On Political Science and the Role of Law in the Process of European Integration' (1996) 2 *European Law Journal* 105. p. 115.

49 For a collection of papers neatly summing up the most critical issues with respect to Brexit, scheduled to occur in 2019, see, Federico Fabbrini (ed), *The Law and Politics of Brexit* (Oxford University Press 2017).

50 Jochen Abr Frowein, 'The European Community and the Requirement of a Republican Form of Government' in Michigan Law Review Association (ed), *The Art of Governance: Festschrift zu Ehren von Eric Stein* (Nomos Verlagsgesellschaft mbH & Co KG 1987). p. 175.

51 See, Federico Fabbrini, Ernst Hirsch Ballin and Han Somsen (eds), *What Form of Government for the European Union and the Eurozone?* (Hart Publishing 2015).

52 Stéphanie Hennette and others, *Pour un traité de démocratisation de l'Europe* (Seuil 2017).

53 See, Thomas Gammeltoft-Hansen and Jens Vedsted-Hansen (eds), *Human Rights and the Dark Side of Globalisation: Transnational Law Enforcement and Migration Control* (Routledge 2017).

54 See, Dimitry Kochenov and Laurent Pech, 'Better Late than Never? On the European Commission's Rule of Law Framework and Its First Activation' (2016) 54 *Journal of Common Market Studies* 1062.

55 See the chapter of Richard Albert ('*Constitutions imposed with consent?* Chapter 5), in this volume.

affection towards European constitutionalism. Global economic conditions have unquestionably brought increasing pressures upon systems of governance which have not absolutely fitted with the nation state model. Yet this challenge brings with it the opportunity to mark a new departure on successful integration within a constitutional system.

Imposed constitutionalism in Europe has accordingly been both an internal and external matter, decided by founding Member States of the European Union. The approval of such steps towards economic integration may have been slow-paced and limited, but its ramifications for future potential were something that continue to expound themselves today. With ongoing development of integration and wider harmony, the decision to proceed with integration through more supranationalism, and not less,[56] can be measured as a success. It can even be said how the Union has the inability to stand still.[57] When bringing together European states in a process of integration, there had been no off-the-shelf model to turn to, thus, providing actors like the Court the legal space to craft a constitutional system with a strong judiciary to support a forum for constitutionalism to develop has been essential. Whether this constitutionalism enhanced by the Court's actions amounts to being an *imposed* constitution is notional, but other theories to support this belief have yet to be sufficiently explored in any great length. Without resorting to the *travaux préparatoires*, which the Court has not fully endorsed,[58] it is thus an open licence for actors to interpret law creatively within the legal order. As Union law continues to become more deeply embedded at a faster rate than it is becoming wider, the general principles of Union law will seep into the foundations of the Union's present underpinning—the treaties.

The treaties elucidate many understandings of European history. Its opening lines marked that it is a step 'resolved to mark a new stage in the process of European integration'. However, in the hundreds of articles that follow the Preamble, it is up to other parties to bring forth respective interpretations when it is attempted to be construed, legislatively or judicially. Furthermore, window dressing in constitutions destabilises other provisions in constitutions that are meant to truly mean something concrete.[59] The transferal of certain areas of competence and its accompanying powers to lawmakers beyond the state has the ability to reshape, or at the very least alter, the very working methods of international law as it progressed since the twentieth century. Whether imposed economic integration through constitutionalism is presentable as an export model for other

56 With certain exceptions. See, Rebecca Adler-Nissen, *Opting Out of the European Union: Diplomacy, Sovereignty and European Integration* (Cambridge University Press 2014).

57 As argued in, Ronan McCrea, 'Forward or Back: The Future of European Integration and the Impossibility of the Status Quo' (2017) 23 *European Law Journal* 66.

58 See, Samuli Miettinen and Merita Kettunen, 'Travaux to the EU Treaties: Preparatory Work as a Source of EU Law' (2015) 17 *Cambridge Yearbook of European Legal Studies* 145.

59 Noah Feldman, 'Imposed Constitutionalism' (2005) 37 *Connecticut Law Review* 857. p. 872.

areas of the world is debatable, as other regional entities willing to integrate may not necessarily opt for a constitutional system of dialogue.

VI Conclusion

Given the foundational steps in forming the European Union, and its supranational law-making, can it be considered an imposed constitution? Has imposed constitutionalism worked in a supranational setting? The primary law of the Union is cognisant of the historical origins of the need to integrate the continent of Europe in a legal way. Whatever way this was subsequently achieved—integration through law[60]—was to be acceptable, as long as it again not lead to the rise of forces intent on destructing other states. The wisdom of early 1950s thought, with first-hand experience of fraught division between European states—brought in, imposed, and laid an early attempt at constitutionalising legal integration as a unifying feature—cannot be forgotten. Without the Union law, it is difficult to know what might have otherwise proceeded in a complicated mixture of states; large and small. For it being near-impossible to fully understand Europe, it is equally less-compelling to fully ponder what might otherwise have been.

The collective understanding of what the European Union is—a post-national legal order—struggles to make full headway in traditional spheres of both international and constitutional law. An aspiration of the European Union was to be distinguished from mere international cooperation through international treaties. With the constitutionalising effects of Union law, and its continuously evolving structure,[61] models of constitutionalism from North America serve the EU well for conceptualising the models and paradigms of constitution-making, given its 'unfinished' status.[62] Whether the European Union has been an imposed constitution, or if it is a self-imposed constitution, cannot yet be fully categorised, yet, on the spectrum of imposition, it can be claimed to be a soft imposition. Given the Union's creation coincided with the formation of other post-war institutions shaping the international world order, questions can too be considered on whether the Union constitutionalism can be truly considered as a form or imposition, or merely a coincidence of its time.

Indicators of supranational constitutionalism in the European Union are evident, albeit that European integration and constitution-building have been slow, and steady-paced. The imposed constitution continues to shape the

60 See the volumes published in the 1980s by, Mauro Cappelletti, Monica Seccombe and Joseph HH Weiler (eds), *Integration Through Law: Europe and the American Federal Experience* (De Gruyter 1986).

61 See, Robert Schütze, *From Dual to Cooperative Federalism: The Changing Structure of European Law* (Oxford University Press 2009); Robert Schütze, *From International to Federal Market: The Changing Structure of European Law* (Oxford University Press 2017).

62 Francis Snyder, 'The Unfinished Constitution of the European Union: Principles, Processes and Culture' in Joseph HH Weiler and Marlene Wind (eds), *European Constitutionalism beyond the State* (Cambridge University Press 2003). p. 58.

constitutionalism and legalism of the European Union. The ever-expanding influence of the Union, through natural growth and judicial interpretation, would suggest that unqualified Member State control has been eroded, and thereby further cementing an imposed constitution. In the Union, the traditional ways of nation states, quite literally, are ever so slowly dissolving, and becoming further integrated, one way or another. There were immense consequences to this, forging institutions capable of providing for supranational law and accompanying rule-making. Integration through law in a post-war situation was inevitable, but also essential for ensuring that another war was not to be waged on the battlefields of Europe. So far, albeit with unsteady times over the most recent decade, the imposed nature of constitutionalism in the European Union, has largely succeeded.

12 Texts in a time of imposition

Lessons from two imposed constitutions in Africa

*James Fowkes**

So much has been imposed on Africa that studying imposed constitutions on the continent can seem like an exercise in the obvious. And sometimes it is. But African cases are of a richness which is neglected by comparative constitutional law, something that is true in many areas but more than usually problematic in this one.[1] Patterns of imposition are pervasive in African experience and scholarship, past and present, constitutional and not. The need to make sense of this tangle of impositions is an important reason why questions about imposed constitutions are so instructive to ask in the African context.

This contribution reports on research into two case studies from Anglophone Africa, Liberia and Botswana, which have received even less scholarly attention than other African cases. The story of Liberia's early independence is often lost amidst the later step up in European colonization efforts in the second half of the 19th Century. Thomas Pakenham's canonical *Scramble for Africa* does not even mention the country.[2] Botswana's independence in 1966 is often displaced by more violent cases that commanded much more international attention around that time, such as the events in Congo/Zaire, now the Democratic Republic of the Congo, and in Southern Rhodesia/Rhodesia, now Zimbabwe.[3] Today, comparative attention, such as it is, tends to be paid mainly to regional hubs like Nigeria or Kenya, or continental constitutional success stories like Benin or the much-cited South Africa.

* I am grateful to the editors, to Alyssa Plesser for exemplary research assistance into many dusty corners, and as ever to Michaela Hailbronner.

1 The neglect has long been obvious and is widely acknowledged as part of a broader global problem with the subjects of comparative constitutional law. See e.g. Daniel Bonilla Maldonado, 'Introduction: Toward a Constitutionalism of the Global South' in Daniel Bonilla Maldonado (ed.) *Constitutionalism of the Global South: The Activist Tribunals of India, South Africa and Colombia* (2013); Ran Hirschl, *Comparative Matters: The Renaissance of Comparative Constitutional Law* (2014). But that does not mean that much has changed yet.

2 Thomas Pakenham, *The Scramble for Africa* (1991).

3 See e.g. Lawrence James, *Empires in the Sun: The Struggle for Mastery of Africa 1830–1990* (2016), ch. 26.

Students of imposed constitutions will find that both cases repay efforts to remedy this neglect. Each is dominated by one imposed text, the 1847 Constitution in the case of Liberia, which was in force until 1980, and the 1966 Botswana Constitution, which remains in operation today. Both are unusually long-lived for an imposed text in Africa. Both are independence constitutions drafted, in their different ways, in a colonial context, but in each case this external relation is accompanied by significant local agency and by complex internal political patterns, including oppressive ones. Coming to terms with these nuances will tell us something about what an adequate concept of 'imposed constitution' should look like, and about which impositions we should and should not use that concept to express. Each of the three sections that follow will draw a lesson of this kind from different aspects of the case studies: first, about the external/internal dynamics of the constitution-drafting; second, about the internal dynamics and differences in local groups' relation to the constitution; and finally, about the significance of post-enactment events and how to understand imposed constitutions in the context of a tangle of other impositions.

Text in a time of imposition: The drafting stage

The events at constitutional time zero are of obvious importance in discussing imposed constitutions, and in neither of the two case studies is the dynamic a simple one of external imposition of a text by colonial powers on local colonial subjects.

Botswana

The case of Botswana offers a drafting story broadly typical of de-colonizing Anglophone Africa. Considerable constitution-drafting occurred before independence, as part of an incremental handover of power. The final instrument in this pre-independence process, the 1963 Constitution, came into force in 1965 and elections were held under its ambit. The 1963 text then formed the basis for the 1966 Constitution, which came into force with Botswana's independence on 30 September 1966.[4]

This process took place under colonial auspices and largely within colonial structures. Both the 1963 and 1966 texts derived their legal force from British enactment. Both were drafted by constitutional conferences of British and Botswanan delegates, the first in Lobatse and the second in London. Colonial officials were thus well placed to exert influence, albeit that British colonialism in Africa was by this point in full and open retreat. Botswana's independence was one among others in this process, and its constitution-drafting drew on earlier

4 For an overview, see Charles Fombad, 'The Republic of Botswana: Introductory Note' *Oxford Constitutions of the World* (October 2011), §1.

efforts, including in Kenya, Nigeria, Uganda and Nyasaland (today's Malawi).[5] These examples, in turn, are connected to the efforts that began the pattern of Commonwealth constitution-drafting under colonial auspices in the Sudan, Malaya (as it was then known) and Ghana.[6] British colonial influence was thus also indirect, via the influence of precedents from other countries in which colonial officials had also exerted significant power.

These colonial influences should not, however, eclipse the role of local agency. Botswana's constitution-drafting was an elite process that included local elites. This is in keeping with the broader narrative of Botswana's colonial and de-colonial experience, which involved a notably small amount of mass mobilization compared to other African examples. Indeed, Botswana's statehood owes itself to local elite action. Bechuanaland (as Botswana was known during its colonial phase) might have suffered incorporation into the Union of South Africa in 1909 but for three chiefs, including King Khama III, whose grandson Seretse Khama would become Botswana's first post-independence leader, who travelled to England in 1895 to obtain a royal assurance of protection.[7]

The first major step towards independence, the Constitutional Review of 1959, was a meeting of colonial officials and chiefs. Political parties entered the mix shortly afterwards, in the form of the more moderate Bechuanaland Democratic Party (BDP), which would govern Botswana after independence and has done so ever since, and the harder-line Bechuanaland People's Party (BPP). Their presence meant that the next major step, the Constitutional Convention of 1963, must be treated as somewhat more inclusive. But this effect remained limited. The main avenue for popular consultation on the 1965 constitution was tribal councils, the *kgotla*, meaning that the expression of public will was largely filtered through the will of important chiefs.[8] Observers described the March 1965 elections, the prelude to independence, as occurring within an "entirely apolitical electorate."[9]

The archetypal revolutionary party of independence based on mass mobilization never emerged in Botswana. The BPP had the necessary ideological aspirations and had, as we will see, some bolder constitutional ideas. But it was a modest force relative to similar parties in other African states at the time. It organized protests and boycotts, but on a limited scale. It faced some repression from

5 James Kirkby, '"Conditional on a Bill of Rights": Race and Human Rights in the Constitution of Botswana, 1960–1966' 4 *Law & History* 30 (2017), 55.

6 On which see generally Charles O. H. Parkinson, *Bills of Rights and Decolonization: The Emergence of Domestic Human Rights Instruments in Britain's Overseas Territories* (2007).

7 Akinola Aguda, 'Legal Development in Botswana from 1885 to 1966' 5 *Botswana Notes and Records* 52 (1973), 52–53.

8 Zibani Maundeni & Kekgaoditse Suping, 'The Politics of Exclusion in Botswana: A Creation of the Independence Constitutional Talks' 27 *PULA: Botswana Journal of African Studies* 325 (2013), 327–328.

9 The observation is that of Peter Fawcus and Alan Tilbury, high colonial officials closely involved in the transition, quoted by Kenneth Good, *Bushmen and Diamonds: (Un)civil Society in Botswana* (Nordiska Afrikainstitutet Discussion Paper 23, 2003), 7.

the colonial authorities, but also suffered from in-fighting and a relatively small black urban constituency.[10] The colonial presence therefore has something, but far from everything, to do with the BPP's modest political effect in these years.

For its part, the BDP worked largely in co-operation with colonial officials. It derived some direct political benefit from this, negatively in not facing the same political repression as the BPP, and positively in being able to take credit for popular pre-independence reforms, for example on multi-racial schools. The BDP's generally moderate positions (including, as we will see, on constitutional issues) presumably owed something to this association. But it would be a mistake, without more, to see those positions as imposed. Rather than boasting of making BDP leaders their puppets, colonial reports sometimes worried that the party's positions might be too weak for local consumption and damage its future electability. This applied even to issues on which colonial officials were generally particularly sensitive, such as racial discrimination and the position of the local white minority.[11] Such concerns are a strong hint that BDP leaders enjoyed a real measure of intellectual independence.

That hint tends to be confirmed by the knowledge that the BDP's positions were, among other things, consciously strategic. In 1966, Botswana was a poor, weak, landlocked state. (Its diamond wealth was discovered only after independence.) It had few international allies and was encircled by the white minority regimes of South Africa, South African-controlled South-West Africa (today's Namibia) and Rhodesia (today's Zimbabwe).[12] The BDP's choices to adopt moderate positions on issues such as race, and join, as we will see, the Commonwealth consensus on rights, were in part exercises in symbolic foreign relations by the clear-sighted leaders of a new state that had few other ways to win international friends. In the words of Quett Mosire, Botswana's first Deputy President and then its second President, '[w]hen you are weak, you have to stick to principles'.[13]

Nor should this strategic awareness be mistaken for cynicism. BDP leaders were also sincerely interested in nation-building. In this, they shared the broader optimism of African post-colonial leaders setting out to build new and better states, which can be hard to recall today.[14] That Botswana has long been a lonely exception to the subsequent collapse of this continental optimism also tells us that the BDP elite's commitments at the beginning deserve to be taken seriously as such. James Kirkby, concluding a rare recent study of primary materials in the years leading up to Botswana's independence, argues that

> [n]on-racialism was just as much an inspiring ideology for the nation to take into independence as it was, conveniently for white residents, a way to pin

10 Kirkby, above n 5, 41–45, 48–50; Maundeni & Suping, above n 8, 328.

11 Kirkby, above n 5, 48–52.

12 Or almost entirely encircled: fastidious geographers will note Botswana's tiny pub quiz question border with Zambia at Kazungula.

13 As quoted by Kirkby, above n 5, 37.

14 Lawrence James, *The Rise and Fall of the British Empire* (1997), 607.

the territory's conceptualization of human rights on individualism rather than African communalism.[15]

The pattern of constitution-drafting amidst de-colonization in Botswana is therefore one in which the power of the departing British met the power of the rising local heirs apparent. The relationship was often co-operative but, especially after World War II, had also involved more local assertiveness against colonial attitudes.[16] In such a setting, no locals can be said to be freely choosing for themselves on their own terms, but a simple story of blunt external imposition will not fit either. If the constitution is imposed, it is as a matter of degree. I take up the complexities of just what degree this should be thought to be at the end of this section, after taking account of the rather different and much earlier drafting dynamic in Liberia.

Liberia

Uniquely in Anglophone Africa, the main external figure in the drafting of Liberia's independence constitution is the United States. Liberia's constitutional enterprise began as a project of white Americans seeking an answer to the question of what to do with US slaves after they were freed. Prior British initiatives suggested resettlement as a solution. Resettlement had long been used as a means for ridding Britain of 'superfluous persons', including religious dissenters, prisoners of war, convicts, and beggars, initially to the sugar islands of the Caribbean.[17] A generation before, the London-based Committee for the Relief of the Black Poor had established the supposed Province of Freedom in today's Sierra Leone.[18] US initiatives of this sort in the area of modern Liberia produced such forgotten novelties as Mississippi-in-Africa and the Republic of Maryland, both founded in the 1830s. They also produced the more well-known efforts of the American Colonization Society (ACS), which began settling freed slaves on what they knew as the Pepper Coast in 1822.

The relationship between white ACS leaders and the freed black settlers who would later declare independence and draft the 1847 Constitution is less straightforward than has sometimes been assumed. Local agency was ultimately even more significant than in Botswana.

Initially, the relationship between the wealthy, politically-connected ACS leaders and the often poorly-educated freed slaves was predictably one-sided, not

15 Kirkby, above n 5, 59.

16 On racial attitudes in this period, see Christopher John Makgala, 'A Survey of Race Relations in Botswana, 1800–1966' 36 *Botswana Notes and Records* 11 (2006), 20–23.

17 James, above n 14, 8–10.

18 Monday B. Abasiattai, 'The Search for Independence: New World Blacks in Sierra Leone and Liberia, 1787–1847' 23 *Journal of Black Studies* 107 (1992), 108–111; Stephen J. Braidwood, *Black Poor and White Philanthropists: London's Blacks and the Foundation of the Sierra Leone Settlement 1786–1791* (1994), 63–128.

least in the original initiative to push for African re-settlement of black people born in America. The constitution that the settlers took along with them in 1822, drafted by the ACS, concentrated power in the Society and its (white) agents.[19] It has therefore long been easy to conclude that the same would go for subsequent constitution-drafting as well. As the close student of early Liberian constitutionalism Carl Patrick Burrowes puts it:

> It was once widely accepted in American academic circles that, in the realm of ideas and values, the white, wealthy and politically powerful ACS leadership had exercised a totalizing, unidirectional hegemony in its relationship with the [Americo-]Liberians, most of whom were illiterate ex-slaves.[20]

The attitude Burrowes describes is probably a reasonable generalization for the dynamic in the 1820s. But by the time of the drafting of the 1847 Constitution and Liberia's declaration of independent statehood on 16 July 1847, the balance of power had changed. The ACS struggled for funds while local black merchants prospered. Local political agitation increased, including in the form of constitutional proposals, and the ACS made increasing concessions to local authority.[21] The 1847 text that ultimately passed was written by a constitutional convention of local settler delegates (who I will refer to from this point as Americo-Liberians). It also came into effect only after being subject to a referendum among the Americo-Liberian community, albeit a problematic one: although 79% of voters were in favour, only 272 people, or slightly over 10% of those eligible to vote, participated.[22]

The changed dynamic is nicely illustrated by the way US sources were used in drafting the 1847 text. Not counting the locally-drafted Declaration of Independence, about two-thirds of the 1847 text was drawn from US sources. Most important among them – at what must surely be the peak of its global influence – was the state constitution of Maine. This reflects the influence that white American lawyers undoubtedly had on the drafting process. The Maine link is explained by the role of Harvard Professor Simon Greenleaf, whose advice on the drafting of the constitution had been solicited by the ACS leadership, and who

19 Abasiattai, above n 18, 112–13.

20 Carl Patrick Burrowes, 'Black Christian Republicans: Delegates to the 1847 Liberian Constitutional Convention' 14 *Liberian Studies Journal* 64 (1989), 81. The original though less comprehensive version of this argument was made by Robert T. Brown, 'Simon Greenleaf and the Liberian Constitution of 1847' 9 *Liberian Studies Journal* 51 (1980–81).

21 Brown, above n 20, 51–53; Abasiattai, above n 18, 112–14; M. B. Akpan, 'Black Imperialism: Americo-Liberian Rule over the African Peoples of Liberia, 1841–1964' 7 *Canadian Journal on African Studies/Revue Canadienne des Études Africaines* 217 (1973), 218–19, 227–28.

22 See the entry for Liberia in the African Elections Database, http://africanelections.tripod.com/lr.html, last accessed 2 February 2018. This feature of the referendum is also emphasized by Brown, above n 20, 53.

had strong prior ties to Maine.[23] But if external influence was the starting point, it was not the end. The Liberian delegates to the constitutional convention that issued both the Declaration of Independence and the new Constitution were educated and sometimes wealthy men of local standing, intent on establishing a new society of their own.[24]

This intent can be seen even in the parts of the 1847 text that borrow closely from US sources, because the Liberian delegates often took it upon themselves to clean up the original language. Burrowes attributes this above all to Hilary Teage, secretary to the constitutional convention that produced the text, editor of the *Liberia Herald* and a published proponent of clear language in legal drafting.[25] This suggests an attitude to US sources that is, to use a phrase more than usually apt in this context, less than slavish.

And outside these borrowed sections, something far more original was going on. The 1847 text tied political power to citizenship and – contrary to the wishes of the ACS leadership – restricted citizenship to people of African descent.[26] It thus pushed back strongly against the earlier pattern of oversight by the ACS and its local white officials. This assertion of black African nationalism is telling evidence of the complex and conscious local project of constitutional nation-building in which the Americo-Liberians were engaged.[27] It was a project at once three things: African nationalist, in what were early days for that idea; Christian, at a time when few Africans were Christians; and republican, in a Jeffersonian small farmer-citizen sense. The latter two elements are clearly borrowed from the ACS and its missionary impulse, and from US paradigms more generally. But the blend of the three, extraordinary for its time, reflects how far the constitution-drafting was from a straightforward imposition of white drafters' ideas on black settlers.

Notwithstanding the settlement's beginnings, then, Liberia's drafting process was sufficiently independent as to raise questions about whether the adjective 'imposed' even applies. Compared to Botswana, it involved a much weaker external colonizer that had been present for a much shorter time and never set up comparable local structures of power, and its text was both locally drafted to a substantial degree and subject to a local referendum.

The most obvious reason for treating the 1847 text as imposed, all this notwithstanding, is because of its status in relation to the local African inhabitants in the territory claimed by the new Liberian state. I consider their position in the

23 Carl Patrick Burrowes, 'Textual Sources of the 1847 Liberian Constitution' 23 *Liberian Studies Journal* 1 (1998), 5.

24 Burrowes, 'Black Christian Republicans', above n 20, provides sketch biographies.

25 Burrowes, 'Textual Sources', above n 23, 5–7.

26 Burrowes, 'Black Christian Republicanism: A Southern Ideology in Early Liberia, 1822 to 1847' 86 *Journal of Negro History* 30 (2001), 39; Brown, above n 20, 54.

27 Burrowes, 'Black Christian Republicanism', above n 26. See also the meditation on early slave-settler correspondence back to the United States by David Kazanjian, 'The Speculative Freedom of Colonial Liberia' 63 *American Quarterly* 863 (2011).

next section. But even if we put that aside, there are reasonable questions to ask about the 'imposed' nature of a constitution drafted in an imposed situation and so obviously within a US frame. These questions closely resemble those that can be raised about the position of the local Botswanan elite, which displayed something of the same independence of mind within a broadly similar context.

Local agency and colonial determinism

Both Botswana and Liberia reflect a key dilemma for the study of imposed constitutions in de-colonizing settings. In each case, a closer look reveals local elite actors with obvious initiative and agency of their own, who cannot be dismissed as puppets or passive subjects. But it is equally obvious that these locals had to operate in a context created and influenced by external actors, in terms broadly set by a constitutional model brought in from outside.

The dilemma arises if we wish to push beyond these twin truths and take a more definite position than the claim that these constitutions are imposed to some degree that is less than total. To what extent should we discount the ostensibly independent constitutional choices of the Americo-Liberian leadership or the Botswana BDP leadership on the basis that they were (pre-)determined by their colonial context? The impulse to turn the dial away from free choice just because the setting was colonial seems disrespectful of local agency, especially since no human enterprise is un-determined by context and previous action in this sense. But to turn the dial the other way seems to misunderstand, and to risk minimizing, the nature of colonialism. It is also difficult to offer answers based on historical sources without making ideologically fraught deductions about the contents of local actors' heads. Thus, any attempt to give more definite answers to questions about imposed constitutions is subject to what is a familiar problem in post-colonial settings. As Mahmood Mamdani has, for example, noted, in commenting on a related problem in two more general approaches to issues of colonialism and the patterns of global development that have formed in its wake,

> if structuralism tended to straitjacket agency within iron laws of history, a strong tendency in post-structuralism is to diminish the significance of historical constraint in the name of salvaging agency.[28]

We could shrug and accept a vague definition on the pragmatic basis that the issue is a muddy one. I am no enemy of this sort of muddling through. But it carries special risks in a context like this one. To say no more than that these constitutions are imposed to some degree is to invite the blurring of these examples with other constitutions in non-colonial settings, and thus potentially to become complicit in efforts to minimize by relativizing. A standard way to downplay the

28 Mahmood Mamdani, *Citizen and Subject: Contemporary Africa and the Legacy of Late Colonialism* (1996), 10.

distinctive experience of the Jews of Europe in the early 1940s is to argue that other groups were also killed in large numbers.[29] Thus the same colonial setting that presents us with definitional difficulties is also a strong reason to want to give more assertive answers in the face of them, to be true to the distinctive experience of colonialism.

In part, this problem is met just by acknowledging it. To use the same analogy, one can and should discuss the experiences of, for example, non-Jewish Belarussians or Poles in the early 1940s, while sincerely disclaiming any intention to minimize distinctive Jewish experiences in doing so.[30] It is no bad thing for the study of imposed constitutions if the connection to dilemmas of agency under and after colonialism is simply noted as a troubled area, whose details (only) are up for meaningful debate, and to leave the discussion to proceed from there.

But I would also contend, more definitely, that the dilemma is best met by doing more work outside the concept of 'imposed constitution'. Many constitutions are products of a legal tradition largely not 'chosen' by their drafters, still less by their subjects. Many drafters use standard formulations as starting points and follow contemporary trends.[31] And many are less sincere than the BDP elites in Botswana and less creative than the Americo-Liberian convention delegates. Accordingly, it seems to me a step towards distortion to try and dial up the degree of imposed-ness in our definition of these two constitutional texts, and others like them, in order to acknowledge the colonial reality.

In the third and final part of this paper, I will follow through on this contention by arguing for a certain mental separation of the concept of imposed constitution from broader social and political impositions, on the basis that many important colonial effects are better filed under the latter and not the former. But I first address a simpler problem that is immediately raised by my argument for classifying these texts as less imposed: that, especially in the Liberian case, in relation to some groups, the text was very imposed indeed.

Imposed constitutions and local political castes

Whether a constitution is imposed raises the question, upon whom? If external actors are dominant and all local actors equally weak, the question has a simple answer. But if local actors stand in different positions in relation to one another, they may also stand in meaningfully different positions in relation to the constitution.

Of course, there are many different ways in which those subject to a constitution might relate to it: every constitution affects some people more than others, or contains more of what some prefer than others or is drafted in ways

29 See e.g. Tony Judt, 'From the House of the Dead: An Essay on Modern European Memory', the epilogue to his *Postwar: A History of Europe since 1945* (2005).

30 As, for instance, in Timothy Snyder, *Bloodlands: Europe between Hitler and Stalin* (2012).

31 For a recent study of these patterns, see David S. Law & Mila Versteeg, 'The Evolution and Ideology of Global Constitutionalism' 99 *California Law Review* 1163 (2011).

that include some more than others. Expressing all these different relationships as slightly different degrees of imposed-ness would fracture the concept beyond utility without our learning anything more than the truism that different individuals can stand in different relations to the same constitution.

But that said, both case studies suggest that there are good grounds to do this to at least a certain extent. I thus defend a relational understanding of imposed constitutions, in which one and the same text is treated as imposed to a different degree relative to different groups. Relational definitions are messier, but are necessary to capture the sharp differences in political status that can exist among those subject to an imposed text.

Liberia

Whatever the degree to which the Americo-Liberian elite felt like free agents in 1847 or should be treated as such, 1847 of course had a very different significance for the African people already living in the territories claimed by the new Liberian state. Albeit that the effects of the new text were not always felt immediately inland, it was an imposition of a foreign system, and no less so for being an early expression of black African nationalism. That fact may complicate the idea of black Americo-Liberians as colonists, but it does not alter the basic nature of the form.[32] As John Mukum Mbuka concludes:

> Despite the fact that modern Liberia was never part of the European colonial project, it was nevertheless, subjected to a form of colonialism that was just as insidious, vicious and damaging as that imposed on other African countries. Liberia was colonized by African-Americans or Americo-Liberians…[33]

The twin elements of racial liberation and colonial paternalism can be seen in the 1847 Constitution's provision confining citizenship to those of African descent, mentioned earlier:

> The great object of forming these Colonies, being to provide a home for the dispersed and oppressed children of Africa, and to regenerate and enlighten this benighted continent, None but persons of color shall be admitted to citizenship in this Republic.[34]

32 See Akpan, above n 21, 217–18, noting uncertainties on this point, but himself concluding that 'the fact remains that [Liberia under the Americo-Liberian regime] must be numbered along with ex-colonial powers in Africa like Great Britain, France and Belgium', Id., 236.

33 John Mukum Mbuka, 'Constitutionalism and Governance in Liberia: Where Is the Love of Liberty that Brought African-Americans to the West African Coast in 1820?' 35 *Liberian Studies Journal* 55 (2010), 55.

34 Constitution of Liberia (1847), Art V s 13.

In subsequent practice, as we will see in the next section, admission to citizenship would be manipulated according to the political calculations of the Americo-Liberian minority. (Citizenship, in turn, was a condition for property and voting rights).[35] But the basic principle never varied: for those whom the constitution called 'native tribes' and 'aborigines', admission to citizenship of their own land would be on the settlers' terms.[36] Only Americo-Liberians participated in the constitutional convention, and only they were entitled to vote in the referendum by which the convention's draft would claim its legal force.

We will therefore have little difficulty in seeing, not only how the 1847 Constitution counts as imposed in relation to the local African inhabitants, but indeed how it was patently more imposed in relation to them than it can be said to have been imposed on the Americo-Liberian community by the ACS. To treat the 1847 text simply as 'imposed', to one degree, on one axis, would be to obscure these very different elements, each of them important.

The Liberian case offers a further novelty, since it is in fact a case of imposition twice over in relation to the local African majority. As we will see in the final section, the high-minded Liberian project turned into an effort to cling to minority dominance, and towards the end of the 19th century, the regime had been driven to adopt a desperate survival plan. It decided to shrink its own jurisdiction to a thin coastal strip known as the 'Constitutional Zone'. Africans within the Zone would have to prove that they had made a complete switch to the Americo-Liberian culture in order to be granted civil and political rights there.[37] In the rest of the territory claimed by Liberia, the inhabitants were ostensibly left to themselves.

Quite what legal situation this might have produced does not seem ever to have become clear, because the desperate strategy was short-lived. It arose at perhaps the last moment in history in which a government could openly withdraw effective government from a substantial territory without more or less automatically forfeiting sovereignty, and that moment was about to end. The Constitutional Zone strategy was overtaken by European efforts to regulate their own colonial scramble for territorial claims over the continent. At the Berlin Conference (1884–85), the European colonial powers agreed to require effective occupation as a condition for recognition of territorial title and borders. The weak Liberian state was thus forced to turn to the British and the United States, and to British and French colonial methods of indirect rule, in order to re-assert its jurisdiction

35 Id., Art I s 11, V s 14.

36 Thus the fact that the local inhabitants were indubitably 'of African descent' did not entitle them to citizenship in the eyes of the Americo-Liberian community; assimilation was required, and later variations to this rule were dictated by Americo-Liberian political strategy. See e.g. Augustine Konneh, 'Citizenship at the Margins: Status, Ambiguity, and the Mandingo of Liberia' 39 *African Studies Review* 141 (1996), 142; Akpan, above n 21, 235–36; Kazanjian, above n 27, 863.

37 Yekutiel Gershoni, 'The First Republic in Liberia: The Evolution of a Single State Society' 28 *Liberian Studies Journal* 65 (2003), 67–68.

over the whole of modern Liberia, losing significant inland territory to British and French control in the process.[38]

In relation to the territory outside the Zone, the 1847 Constitution is thus a rare example of an imposed constitution being temporarily de-imposed without being abolished. From the perspective of Africans living in this area, the text was imposed not once but twice. Neither moment can be separated from broader white colonial patterns: the ACS was largely responsible for the initial steps to establish a settlement on African land, for example, and the Zone is an episode all about broader colonial pressures.[39] But at each moment the Americo-Liberian elite has a significant status as an imposer in its own right.

Botswana

The Liberian case is unusually clear-cut, representing as it does a case of colonialism-within-colonialism. The closest Botswanan analogue, more conventionally, concerns the position of minority cultural groups. While the dominant ethnic group, the Batswana, makes up just under 80% of Botswana's population (with internal subdivisions), the population also includes various cultural and ethnic minorities, most vulnerable among them smaller African ethnic groups such as the Bakgalagadi and the Basarwa or San. Concerns over the treatment and marginalization of these groups represent perhaps the largest question mark hanging over the BDP's proud record of post-independence government.[40] And although multiple factors are in play, the position of these minority tribal groups is readily linked, in part, to features of Botswana's constitutional text and the circumstances of its drafting.[41]

As noted, tribal structures were the main avenue for public participation in the constitutional drafting process, and in practice this largely meant the tribal structures of the majority. We should not therefore be surprised to learn that this dominant position was built into the new constitutional structures for customary leadership.[42] Part III of the 1966 Constitution established a council of tribal

38 Yekutiel Gershoni, 'Minority Rule and Political Trade-In' 27 *Liberian Studies Journal* 63 (2001), 69–73; Akpan above n 21, 229–35.

39 Akpan, above n 21, 220–21; Kazanjian, above n 27, 864–65.

40 See e.g. Amelia Cook & Jeremy Sarkin, 'Is Botswana the Miracle of Africa? Democracy, the Rule of Law, and Human Rights Versus Economic Development' 19 *Transnational Law & Contemporary Problems* 453 (2010), 455.

41 This link has been emphasized by, among others, the UN Special Rapporteur, James Anaya: see most recently *Report of the Special Rapporteur on the Situation and Human Rights of Indigenous Peoples, Addendum: The Situation of Indigenous Peoples in Botswana* A/HRC/15/37/Add.2 (2 June 2010), §9–10.

42 That is not to say that the structures for customary governance were themselves dominant; the marginalization of customary law is a part of the Botswana story as it is of so many others. For a contemporary account of the House soon after its formation, noting its weaknesses (and wrongly predicting its demise), see J. H. Proctor, 'The House of Chiefs and the Political Development of Botswana' 6 *Journal of Modern African Studies* 59 (1968).

chiefs, the Ntlo ya Dikgosi. Tswana chiefs received eight seats in a fifteen seat-body by permanent right where other members had to be elected, in a provision that openly singles out the main Tswana subdivisions:

> The ex-officio Members of the House of Chiefs [those who did not need to be elected] shall be such persons as are for the time being performing the functions of the office of Chief in respect of the Bakgatla, Bakwena, Bamalete, Bamangwato, Bangwaketse, Barolong, Batawana and Batlowka, respectively.[43]

After a long period of silence on minority cultural rights during which this arrangement would persist, public debate increased sharply in the late 1990s. The structure was amended in 2006, becoming both somewhat more equitable and somewhat more opaque.[44]

We will have little difficulty, in turn, in linking this situation partly to British colonial influence. Throughout Anglophone Africa, colonial officials structured their relationship with tribal authorities according to their own interests, including by elevating customary rulers above their traditional checks and balances. In other Anglophone African societies, the foremost legacy of this interference was often a post-independence story of vicious inter-ethnic politics marked by selective patronage and periods of grim authoritarianism. In Botswana, it meant entrenching the dominance of the Batswana, who in turn governed with a sufficiently responsible hand not to fracture or forfeit their position after independence.[45]

This dynamic is also borne out by the absence in the Botswanan case of the concern for the constitutional position of minorities that British colonial authorities showed elsewhere. Colonial authorities were always concerned about the position of white settlers, but they also sometimes made bids to include constitutional protections for the post-independence position of African minorities: Ghana, Nigeria, Kenya and Tanganyika (later part of Tanzania) are all examples.[46] Such guarantees were not included in the 1966 Botswana Constitution and I know of no evidence that the British colonial officials there pushed for them. The post-independence position of minority cultural groups is also plausibly linked to this omission.

From the perspective of minority groups like the Bakgalagadi and the Basarwa, then, the 1966 Constitution was a project of elites thinking primarily of other interests. Its provisions at the very least made no attempt to structure the post-independence state in a way that might compensate for the vulnerable social position of these groups. Their political exclusion was not total, as it was for the

43 Constitution of Botswana (1966), s 78 read with s 77, prior to 2006 amendments.

44 Id., ss 77–79, as amended; on the surrounding political dynamics see Jacqueline S. Solway, 'Navigating the "Neutral" State: "Minority" Rights in Botswana' 28 *Journal of Southern African Studies* 711 (2002), 711–12.

45 Maundeni & Suping, above n 8, 329; Good, above n 9, 7; Solway above n 44.

46 See the discussion of these cases in Parkinson, supra n 6.

local African population in Liberia in 1847. The 1965 elections in Botswana were not restricted on communal lines, unlike the Liberian referendum on the 1847 Constitution. Minority African groups were not shut out of representation in bodies such as the Ntlo ya Dikgosi. The provisions on tribal leadership aside, the 1966 text was neutral on ethnic matters, albeit that neutrality invariably favours socially dominant groups. And all elite transitions involve important decisions being made for everyone else by a distant group in a small room with closed doors. But differences of political caste make it hard to treat these most vulnerable and marginal groups just as normal, elite-represented citizens. Compared to other groups in Botswanan society, there is a notably stronger sense in which these minorities might claim to have been made subject to someone else's constitution in their own land, albeit in a weaker sense than was true of the African majority in Liberia.

Relational definitions and their limits

The argument just made sets up a sliding scale, in which the Liberian text was more imposed, relative to the African majority, than the Botswana one is in relation to the Basarwa. Does this logically imply that we should carry on using 'imposed' to diminishing degrees all the way down the scale? I have been discussing the strongest examples in each case, but there are of course other cultural groups to take account of, as well as other possible groupings, such as by gender or class. Should we understand the two constitutions as differently imposed in each of these dimensions as well, and will we not hopelessly fracture the concept, or render the term 'imposed' meaningless by over-use, if we do so?

This problem, though real, strikes me as only formally problematic. The only reason to care about the imposed nature of constitutions in the first place is because we care about degrees of agency and representation enjoyed by those who are subject to them versus those who put them in place. If so, it seems perverse not to take account of local disparities in these respects as well as those between external and internal actors. It is undoubtedly true that, in theory, such a move could end up drawing a tree of imposed-ness of ever-branching complexity. It is true that the branches would soon reach degrees of imposedness that are found in many countries, and soon thereafter, degrees that will be inescapably present in all constitution-making exercises of any scale. And it is true that it might imply that many constitutions should be treated as imposed because of their differential relation to, say, women or poor people. But the problem with any of these results will not be that they are descriptively false. It is only that they might be unwieldy, for which common sense usage can correct. Permitting ourselves to talk conceptually in many different degrees of imposed-ness in relation to many different groups will not change the fact that most of these are too attenuated to command attention. So constrained, relational definitions simply permit us to speak to cases where more than one axis of imposed-ness merits separate consideration. Concepts should simplify, but not over-simplify.

Imposed constitutions and other impositions

The argument just made does, however, begin to illustrate a different problem of line-drawing to which I support a less open-armed approach. When talking about vulnerable social groups, one inescapably ends up talking not only about their treatment in the text but also about their experience in the society after the moment of constitution-drafting. This can be relevant: for instance, to understand the significance of the imposed constitution. But is it relevant to the question whether the constitution counts as imposed in the first place, or to what degree we should understand it to be imposed? This issue of the relevance of post-enactment facts is part of the larger question that I noted at the outset of keeping control of the concept of imposed constitutions amidst the tangle of other impositions.

Botswana

To consider the relevance of post-1966 events to our assessment of the 1966 Constitution requires first having a brief sense of what these events have been. Several features of the Botswanan state that has established itself since independence can be linked more or less confidently to features of its imposed constitution and to the circumstances of its drafting.

Perhaps the clearest way in which the 1966 text still speaks of its time is in its Bill of Rights. Creativity in this regard during the drafting came only from the rival BPP politicians, and none of the BPP's main proposals made it into the text. Most notable among them were arguments for communal rather than individual land rights, a focus on rights for those of African descent rather than multi-racial rights, and a call for socio-economic rights.[47] In the face of such ideas, both the colonial officials and the BDP leadership preferred to locate themselves squarely within the emerging, and much more cautious, consensus for de-colonizing Commonwealth states.[48] The result is a surviving example of de-colonizing British Commonwealth boilerplate, comprising only a limited set of traditional civil-political rights.

This consensus also included a modest role for courts. Whatever our abstract speculations about the value the BPP's bolder experiments might have had, even if they had been included it is unlikely that the Botswana judiciary would have implemented them very boldly. Botswana's courts have long upheld the rule of law and the dominant party nature of the state has not served to undermine the judiciary.[49] But constitutional adjudication is not at the centre of Botswana's post-independence story. For good and ill, that story is above all one about the decisions of the BDP in government, rather than a story about constitutional

47 Kirkby, above n 5, 39–40, 44–45, 59.

48 See generally *Ibid*; Fombad, above n 4, §3.

49 This is part of a broader pattern in Southern Africa: see also Peter VonDoepp, *Judicial Politics in New Democracies: Cases from Southern Africa* (2009).

constraint by judges of a lawless regime, still less one of transformative constitutionalism.[50] This judicial restraint, too, speaks to the traditional attitudes of the English common law, which tended to be even stronger in colonial settings where judges were usually trusted less.[51] The restraint should also be linked to the tenor of constitutional debates in the Commonwealth in the 1950s and 1960s, when British thinkers (and by no means all of them) were only just warming to the idea of including entrenched rights in constitutions at all.[52]

The elite features of the de-colonial transition have also echoed down the years after 1966. Botswana has generally fair elections and the rule of law prevails in a robust sense, but it has been a dominant party state for over half a century. Opposition party and civil society activity is often weak; political engagement generally is low. As a result, though BDP leaders are fairly elected, weak competition and limited scrutiny make that democratic credential less meaningful than it would in a more competitive environment. The government's leaders can sometimes display intolerant, authoritarian streaks, including resistance to open discussion of issues deemed sensitive.[53] All this can trouble democratic classifiers.[54]

Local observers trace these contemporary features of the state back to the transition. For example, civil society activist Alice Mogwe observes that Botswana displays a 'lower level of political consciousness' compared to its southern African neighbours and attributes this to the fact that 'we haven't a struggle culture'.[55] The scholars Zibani Maundeni and Kekgaoditse Suping see a similar connection, concluding that forms of political exclusion in Botswana's political system [today] were unintentionally created by the constitutional negotiations in the pre-independence era.[56]

Completing the picture, more specific arguments of this sort can also be made about the cultural minorities discussed in the previous section. For example, while all Botswana's other cultural groups have suffered somewhat from the dominance of Tswana culture and language, it is groups like the Basarwa that have climbed

50 See further James Fowkes, 'Relationships with Power: Re-Imagining Judicial Roles in Africa' in Charles Fombad (ed.) *Stellenbosch Handbooks in African Constitutional Law, Vol. 1* (2016).

51 See e.g. Rachel L. Ellett, *Pathways to Judicial Power in Transitional States: Perspectives from African Courts* (2013), 36–37 and earlier sources there cited; Jennifer A. Widner, *Building the Rule of Law: Francis Nyalali and the Road to Judicial Independence in Africa* (2001), 77–79.

52 A general lesson of Parkinson, supra n 6; see also A. W. Brian Simpson, *Human Rights and the End of Empire: Britain and the Genesis of the European Convention* (2001), 8–53.

53 See e.g. generally Good, above n 9; Cook & Sarkin above n 40; Kebapetse Lotshwao, 'The Weakness of Opposition Parties in Botswana: A Justification for More Internal-Party Democracy in the Dominant Botswana Democratic Party (BDP)' 5 *African Journal of Political Science and International Relations* 103 (2011); David Sebudubudu, 'Factors that Impede Democratic Consolidation in Botswana' 13 *Taiwan Journal of Democracy* 137 (2017).

54 See e.g. Steven Levitsky & Lucan A. Way, *Competitive Authoritarianism: Hybrid Regimes After the Cold War* (2010), 254–58; Larry Diamond, 'Facing up to the Democratic Recession' 26 *Journal of Democracy* 141 (2014), 146; generally Sebudubudu, above n 53.

55 Quoted by Good, above n 9, 7.

56 Maundeni & Suping, above n 8, 326.

least into the middle class, that have tended to require the most external assistance to mobilize in support of their interests, and that remain the most vulnerable groups in today's Botswana.[57]

Arguments like these are naturally relevant to understand contemporary Botswana, but they are relevant to a discussion of imposed constitutions for two reasons.

First, these post-enactment arguments are obviously about the text in some important way, but they are also about broader constitutional or legal or political culture. The imposed text, in these respects, must be seen as part of a broader pattern of imposition. In Botswana's case, the longevity of the 1966 text means that these two things do not come apart. But a glance at the rest of Anglophone Africa will remind us that they easily can, and that factors like inherited legal cultural and colonial manipulations of traditional political structures can have a powerful influence long after formal elements like colonial-era constitutions are replaced. In other words, a case like Botswana's can make it easy to assign to the imposed text consequences that we should instead assign to broader political categories.

Second, the same glance elsewhere will remind us that other post-colonial countries in Anglophone African have chosen to change their constitutional texts after independence much more than Botswana has. Almost all other constitutional texts in Anglophone Africa date from 1990 or later, and the exceptions do not dislodge Botswana's clear claim to greatest endurance.[58] Botswana is notable for the degree of continuity between the patterns in the de-colonizing years in the mid-1960s, and those that have prevailed in independent Botswana ever since. That continuity includes the government – the BDP has been continuously in power for 52 years – but also more general features of political and legal culture. Since other formerly colonized states in Anglophone Africa and elsewhere have generally changed more or at least tried to, despite the stubbornly powerful effects of legal culture, there is a meaningful sense in which this continuity is something that Botswana or its leadership chose, when it could have chosen otherwise.

The case of Botswana therefore poses difficult questions about responsibility and ownership that resonate with much better-known cases like Germany and Japan. Granted that some colonial legacies can be very persistent, is there nevertheless a point beyond which the decision to retain a constitution should make us classify it as less imposed? The earlier dilemma of being true to local agency while remaining conscious of colonialism's lingering effects is also strongly present here. But Botswana is a useful site for asking this question because Botswana, like postwar Japan and Germany, is a success story. It has done better, relative to its starting point and over a continuous period, than any other Anglophone

57 See generally Solway, supra n 44.

58 The only two exceptions to the post-1990 rule are the 1986 Constitution of Liberia that replaced the 1847 text, and the 1977 Constitution of Tanzania. Both, in addition to being more recent, are the subjects of current (if drawn-out) efforts to re-draft or replace them.

African example. To pose this question in this context, then, is importantly about giving credit to local actors for this success, rather than about assigning blame to locals in a move that is often also about trying to deflect colonial responsibility. If Botswana deserves credit for what it has made of itself, should we not give it ownership of its constitution?

In my view, it is better to express this important point in another way. Botswana's constitution should be treated as an imposed text, because of its origins (factoring in local agency in those origins by treating that property as a matter of degree). What has been done since is most naturally described as a story of what the country has done with an imposed text, and credit can be assigned accordingly. What has changed, to the extent that it has, is not that the text was imposed, but that this historical fact is of blessedly diminished significance. If less has gone wrong, there is less to blame on, inter alia, the constitutional text, and less reason to emphasize its imposed nature and to make that a symbol of the broader problem. There is also presumably less reason to seek the symbolic benefits of replacing it, which would explain why Botswana's text is an outlier in Anglophone Africa in its longevity. If we wish to go beyond this, and argue that not merely the salience but the fact of being imposed has changed, we should require a more overt (re)-enacting or ratifying act by the Botswanan people. Pending that, we should treat theirs as a story of partially surmounting and moving beyond their constitutional history, not re-writing it.

Liberia

If Botswana is the success story, Liberia under the 1847 Constitution is something like the opposite, but the same two lessons are borne out when analyzing its unhappier history.

The value of mentally distinguishing imposed constitutions from other broader impositions is apparent when considering the position of the Americo-Liberian community in relation to the ACS. The Americo-Liberian elite drafters really did write a constitution for themselves to a large extent, and to some extent in the interests of their community, that community's lack of interest in the constitutional referendum notwithstanding. Accordingly, as argued earlier, the 1847 text cannot be treated as very imposed constitution, in this relation. And that makes it hard to treat the text as imposed to the degree where we might feel we have adequately expressed the responsibility of actors like the ACS for the events that followed.

If we separate imposed text from other sorts and sites of imposition, however, we can be accurate about the narrower circumstances of the drafting, while being adequate to the position in which the original Americo-Liberian settlers were put. Like the erstwhile white minority states in the south around Botswana, which it most closely resembles in Africa, the Americo-Liberian regime has its own long record of oppression. But the status of its people as a precarious minority of cherished but precarious identity was heavily pre-destined by broader colonial patterns over which they had even less control than the white regimes in the south. Their broader predicament was imposed on them far more, and far more damagingly, than the constitutional text that represented their most optimistic response to it.

The second argument, about the significance of subsequent events for the imposed status of the constitution, is also borne out by the Liberian case. I have just argued that the subsequent unhappy history of the Americo-Liberian community should not lead us to dial up the degree of imposed-ness of the 1847 text in order to express the ACS's degree of responsibility for that later history, and the position of the African majority in the Liberian story is best understood in a similar way.

The Americo-Liberian civilizing mission, colonial in principle, was a failure in practice. It depended on assimilating the local African people by education. The funds to pay for that education in turn depended on economic growth, itself a part of the republican blueprint for raising one's station. Economic growth also depended on fresh settlers. As it turned out, none of these virtuous cycles really transpired. Migration and economic growth were often anaemic, and most educational (and other) projects aimed at the local African population soon withered.[59] As a result, the Americo-Liberian regime became a precarious minority state, employing all the standard tactics of such regimes. At various times, it tried to co-opt the black African majority with limited political rights and to distract them with economic growth. As in other similar political systems, these strategies could often claim a measure of success in their own terms. The regime they served endured for 133 years. But they came at the cost of cementing Liberia's status, in Yekutiel Gershoni's nice phrase, as a 'one society state', in which the earlier ideals of black nationalism and liberty became secondary at best and 'the need of the minority to survive in power would become the raison d'etre of the Liberian Government'.[60] That dynamic persisted, in various guises, until the minority regime was forcibly dislodged by the coup d'état of April 1980.

Set aside the special case of the Constitutional Zone, which as already argued counts as a fresh episode of de- and re-imposing. What effect does the rest of this subsequent ugly history have on the nature of the 1847 Constitution as an imposed text? We might at first glance be reluctant to treat it as irrelevant. But as with the Botswanan case, it is natural to say that the black African majority was subjected to an imposed text, and then to a good deal of additional imposition of other kinds thereafter. The later events show why imposed constitutions can be bad things. But they do not make the 1847 text any more imposed, and should be kept out of that variable.

59 Akpan, above n 21, 228–29, 234, also noting some exceptions; on these and patterns of inter-mingling more generally see William E. Allen, 'Liberia and the Atlantic World in the Nineteenth Century: Convergence and Effects' 37 *History in Africa* 7 (2010), 30–41.

60 Gershoni, 'First Republic', above n 37, 65 (Gershoni also uses 'single-society state', Id., p. 68); Gershoni, 'Minority Rule', above n 38, 74.

Conclusion: Lessons about imposed constitutions in African cases

On the strength of these two case studies, the concept of an imposed constitution should have three features. First, as other contributors to this volume have also argued, it should be recognized as a matter of degree. This permits us simultaneously to acknowledge the insidiousness of colonialism, and to take local initiative and thought seriously. That degree stands as a placeholder for a difficult post-colonial debate about determinism and local agency, which is hard to resolve precisely but which is unavoidable in this context.

Second, the concept should be relational, so that we can recognize that one text can be imposed differently in relation to different groups. This is admittedly messy. It threatens to break down the property of imposed-ness into a widening series of bids by various groups to show that their less than ideal relation to the text and its enactment merits separate specification of its imposed-ness on them. But the two case studies show why we should not buy conceptual neatness at the price of lumping all the inhabitants of 1960s Botswana or 1840s Liberia together. Concepts should simplify, but not over-simplify.

Third, we should distinguish between the imposed text and other imposed things, including broader patterns of legal and political culture. These can survive long after the text is gone, so it is helpful to be able to talk about them separately. Local agency can also be much less able to alter these more intangible inheritances even in a context where local actors have significant control over the drafting of the constitutional text. And the distinction allows us to be true to a broader African (and colonial) reality in which colonial constitutional texts are usually better treated as symbolic of external imposition rather than its sum. The greatest evils of colonialism, as with other forms of state oppression, do not lie in the constitutional texts written under its hand. An approach that is able to keep text and drafting mentally separate from the broader social and political influences of colonialism has the final advantage of allowing us to emphasize that. It permits us to talk about imposed constitutions in Africa in colonial context without every use of that category having to carry the full weight of the colonial legacy, and so permits us to treat these texts as the richly complex human enterprises a closer look reveals them to be.

Index

For Product Safety Concerns and Information please contact our EU
representative GPSR@taylorandfrancis.com
Taylor & Francis Verlag GmbH, Kaufingerstraße 24, 80331 München, Germany

www.ingramcontent.com/pod-product-compliance
Ingram Content Group UK Ltd.
Pitfield, Milton Keynes, MK11 3LW, UK
UKHW020149200926
475702UK00016B/2627

* 9 7 8 0 3 6 7 5 1 9 9 2 6 *